T0310460

"Patrick Naim and Laurent Condamin articulate the most comprehensive quantitative and analytical framework that I have encountered for the identification, assessment and management of Operational Risk. I have employed it for five years and found it both usable and effective. I recommend this book as essential reading for senior risk managers."

–C.S. Venkatakrishnan, CRO, Barclays

"I had the pleasure to work with Laurent and Patrick to implement the XOI approach across a large multinational insurer. The key benefits of the method are to provide an approach to understand, manage and quantify risks and, at the same time, to provide a robust framework for capital modelling. Thanks to this method, we have been able to demonstrate the business benefits of operational risk management. XOI is also well designed to support the Operational Resilience agenda in financial services, which is the new frontier for Op Risk Management."

–Michael Sicsic, Head of Supervision, Financial Conduct Authority; Ex-Global Operational Risk Director, Aviva Plc

"The approach described in this book was a 'Eureka!' moment in my journey on operational risk. Coming from a market risk background, I had the impression that beyond the definition of operational risk, it was difficult to find a book that described a coherent framework for measuring and managing operational risk. Operational Risk Modeling in Financial Services is now filling this gap."

–Olivier Vigneron, CRO EMEA, JPMorgan Chase & Co

"The XOI methodology provides a structured approach for the modelling of operational risk scenarios. The XOI methodology is robust, forward looking and easy to understand. This book will help you understand the XOI methodology by giving you practical guidance to show how risk managers, risk modellers and scenario owners can work together to model a range of operational risk scenarios using a consistent approach."

–Michael Furnish, Head of Model Governance and Operational Risk, Aviva Plc

"The XOI approach is a simple framework that allows to measure operational risk by identifying and quantifying the main loss drivers per risk. This facilitates the business and management engagement as the various drivers are defined in business terms and not in risk management jargon. Further, the XOI approach can be used for risk appetite setting and monitoring. I strongly believe that the XOI approach has the potential to become an industry standard for banks and regulators."

–Emile Dunand, ORM Scenarios & Stress Testing, Credit Suisse

Operational Risk Modelling in Financial Services

Founded in 1807, John Wiley & Sons is the oldest independent publishing company in the United States. With offices in North America, Europe, Australia and Asia, Wiley is globally committed to developing and marketing print and electronic products and services for our customers' professional and personal knowledge and understanding.

The Wiley Finance series contains books written specifically for finance and investment professionals as well as sophisticated individual investors and their financial advisors. Book topics range from portfolio management to e-commerce, risk management, financial engineering, valuation, and financial instrument analysis, as well as much more.

For a list of available titles, visit our website at www.WileyFinance.com.

Operational Risk Modelling in Financial Services

The Exposure, Occurrence, Impact Method

PATRICK NAIM
LAURENT CONDAMIN

WILEY

This edition first published 2019.

Registered office.
John Wiley & Sons Ltd, The Atrium, Southern Gate, Chichester, West Sussex, PO19 8SQ, United Kingdom

Library of Congress Cataloging-in-Publication Data

Names: Naim, Patrick, author. | Condamin, Laurent, author.
Title: Operational risk modeling in financial services : the exposure, occurrence, impact method / Patrick Naim, Laurent Condamin.
Description: Chichester, West Sussex, United Kingdom : John Wiley & Sons, [2019] | Includes index. |
Identifiers: LCCN 2018058857 (print) | LCCN 2019001678 (ebook) | ISBN 9781119508540 (Adobe PDF) | ISBN 9781119508434 (ePub) | ISBN 9781119508502 (hardcover)
Subjects: LCSH: Financial services industry—Risk management. | Banks and banking—Risk management. | Financial risk management.
Classification: LCC HG173 (ebook) | LCC HG173 .N25 2019 (print) | DDC 332.1068/1—dc23
LC record available at https://lccn.loc.gov/2018058857

Cover Design: Wiley
Cover Images: © Verticalarray /Shutterstock, © vs148 /Shutterstock, ©monsitj / iStock.com, © vs148/Shutterstock

Set in 10/12pt TimesLTStd by SPi Global, Chennai, India

Printed in Great Britain by TJ International Ltd, Padstow, Cornwall, UK

10 9 8 7 6 5 4 3 2 1

Contents

PART TWO
Challenges of Operational Risk Measurement

PART THREE
The Practice of Operational Risk Management

PART FOUR

The Exposure, Occurrence, Impact Method

List of Figures

List of Tables

Foreword

I met Patrick and Laurent at a conference on operational risk in 2014. This meeting was a "Eureka!" moment in my journey on operational risk, which had started a year earlier.

I had been asked to examine operational risk management from a quantitative perspective. Coming from a market risk background, my first impressions were that, beyond the definition of operational risk, it was difficult to find a book that described a coherent framework for measuring and managing operational risk. *Operational Risk Modelling in Financial Services* is now filling this gap. Nevertheless, in the absence of such a book available at the time, I became familiar with the basic elements of operational risk: the risk and control self-assessment process (RCSA), the concept of key risk indicators (KRIs), and the advanced model approach (AMA) for capital calculation under Basel II.

In examining the practices of the financial industry, I had the impression that these essential components existed in isolation from each other, without a unifying framework.

The typical RCSA is overwhelming because of the complexity and granularity of the risks it identifies. This makes individual risk assessment largely qualitative and any aggregation of risks problematic.

KRIs were presented as great tools to monitor and control the level of operational risks, but in current practice they appeared to come from heuristics rather than from risk analysis or a risk appetite statement.

Finally, at the extreme end of the quantitative spectrum, all major institutions were relying on risk calculation teams specialising in loss distribution approaches, extreme value theories, or other sophisticated mathematical tools. Financial institutions have fuelled a very sustained activity of researchers extrapolating the 99.9% annual quantile of loss distributions from sparse operational losses data.

As difficult as this capital calculation proved to be, it was generally useless for risk managers and failed to pass the use test, which should ensure that risk measurement used for capital should be useful for day-to-day risk management. This failure should not be attributed to the Basel II framework, as AMA has tried to combine qualitative and quantitative methods in an interesting way and has introduced the important concept of operational risk scenarios!

In summary, I was confronted with an inconsistent operational risk management framework where the identification, control, and measurement of risks seemed to live on different planets. Each team was aware of the existence of the others, but they did not form a coordinated whole.

This inevitably raised the question of how to bridge the gap between risk management and risk measurement, which was precisely the title of Patrick's speech at the Oprisk Europe 2014 conference! *Eureka!* Never has a risk conference proven so timely.

The question is fundamental because it creates a bridge between an operational risk appetite statement and KRIs, and establishes a link between major risks, KRIs, and RCSA by leveraging the concept of operational risk scenarios.

The quantification of these risks (the risk measurement) can be compared to the stress testing frameworks used in other risk disciplines such as market risk. It can also be used to build a forward-looking economic capital model.

Once a quantitative risk appetite is formulated, once KRI are put in place to monitor key risks, and once an economic capital consistent with this risk measure is established, better risk management decisions can then be made. Cost-benefit analyses can be conducted to establish new controls to mitigate or prevent risk.

In other words, a useful risk management framework for the business has emerged!

I believe that *Operational Risk Modelling in Financial Services* is a book that will help at every level from the seasoned operational risk professional to the new practitioner. To the former, it will be an innovative way to link known concepts into a coherent whole, and to the latter it will serve as a clear and rigorous introduction to the operational risk management discipline.

Olivier Vigneron
Managing Director | Chief Risk Officer, EMEA |
JPMorgan Chase & Co.

Preface

Thank you for taking the time to read or flip through this book. You probably chose this book because you are working in the area of operational risk, or you will soon be taking a new job in this area. To be perfectly honest, this is not a subject that someone might spontaneously decide to research personally, as can be the case today for climate change, artificial intelligence, or blockchain technologies.

However, we quickly became passionate about this subject when we first started working on it over 10 years ago. The reason for this is certainly that it remains a playground where the need for modelling, that is, a simplified and stylized description of reality, is crucial. Risk modelling presents a particular difficulty because, as the Bank for International Settlements rightly points out in a discussion paper in 2013[1]: "Risk is of course unobservable".

Risks are not observable, and yet everyone can talk about them, and have their own analysis. Risks are not observable, yet they have well observable consequences, such as the 2008 financial crisis. It can be said that risks do not exist – only their perceptions and consequences exist.

Risk modelling therefore had to follow one of two paths: modelling perceptions or modelling consequences. In the financial field, quantitative culture has prevailed, and consequence modelling has largely taken precedence over perception modelling. For a banking institution, the consequences of an operational risk are financial losses. The dominant approach has been based on the shortcut that since losses are the manifestation of risks, it is therefore sufficient to model losses.

As soon as we started working on the subject, we considered that this approach was wrong, because losses are the manifestation of past risks, not the risks we face today. We have therefore worked on the alternative path of understanding the risks, and the mechanisms that can generate adverse events. This approach is difficult because the object of modelling is a set of people, trades, activities, rules, which must be represented in a simple, useful way to consider – but not predict – future events, and at the same time seek ways to mitigate them. This is more difficult than considering that the modeling object is a loss data file, and using mathematical tools to represent them, while at the same time, and in a totally disconnected way, other people are thinking about the risks and trying to control or avoid them. This work on mechanisms that can lead to major losses bridges the gap between risk quantification and risk management,

[1] Basel Committee on Banking Supervision. Discussion Paper BCBS258, "The Regulatory Framework: Balancing Risk Sensitivity, Simplicity and Comparability," July 2013, https://www.bis.org/publ/bcbs258.pdf.

and is more demanding for both quantification and management, since modellers and business experts must find a common language.

It is only thanks to the many people who have trusted us over these 10 or 15 years that this work has gone beyond the scope of research, and has been applied in some of the largest financial institutions in France, the United Kingdom, and the United States. We have worked closely and generally for several years with the risk teams and business experts of these institutions, and for several of them we have accompanied them until the validation of these approaches by the regulatory authorities.

This book is therefore both a look back over these years of practice, to draw a number of the lessons learned, and a presentation of the approach we propose for the analysis and modelling of operational risks in financial institutions. We believe, of course, that this approach can still be greatly improved in its field, and extended to related areas, particularly for enterprise risk management in nonfinancial companies.

This book is not a summary or catalogue of best practices in the area of operational risks, although there are some excellent ones. In any case, we would not be objective on this subject, since even though we have been privileged observers of the practices of the largest institutions and have learned a lot from each of them, we have also tried to transform their practices.

The first part of this book is both a brief presentation of the method we recommend and a summary of the lessons learned during our years of experience on topics familiar to those working in operational risks: RCSA, loss data, quantitative models, scenario workshops, risk correlation analysis, and model validation. In this section, we have adopted a deliberately anecdotal tone to share some of our concrete experiences.

The second part describes the problem, that is, operational risk modelling. We go back to the definition of operational risk and its growing importance for financial institutions. Then we discuss the need to measure it for regulatory requirements such as capital charge calculation, or stress tests, or nonregulatory requirements such as risk appetite and risk management. Finally, we discuss the specific challenges of operational risk measurement.

The third part discusses the three main tools used in operational risk analysis and modelling: RCSA, loss data models, and scenario analyses. We present here the usual methods used by financial institutions, with a critical eye when we think it is necessary. This part of the book is the closest to what could be considered as a best-practice analysis.

Finally, the fourth part presents the XOI method, for Exposure, Occurrence, and Impact. The main argument of our method is to consider that it is possible to define the exposed resource for each operational risk considered. Once the exposed resource is identified, but only under this condition, it becomes possible to describe the mechanism that can generate losses. Once this mechanism is described, it becomes possible to model and quantify it.

The method we present in this book uses Bayesian networks. To put it simply, a Bayesian network is a graph representing causal relationships between variables; these relationships being quantified by probabilities. You go to the doctor in winter with a fever and a strong cough. The doctor knows that these symptoms can be caused by many diseases, but that the season makes some more likely. To eliminate some serious viral infections from his diagnosis, the doctor asks you a few questions about your background and in particular your recent travels. The following graph can be used to represent the underlying knowledge.

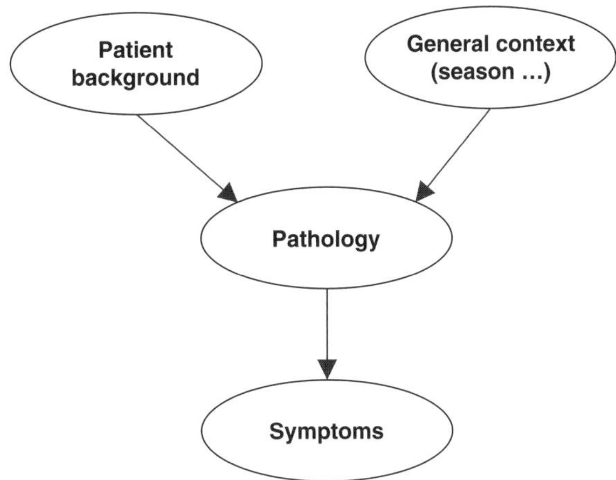

Nodes are the variables of the model, and links are represented by probabilities. The great advantage of Bayesian networks is that ... they are Bayesian, that is, that probabilities are interpreted as beliefs, not as objective data. Any probability is the expression of a belief. Even using an observed frequency as a probability is an expression of a belief in the stability of the observed phenomenon.

Bayesian networks are considered to have been invented in the 1980s by Judea Pearl of UCLA[2] and Stefen Lauritzen[3] of University of Oxford. Judea Pearl, laureate of the Turing award in 2011, has written extensively on causality. His most recent publication is a non-specialist book called *The Book of Why*[4]. It is a plea for the understanding of phenomena in the era of big data: "Causal questions can never be answered by data alone. They require us to formulate a model of the process that generates the data".

Pearl suggests that his book can be summarized in a simple sentence "You are smarter than your data". We believe this applies to operational risk managers, too.

[2]Judea Pearl, *Probabilistic Reasoning in Intelligent Systems: Networks of Plausible Inference*)(San Francisco: Morgan-Kaufmann, 1988).

[3]R. G. Cowell, P. Dawid, S. L. Lauritzen, and D. J. Spiegelhalter, *Probabilistic Networks and Expert Systems: Exact Computational Methods for Bayesian Networks* New York: Springer-Verlag, 1999.

[4]Judea Pearl and Dana McKenzie, *The Book of Why: The New Science of Cause and Effect* (New York: Basic Books, 2018).

PART One

Lessons Learned in 10 Years of Practice

CHAPTER 1

Creation of the Method

This first part of the book presents our experiences in operational risk modelling from a subjective point of view over the past 10 years.

1.1 FROM ARTIFICIAL INTELLIGENCE TO RISK MODELLING

We are engineers specialized in artificial intelligence. We have been working together for about 25 years, and early in our careers we spent a lot of time on applications of neural networks, Bayesian networks, and what was called data mining at this time. It was almost a generation before the current popularity of these techniques.

Back in the 1990s, few industries had the means to invest in artificial intelligence and data mining: mostly banking, finance, and the defense sector, as they had identified applications with important stakes. The defense usually conducts its own research, and so, quite naturally, we spent a lot of time working in research and development with banks and insurance companies, for applications such as credit rating, forecasting financial markets, and portfolio allocation. We were fortunate enough that the French Central Bank was our first client for this service, for several years. Thanks to a visionary managing director, the French Central Bank created in the early 1990s an AI team of more than 20 people working on applications ranging from natural language processing to credit scoring.

Our conclusion was mixed. Machine-learning techniques were generally not better than conventional linear techniques. This mediocre performance was not related to the techniques themselves, but to the data. When you try to predict the default of a company from its financial ratios, you will always have several companies with exactly the same profile, but that will not share the same destiny. This is because the observed data do not include all of the variables that could help predict the future. The talent and the pugnacity of the leader, the competitive environment, and so on, are not directly represented in the accounting or financial data. However, these nonfinancial indicators are the ones that will make the difference, all things being equal otherwise. Finally, in rating or classification applications, and whatever the technique used, the rates of false positives or false negatives were usually very close.

This is even more applicable when you are trying to predict the markets. We were most of the time trying to forecast the return of one particular market at various horizons, using either macroeconomic variables, or technical variables. We would have been largely satisfied with a performance just slightly better than flipping a coin. Again, the performance of nonlinear models was comparable to other techniques. In a slightly more subtle way here, the limitation was expressed through the dilemma between the complexity of the model and the stability of its performances: to get a model with stable performance, this model must be simple. The best compromise is often the linear model.

About 10 years ago, a Head of Operational Risk for a large bank asked us to think about the use of the Bayesian networks to model the operational risk, and to seek to evaluate possible extreme events. Not surprisingly, she was advised to do so by the former managing director of the French Central Bank, which we mentioned previously.

We were immediately intrigued and interested in the subject. We liked the challenge of leaving aside for a while the "big data" analysis to work on models based on "scarce data"! We thought, and continue to think, that the work of a modeler is not to look for mathematical laws to represent data, but to understand the underlying mechanisms and to gain knowledge about them. It is not surprising that one of us wrote his PhD thesis on the translation of a trained neural network into an intelligible set of rules.

Going back to operational risks, or more precisely to one of the requirements of AMA (advanced measurement approach), the problem was formulated mathematically quite simply, but seemed to require an enormous work.

The mathematical problem was to estimate an amount M such that it could only be exceeded with a probability of 0.1%, regardless of the combination of operational risk events that could be observed in the forthcoming year.

In practical terms, this meant answering several questions, all of them more difficult than the other:

1. *Identification.* What are the major events that my institution could be exposed to next year? How to identify them? How to structure them? How to keep only those that are extreme but realistic (that is, how not to quantify a *Jurassic Park* scenario!).
2. *Evaluation.* How to evaluate the probability that one of them will occur? If it occurs, how to evaluate the variability of its consequences?
3. *Interdependencies.* All adverse events will not happen at the same time. However, certain events can weaken a business and make other extreme events more likely. For example, a significant natural event can weaken control capabilities and increase the risk of fraud. How to evaluate the correlations between these events?

Once we became acquainted to the problem, we did two things:

1. As consultants, we studied closely the risk management system of the bank.
2. As researchers, we studied the state of the art on the question of quantification.

We must admit that if we were impressed by the work done by our client, this was not the case on the state of the art.

This customer, which is one of the largest French banks, serves today nearly 30 million customers with more than 70,000 employees, and covers most of the banking business lines, even if it does not compare in that with the large investment banks in Europe or in the United States.

The Head of Operational Risks had put in place a set of risk mappings.

This work was based on a breakdown of the bank's activities. The breakdown did not use processes – as we found later that most banks do – but objects. The objects were of different nature: products, people, systems, buildings, and so on. This approach was consistent with the overall risk analysis approach proposed by the ARM method.[1] According to this approach, a risk is defined by a combination of Event, Object, and Consequence. A risk is therefore defined by the encounter of an event and a resource likely to be affected by this event. We will come back to this, but this approach, common to ARM and ISO 31000 and shared by most industries and research organizations working on major risks, is extremely structuring and fertile for modeling.

This mapping was not only a catalog. For each type of exposed object, the Operational Risk department of this bank had established a working group consisting of a risk manager and several experts to identify and assess risks in a simple way. Contrary to what we have seen later in sometimes more prestigious organizations, this work was not only an expert evaluation obtained during a meeting, but was a structured and well-argued document, which could be reviewed and discussed by the internal audit bodies and by the regulator. As a conclusion of each study, each of the risks identified and considered significant by the working group for the type of object considered, was the subject of a quantified evaluation. This assessment was in the form of a simple formula that evaluated the cost of risk.

The analysis was describing a mechanism by which a loss could be observed, and the indicators used made it possible to quantify it. For example, the default or disruption of a supplier could impact the business during the time needed to switch to a backup supplier. The switching time would of course depend on the quality of prior mitigation actions. This helps defining the outline of a "Supplier Failure" model: list all the critical suppliers, evaluate for each of them a probability of default, evaluate the impact of the supplier unavailability on the bank's revenue, and assess the time to return to normal operations. The combination of these different factors, all assessed with a certain degree of uncertainty, made it possible to consider building a model. We have subsequently validated this approach for all types of risks, irrespective of the type of exposed objects: people, buildings, products, stock market orders, applications, databases, suppliers, models , and so on.

1.2 MODEL LOSSES OR RISKS?

The other part of our preparatory research concerned the state of the art on modeling. We were surprised to find that the dominant model was called the LDA, for Loss Distribution Approach, and was actually a statistical model of past losses, not a risk model.

The point that surprised us the most is the effort statisticians made to search for laws that would fit the data, without seeking any theoretical justification for choosing the law. We had some theoretical knowledge of the modelling of financial markets, in which the use of a normal law results from the theoretical framework of efficient markets. This framework, proposed by Bachelier, demonstrates that if the markets are efficient, then the distribution of returns follows a normal distribution. This theoretical hypothesis is clear and debatable. We can accept or reject the hypothesis of efficient markets. It can be considered that there exists insider information that distorts the markets. This discussion regards the validity of the models, of the same nature

[1] The method taught by "The Institutes" to obtain the qualification of Associate in Risk Management. See https://www.theinstitutes.org (accessed 5/10/2018).

as the discussions that one may have in physics, on the fact that the hypothesis of perfect gases, or incompressible fluids is or is not acceptable, and therefore that the associated equations are applicable.

On the modelling of operational risks, nothing like that. The choice of a law did not come from a theoretical discussion, but only from its ability to fit to the data, which seemed to us contradictory to any modelling logic. Moreover, the data considered in the adjustment are not of the same nature.

The principle of the LDA is (1) to assume that the average number of losses observed in one year will also be observed in the following years although with some variance (this is represented by the use of a frequency law, for example a Poisson law), and (2) to adjust a theoretical distribution on the amounts of observed losses.

Taken literally, this approach means that the only variability of the losses lies in their number and in their arrangement (an unfavourable year can suffer several significant losses). In other words, randomness would lie only in the realizations, and not in the nature of the risk scenarios. According to this principle, a tsunami would be then only an unexpectedly big wave. Even if the adjustment of a theoretical distribution on the height of the waves makes it possible mathematically to calculate the probability of a wave of 20 or 30 meters of height, it does not account for the difference of nature of the two phenomena: tsunamis are not caused by the same process as waves.

This approach seemed to be wrong for several reasons. Regardless of the possibility of statistically adjusting a law without knowing the theoretical form that this law must take, what would be the logic to use past losses to anticipate future losses, even as technologies evolve, risks evolve, and banking activities evolve?

Why use credit card fraud loss history before EMV chips implementation, in a context where EMV chip cards are now widespread and being used? How not to see that the regulatory pressure on the risks related to the conduct of banks depends on the political climate? Would the political will to punish the banks for the economic and human disaster of the subprime crisis be applied with the same rigor if Barack Obama had not been president at that time? How about losses related to sold or obsolete activities? For example, our French client had in its accounts a significant loss related to a model error on market activities, which led the management of the bank to sell these activities: was it then justified to consider this loss in the history used to extrapolate future losses?

Of course, we know the argument of "quants" in banks, which can be summarized in a few words. Even if things change, past losses are representative of an institution, its size and its culture, and therefore they can be validly used, even to predict losses of another nature. In other words, a loss observed on market activities contains information to anticipate a possible loss on the use of cryptocurrencies, because the risk profile of a bank has a certain stability, which gives it a certain propensity to take risks, a certain appetite for risk, independent of activities and technologies. This sounds like an attempt to give a soul to a banking institution that would remain stable through all the changes. We will not engage in this metaphysical terrain of the soul of organizations, but to consider that this soul would manifest itself through the taking of operational risk, seems to us to be fanciful at best.

CHAPTER 2

Introduction to the XOI Method

2.1 A RISK MODELLING DOCTRINE

From these observations and reflexions, we have formulated an Operational Risk Modelling doctrine. This doctrine proposes to adopt a statistical method for recurrent risks, and a scenario analysis method for rare risks.

It can be summarized in two sentences.

> *What has happened quite often will happen in similar conditions, in the absence of new preventative actions. For what has never happened, or very rarely occurred, we need to understand how this can happen and unfold, and assess the consequences in the absence of new protective actions.*

If we interpret this in the space of risk represented in a usual way on a "Frequency – Severity" map (Figure 2.1), this doctrine is expressed as follows:

Potential losses due to high severity and low frequency risks are addressed through the development of probabilistic scenarios based on the analysis of the loss generation mechanism.

This approach can be extended to frequency risks with a potential for high severity, and for which an in-depth study of the possible evolutions of the risk is necessary (prevention and protection).

Potential losses due to low severity and high or medium frequency risks can be addressed by statistical models. In this context, the use of the LDA is acceptable. In fact, frequent losses can be validly modelled by a statistical law.

We present now in detail this approach of modelling, without insisting on the modelling of frequent risks through LDA, because this method is usual today and is not therefore specific of our approach. We first present the methodology of qualification, selection, and quantification

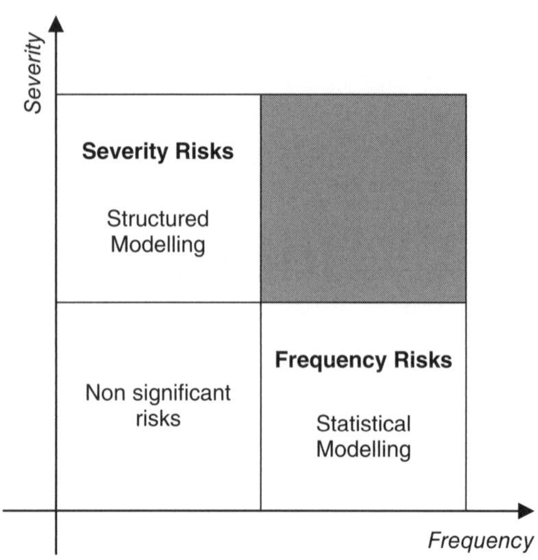

FIGURE 2.1 Modelling Approach by Risk Type

of risk scenarios. Then we explain the principle of integration, to produce a valuation of capital for operational risks in each cell of the matrix of Basel, from scenario models and historical loss data.

2.2 A KNOWLEDGE MANAGEMENT PROCESS

Operational risk modelling should be viewed as a knowledge management process that ensures the continuous transformation of human expertise into a probabilistic model. The model allows us to calculate the distribution of potential losses, identify reduction levers, and perform impact analyses of contextual evolutions and strategic and commercial objectives.

The process is continuous in order to avoid any gap between the expertise and the model. The model must remain controllable and open to criticism by experts, as well as auditable by regulators. For the sake of transparency, each step of the process must be documented.

This process consists of two main steps: (1) the definition of the scenarios and (2) the quantification of the scenarios. We will detail the content of these steps later, but it is essential to remember that probabilistic modelling only makes sense if it is based on the foundation of the scenarios defined in the first step.

The three actors in the process are the expert, the risk manager, and the modeller (Figure 2.2). The expert holds the technical knowledge on a specific field or profession. For example, experts in electronic banking fraud, computer network specialists, lawyers, and so on will be consulted. The expert is not necessarily sensitive to the problem of risk assessment. The risk manager should have a double competence: he or she knows the bank activities and obviously masters the foundations of risk management and assessment. He or she is responsible for the scenario definition phase during which he or she consults the experts to identify and select the relevant risks. The modeller is in charge of the risk quantification phase. Even if its main competence is the modelling of the knowledge, it is illusory to entrust the quantification to modellers who do

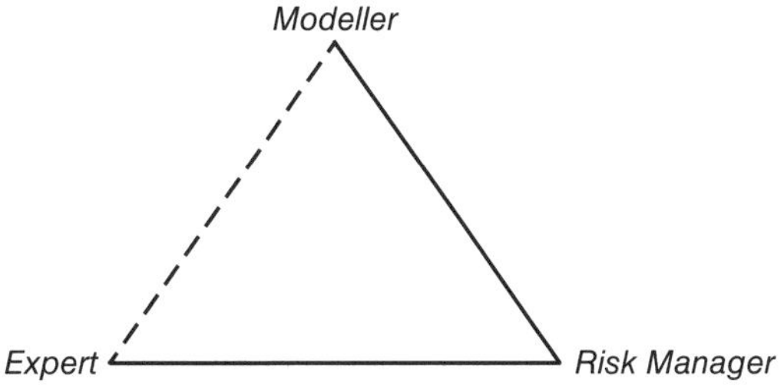

FIGURE 2.2 The Three Actors of the Risk Modelling Process

not have at the same time a minimum knowledge of the bank activities and in-depth expertise on risk management.

The first phase of the process involves only the risk manager and the expert while the second involves mainly the risk manager and the modeller, even if the expert can be involved by the modeller for technical questions. *The overlap of the skills the three actors ensures the continuity of the process.*

2.3 THE EXPOSURE, OCCURRENCE, IMPACT (XOI) APPROACH

As we have already mentioned, the risks to be considered are numerous, heterogeneous, and have very different realization profiles. It is therefore important to define a unified formalism that will make it possible to define risks during the scenario definition phase and to quantify them during the scenario quantification phase. This is the purpose of the XOI approach (eXposure, Occurrence, Impact). This model defines precisely the concept of risk borne by the bank as well as the quantified form of risk.

A bank is exposed to risks if it has vulnerabilities. Vulnerability is the central concept of the approach presented here. This notion is discussed in detail in ARM,[1] we give here the definition and illustrate it with examples.

A vulnerability is defined by three elements:

1. *The Peril*, or event, is the threat to the bank. Examples: fraud, data entry errors, natural disasters, epidemics, and so on
2. *The Object* or resource is the entity of the bank that can be struck by the peril. Objects can be material, immaterial, human resources, an operating figure, and so on
3. *The Consequence* is the impact of the occurrence of the peril on an object. We generally limit ourselves to the financial impact.

There is no vulnerability when a peril can strike an object without financial consequences. For example, if a building is built to withstand a level 5 earthquake on the Richter scale in a city where the maximum potential earthquake is at level 3, no vulnerability is to be considered

[1] Op. cit.

even if the peril "Earthquake" exists for the object "Building" because no consequence is to be feared.

Given this definition, we can clarify the meaning of the notions of risk, loss, and scenario, as we envision them.

The *risk* is the possibility that a *peril* strikes an *object.*

The *loss* refers to the observed occurrence of a peril on an object.

The *scenario* designates how a vulnerability materializes. Each scenario defines a unique vulnerability for which the XOI triplet is the cornerstone.

The three components of the XOI model are:

1. *Exposure (X).* This is the number of independent objects exposed to a peril given during the year. The independence of objects is defined in relation to the peril. For example, market trades are independent of the peril "Data Entry Error", because a data entry error only hits an order. On the other hand, the clients of product are not independently exposed to "Mis-Selling," as this is usually a systemic flaw in sales processes.
2. *Occurrence (O).* It is the occurrence of a peril on one particular instance of the object for the forthcoming year. This is a Yes/No variable quantified by its probability.
3. *Impact (I).* This is the cost following the occurrence of the peril on one particular instance of the object. This cost may depend on the object and on circumstances.

The triplet (eXposure, Occurrence, Impact) is the exact transposition of the triple (Peril, Object, Consequence). This helps ensuring the continuity of the knowledge modelling process.

Therefore the two steps of the modelling process can be reformulated:

1. Define Scenarios = Identify Vulnerabilities
2. Quantify Scenarios = Quantify Exposure, Occurrence, and Severity

2.4 THE RETURN OF AI: BAYESIAN NETWORKS FOR RISK ASSESSMENT

Reducing uncertainty through knowledge to better understand and evaluate our risks is the challenge of quantitative risk modelling.

Introduced in the 1980s in the field of medical diagnostics, where the fusion of theoretical knowledge and statistical data is essential, Bayesian networks have since been applied in fields as varied as the safety of operation, fault diagnosis, credit scoring, predictive maintenance, and so on.

As a modelling tool, Bayesian networks have the significant advantage of allowing the fusion of statistical data and human expertise. From the mathematical point of view, Bayesian networks use graph theory and probability theory, and are supported by strong theoretical results.

It is therefore a particularly suitable tool for *modelling* and *quantifying* risks in general and operational risks in particular.

We briefly introduce Bayesian networks, which will be discussed in more detail in Part IV of this book.

A Bayesian network is a probabilistic graph. The graph represents the causal structure of a domain, that is, the cause-and-effect relationships between the variables describing the domain. Knowledge is quantified by probabilities.

To construct a Bayesian network is thus to (1) construct the graph, (2) to inform the marginal and conditional probabilities connecting the nodes of the graph between them.

The construction of the graph is usually done with the help of experts. Although there are algorithms to discover the optimal structure of a graph to account for observed data, in the case of operational risk modelling, we first look at causalities as they can be described by the experts.

The quantification of probabilities is based on two nonexclusive methods.

1. The *frequentist* method is applicable if data is available. It consists of estimating the probabilities by calculating the percentages of each category for each variable. The frequentist method can be implemented manually by performing counts on the database, or automatically by learning the Bayesian network.
2. The *subjective* method consists in assigning probabilities a priori that is based on beliefs rather than on a data history. It will be applied when the historical data is insufficient or in the case of a change of context rendering the history unusable. These probabilities are provided by experts.

Frequency probabilities and subjective probabilities can be combined in a Bayesian network.

A Bayesian network can be seen in a very simple way as a *conditional probabilities* calculator.

The distribution of any node of the network can be computed unconditionally, that is, without knowing the state of the other nodes, or conditionally, that is, by knowing the state of some of the nodes of the network, using Bayesian *inference*. The internal mechanics of inference is complex but is beyond the scope of our discussion here.

As soon as the state or distribution of a node is known, we can deduce the distribution of the other nodes by inference. As soon as information is known on one node of the network it is used to recalculate the distribution of all the other nodes.

Both an intuitive knowledge representation tool and a conditional distribution calculator, Bayesian networks have the following advantages for operational risk modelling.

The model is the opposite of a “black box”, as its structure and quantification assumptions are clearly documented:

- The models are controllable by the experts and auditable by the regulatory authorities.
- Probabilities are always the result of simple calculations (counts) or expertise, thus increasing the transparency of the calculations made.

- Bayesian networks can represent all the factors that condition the different components of a scenario and will thus make it possible to identify the levers of reduction and to quantify their importance.
- They propose a common formalism for the representation of knowledge that will be applied to all types of risk.

Obviously, their implementation implies the availability of experts, but this availability, which could be a practical obstacle in certain cases, is for us an essential condition for the success of operational risk modelling.

CHAPTER 3

Lessons Learned in 10 Years of Practice

3.1 RISK AND CONTROL SELF-ASSESSMENT

Any risk quantification project should be thought about as a knowledge management project. Risk quantification is a continuous process of knowledge transformation that begins with risk identification and ends with a quantified risk profile. The identification of risks which results in a risk mapping is the first step in this process. Although we are rather quantitative people, we consider this qualitative step as the most important.

We have been working with financial institutions as well as with nonfinancial institutions, and although we observed that risk identification is probably too much a kind of administrative process in many companies, we must acknowledge that many resources, both human and technical, are devoted to this task. A myriad of software has been developed by external vendors or internal IT teams to facilitate the RCSA[1] process. Second and first lines of defense are fully committed to those tasks for significant periods of time.

We intentionally split RCSA into two subtasks: risk identification and risk assessment.[2] We are aware that the boundaries between these two processes are usually blurred, or that the identification of significant risks is considered as a result of the RCSA, but in the best practices that we have encountered they were separated and each of them led to specific deliverables.

Risk identification is the process that aims at identifying the exposures of the firm and the adverse operational events that could strike them. Risk assessment is the process that aims at scoring the frequency and impact of the risk previously identified as well as the efficiency of the controls. Risk assessment delivers some results that are of importance for the further quantification exercise as it makes it possible to determine which risk is frequent and could be addressed with a data-driven model and which risk is severe and should be addressed with scenario-based approaches.

[1]Usual acronym for "Risk and Control Self-Assessment."

[2]For simplicity, we will often write "risk identification" to speak about risk and control identification and "risk assessment" or "risk scoring" to discuss risk and control scoring.

Being identified as modelers, we rarely took part to RCSA exercises, but using their results, we spent a lot of time analyzing the methodologies and the risk registers. We have also been involved in further work to ensure consistency between RCSA and scenario analysis. Furthermore, having participated in major operational risk projects, we have witnessed all the project cycles and have been close to the risk management team at all stages of risk mapping. Our experience is therefore not that of a practitioner, but that of a privileged observer.

3.1.1 Risk and Control Identification

Summary of the lessons learned:

- There are many different practices for designing a risk taxonomy.
- The quality of the risk taxonomy is a key success driver of risk quantification.
- Risk identification should be driven by risk awareness and expertise rather than by administrative processes and automated tools.

The most usual and simple version of risk identification aims at providing a comprehensive list of risks, more or less structured, that the firm could face in the future. Usually, the scope of the identification is firmwide, but it could also be limited to a single business unit for prototyping or specific risk management projects. The result of risk identification is a spreadsheet or a more sophisticated database typically containing five types of information (see example in Table 3.1):

1. The business line or process or any exposure unit
2. The event category
3. The name of the risk
4. The description of the risk
5. The type of consequences

Of course, this information can be more or less detailed. It is not uncommon to have dozens of properties that identify the business line or the process or the event: the root cause, the secondary cause, and so on.

3.1.1.1 Building a Good Risk Taxonomy Is Not Easy Defining the risk taxonomy is basically providing a breakdown of business resources and events in order to organize

TABLE 3.1 Example of Risk Definition

Line of business/process	Retail brokerage/Corporate action processing
Event category	Execution, delivery, and process management/Transaction capture, execution, and maintenance
Name of the risk	Corporate action error
Description	Failure to execute a corporate action as requested by the client
Consequences	Compensation to client

TABLE 3.2 Basel Loss Event Categories

Loss Event Category (Level 1)	Label Type
Internal fraud	Event
External fraud	Event
Employment practices and workplace safety	Processes
Clients, products, and business practices	Resources (client, product)/processes
Damage to physical assets	Event/resource
Business disruption and system failures	Event/resource
Execution, delivery, and process management	Processes

the risks that will be identified. Although some high-level risk repositories have been defined by the regulator for reporting purpose, there is no mandatory standard shared by all the institutions.

To figure out that it is not an easy exercise to define a consistent taxonomy, we just need to have a look at the names of the Basel loss event categories (Table 3.2).

In this simple example, it appears that some categories focus on events, others focus on resources, still others focus on processes and some are a mix of those. Consistency sounds quite a difficult objective to reach.

As a consequence, risk repositories vary a lot across institutions by many aspects. One that may be of concern as far as knowledge management is concerned is the breakdown of the activities. A few years before the raise of the operational risk management, business process management was a very topical issue in large institutions. Helped by consulting firms, institutions have conducted some very resource-consuming business process analyses that delivered plenty of documentation and more importantly some repositories of business processes.

When it came to proposing a breakdown of exposures in the firm, it was natural to leverage those business process repositories. However, we believe that this was not a good idea as business processes are transversal to the firm. Business processes are a useful engineering concept to identify inefficiencies and improve performance. However, from a knowledge management perspective, a business process is not very concrete or observable. For instance, it is sometimes difficult to identify the business processes owners. From what we have seen, the organization of a company is articulated more around business lines and product lines than processes. People work for business units, not for business processes.

Fortunately, the process-based repositories are the exception. Most of the institutions we have been working for use a business breakdown that is either a refined version of the Basel list of business lines (see Table 3.3) or a refined version of the firm business structure as presented in their annual report.

3.1.1.2 A Bottom-Up Approach Can Become Intractable When designing the taxonomy or naming the risks, institutions that have the same activities run in many different locations should be cautious about using a bottom-up method. We will illustrate this point with an experience we had in 2008.

Our client was a large French retail bank organized into relatively independent regional banks.

TABLE 3.3 Basel Lines of Business

Level 1	Level 2
Corporate finance	Corporate finance Municipal/Government Finance Merchant banking Advisory services
Trading and sales	Sales Market making Proprietary positions Treasury
Retail banking	Retail banking Private banking Card services
Commercial banking	
Payment and settlement	
Agency services	Custody Corporate agency Corporate trust
Asset management	Discretionary fund management Nondiscretionary fund management
Retail brokerage	

A major consulting firm had advised this bank to carry out an independent risk mapping in each regional bank before merging the risk maps at the central risk management team level.

This was probably a good idea for the consulting firm as this type of bottom-up mission needs a lot of human resources. But the result of this important work was totally useless.

The project had collected thousands of risks from the regional banks, but it was not possible to reconcile similar risks between them, other than by reading and interpreting the risk descriptions. As we had been recruited to build scenario models, we still had to select candidate scenarios from this heterogeneous taxonomy. For this purpose, we used natural language processing algorithms. The result was not perfect, but at least it was usable.

A few months later, the bank decided to restart the definition of its risk taxonomy from scratch. Although some iterations may be necessary to validate the choices made by the central risk management team, a centralized definition of the risk framework is needed before distributing it to all business units, to ensure overall consistency from the outset.

3.1.1.3 Is Completing the Risk Register Just Checking Boxes? Once the risk taxonomy has been defined, the usual practice is that the first line of defense has to populate the risk register. Business lines are requested to establish a list of the risks that could affect them. It would not be an exaggeration to classify the methods used to populate the risk register between two extremes: the risk-aware practice and the administrative practice.

Let us start with the administrative method: the person from the first line of defense dedicated to risk identification goes through the list of risks proposed by the taxonomy that pertain to his or her line of business and checks those that he or she believes could occur. This process implies that the risk taxonomy is very granular and encompasses all specific situations.

As far as we know, this approach is frequently used when the firm has already run many exercises and has built up a reliable taxonomy. However, we doubt it is a good method because it is biased toward past risks and doesn't contribute to risk awareness. It becomes a tick-the-box activity, with little or no thinking.

But we must acknowledge that this kind of industrial process makes it possible to reduce the workload of the first line of defense during risk identification and to re-allocate this resource for later scenario analysis of major risks. At least, it would make sense to come back to a more risk-aware approach on a periodical basis.

The risk-aware method can be illustrated by the example of the first client we worked with for an AMA project. When the client contacted us, she had already built "the firm's risk map". Interestingly, she called this risk map "Expert Based Risk Model" rather than simply "Risk Mapping". But this was intentional, as this meant that she considered this risk mapping as the first step in a modelling process. And this perspective had changed a lot in the way the firm conducted their risk mapping.

Of course, they had defined a risk taxonomy and built a corresponding risk register, but they had done more than that. The risk management team, together with the business people, had defined a list of 22 core activities. For each of them, an operational risk manager had been in charge of establishing a very detailed document to describe the activity and its vulnerabilities as well as the controls in place. The list of risks was only one outcome of this high-added-value work.

This thoroughly documented analysis of the firm's exposures contrasts with traditional practice that is more focused on the event side of the risk. But it was a great experience to achieve a full understanding of the operational risk profile by reading a document written in natural language instead of looking at a spreadsheet or a table in a database.

3.1.1.4 Some Risks Are Not Risks! No tools or methodology can grant that the list of your risks is relevant.

Here are some examples of the strangest or funniest risk names we have encountered in our projects:

- "Change Management": This is not a risk but a cause of risk. A change in a process or a software could increase the probability of an error for example.
- "Project Peak": Project peaks are part of the lifecycle of projects, they are not operational risks. However, a project peak can lead to work overload and increase the probability of errors.
- "Product Governance": This name doesn't indicate any explicit event. What are we talking about? One can guess that the firm uses a light formulation to talk about "mis-selling," but this is definitely not a self-explanatory naming.
- "Operational Precision": This is neither a risk nor a cause of risk, but a consequence. This name is too broad, as it would cover all possible errors.

- "Business Protection": Again, the event is not explicit. This name could cover almost all operational risks.
- "Unexpected payment to customers": This is a kind way of saying "mis-selling"!

We often give one simple example to our clients for defining a risk. Ask yourself if it could actually happen. Ask yourself if you would enter the office of your CRO and announce: "Madam/Sir, a major change management event has occurred".

3.1.2 Risk and Control Assessment

Summary of the lessons learned:

- Defining consistent scores for frequency and severity is critical for RCSA.
- Aggregation of scores must be handled with care.
- The measurement of inherent risk is generally artificial.

This step aims to assess the risks and the controls that have been identified. Practically, the two tasks might be performed in parallel: once one individual risk and its controls are identified, they can be scored without waiting for the completion of risk identification.

The objective of the risk scoring process is to propose a qualitative rating for:

- The frequency of the inherent and residual risk
- The severity of the inherent and residual risk
- The efficiency of the controls that apply to the risk

Companies face many problems in achieving this objective.

3.1.2.1 Rating Scales: Ranks versus Ranges The first problem is the choice of the rating scales.

The exercise is not to provide a very precise assessment of each identified risk, as the number of possible risks may be in the tens of thousands for large institutions. Therefore, the rating need not be very granular. Generally, we observe around 4 to 6 categories, including frequency, impact, and control efficiency.

The rating scale presented in Table 3.4 is a typical example of such a scoring grid and was used by a specialized brokerage firm focused on fairly frequent risks.

This example is interesting, as it illustrates the many issues that need to be addressed when designing a risk or control scale. Each firm uses its own scale. We did not see any standardized approach to score the risks.

The reader has probably noticed that the scale used in the example is both qualitative with subjective labels – "Rare", "Not frequent" – and semi-quantitative, as level names are supplemented with descriptions that contain quantitative information like "multiple of $1,000" and so on.

TABLE 3.4 Scales for Frequency, Severity, and Control Efficiency

Frequency	Severity	Control Efficiency
Very rare *Less than 1 in 5 years*	Low *Less than $1,000*	Inefficient *Less than 25% of losses avoided*
Rare *Less than one in a year*	Moderate *Multiple of $1,000*	Insufficient *25% to 50% of losses avoided*
Likely *Several times a year*	Medium *Multiple of $10,000*	Medium *50% to 75% of losses avoided*
Frequent *Several times a month*	High *Multiple of $100,000*	Efficient *75% of losses avoided*
Very frequent *Several times a week*	Major *Multiple of $1,000,000*	
Continuous *Several times a day*	Critical *Multiple of $10,000,000*	

The level names alone don't contain enough information to be useable for a rating exercise. We have used some scales where the "Rare" event meant a less than 1 in 20 years event, or where the "High" severity meant losses above $10 million.

A word is meaningful in a specific context only. And even if the scope of the scale is limited to the context of the firm, it is likely that the same word ("rare", "high", "efficient") won't be interpreted in the same way by different business units. One must always keep in mind that at the end of the scoring exercise, the ratings have to be comparable in order to rank the risks and identify the most material ones.

Therefore, any rating scale that is intended to be actually used should be semi-quantitative. About that, we would like to raise a warning: integer numbers that are sometimes assigned to the levels of the scale to rank them can't be considered as semi-quantitative information.

Let us consider for instance the scale presented in Table 3.5 with six levels for frequency and severity.

Those integers are ordinal numbers, not cardinal numbers. They can be used for comparison purposes only! This remark may seem self-evident, but we have encountered many cases where

TABLE 3.5 Scales Are Based on Ordinal Numbers

Frequency	Severity
1. Very rare	1. Low
2. Rare	2. Moderate
3. Likely	3. Medium
4. Frequent	4. High
5. Very frequent	5. Major
6. Continuous	6. Critical

such integers were inappropriately multiplied together to infer an estimate of the risk, for example, "A level 3 Frequency multiplied by a level 4 Severity results in a level 12 risk". We have learned at school, when we were young children, that ordinal numbers could not be combined together within arithmetic expressions, but we have since forgotten.

A semi-quantitative scale should be expressed within a time period for frequency and in a local currency amount for the severity.

Is a semi-quantitative scale appropriate for controls? It would be great if one could say that a control can reduce the risks by 25% or 50% or 75%. For most of the controls we know, this is impossible. Being in a position to say that a specific control can reduce the average loss by 25% or 50% is unrealistic, except in the case of very targeted and simple controls. If you have a human doublecheck on the dollar amount of wire transfers, and if you know, based on external research, that the probability of not detecting an error is 5%, then you could claim that the control divides the risk by a factor of 20. But most of the controls are not that simple.

For controls assessment, we recommend the use of very simple and subjective scales.

3.1.2.2 Rating Scales: Relative versus Absolute For institutions with several business lines or with geographically distributed activities, one of our clients was using a method for severity scale that is worth mentioning. Instead of using the same scale for all the business units, its framework was proposing a relative scale method. Each level was covering a range for severity expressed in a number of days of revenue (see Table 3.6). This makes a lot of sense, as each business unit has its own perception of the risk and can use the full rating scale. With an absolute scale, small business units would use the lower levels while large ones would use the upper levels.

The relative scale simultaneously addresses two problems: the local assessment of risks within a business unit and the overall comparison of the risks at the firm level.

3.1.2.3 Severity Rating: Average versus Extreme The firms can also have different requirements regarding which "severity" should be assessed. Some frameworks are requesting the assessment of the maximum severity while others are requiring the assessment of the average severity or even both of them.

In determining the best option, it should be remembered that people assessing risks are generally not statisticians. Their assessment will be based on their perception or experience. Those who are exposed to frequent risks (credit card fraud, transaction errors, etc.) will be

TABLE 3.6 Relative Severity Scale

Label	Magnitude
1. Negligible	Loss ≤ 1 hour of revenue
2. Low	1 hour of revenue < Loss ≤ 1 day of revenue
3. Medium	1 day of revenue < Loss ≤ 1 week of revenue
4. Serious	1 week of revenue < Loss ≤ 1 month of revenue
5. Very serious	1 month of revenue < Loss ≤ 1 year of revenue
6. Major	1 year of revenue < Loss ≤ 3 years of revenue
7. Fatal	3 years of revenue ≤ Loss

able to estimate the average impact because they have experienced many events and can average them. On the other hand, when it comes to rare and severe risks, people's perception is generally biased toward extreme losses and the estimation of average severity is out of reach as the average is not directly experienced.

For example, if, as an IT subject matter expert (SME), you had to rate the risk of a massive cyber-attack on your trading system, since this has probably not happened frequently in your firm, you might imagine one specific adverse situation that you could experience, but it is very unlikely that you would think of all the situations in order to come up with an average severity. You may have the opportunity to do so during scenario workshops, but not during the RCSA.

Therefore, scoring average severity makes sense for frequent risks, while assessing the maximum severity makes sense for severity risks.

When a firm has chosen to assess both the maximum and the average severity, there are always some later doubts on how people have actually interpreted the two metrics, and as result on how we should use them for major risk selection or risk management decisions.

3.1.2.4 Does Inherent Risk Really Make Sense? To be honest, we don't know why this practice of assessing the residual and inherent risk has been disseminated in the financial industry. But it is a fact nonetheless, and most of the consulting firms have contributed to this dissemination.

This practice is supported by a logical reasoning that can be summarized through the following equation:

$$\textit{Residual risk} = \textit{Inherent risk} - \textit{Controls}$$

This equation relates the residual risk, that is, the current risk to your business, to the inherent risk, that is, the risk to your business if there were no control, and the controls currently in effect. From a theoretical point of view this equation makes sense, but from a practical point of view it is not applicable.

As we have worked on industrial risks, with nuclear industry or transportation industry for example, we guess this approach is transposed from industrial risk assessment, where it makes sense because risk mitigation devices – sprinklers, containment cells, safety valves, and so on – are clearly identified, and their impact on the reduction of probability or severity is accurately modeled.

The general problem that is posed to anyone in charge of assessing the inherent risk can be formulated as follows: Currently you work in a firm with a control environment; now imagine that these controls are removed. What do you think the risk level be? Actually, the question is asked for each risk individually.

The difficulty of this thought exercise depends on the type of risk, as illustrated by the examples given in the following paragraphs.

If a fire door between two server rooms is the only device that has been installed to prevent a fire from spreading, you could easily imagine that removing it would lead to an inherent maximum severity equivalent to the total destruction of the two rooms. In the real world, even for this very simple type of event it would not be so easy, as there can be multiple controls:

What about the annual training session with the fire department, the sprinklers, and so on? How should you combine the controls and then imagine the results if you remove them?

Let us now consider another risk: the breaching of antitrust regulation. This risk belongs to the category of Conduct Risks. The controls related to this type of risk are mostly cultural, imagining their removal is impossible, as they are very difficult to identify. Therefore, distinguishing between inherent risk and residual risk is practically impossible for this kind of risk.

Except for very technical risks, it is not a good practice to ask the first line of defense to assess the inherent risk. They may be asked to assess the residual risks because they reflect the existing risk profile. They may be asked to assess the controls because they are part of the business environment and can be observed. But the inherent risks are not observable and should be inferred.

We do not recommend carrying out inherent risk assessment, but if the risk assessment framework requires it, we want to warn against a bad practice that we have observed. As we have already noted, scores are not actual measures that can be processed through usual arithmetic expressions: It is wrong to calculate the inherent risk score (frequency or severity) by subtracting the residual risk score from the control efficiency score, as the equation above may suggest.

3.1.2.5 Keeping Track of Information Used for Rating Let us discuss briefly the nature of information that should be considered for risk rating.

Ideally, the rating should be a judgement made by the business about the future. To inform this judgement, one should use the following information:

- Internal losses: What has already happened could occur again
- External losses: What had already happened to others could happen to the firm.
- New regulations: To determine the next regulatory issue
- Internal and external surveys: To forecast changes in risk factors (market, social, etc.)

Clear statements must be made in the methodology documents about which source of data must be used. When a score is used for risk ranking or risk selection, it must be clear if this score only summarizes forward-looking information or if it combines both backward-looking and forward-looking information.

If this statement is not clear, which is unfortunately quite common, it can't be assumed that the RCSA reflects all the available knowledge about the risks. As a consequence, for a subsequent stage of risk ranking and risk selection, internal and external losses must again be relied on. This makes the whole process a little bit more complex and takes more time.

3.1.2.6 Using the Rating Matrix The result of any useful RCSA could be displayed on the following type of graph:[3]

- The horizontal axis contains the levels of frequency
- The vertical axis contains the levels of severity (average or max)
- Each small circle represents a risk that has been identified.

[3]This matrix might be transposed to be aligned with the usual distribution presentation, where horizontal axis is for severity and vertical axis is for frequency.

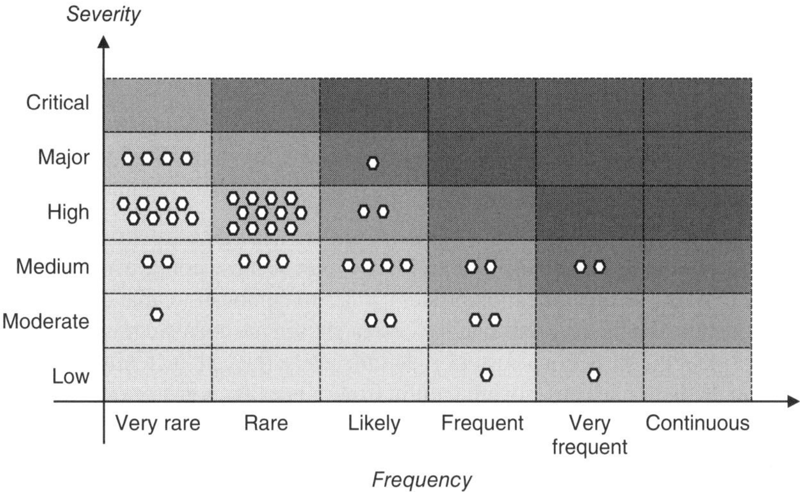

FIGURE 3.1 A Risk Matrix

If a consistent semi-quantitative scoring scale has been defined, as discussed above, all the risks identified by the firm could be put in the same matrix and could be compared (see Figure 3.1). This matrix could also include some specific colors to represent the efficiency of the controls.

If the rating scale is not consistent, this objective is out of reach and the RCSA would require a very costly re-engineering to become a useful part of the risk quantification process. This is not a theoretical issue – we have faced this kind of late redesign when a firm became aware that its RCSA was not able to identify the major scenarios of risk.

However, before placing the risks in this matrix, some aggregation operations might be needed. To give a flavor of what we mean by aggregation, let us imagine the situation where a trading error risk has been identified by many trading desks separately. Thus, one risk would be assigned several scores depending on the trading desk that has rated it.

When it comes to decide, at the level of firm, whether the risk has a high severity or high frequency, these ratings must be aggregated. For instance, let us assume that one trading desk has decided to rate the trading error [Frequency = Usual – more than 1 per month, Severity Max = High – around $10m] and another business unit has rated this as [Frequency = Rare – less than one in five years, Severity Max = Major – around $100m]. In this case, we could logically consider that the maximum severity is the maximum of the two assessments, that is, "Major", and that the frequency is the sum of the frequencies, that is, "Usual" (Table 3.7).

With a few precautions, aggregation is not so difficult when the rating scale is consistent.

TABLE 3.7 Aggregation of Two Assessments

Assessment	Frequency	Max Severity
#1	Usual (≥ 1 per month)	$10m
#2	Rare (< 1 in 5 years)	$100m
Aggregation	Usual (≥ 1 per month)	$100m

Once the risks are placed in the matrix, the good but not necessarily usual practice is to define a set of rules based on the frequency, the severity and the control level that enable to tell which risks should be quantified by scenario-based approaches and which risks should be quantified by data-driven approaches.

We have experienced this very consistent usage of the RCSA in practice and this led to very consistent selection of the scenarios that is not easy to challenge by regulators.

But we also experienced some less successful approaches where the scenario selection process was loosely coupled with the RCSA. The problem is that at some point, when the firm applies for an approval of its risk quantification process, it has to demonstrate that the list of risks that have been modelled and the methods that have been chosen are consistent with the RCSA outputs. Late rework of the RCSA or a posteriori definition of a relevant matching process between the RCSA and the list of scenarios were painful experiences for some of our customers.

3.2 LOSS DATA

Summary of the lessons learned:

- Operational risk assessment relies too much on internal losses.
- External loss data should be used more for extreme risk assessment.
- When available, business event databases should contribute to risk assessment.

In terms of risk assessment, knowledge is essential. From our perspective, assessing a company's risks is nothing more than building a solid body of knowledge about risks. Along with the RCSA,[4] the loss data have long been considered as a core piece of knowledge by operational risk teams. While we certainly agree that loss data are important to inform the perception a firm has of its risks, this importance has probably been overweighted over the past years because a statistical culture has dominated in this area until recent pushback from the regulator on the use of internal models.

Beyond simply meeting certain regulatory requirements that require firms to collect their loss data on a regular basis, we observed three main uses for loss data:

1. *Risk analysis:* Since what has happened in the past could occur again in the future, it is reasonable to consider the past events as a good source of information to analyze future potential losses. This implies that a sufficient description of each material loss must be provided. Theoretically, on the basis of a good description, it should be possible to identify the drivers of a risk.
2. *Model Building:* Loss data, provided that they are of good quality, can be used to inform the assessment of the frequency, the severity or the components of the severity of a risk. Losses are more useful to frequent risk models than they are to extreme risks models.

[4]Risk and Control Self-Assessment database.

3. *Model Validation:* Loss data can also be used to challenge the results of the risk models. For this purpose, it is generally useful to use external loss data as well as internal loss data, especially to address the validation of extreme risk models.

To be comprehensive when discussing loss data, operational risk events that have not resulted in actual financial losses (i.e., near misses) or that have resulted in financial losses that are difficult to measure (i.e., loss of revenue due to business disruption) should be considered.

Four types of operational risk event data can be used in the context of operational risk quantification:

1. *Internal loss data (ILD):* These data correspond to financial losses due to operational events as reported by the firm's business lines. Due to regulatory requirements and especially because of the LDA[5] models, firms have made a lot of efforts to create such databases. As a result, most companies have very good internal loss data.
2. *External loss data (ELD):* This data is provided by external suppliers, whether they are industry consortia (e.g., ORX, ORIC) or companies (e.g., FIRST by IBM). These services are subscribed to by most companies.
3. *Internal specific loss data (ISD):* Companies also have databases in which events related to specific activities or types of events are recorded. For example, trading errors or algorithm errors are recorded by market risk management teams as part of their normal activities. Similarly, the legal teams regularly monitor all events related to legal matters (increase in provisions, settlements, etc.). These data are used to feed the internal loss database, but they transmit much more knowledge than the internal loss data.
4. *External specific loss data (ESD):* These data, built by external companies or research laboratories, can be useful to address specific risks. As an example, the Global Terrorism Database[6] can be a reliable source of information to address the risk of a terrorist attack, the Securities Class Action Clearinghouse[7] database may be used to cover Securities Class Action scenarios.

Let us now talk about our experience on the use of these different type of data in the context of operational risk quantification. Different institutions may have different usages that we have not experienced, but since we have worked closely with different types of financial institutions, and in particular with some of the most important ones, over the past 10 years, we can reasonably assume that the picture we are giving is representative.

3.2.1 Internal Loss Data

As mentioned above, much effort and resources have been devoted to the development and the maintenance of good quality internal losses databases.

Before describing how loss data are used in quantitative assessment of risk, it is important to remember how losses are organized and recorded in databases. To put it simply, losses are recorded along two dimensions: the business line where the event has occurred and the type

[5]Loss Distribution Approach.

[6]www.start.umd.edu/gtd/ (accessed 4 October 2018).

[7]securities.stanford.edu/ (accessed 4 October 2018).

of event. The granularity of the taxonomy depends on the institution. Some institutions can have more than five levels of business lines. Regardless of granularity, the loss taxonomy is generally designed to be consistent with regulatory reporting requirements. Since most internal losses databases were established in accordance with Basel regulation, loss taxonomies are generally consistent with the Basel matrix.

What we want to emphasize is that, although loss taxonomies may be relevant for developing statistical models of frequent risks, they are often difficult to use in the case of extreme risk scenarios. Why? Because when it comes to scenario assessment, the categories provided by loss data are too broad and fail to address the specific situations described by the scenarios.

To understand how the loss data are used, a distinction needs to be made between the types of quantitative frameworks that have been designed by the firms to assess risks: statistical and scenario-based frameworks. Most firms use both, but the importance given to each part depends on the firm.

The statistical framework makes extensive use of internal loss data to build and validate models. For example, LDA approaches, used for AMA[8], or loss projection approaches, used for CCAR[9], rely on past observed losses to fit the models and assess their quality. It has always been a concern for us that modelers use only statistical metrics – frequency, amount – on observed past losses to extrapolate future extreme losses. Indeed, we acknowledge that the number and amount of past losses may contain information on the frequency and severity of frequent risks, but they certainly do not contain information on extreme risks, as those could exceed what has happened in the past and should therefore be analyzed through a more expert-based approach.

On the other side, scenario-based frameworks generally make a more flexible use of loss data. For this type of approach, it is reasonable to assume that the loss data may contain descriptive information on the loss generation mechanism and its drivers, may convey information about the probability of occurrence, but also offer very little information about the severity of future losses.

In our opinion, operational risk practitioners could leverage the description of the losses to a greater degree, to support their risk analysis. Moreover, although the past losses can provide information about the frequency, it is recommended not to use these losses as they are. First, as explained above, it is quite common for internal loss categories not to be fully consistent with the scope of the risk under consideration. For example, when you want to assess a risk of "fat finger error"[10], you don't want to assess any type of error that can be done in trading business. Therefore, relying on the loss data from a broad event category, without a specific manual selection process, can be very misleading, especially when it comes to frequency. Second, an analysis of the factors of the occurrence should be carried out before considering that the past may reflect the future.

---

[8]Advanced Measurement Approach was defined as a possible method to quantify operational risks by the Basel committee. See Basel Committee on Banking Supervision, "Operational Risk – Supervisory Guidelines for the Advanced Measurement Approaches," June 2011.

[9]Comprehensive Capital Analysis and Review is a United States regulatory framework introduced by the Federal Reserve for large banks and financial institutions. https://www.federalreserve.gov/supervisionreg/ccar.htm (accessed 4 October 2018).

[10]The risk that a trader sends a wrong order (error on price, quantity, currency, etc.) .

3.2.2 External Loss Data

What kind of useful information could be found within external loss data? Nearly the same as in internal loss data, but precautions are necessary since they do not represent the specific context of the firm.

More precisely, external loss data contain very useful information on the loss generation mechanism and its drivers. They are worth using when analyzing extreme risk events as those may be missing from internal loss data.

Moreover, they may provide quantitative support to frequency evaluation, provided that the firm is able to define an appropriate scaling method.

With respect to severity, external loss data are more likely to capture extreme events than internal loss data. Provided that a scaling method is applied to take the size of the company into account, external losses can be used as input data to estimate the distribution of the severity and its drivers.

In the early developments of the LDA, much research has been done to find good scaling methods for operational risk loss events. It has been empirically demonstrated, at least for frequency, that the firm's revenue could be a good scaling factor for the number of losses.[11]

Provided that a good scaling method is defined, the use of external loss data should lead to more robust models, at least for extreme risks, as it allows overcoming the difficulties related to the lack of data for a specific firm and increases the likelihood of capturing extreme events. Indeed, it is likely that a firm in the world has experienced the considered extreme risk.

When they are not used as inputs to the models, they could at least be used to challenge the results of the model. For example, if you have built a model for the risk of "Rogue Trading"[12], it is very unlikely that the model validation team or an external challenge panel would not ask you to check whether your model could take into account the worst known case, the Société Générale 2008 Jérôme Kerviel fraud case.

Although this type of validation should not be considered statistically valid, it is very important to ensure that your model does not miss some key assumptions.

For statistical models, two main difficulties can arise when using external loss data. First of all, as we have seen above, an appropriate scaling method needs to be applied. To do this, it is necessary to design and fit a scaling model. A new model is a new source of error and instability. Since, the results of a risk model are very sensitive to the largest losses present in the database, adding some new scaled losses that could be very large is a concern for firms that do not want to produce operational risk numbers that are too large or too unstable. Second, another potential problem, more practical, is that external losses have their own taxonomy thay may differ from the internal one. For this reason, some work needs to be done to establish an appropriate match between the two databases. This work cannot always be automated, and often requires time-consuming manual work, which exposes the modelling team to challenges from the validation teams.

[11]See for instance: H. S. Na, L. Miranda, J. Van den Berg, and M. Leipoldt (2006), "Data Scaling for Operational Risk Modelling", Erasmus Research Institute of Management (ERIM).

[12]The risk that a trader builds and conceals large directional positions for several days or weeks.

For scenario-based models, we believe that in general, one doesn't make best use of the loss description. The description is commonly used to assign the loss to a given risk when it is not straightforward from the risk taxonomy, and, less often, as a narrative for a possible situation covered by a scenario.

One very questionable practice that we have experienced is the following: an external loss is used as a point estimate in a scenario analysis without justification or scaling. For example, the 2012 Knight Capital $440 million loss[13] is considered as the maximum loss for the "Trading Algorithm Error"[14] scenario, regardless of the size of the trading algorithm business in the firm.

It cannot be said without a thorough analysis that $440 million represents the worst possible loss. Only an expert could legitimately make this decision, after analysis, and on this basis, identify the main drivers of this external event (position, detection time, etc.) and adjust these drivers to the context of the firm to produce a relevant estimate.

When using the loss amount, either scaled or not, of external loss data does not bring much new knowledge to the firm, reading and analyzing the narrative of external loss events opens the way to a deeper understanding of the loss generation mechanism. In our opinion, this is how external loss databases should be leveraged.

3.2.3 Internal and External Specific Loss Data

These data have a focus on a specific area: litigations, trading errors, applications disruptions, terrorist attacks, natural disasters. They contribute to the usual activity or are compiled by external third parties for commercial or research purpose.

These data convey much more information on the drivers of the loss generation mechanism than the internal and external loss data presented above.

As an illustration, let us consider the 9/11 terrorist attack. In a classical external loss database, we would find the date, the description of the event, the cost of the buildings that have been destroyed. If you search the Global Terrorist Database,[15] you will find much more information on the event: the type of weapons, the type of terrorist group, the number of people killed or injured, the range for the damage amount, the specific location and many other criteria (more than 50 per event). This information is very useful when it comes to filtering some specific events. If, for example, you intend to estimate the probability of a serious terrorist attack in London, you could select all the terrorist attacks that have occurred in iconic capitals over the past years, and you could even exclude from the scope the terrorist attacks perpetrated by the IRA[16] organization, if an expert considers that this type of attacks is no longer possible.

Internal specific loss data and to some extent external loss data are used by businesses. These data are never used to build or validate statistical models which is not surprising as they don't

[13]https://dealbook.nytimes.com/2012/08/02/knight-capital-says-trading-mishap-cost-it-440-million/ (accessed 4 October 2018).

[14]The risk that a trading algorithm contains an error that causes an abnormal behavior and results in market losses.

[15]www.start.umd.edu/gtd/ (accessed 4 October 2018).

[16]Irish Republican Army.

TABLE 3.8 Assessment of Loss Data Information Value

Column	Description	Possible Values	
Data	Type of loss data	Internal loss data External loss data Internal specific loss data and external specific loss data	
Risk type	Type of risks to be assessed	Frequent risks Extreme risks	
Step	Phase of the assessment process	Risk analysis Assessment of the frequency Assessment of the severity Validation of the model	
Conveyed information	Availability and quality of the information for the specified use	- * ** ***	No information Poor Medium Rich
Use of information	Use of the information to inform or as input of the assessment process	- * ** ***	No use Rare or loose coupling Medium Extensive or tight coupling

necessarily contain the information needed by statistical models. But what was more surprising for us is that they are rarely leveraged to inform risk analysis or scenario analysis.

In Table 3.9, we summarize how each type of loss data can be used for risk assessment by statistical models and scenario-based approaches. For each type of data, and each type of use, it describes the information conveyed by the data for this specific use, and to which extent this information is actually used by the firms. This table summarizes our experience, and, as such, may not reflect all particular cases.

The columns of Table 3.9 are listed and described in Table 3.8.

This reads as:

- No real risk analysis is carried out for frequent risks; they are addressed statistically per business line and event type category. "n/a" is applied to every row corresponding to risk analysis for frequent risks.
- There is no real risk analysis performed in the context of statistical models, even when modelling extreme risks.
- Scenarios are not used for the assessment of frequent risks. The corresponding cells are set to "n/a."
- External Loss Data conveys high information for frequency assessment of extreme risks (***) but this information is not leveraged by scenario-based models (*).
- Internal Loss Data conveys medium information about frequency of extreme risks (**), but this information is overly relied on by statistical models (***).

TABLE 3.9 Value of Information for Different Types of Loss Data

Data	Process		Information Conveyed	Information Used	
	Risk Type	Step		Statistical	Scenario
ILD	Frequent	Risk analysis	n/a	n/a	n/a
		Frequency	***	***	n/a
		Severity	***	***	n/a
		Validation	***	***	n/a
	Extreme	Risk analysis	***	n/a	*
		Frequency	**	***	**
		Severity	*	***	**
		Validation	*	***	*
ELD	Frequent	Risk analysis	n/a	n/a	n/a
		Frequency	**	–	n/a
		Severity	**	–	n/a
		Validation	**	–	n/a
	Extreme	Risk analysis	***	n/a	*
		Frequency	***	–	*
		Severity	**	–	*
		Validation	**	–	*
ISD/ESD	Frequent	Risk analysis	n/a	n/a	n/a
		Frequency	–	–	n/a
		Severity	–	–	n/a
		Validation	–	–	n/a
	Extreme	Risk analysis	***	n/a	–
		Frequency	**	–	–
		Severity	–	–	–
		Validation	–	–	–

3.3 QUANTITATIVE MODELS

Summary of the lessons learned

- Over the past decade, loss data models have become the dominant approach to quantifying operational risks and have been promoted by regulators.
- Nevertheless, LDA models are not justified by any theory, and have many practical shortcomings.
- Scenario-based approaches are generally too qualitative or meant only to add new data points to internal loss data.
- A new generation of scenario-based approaches that will bridge the gap between risk management and risk quantification is now possible.

With regard to quantitative models of operational risks, we will be deliberately provocative by stating that the past 10 years have been dominated by approaches that could probably be considered quantitative, but that can in no way claim to be modelling approaches.

This is expected to change in the short term as regulation, which is the most powerful driver for the operational risk modelling, is rapidly evolving.

To better understand the landscape of operational risk models in recent years it is necessary to go back to 2001, when the first documents about the Internal Measurement Approach, the early designation for the future Advanced Measurement Approach, were issued by the Basel Committee on Banking Supervision[17]. As far as risk modelling is concerned, what could the banks read in those documents? First, the quantitative standards for internal operational risks measures stipulate that:[18]

> The bank must be able to demonstrate that the risk measure used for regulatory capital purposes reflects a holding period of one year and a confidence level of 99.9 percent.

There was no doubt about the quantitative nature of the objective. This very demanding requirement could be considered as the official birth certificate of the operational risk modelling domain. At the time, the regulator was trying not to be too prescriptive about the methods to be used. But if we take a closer look at these documents, we can clearly identify the drivers for the future biases we have experienced over the past 10 years.

In early 2001 BCBS papers, the regulator proposed a general framework inspired from the Credit Risk Model framework by encouraging banks to define an appropriate breakdown of activities and risks in order to assess an exposure indicator (EI), a probability of a loss event (PE) and a loss given event (LGE) for each business and each type of risk.

This idea was very interesting, because it aligns operational risks with other types of risks, in particular credit risk, but above all because it explicitly introduces the concept of exposure to operational risks. Unfortunately, this concept, which is key to any relevant modelling approach, would be totally ignored by most modelers.

But these early 2001 documents also contained the seeds that have strongly skewed operational risk modelling approaches. The regulator explicitly suggested the Loss Distribution Approach as a good modelling tool for future AMA[19] banks. This method is well known in actuarial sciences[20] but was introduced for operational risk modelling by Antoine Frachot and Thierry Roncalli from Credit Lyonnais Operational Research Group.[21] This support from the regulator

---

[17]See Basel Committee on Banking Supervision, "Consultative Document, Operational Risk, Supporting Document to the New Basel Capital Accord," January 2001.

[18]See Basel Committee on Banking Supervision, "Working Paper on the Regulatory Treatment of Operational Risk," September 2001.

[19]Advanced Measurement Approach was defined as a possible method to quantify operational risks by the Basel committee. See Basel Committee on Banking Supervision, "Operational Risk – Supervisory Guidelines for the Advanced Measurement Approaches," June 2011.

[20]See H. Bühlmann (1970), *Mathematical Methods in Risk Theory*, Grundlehren der Mathematischen Wis-senschaften in Einzeldartstellungen, Band 172, Springer-Verlag, Heidelberg.

[21]See A. Frachot, P. Georges, and T. Roncalli (2001), "Loss Distribution Approach for Operational Risk," Working Paper, Crédit Lyonnais, Groupe de Recherche Opérationnelle.

together as well as numerous requirements related to the use of internal or external loss data made the Loss Distribution Approach the ultimate objective of any AMA bank.

This method has deeply shaped the landscape of operational risk modelling over the past decade and this statement is not only theorical for us. The liveliest discussions we had in recent years, whether with the regulator or with the quantitative teams or even with model validation team, have been linked to our criticism of the loss-based models.

We will present the Loss Distribution Approach in more detail in Part III, but at this point we only need to know that this method is based on statistical modelling of loss frequency distribution and loss severity distribution. Regardless of the complexity of the underlying mathematics, the key point is that this method aims to model the risks, that is, the potential future losses, by finding the distributions that best match the past losses. We will come back to this point later.

It is in this context that we started working on operational risk modelling for a French bank in 2006. We were fortunate that this bank, which targeted AMA, had done significant work on risk analysis but was only in the very early stages of risk quantification. Moreover, we were new to the business and not aware of the dominant approaches. For these reasons, we were naïve but also free of preconceived ideas.

As we were quite serious engineers, we began to review the existing books and research papers on risk quantification. What surprised us when we read books on risk quantification was that, in general, they were not addressing their topic, that is, the risks. Most of these books were a pretext to present a collection of mathematical methods (Statistical Modelling, Monte-Carlo simulation, Bayesian Inference, etc.) likely to be of interest for operational risk modelling. The research topic, risk modelling, was generally addressed quickly in the first chapter, followed by hundreds of pages with mathematical formulas. In fact, it was as if there were no problem or issue to resolve. Perhaps we had missed something and the problem had already been solved!

We can certainly find some very good books on risk modelling, but they generally pertain to alternative scientific fields, for example, Reliability Theory, where risk analysis is more important than mathematics tools. We also found some valuable literature on specific topics (natural catastrophes, human errors, etc.), but to be honest it was quite difficult to find useful literature that covers the modelling of the full range of operational risks.

What was even more surprising is that the modelling techniques were assuming the existence of a large amount of data, even though we had learned that the most important risks are rare events. Finally, it was clear that we would have to build our own foundations to solve the problem.

Why was the culture of statistical modelling predominant in the field of operational risk for financial industry?

On the basis of the many discussions we had with professionals during conferences or during our missions, we can offer some explanations. First, quantitative modelling approaches for operational risk are inspired by market risk models and credit risk models but have been poorly translated. Second, the culture of quantitative modelling is dominated by data-driven models. As a new area of research under strong regulatory pressure, the operational risk field has been tempted to borrow ready-to-use approaches rather than building its own theory.

Let's dwell on the two previous statements to help us understand the methodological shortcomings in the current loss data-based approaches.

In the banking sector, most of the quantitative teams come from investment banking business and are highly qualified to build market risk models. Much theoretical and empirical work has been done in this field, but the roots of market risk modelling approaches can be found in the Louis Bachelier's Theory of Speculation, published in 1900. Bachelier can be considered as the father of the financial mathematics. He was certainly a mathematician but his approach is worth briefly recalling, as it contains the characteristics of an ideal modelling approach. Bachelier,[22] like a physicist, made assumptions about the investor and market behavior and derived a Gaussian random model for stock returns. This model was then tested against historical data.

Since then, this model has faced many challenges, but it has fueled most of the financial models that flourished during the twentieth century. Most of the financial models rely on some kind of structural assumptions on the world or on the behavior of the markets.

Where are the structural assumptions about the world that allow us to say that: operational risk losses follow a log-normal distribution, or a Pareto distribution or any specific fat-tail law? Perhaps we have missed a very important book or research paper, but we are not aware of such work. While market risk "quants" can legitimately rely on pre-existing probabilistic models, operational risk modelers cannot because they have not built a reliable theory of the underlying phenomenon.

Trying to find the best distribution among a list of potential candidates based on loss data could be a method to try to identify an underlying generating process, but this is certainly not a modelling approach.

This logic has a profound impact on the governance of the models within the organization. As modelling was purely data-driven, it could be delegated to quantitative teams who would try to find the magic distribution. Although those approaches were not theoretically sound, we could have explained their longevity by their ability to do the job. But where are those pragmatic methods able to provide some robust assessments of the future losses? We spent many hours arguing about the intrinsic instability of those statistical methods with practitioners.

Proponents of these data-driven approaches argue that they are more robust than scenario-based approaches because they have less parameters. Their argument is that distribution laws have few parameters[23] and thus avoid capturing the noise contained in the loss data. This argument makes sense and is theoretically grounded by the Statistical Learning Theory.[24] For us, this argument was quite strong because as machine-learning researchers in the 1990s, we always sought for neural networks with the smallest number of parameters.

We observed many practices that contradict this argument. Let us examine the two most common ones. First, many distribution candidates are possible to fit the losses. If you have five distributions, each of them with two parameters, this gives 10 parameters instead of the two. Second, one model is built per type of risk and business. If you use the Basel matrix with seven

[22]See Louis Bachelier, "Théorie de la speculation," *Ann. Sci. Ecole Norm.* Sup. 17, 21–86, 1900.

[23]For example, two parameters for the log-normal distribution.

[24]See Vladimir N. Vapnik, *Statistical Learning Theory* (New York: Wiley, 1998).

event types and eight lines of business, this would lead to 56 models. We reach 560 parameters for the overall model!

Two additional techniques, frequently used by modelers, contribute to increase this complexity. Some algorithms optimize the breakdown of the losses to be used. This adds complexity. One practice that is not unusual for loss data-based modelling is to treat the larger losses before they are adjusted with distributions. This practice is intended to ensure the stability over time of the capital derived from the model. For example, it could be decided to remove a very large loss based on risk management decision, or to split a large loss because it was considered to be several independent events. This way, some additional freedom degrees are added to the model to capture some expert-based assumptions on the individual losses. If, in the worst case, all large losses were analyzed and manually selected, this would significantly increase the number of model parameters.

In addition, these so-called quantitative models actually include many assumptions that are not necessarily based on data but are necessary to ensure that the models results are aligned with some reasonable numbers that senior management has in mind.

We think this is a good thing for a modelling process to gather feedback from an external challenge panel; we don't consider this type of retrofit as a manipulation of numbers. But we believe that when a model is challenged because it does not meet the management's expectations, the only levers that a modeler should have would be to refine the assumptions of the business experts, not to reoptimize mathematical parameters that nobody can challenge.

What seemed strange to us was these data-driven approaches, although they had many flaws, had been so widely disseminated in the world of the operational risk modelling that a significant gap had widened between risk management and risk quantification. This contributed to keep the business expert's common sense away from the "quants".

As a perfect illustration of this point, let us examine the answer that was brought by the modelers to the Basel requirement. According to AMA, internal models must include scenario analysis to capture plausible but severe losses. Indeed, scenarios are one of the four mandatory elements to be used to build an internal model.

The cost of operational risk is generally explained by a small number of major events. This is visible by observing the loss database of different institutions, and externally – for example, by examining the ORX[25] public report – showing that 0.5% of events account for almost 70% of the total loss amount.

This should have encouraged modelling teams to design specific approaches for scenario assessment. But on the contrary, they have done their best to adapt the loss distribution approach to this requirement.

So, what can you do if you want to model potential severe losses with a loss distribution approach? Two solutions were proposed and used in capital models: use a class of very heavy-tailed distributions, or create new artificial points.

[25]From ORX public report "Beyond the Headlines," November 2017.

As there is no underlying theory to support the use of a specific distribution, why not use the family of distributions of the Extreme Value Theory? This is a purely mathematical idea, there is no possible challenge by the experts, there is some sweat every year when it comes to updating the model with new data – but why not?

But if this method could answer the problem of capturing extreme losses it did not really answer the requirement of including scenarios in the calculation. This is where the second method joins the game. In order to add artificial points representing potential losses, business experts were requested to tell a story about what might happen in the future, such as "The bank is fined \$200m for violating the Client Asset Protection rules on a volume of approximately \$25bn of clients' custodian assets". Then, and this was not the easiest part, this adverse situation needed to be assigned a probability.

This type of scenario assessment can generate dozens of points to add to the observed losses. And then, the usual loss data-based modelling can be applied by the "quants." Note that these additional artificial points are of course new degrees of freedom for the overall model!

In summary, quantitative modelling has been largely dominated over the past 10 years by loss data-driven models, that is, empirical models that are calibrated from loss data. Other approaches, such as scenario-based approaches, although they might be quantitative, are not eligible for quantitative models in most current risk modelling frameworks.

For us, this domination may be explained by cultural biases in favor of statistical modelling because quants teams were generally composed of statisticians, but it was implicitly supported by regulatory requirements that recommended extensive use of internal or external losses. However, in recent years, a significant change has been initiated by the regulator. In response to a growing concern on the complexity of the loss-based models, which made them unstable, unchallengeable, and unsuitable for risk management, the regulator decided in March 2016 to replace the Advanced Measurement Approach with the Standardized Measurement Approach, which gets rid of internal model for regulatory capital assessment.[26]

For many reasons, this method has received a pushback from the banks and is not currently applied by the financial institutions. However, it is likely that the framework for regulatory capital calculation will be simplified and standardized. This doesn't sound the death knell for the operational risk models. Indeed, the focus is now switching from regulatory capital to risk management applications and stress testing, and models are now expected to be both quantitative, in the sense that their results are numbers and even distributions, understandable to business experts, and useful for risk management.

Therefore, there are opportunities for a new generation of models to emerge. These models should be more based on assumptions made by business experts and less driven by statistics. Among these models, scenario-based approaches are quite good candidates, because many banks have already implemented them. However, many current scenario-based approaches need to be upgraded to move to more structured and less qualitative methods.

[26]See Basel Committee on Banking Supervision, "Consultative Document, Standardised Measurement Approach for Operational Risk," March 2016.

3.4 SCENARIOS WORKSHOPS

Summary of the lessons learned:

- It is difficult to identify experts and even more difficult to set up stable working groups for scenario workshops.
- Most institutions use a unstructured approach for scenario workshops that deliver poorly articulated quantitative results.
- Some institutions use an incremental and iterative working group approach. This approach can deliver good results if properly formalized.

Scenario workshops are the usual method to elicit and collect the knowledge required to inform scenario assumptions and provide some estimates for basic risk metrics. Scenario workshops must be considered as knowledge transformation processes.

Knowledge is distributed throughout the organization and sourcing, gathering and processing this knowledge in order to produce some results that can be used for risk measurement is very challenging but is essential to the success of any scenario-based approach.

We have built scenario-based models in several industries – financial, energy, transport, real estate, and so on – for various type of applications – decision making, regulatory. Regardless of the context, setting up and facilitating effective workshops has always been a very difficult and time-consuming task. A simple rule one can keep in mind is that if you have low expectations on measurement, a workshop should be easy to organize and conduct. But if you want to carry out a detailed and quantified analysis of your risk, the choice of the attendees and the conduct of the meeting are the keys to success.

3.4.1 Where Are the Experts?

The scenario workshop aims at building knowledge on a specific risk, usually a significant risk. Regardless of the type of scenario approach, the general problem that a workshop attempts to solve is to provide some reliable justifications for what could happen, how it could unfold, and how much it could ultimately cost. The workshops are intended to bring reliable justifications to the table.

And reliable justifications can only be provided by the company's people who are reliable for their recognized expertise, the so-called experts or SMEs. Niels Bohr, the famous physicist, once said that "an expert is a person who has made all the mistakes that can be made in a very narrow field". This definition is perfectly suited to the area of operational risk, as it implies that the expert should have a deep understanding of what could go wrong, but it also clearly indicates that an expert's scope is very narrow.

On one hand, this means that for a single risk, many experts may be required. On the other hand, some people with broad knowledge are needed to embrace the full picture for one risk. If you are facing a risk that could impact many businesses in the company, say a cyber-attack on critical applications, you normally need around the table experts from IT, experts from wire-transfers, experts from trading applications and many others. But it would also require, in addition to that, someone with a general and transversal knowledge because each of the experts would have only a narrow vision of the problem.

We will come back later on to how institutions identify people with a broad overview and knowledge. For now, let us start with the first issue that must be overcome: finding out the right experts.

The larger a financial institution is, the more difficult it is to identify experts. There is no directory of experts that could be could be relied upon to reach the right person. You may find many information about an employee's profile in the phone book, but as far as we know, the "expert" status doesn't exist. The concept of "expert" is not clearly defined or framed as it could be for industries where knowledge management is a critical issue[27].

Furthermore, as discussed previously, for the same risk, many business units might be exposed. Even risks that might a priori look like to have a very narrow exposure may involve many potential SMEs.[28] For example, if one considers the risk of error on a trading algorithm in a large institution, there are usually many trading desks in different geographical locations using such algorithms. Finding the right SMEs among employees will depend on the connections, sometimes even the personal connections, of the risk management team with the targeted business units.

Not only must the SMEs be identified, but they must also be committed to the scenario assessment project. Most of them are very busy and not dedicated to risk management tasks. They are involved in the daily business, and that is precisely what makes them experts. While these experts can be invited to a meeting, it is much more difficult to involve them in a stable working group.

When it comes to developing a complete set of scenarios, the potential problems listed above could be even worse, as the process of identifying experts should be replicated for several scenarios.

3.4.2 The Working Group Method

Nevertheless, these workshops must be carried out. So, what are the options for the risk management team? The practical approaches we have experienced so far can be split into two categories:

1. The stable working group method
2. The incremental working group method

One bank can use both depending on the type of risk and the availability of experts. While we recommend the first method, we recognize that the second method can be effective, subject to certain precautions.

[27]See, for example, the report published by the International Atomic Energy Agency: IAEA (2006), *Knowledge Management for Nuclear Industry Operating Organizations*, IAEA-TECDOC-1510, Appendix X.
[28]Subject matter expert.

If we could draw this parallel, we would say that the incremental working group method for scenario assessment is equivalent to the agile programming method for software engineering. Instead of considering that a complete design documentation should be written before software development begins, it is recognized that users' needs can't be frozen until they have used a software, and therefore an iterative approach, with many short design-development loops, is preferred. This is a very practical solution to a practical problem but it has to be formalized to be effective.

We have seen the use of incremental methods with very different results; the following lists some situations for which this method was appropriate:

- The scenario involved many experts either because the event is complex or ill-defined, or because it impacts many business units. Cyber-risk is a good example of such a type of risk because it is multiple and can affect the entire company.
- The scenario was in its first round of assessment, as recently identified, or the scenario assessment project was in the early stages, and the timeline was tight.
- The experts had not been identified and it would have taken a long time to recruit them, or they were identified but couldn't be involved in the long term.

The incremental method was led by the risk management team in an iterative way as follows:

1. Set up a new group of SMEs
2. Share the current version of the scenario documentation
3. Run the meeting
4. Update the documentation
5. Go to step 1

This process is usually stopped when the risk management team considers it has reached all the SMEs concerned. For us, the main advantage of this approach is the fact that it reduces the risk that one expert will bias the scenario too much with her or his opinions. Moreover, it is a self-validating process as each iteration can challenge the previous one.

However, the main potential shortcoming of this method is that it may not converge toward a stable assessment. The leader's ability to recruit the right persons in the right order, to understand the assumptions and ensure consistency between the meetings, is a key success factor for this approach. Otherwise "the last to speak is right" issue might cancel out all the benefits of the method.

We have been through some funny situations in this context. After three iterations on a cyber-risk scenario, we had reached an assessment that was considered reasonable by most experts. The fourth meeting included senior executives and people with broad firm knowledge. This meeting did not go well, because the risk manager who led the scenario evaluation did not sufficiently support the work done to date. When it came to presenting the estimate of potential extreme loss, he was asked to completely rework the scenario assumptions, as the result was 10 times lower than senior management's expectations.

In this case, it is likely that the result of the assessment would have been very different if all the SMEs had been involved together in the same meeting.

TABLE 3.10 Working Groups for Scenario Assessment

Application	Unit Type	Description
AMA	Medium bank	We had to attend and lead scenario workshops with the support of risk management for the 60 major risks identified by the bank. Previously, a comprehensive risk mapping had been carried out for each business line and each support activity. Each subrisk mapping had been established by a clearly defined working group including SMEs and risk managers. As there was no gap between risk mapping and risk quantification, the same working group participated in all workshops on scenarios related to its business line or activity, from scenario description to driver quantification.
Economic capital	Specific business unit	As a technical service provider, this business unit of a medium-sized bank aimed to assess the economic capital required by some of its processes. We had been hired to develop scenario-based models to assess the technical risks associated with payment and settlement facilities. A group of highly qualified experts had been identified to attend all of the scenario workshops. In this specific context of technical risks, it is critical that a group is formed because the analysis can be very granular and discussions must remain consistent between two workshops.
CCAR[29]	Specific business unit in large bank	For a scenario addressing an advisory failure of the Asset Management team, a group of SMEs was formed that contributed to all the workshops. This commitment of a stable group of people made it possible to refine the models in order to include some control drivers and carry out some sensitivity analyses we could not perform for other scenarios processed through incremental approach.

Whenever possible, we recommend that working groups be formed before launching the scenario workshops. We have really achieved good results with this method whenever the scenario is well targeted or the activity affected by the scenario is clearly defined.

Some illustrative examples are described in Table 3.10.

3.4.3 Structured versus Nonstructured Approaches

Whatever the method, the typical practice for a scenario workshop can be summarized as follows. A meeting with business experts is facilitated by the risk management team and sometimes involves members of the modelling team. Prior to the meeting, the risk management and the business experts prepare the list of internal and external losses related to the scenario to help determine the potential magnitude of the event.

[29]Comprehensive Capital Analysis and Review is a United States regulatory framework introduced by the Federal Reserve for large banks and financial institutions.

The discussion generally begins by re-scoping the scenario as the initial definition can sometimes be a bit of a catch-all. This type of discussion might reveal some gaps during the risk identification process. Sometimes the names of the scenarios are capturing a too broad reality or represent risk category rather than risk events: "Cyber Risk", "Conduct Risk", and so on. Sometimes the names of the scenarios are misleading or do not even contain an event name: "Change Management", "Conflict of interest", and so on. How could it be possible to analyze such scenarios without being more precise about their scope?

Then, the discussion focuses on what has happened within the firm or in other companies and how these external events should be adapted to the size and business of the firm.

These simple assessments can help justify an estimate for the most severe cases. A breakdown of the potential loss into different cost components – direct cost, fine, and so on – is common practice during this "quantitative" phase of the workshop.

Then the workshop continues with a qualitative discussion about the controls that may reduce the frequency or the severity of the risk.

Less often, a simple driver-based formula is proposed to evaluate the potential loss. By providing a range of more or less extreme situations for the drivers, experts can come up with a reasonable and justified estimate of the worst cases.

The usual outcome of a series of workshops is either an estimate of frequency and severity, or a set of several extreme situations with their probability and severity: 1 in 10 years, 1 in 50 years, 1 in 100 years, and so on.

The best way to determine the quality of the workshop is to examine the main outcome of this process: the scenario documentation. When reading this documentation, you can easily distinguish between two categories of approaches for scenario assessment: the structured assessment and the unstructured assessment.

If you feel that the quantitative results of the scenario analysis are loosely linked to all the statements or the assumptions articulated by the experts, then it is likely that the scenario approach is not structured. We do not support this type of approach, as the final figures seem to be discerned by holding a "finger in the air" and rather difficult to justify. It could be useful in early stages when the firm is not mature enough and has not yet developed a robust methodology. But if the numbers have to be used as inputs for real applications, regulatory or not, we don't consider that this type of workshop produces anything other than literature and qualitative judgements.

And the more quantitative the expectations, the less relevant this approach is. It is definitely not possible to come up with percentile estimates ("This scenario could result in a $100 million loss with a probability of 10%") without conducting some very structured knowledge elicitation during the workshop.

To be honest, our experience is that the nonstructured elicitation method is not the exception.

In structured approaches, experts are guided to build a quantitative story on the scenarios. They are not expected to speak in an informal way, but rather to identify and assess some drivers and to propose a rationale to combine these drivers. Of course, this type of workshop requires higher skill for the leader, who should be able to structure the knowledge shared by the experts. But the results can meet the high expectations of regulatory risk measurement frameworks.

TABLE 3.11 Loss Equations for Sample Scenarios

Scenario	Formula
Data compromise	Size of Compromise × Cost per Record
Wire transfer fraud	Average Transfer Amount × #Fraudulent Transfers × Recovery Rate
Trading error	Order Amount × Market Volatility × $\sqrt{\text{DetectionTime}}$

The simplest version of the structured approach is to build a simple equation that helps in assessing the loss for a given scenario. Table 3.11 gives a few examples of real or simplified formulas that we have seen in structured approaches for the assessment of the severity.

In a more sophisticated approach, such as the one presented in this book, we conducted four workshops, each with a specific objective:

- Workshop #1: Definition of the loss generation mechanism and its drivers
- Workshop #2: Presentation of the data requested to assess the drivers
- Workshop #3: Validation of the data collected for the drivers
- Workshop #4: Validation of the scenarios results

3.4.4 Key Success Factors for a Workshop

To conclude this topic, we are aware that the method to conduct the workshops may depend on the size of the firm, the scope of the exercise as well as the measurement objective and methodology. However, we would like to highlight the three factors that we believe are key for the scenario workshop to produce meaningful results for risk management decision purpose or regulatory requirements.

1. The identification of a group of experts that is stable over time to ensure a consistent scenario analysis
2. The use of a structured scenario approach to support the knowledge elicitation process
3. The involvement of three complementary groups of skills: the risk manager, the experts, the modellers. The experts provide the business knowledge. The risk manager ensures that the granularity of the analysis is good by balancing the experts' tendency to go into too much detail. The modeller ensures that the analysis remains consistent with the quantification objectives.

3.5 CORRELATIONS

Summary of the lessons learned:

- Correlation is the most important driver of the overall risk estimate and, as such, is subject to scrutiny by both the independent validation units and the regulator.

(*Continued*)

- Correlation assessment methods range from causality analysis to statistical estimation.
- Correlation assumptions are difficult to justify and a conservative overlay is usually necessary.

The worst-case situations are very unlikely to occur at the same time. This commonsense statement could be considered as the justification for all the work done on correlation assessment. The challenge of this work is to quantify to what extent the aggregation of several risks could result in an overall risk that is lower than the sum of the individual risks.

For example, if you have a cyber attack scenario that you have estimated at $100 million and a rogue trading scenario that you have estimated at $200 million, each of them with a 95% probability, you would like to know if the overall risk will be less than, equal to, or greater than $300 million.

Insurance companies base their business model on the aggregation of independent individual risks. They know that among the clients who have paid a premium to be covered in case of a fire event, only a few of them will have a fire at home and will be compensated. Their gain is based on a zero-correlation assumption between the individual risks. If an insurer covered all individual homes located in the same narrow area exposed to forest fires, then the zero-correlation assumption would no longer hold because all homes would be exposed to the same fire event at the same time.

We have named this section "Correlations," whereas it actually deals with the aggregation of risks. This is intentional as "Correlation" is the usual method for aggregating multiple risks. But, as we will see in the following, another type of method can be applied, based on causality analysis.

Risk Aggregation is a significant part of the risk quantification process. Our experience of aggregation is related to the quantification of the operational risk regulatory capital for large banks or large insurance companies that had chosen the Advanced Measurement Approach[30] or the Internal Measurement Approach.[31]

We can classify our experiences into three categories based on our involvement in the design of the aggregation framework:

1. *Designer:* We had to propose an aggregation methodology without any constraints defined by an existing framework. This aggregation methodology had to address both data-driven models and scenario-based models.
2. *Constrained design:* An aggregation framework based on correlation matrices between different types of risks was defined and we had to adapt this framework by designing a correlation matrix for scenario-based models.
3. *Contributor:* We had to feed an aggregation process based on an existing correlation matrix with distributions calculated by scenario-based models.

[30] AMA as specified by the Basel II regulation for banking industry.

[31] IMA as specified by Solvency II regulation for insurance industry.

Before presenting some lessons learned with different methods, let us recall in simple terms the practical problem to be solved at this stage. Whatever the method, the typical situation before carrying out an aggregation process is the following one. The firm has defined a set of units of measurement. A unit of measurement represents a set of risks that will be modelled together. For each unit of measurement, a method is chosen to model the potential losses associated with the unit of measurement. Typically, scenario-based models could be used for the units of measurement that represent rare and high severity risks, while data-driven models could be used for units of measurement that cover frequent risks.

3.5.1 The Correlation Method

From there, the most common method is to use a correlation matrix. This method assumes that the distributions of potential losses are calculated for each unit of measurement. Then two parameters must be defined:

1. The correlation matrix, which contains for each pair of units of measurement the correlation rate between the amount of losses over a given period of time. While 0% means that the units of measurement are independent, 100% means that they are fully correlated.
2. The multivariate probability distribution, also called "copula", determines how the correlation will be applied to individual loss distributions of each unit of measurement.

The correlation matrix is generally estimated from two sources: an estimation based on internal loss data is overlaid by expert judgement. Why should a loss data-based estimation be supplemented by an expert judgement? To answer this question, let us quickly examine all the uncertainties involved in assessing a correlation matrix with loss data.

To estimate correlation rates, a table similar to Table 3.12 must be completed with the cumulated loss amount for each period of time for each unit of measurement.

Before generating this table, the first prerequisite is that the losses must be identified for all units of measurement. For internal losses, at least, this is easy when the structure of the loss database is consistent with the risk taxonomy. For external losses, it would be much more difficult because the external losses taxonomy needs to be mapped onto the internal risk taxonomy and, in addition, the loss data must be scaled. We did not see any of our clients using external loss data for assessing correlations.[32]

TABLE 3.12 Table of Losses Used for the Correlation Matrix

Period / UoM	P#1	P#2	...	P#n
UoM #1	Loss(UoM #1, P#1)	Loss(UoM #1, P#2)	...	Loss(UoM #1, P#n)
UoM #2	Loss(UoM #2, P#1)	Loss(UoM #2, P#2)	...	Loss(UoM #1, P#n)
...				

This table contains, for each unit of measurement, the total amount of losses per period.

[32]To be perfectly accurate, in one project we used correlations observed on external data as a benchmark of the overall correlation level.

Another prerequisite for assessing a correlation between two series of losses is that the loss dates are correctly defined. And, as far as we know, this is quite difficult to set a date for multiyear events. For instance, what date should a firm set for a mis-selling case? Should it be the date of the first claim, the date of the settlement or the date of the last payment? That makes a lot of difference as there could be 10 years between these dates. As a result, some significant amounts of losses may be recorded at different dates depending on the policy chosen.

Moreover, since the comprehensiveness of the loss database is generally ensured for at most 15 years, the number of points used in the estimation of the correlation rate is very limited and may justify the use of large confidence intervals around estimations. One solution often used to circumvent this problem is to consider a shorter period of time, for instance a quarter instead of a year. This may apparently solve the problem of statistical significance by increasing the number of periods but this also amplifies the effect of uncertainty on dates.

Finally, for units of measurement with few or no losses, no correlation rate can be computed directly. Such units of measurement have to be merged with others in order for the calculation to be possible.

All these uncertainties justify why the correlation matrix based on loss data should not be used as is. What we have observed in practice is that this matrix serves as a floor for the experts who will propose a conservative overlay. This overlay is based on a belief that they have about dependencies between high-level classes of risk. This belief is expressed on a quantitative scale.

From our point of view, it makes no sense to ask an expert to have a belief about the correlation between two risks. The interpretation of the question may vary a lot from one expert to another, as we have observed. Most of them have in mind the correlation between the occurrence of two risks, few of them consider the correlation between the amounts of the risks. Some experts even think implicitly of simple causality: would the occurrence of one risk increase the likelihood of the occurrence of another risk?

The concept of correlation is fuzzy to most of us, even for people with a good statistical background. There is a good reason why the mantra "correlation is not causation" is taught to students in statistics and introductory textbooks. But not all of us are statisticians, and experts' estimates can vary considerably depending on how they understand or interpret the notion of correlation.

Fortunately, given that regulators are very concerned about the potential benefits of diversification due to risk aggregation, experts generally provide fairly conservative assessments of the correlation.

Once the correlation matrix has been estimated, the second parameter to choose is the copula. Two main types of copula are of practical interest: the Gaussian copula and the Student copula. There is not much saying about that topic from a practical point of view. A very qualitative argument supports the selection of the copula. The Gaussian copula is known to capture the correlations between low to medium risks, while the Student copula is better able to capture correlations between extreme risks. This means that, for the same level of correlation, you are more likely to sample a large loss in the same year in two different units of measurement using a Student copula than a Gaussian copula.

The Student copula is more conservative than the Gaussian one. This is why the Student copula is often used in practice. There is just one more detail: When using a Student copula, the modelling team must also define the number of degrees of freedom from one to infinity. That's a pretty wide interval! How to choose the right level? The only rule to keep in mind is that the larger this parameter, the closer the Student copula is to the Gaussian copula. Therefore, the larger the parameter, the lower the probability of major losses occurring in two units of measurement in the same year. Therefore, this parameter determines the conservativeness of the aggregation: the lower it is, the higher the aggregated risk.

Practically, most firms are using three or four degrees of freedom as advised by the European Bank Authority in a consultation paper.[33]

3.5.2 The Causality Method

When we had the opportunity, we proposed an alternative approach to the correlation method described below. About 80 scenarios[34] had been identified for which an XOI[35] model had been calibrated. Then we had to aggregate those 80 scenarios to obtain an overall risk figure. To achieve this objective, we first defined with SMEs a set of seven business environment and internal control factors (BEICF):

1. Corporate strategy
2. Compliance and relations with regulators
3. Legal and relation with customers
4. Human resources and competence
5. Internal control resources
6. IT and logistics resources
7. Economic environment

Then we identified two types of probabilistic dependencies between a factor and a scenario:

1. The occurrence of a scenario increases the probability of deterioration of a factor
2. The deterioration of a factor increases the probability of occurrence of a scenario

From this analysis, we built a dependency probabilistic graph including all XOI models and BEICFs. The aggregated risk distribution was calculated by sampling this graph. The technical details of this approach are discussed in Part IV of the book. Let us just mention here that some parameters still have to be calibrated, such as the increase in scenario occurrence probability resulting of the deterioration of a given factor.

If we tried a simple comparison between causality and correlation methods for aggregation, we would argue that causality methods are more consistent and better in term of risk analysis, because they propose a structured approach to dependency assessment. However, correlation

[33]See European Bank Authority, "Consultation Paper, Draft Regulatory Technical Standards on assessment methodologies for the Advanced Measurement Approaches for operational risk under Article 312 of Regulation. (EU) No 575/2013," 12 June 2014, EBA/CP/2014/08.

[34]Each scenario can be considered as one unit of measurement.

[35]Exposure Occurrence Impact model presented in Part III.

methods are easier to implement and challenge, because correlation matrices can easily be compared and copula mathematics are widespread among the "quants" community.

In our view, the main problem of correlation methods is that experts, whether second or first lines of defense, are asked some questions for which they are not qualified. Assessing a correlation is like evaluating the percentile of a distribution: it cannot be done by a human brain!

3.5.3 Are the Methods Equal to the Challenge?

To understand the challenge of aggregation in terms of monetary value, let us share an observation we made. The aggregated risk[36] could be multiplied by three or four if we increase the average correlation from 0% to 100%. As an illustration, for a large bank, depending on the aggregation assumptions, the operational risk capital could vary between \$5 billion and \$20 billion. The stakes are very high!

It also means that no matter how accurate your individual models are, this accuracy may be cancelled out by the large uncertainty on correlation rates. More important, any conservative overlay applied to these models could be offset by the aggregation method. The regulators are of course fully aware of this problem.

On the other hand, aggregation methods of all types contain several parameters that are difficult to evaluate and can be easily challenged. For this reason, the firm must be prepared for a kind of negotiation process around the aggregation method.

In our experience, a lot of work is done to justify that the aggregated risk is conservative enough. Many sensitivity analyses are performed by the modelling team or by the independent validation team on the parameters of the aggregation method – correlation matrix, dependencies strength – to reinforce the justifications of the most sensitive assumptions.

The *implicit uniform correlation* rate is a simple benchmarking method:

- Use of a copula and a *uniform correlation matrix* (Figure 3.2) to sample the aggregated risk distribution for each correlation level between 0% and 100%.[37] The implicit uniform correlation rate is obtained when the resulting aggregated risk is equal to the aggregated risk calculated by the actual aggregation method.
- Use of a closed formula[38] to calculate which uniform correlation rate should be applied to obtain the observed aggregated risk given the observed individual risks if all individual risks followed a Gaussian distribution.

If we wanted to summarize our experience about operational risk aggregation with financial institutions, we would say that although the firms make their best efforts to develop consistent aggregation methods, they are conscious that these methods are, in many respects, challengeable and supplement these methods with a series of studies to demonstrate that they have considered all possible options to make informed decisions on the parameters.

---

[36]Measured by the 99.9% percentile of the aggregated risk distribution.

[37]A 1% step could be used: 0%, 1%, 2%, …, 98%, 99%, 100%.

[38]The implicit uniform correlation rate is solution of the closed formula: $VaR_{ag}{}^2 = \sum_i VaR_i{}^2 + \rho \sum_{i,j} VaR_i VaR_j$, where VaR_{ag} is the aggregated value at risk as calculated by the aggregation method, VaR_i is the value at risk for the ith unit of measurement, ρ is the implicit uniform correlation rate.

100%	ρ	ρ	ρ
ρ	100%	ρ	ρ
ρ	ρ	100%	ρ
ρ	ρ	ρ	100%

FIGURE 3.2 Example of a Uniform Correlation Matrix

3.6 MODEL VALIDATION

Summary of the lessons learned:

- Model validation is designed for data-driven models, and the requirement level is higher for quantitative models than for expert-based assessment.
- As a consequence, validation effort is not always proportional to the stakes.
- More time is spent to validate a model than to verify it is fit for purpose.
- The boundary between model building and model validation is sometimes blurred.

Over the past years, we have built many types of models – data-driven or expert-based – in many contexts – research, risk management, regulatory – and we have had the opportunity to address many different situations during the validation stages.

Before going into the details of the discussion, we would like to mention that the XOI method, described in Part IV of this book, has enabled several large institutions to obtain a formal approval of an internal model by regulators, despite some obstacles encountered during the validation process. This is why we strongly believe that some of the difficulties described below were contextual, and related in particular to the use of an innovative method in a market where the LDA was the dominant method.

3.6.1 Model Validation in Data Science

Our first experience of model validation is related to our early research and professional life. As researchers and then engineers in AI, we have built various neural networks-based forecasting models or classifiers in different areas: financial forecasting, credit scoring, pollution predictive assessment, customer churning, and so on.

At this time, in the 1990s and the early 2000s, the learning databases were not as huge as those currently being processed by the so-called deep learning algorithms.[39] However, it was not unusual to process several thousand examples for learning.

[39]See J. Schmidhuber, "Deep Learning in Neural Networks: An Overview", *Neural Networks* 61 (2015): 85–117.

In this context of empirical learning, model validation was relatively easy to formulate. A model was "good" if it met an error criterion on a set of examples called the validation database. Actually, the process of building and validating a model was quite simple, at least in theory. A dataset of examples was split into three subsets: the learning dataset, the testing dataset, and the validation dataset. The learning dataset was used to calibrate the model parameters, the testing dataset was used to select the fitted model with the best generalization capabilities, and the validation dataset helps to assess the quality of the selected model.

Therefore, to build and validate a data-driven model, you need only a sufficient number of learning data to estimate its parameters and a sufficient number of out of sample data to check the model quality. This approach of validation is based on solid theoretical basis derived from the *Statistical Learning Theory*.[40]

Even in this apparently easy-to-handle situation, "pure" validation is not possible. Indeed, what happens if the model is not validated? If you need to use the model, you have no choice but to update it. As a consequence, the validation dataset becomes part of the model building process and the so-called validation is no longer validation but model building.

In the risk quantification space, as many of the models used by the banks for credit and market risk are data-driven, this type of model has strongly influenced model validation approaches in recent years. In the area of operational risk, the prevalence of the Loss Distribution Approach has not challenged this thought pattern.

As a consequence of this bias, we observed that a lot of resources, people, skills, and tools were available to challenge data-driven models, but very few resources when it came to validate expert-based models.

Let us tell you some stories from the field with our customers to give you a more accurate picture of the validation landscape. As always in this part of the book, we do not claim that our experience reflects what is happening in all institutions, but as these stories relate to different contexts, large institutions and different classes of models, these stories can highlight some of the typical characteristics of the validation process.

3.6.2 Validation Efforts Are Not Proportionate: An AMA example

> *The validation process is very resource-intensive for low-stake data-driven models but is very light for high-stake scenario-based models.*

We had been hired by a French bank that was planning to use AMA for operational risk. According to our customer's requirements, we had built a model with two components. A scenario-based component to address high severity risks and a Loss Distribution Approach to address frequent risks. The scenario-based component consisted of 60 XOI[41] models that covered the most significant risks identified by the bank. The data-driven component was a combination of statistical models, each oneadjusted to a homogeneous set of frequent losses.

Several items of the model were requiring a validation. They are summarized in Table 3.13.

[40] See T. Hastie, R. Tibshirani, and J. Friedman, *The Elements of Statistical Learning* (Springer-Verlag, 2009).

[41] eXposure, Occurrence, Impact models will be described in detail in Part IV.

TABLE 3.13 Validation of Model Components

Model Component	Item	Description
Overall	Methodology	Document that describes how to calculate the overall operational risk distribution
	Results	Overall operational risk distribution
Frequent risks	Loss data	Underlying data used for the Loss Distribution Approach
	Loss data breakdown	How the loss data are broken down into independent and homogeneous subsets of loss data
	Calculation engine	Software program implementing model fitting and model simulation
	Results	Resulting distribution for each Loss Distribution Approach
Scenarios	Expert-based assumptions	Assumptions on drivers made by SMEs
	Quantitative assumptions	Assumptions on drivers that are supported by statistical data processing
	Calculation engine	Software program implementing the model inference and simulation
	Results	Resulting distribution for each scenario
Aggregation	Assumptions on the dependency structure	Dependency between individual models (Scenarios and Loss Distribution Approach)
	Calculation engine	Software program applying the dependency structure to individual models in order to calculate the overall distribution of operational risk

While the scenario-based component covered about 80% of the operational risk capital, the Loss Distribution Approach covered only 20%. And, consistently, our efforts had prioritized the design and construction of the XOI models. For this reason, we were somewhat surprised by what happened in terms of validation and approval.

A four-step validation process was conducted:

1. Validation by the model team
2. Preparation of the independent validation
3. Independent validation
4. Regulator review for the approval

The first step of validation was conducted by the internal modelling team. This team was composed of statisticians who did a very good job of verifying the calculation engines, validating the data-driven model building process and its outcomes. They also tested the quantitative assumptions of the scenarios when they involved some data processing. But they totally ignored the experts' assumptions.

For the scenario component, the accuracy of the validation process was certainly not driven by considerations of materiality, but by the fact that people were statisticians, and, as such, they were very good at verifying the data. We had memorable challenges on errors in the order of

0.1%, while the uncertainty of the experts' assumptions was more in the order of 10%. In the end, this validation step proved that the models were very good for 20% of the risks, that is, the fraction covered by the data-driven models, but that they had not properly addressed the largest part of the risks.

The second step was preparatory work for the independent validation that would be later conducted by the General Inspection. It was carried out by a large consulting firm. Their work was mainly to ensure that models could be validated, not to validate them. However, they attempted to challenge the models at a very high level, identifying potential inconsistencies between the results and the observed internal or external losses. Their work was driven by risk materiality, but it was such a high-level approach that we cannot consider it contributed directly to validating any of the items listed above. Their main deliverable was a list of requests for change on the supporting documentation.

The third step was carried out by the General Inspection. They focused mainly on one of the most important pieces of the model: the assumptions on the dependency structure and the associated methodology to address them. As far as scenarios are concerned, they requested some sensitivity analyses on some of the most severe scenarios and checked whether our models took the controls into account.

Therefore, before meeting the regulator, most of the elements had been reviewed and validated, with the exception of the expert-based assumptions for the scenarios, and these assumptions were probably, along with the dependency assumptions, the main drivers for the overall outcome. While these assumptions had been carefully examined by the SMEs during the model development process, no validation by independent experts had been carried out.

We expected to be questioned on this point during the last stage of the validation process: the audit by the regulator. We consider this audit as the ultimate validation step as it determines whether the bank can use its model in real life. We had prepared for the review for months and spent a lot of time improving the documentation on both components of the models. Naturally, we had put most of our resources on the scenario-based component, because it was the most material.

If our only objective had been approval, we should have spent more time learning about the auditors' profile, academic background and professional skills. The members of the team who conducted the review of the models were all statisticians. And people like to question what they know. So, they spent 80% of their time challenging the Loss Distribution Approach model and 20% challenging the scenario-based models.

Even when reviewing the scenario-based models, their effort was not driven by materiality. They picked up a random sample of scenarios and focus on quantitative assumptions to find out some potential statistical flaws that, for the most part, would not affect the results.

At the end of the day, 80% of their time had been devoted to reviewing 20% of the capital. For sure, this was not the most effective allocation of resources, but above all, some very important assumptions had not been challenged. The model could have been very poor on the most material risks without any warning from the auditors.

The whole process involved many people over a long period of time. But we can say with certainty that they had not grasped the main feature of the specific model we proposed. They focused on what they were able to validate, that is, calculations and statistics, rather than designing approaches to deal with the most subjective parts of the model.

This first experience relates to the first generation of AMA models in Europe. Since then, the validation process of operational risk models has been formalized by internal guidelines to cover qualitative and quantitative approaches for risk assessment.

Regardless of the sophistication of the validation process, it seems that at least three statements remain true. First, expectations and requirements for quantitative models are very high, while they are low for qualitative models. Second, any model that produces a distribution of risks is called a quantitative model. Third, quantitative models that are not based on data are not properly validated.

3.6.3 Validation Frameworks Are Too Specific: A CCAR[42] Example

To illustrate this, let us briefly review another experience we had, some years later, with a large financial institution in the context of the CCAR regulatory framework. We had been engaged to contribute to one component of the operational risk assessment: the scenarios for the most significant risks.

For model validation teams, this model was a strange thing. It combined both expert and quantitative assumptions, and, moreover, it generated a loss distribution with a Bayesian network and a Monte-Carlo simulation. Because of the last feature, it was naturally considered as a quantitative model by the independent validation unit.

An attempt to validate this quantitative model involved three tasks:

1. Numerical validation of the calculation engine by the quant team
2. Review of the quantitative assumptions on a sample of models by the quant team
3. Validation of a sample of models by the independent validation unit

The modelling team was composed of quantitative modellers with risk expertise[43] who were naturally unable to challenge the experts' assumptions.

For the third task, since our model did not fit perfectly into the categories defined by the validation framework, instead of designing some new set of methods to handle this type of model, they simply tried to interpret our model as a statistical model.

For them, the drivers in our models (e.g., market volatility, income, number of merchants, number of trading orders, etc.) were interpreted as the parameters of a data-driven model (e.g., μ and σ of a lognormal distribution). This interpretation was conceptually wrong, but it was a convenient way of recycling existing validation methodologies.

We spent a lot of time arguing that no a priori shape was assumed for the loss distribution, unlike statistical methods, and that our drivers were not mathematical parameters that could be fitted from the data. We don't know if we convinced them, but they had to acknowledge that they would not be able to validate these models with the usual method.

It was therefore decided that the model should not be considered as a standard quantitative model and that it would require a separate treatment of quantitative and qualitative assumptions, which we thought was the right option.

[42]Comprehensive Capital Analysis and Review is a US regulatory framework introduced by the Federal Reserve for large banks and financial institutions.

[43]They certainly had an expertise in risk modelling but no knowledge about the risks facing the business.

In addition, to avoid that the quantitative part of the scenarios be subject to the demanding criteria used for the validation of quantitative models, a simplified version of the scenarios has been created.

For this project again, and although it followed a very different path, the validation of the most significant contributions to stressed capital was much lighter and less demanding.

3.6.4 Toward a New Generation of Model Validation Frameworks

We are convinced that model validation frameworks are not adapted to operational risks.

Validation methods are very elaborate and demanding for data-based models, while requirements for expertise-based approaches are quite low.

However, material operational risks cannot be represented by data-driven models, precisely as there is little or no representative data. Any reasonable approach to operational risk modelling should include a quantified judgment about the future. Any model should be a combination of strongly justified beliefs. Theoretical foundations for this type of approaches already exist[44] but model validation frameworks have to move away from the misconceptions that undermine their efficiency.

One of the key components of a new generation of validation frameworks is the “expert”. The concept is overused and not clearly defined. Everything that is not observable is said to be expert-based. For this expert-based assessment to be reliable and validated, the concept of an expert should be clearly scoped as it is in other industries (e.g., nuclear industry). In a bank, many people have high skills and expertise but they should be clearly identified as experts at the bank level. This would avoid considering any person available to attend a meeting as an expert. These identified experts could participate in the validation process and give this new generation of operational risks models real legitimacy.

[44] For example, Bayesian Networks are a promising probabilistic framework for this type of model.

PART Two

Challenges of Operational Risk Measurement

In this part of the book, we will discuss the problem of measuring operational risk in the financial industry, focusing principally on the banking sector.

In the first chapter in this part, we will try to define operational risk – not immediately adopting the usual definitions such as the one used by the Basel accords, but trying to find a rationale to justify this definition. We have experienced a lot of discussions on the boundaries of operational risk, so we believe it is useful to take a closer look at these boundaries, in particular with strategic risk.

In the second chapter, we will discuss the importance of operational risk. Operational risk has gained in significance in the past decade, by an order of magnitude for the amount of losses, by a factor of three in terms of regulatory capital, and by a factor of two for the share of regulatory capital it represents. In this second section, we will also discuss the empirical relation between operational risk and profitability. This analysis will support the further discussion of operational risk appetite.

In the third chapter, we will discuss the need for operational risk measurement. This is of course a regulatory requirement, and although the most apparent trend of the regulation is to go back to a simple and comparable measurement through the SMA, we believe that the requirements will increase when it comes to demonstrating the adequacy of the regulatory capital to the actual risk profile of each institution.

In addition, the strong expectation set by regulators to produce an articulated risk appetite statement also requires that operational risk is measured. We anticipate that although qualitative appetite statements will always exist, at least for emerging risks, more quantitative assessments will become preferable.

Finally, the management of operational risks also requires measurement. Our experience is that operational risk management, in particular in terms of control, is usually focused on business-as-usual types of risks. In a very few cases only, there is a specific set of controls addressing extreme events, as the implicit belief is that business-as-usual controls prevent the occurrence of extreme events. This belief is possibly rooted in the use of the loss distribution approach as a measurement method. As the LDA assumes that extreme losses are the extrapolation of current losses, it seems reasonable to believe that controls mitigating current losses have also an effect on their extreme realizations. But we believe both statements are, in general, wrong.

Finally, in the fourth chapter, having established the importance of operational risk, and the need for its measurement, we will analyse the challenges of risk measurement.

We will in particular discuss the difference between the analytical measurement approach and the statistical measurement approach. As far as risk is defined as the effect of uncertainty on objectives, we can indeed use various statistical approaches to assess the dispersion around the objective; or try to identify all the possible events that could impact the achievement of this objective and assess their consequences. Simply put, this is the difference between observing the performance of 1,000 archers and assessing how far the arrow can deviate from the target, on the one hand; and enumerating all the events that perturbate the next shoot (an unexpected breeze, a flash of sunlight, the flight of a bird, etc.), on the other hand.

We will try to demonstrate that, in most cases, there is a clear line between these two approaches: when measuring a manageable risk, the analytical approach is preferred, and when measuring a external risk, the statistical approach is preferred. This applies to project risk: a project manager will try to identify all the risks of her project, measure and mitigate them, while a programme manager, in charge of a portfolio of projects, will prefer to use a statistical approach for each project. This applies to credit risk. As the default of borrowers is not a risk directly manageable by the bank, the probabilities of default will be assessed statistically. But the level of risk of the overall portfolio can be managed through a rational allocation, taking into account the different probabilities of default, and the correlations between defaults. For this purpose, the enumeration and impact analysis of stress scenarios will prove extremely useful. This applies also, and this is probably the most obvious, to market risk. The distribution of market returns is not something a bank can manage, but it can design an appropriate portfolio structure to optimise the risk/return trade-off. In market risk, also, stress testing has become a usual tool to effectively assess the risk.

For some reason, this did not apply to operational risk until recently. Indeed, the loss distribution approach, or LDA, is a statistical approach. As statistical approaches are considered adequate to measure risks that cannot be managed, measuring operational risk using a statistical approach would mean, from this perspective, that operational risk is beyond the control of the bank, that is, not manageable.

Finally, the regulators, in their attempt to improve the Basel III accord, have clearly expressed the trade-off between the risk sensitivity of a measurement and its simplicity and comparability. This is fully consistent with the logic of analysing what is under control, and statistically assessing what is beyond control. The regulator does not manage the risk of the banks;

therefore, the regulatory requirements should be simple and comparable. In general, this means using a statistical approach. On the other hand, the regulator should encourage banks to assess more analytically their own risks. This is precisely the trend we see through the simplification of regulatory capital measurement and the development of stress testing or capital adequacy programmes.

For all these reasons, we believe that the recent debate around the end of the AMA was flawed. The LDA was the mainstream method used for AMA. The LDA is neither risk sensitive nor analytical, on the one hand; and neither simple nor comparable, on the other hand. So it helps neither the regulator to assess the regulatory capital, nor the bank to manage operational risk. The combination of SMA and ICAAP or SMA and stress-testing is, from this point of view, true progress.

CHAPTER 4

Definition and Scope of Operational Risk

4.1 ON RISK TAXONOMIES

It seems challenging to reach a consensus on the taxonomy of risks. This is probably due to the fact that different taxonomies are generated from different perspectives. The taxonomy may be based on the adverse event, on the nature of the resource exposed, on the nature of the consequences, and so on. The taxonomy may also be based on the supposed cause of the event, or even on the insurability of the loss.

In this section, we will analyse existing taxonomies to try to get a reasonable definition and scope of operational risks.

4.1.1 Strategic versus Operational Risk

It is probably best to start with a definition of *risk*. We will use the ISO definition of risk, as the "effect of uncertainty on objectives."

This definition has the advantage of being extremely concise, and at the same time to contain several important components: "objectives", "effect", and "uncertainty".

The first interesting point to notice is that the definition does not explicitly specify whether the supposed effect of uncertainty is considered when *setting* the objectives or when *achieving* or trying to achieve the objectives. Although the ISO standard mentions in a further note "an effect is a deviation from the expected", therefore putting focus on the execution rather than on the definition, we believe that both effects should be considered. On one hand, the perceived uncertainty may influence the definition of objectives, and on the other hand, the uncertain events that will occur in the future will impact the achievement of the objectives.

An insufficient perception of potential events or difficulties ahead may result in setting unrealistic objectives. Perceived risks should inform the definition of objectives and of the strategy. This does not mean that an optimal strategy can be determined from the initial risk analysis, but conversely, a strategy which is not informed by a thorough risk analysis can be considered as non-rational. However, a non-rational strategy, based on an intuition or a bet on the future, can still be effective.

At this stage we have two dimensions to take into account:

1. For Objective/Strategy: Definition/Execution
2. For Risks: Perception/Occurrence

Perceptions of risks influence strategy definition. The prior analysis of the risk events that may occur during the further execution of the strategy are useful to assess the strategy and to make it more robust.

After the design phase, once the strategy has been defined and is implemented, some risk events will actually occur. Some risk events will only delay or alter the achievement of the objective, but this objective will remain achievable, at maybe a higher price. These events only impact the execution of the strategy, and not the strategy itself. We call these events operational risks, as they impact only the operations that concur to deliver the objective.

Some events will have a more significant impact and will require a redesign of the strategy, or even will make the strategy irrelevant, or the objective set unreachable. We call these events strategic risks (see Figure 4.1).

Obviously, the more comprehensive the perception of risks is during the strategy design phase, the less likely it is to incur strategic risks. But as was said previously, a more robust strategy is not necessarily the most successful, it is only more rational. Building a riskier strategy by betting on the future is likely to be more successful if the initial bet is correct.

This initial dichotomy is important, but it is probably too general to be usable in practice. We will now examine the basis of more detailed taxonomies. We need to keep in mind

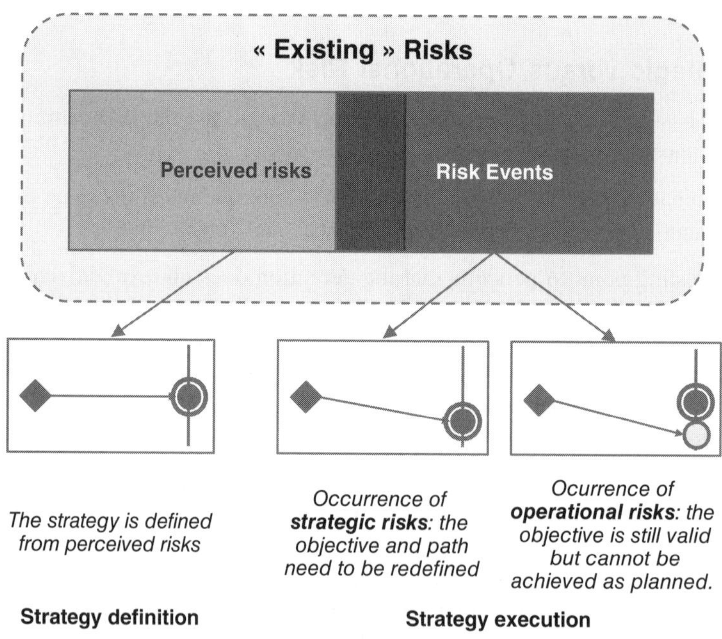

FIGURE 4.1 Strategic versus Operational Risks

however that the question of the boundary between strategic and operational risks often arises in practice, and that the previous analysis will be useful.

Going back to the ISO definition, we can derive the foundations of risk taxonomies from the three components used in the definition.

Defining risk as "effects on objectives" means, as also explained in the note 1 of the ISO 31000 – 2018, that "an effect is a deviation from the expected". Objective and effect are therefore of the same nature, of the same dimension is they are quantifiable. Put in mathematical terms, this can read simply "risk is the variance of the objective around its expected value". Note that this is not necessarily a financial objective. The objective can be defined as revenue or profit but also of course as safety, impact on environment, reputation, and so on. Note also that the consequences of risk are not necessarily negative. The effects are of the same dimension than the objectives (revenue, profit, safety, impact on environment, reputation, etc.) and therefore do not define two different dimensions. The nature of the objective, or the variable measuring the objective, can therefore be a first dimension on which to build risk taxonomies.

Linking risk to the *objectives* implies, as discussed earlier, the existence of a strategy and of an implementation of this strategy. An implementation of a strategy requires resources. The nature of the resources potentially exposed to the risk events is a second dimension that we can use to build a risk taxonomy.

Finally, defining risks as being related to *uncertainty* encompasses the intrinsic uncertainty of the future, but also the uncertainty that results from incomplete knowledge. The different types of uncertainties is the third dimension that we can use to define risk taxonomies.

The three components proposed in the ISO definition can help us envision the axes that could be used for taxonomies:

- Taxonomies based on the nature of the objective/effect variable
- Taxonomies based on the nature of resources used to reach the objectives, or on the nature of the events that can harm these resources
- Taxonomies based on the nature of the uncertainty
- A combination or a refinement of one of the three dimensions above

4.1.2 Taxonomies Based on the Nature of Uncertainty

The uncertainties can be classified according to the now common Know/Unknown approach.

- Known Knowns are certitudes, and therefore are out of the scope of uncertainty
- Known Unknowns, or things we know we don't know. Part of know unknowns can be addressed using probabilities. These are identified variables or events, for which we can characterize our uncertainty. This is the uncertainty due to unreachable knowledge.
- Unknown Knowns may seem contradictory, but "things that we don't know that we know them" could mean some knowledge that is accessible to us, but for which we need to engage in some work to make it explicit – this is the uncertainty due to laziness.
- Finally, the "Unknown Unknowns" or "things we don't know we don't know", are the events that are not even identified, such as technological disruptions, geopolitical changes, and so on.

This dimension is usually not present in business risk taxonomies. This is quite normal as it would be difficult to designate someone as the Unknown Unknowns manager.

There is however a similar, although not equivalent, distinction as proposed by Knight.

The author of Risk, Uncertainty, and Profit[1], designates the measurable uncertainty by risk and keeps the term uncertainty for the unmeasurable one. According to Knight, profit is the result of true uncertainty, while risk management yields only a form of wage.

"Profit arises out of the inherent, absolute unpredictability of things, out of the sheer brute fact that the results of human activity cannot be anticipated and then only in so far as even a probability calculation in regard to them is impossible and meaningless."

Knight links entrepreneurship to true uncertainty, and for this, values uncertainty as the driver of business. On the other hand, he does not necessarily recognise an intrinsic value to entrepreneurs:

"The receipt of profit in a particular case may be argued to be the result of superior judgment. But it is judgment of judgment, especially one's own judgment, and in an individual case there is no way of telling good judgment from good luck, and a succession of cases sufficient to evaluate the judgment or determine its probable value transforms the profit into a wage."

The Knightian distinction between risk and uncertainty does not exactly match the distinction between know unknowns, and unknown unknowns (Figure 4.2). Indeed, some known unknowns, such as the outcome of some geopolitical tensions, or the success of new technologies, pertain to true Knightian uncertainty.

The recent global crisis in 2008 has cast new attention on Knightian uncertainty, and this type of distinction now appears in high-level discussions. It arises typically when senior executives or board of directors try to redefine or improve the foundations of the risk organization within their firm. We don't believe that this type of discussion is undertaken only for

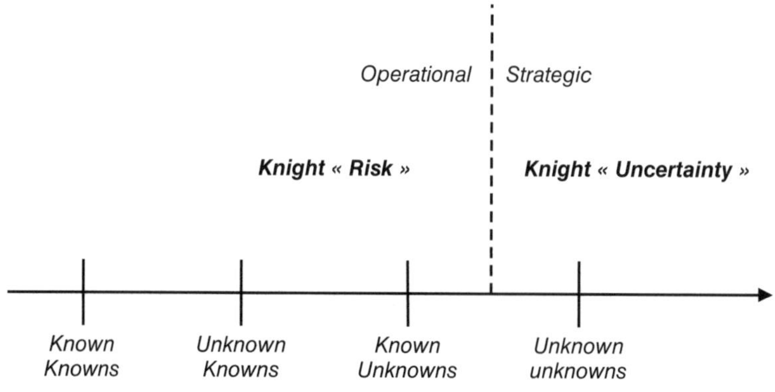

FIGURE 4.2 Knightian Uncertainty

[1] See for instance https://fraser.stlouisfed.org/files/docs/publications/books/risk/riskuncertaintyprofit.pdf (accessed 5/10/2018).

philosophical reasons. It might sometimes be convenient to move the bar from right to left, and to qualify as fundamentally uncertain some events that would have required more analysis.

As a conclusion, taxonomies based on the nature of uncertainty are not operative, as they result merely in the separation between strategic and operational risk, as discussed previously. And furthermore, operational risk is here defined as related to the possibility of prior measurement and is not opposed to financial risk such as credit or market risk. In other words, this dichotomy separates what is measurable a priori, from what is not, and thus would induce categories such as strategic credit risk, and operational credit risk. As relevant as they may be, since credit default certainly entails a dimension of risk and a dimension of uncertainty in the Knightian sense, they do not correspond to the categories commonly accepted.

4.1.3 Taxonomies Based on the Nature of Objectives

Most of the risk analysis frameworks are based on objectives of financial nature. Revenue and profit are the most straightforward financial objectives, but stability of revenue, or geographic balance of revenue, can also be part of the objectives.

Nonprofit organizations will of course rely on nonfinancial objectives, such as population outreach, contribution to job creation, empowerment of minorities, and so on. However, profit driven firms will also set nonfinancial objectives such as passenger safety for transportation firms, workers safety, environmental impact, compliance with laws and regulations, and so on.

Of course, all objectives are interrelated as they all are constrained by available resources – increasing passenger safety will require financial resources that cannot be used for business development, and so on. But this does not mean that all objectives should be considered as reducible to a financial objective.

At a broad level, we can consider four types of objectives an organization should maintain, and for which it is necessary to minimize uncertainty:

1. The firm must be economically viable, which can be interpreted in terms of revenue, profit, or stability of revenue and profit. Of course, most of the focus of risk management is on events impacting the economic viability.
2. The firm must act legally and in compliance with laws and regulations of the different jurisdictions it operates in. Events impacting legality can impact the licence to operate, and correspond to a level of uncertainty that cannot be tolerated.
3. The firm must be a responsible actor in society. Social responsibility can be focused on the workers and therefore on occupational safety and health, or it can be wider and consider the global footprint of the enterprise. Of course, these objectives are in general connected with the compliance to laws and regulations and should go beyond their minimal requirements.
4. The firm must safeguard its reputation. Again, any event impacting significantly one of the three objectives mentioned earlier will also impact reputation.

It is clear that although these objectives can be managed separately, significant events usually impact more than one dimension. For this reason, taxonomies based on only the nature of objectives are not operative either.

4.1.4 Taxonomies Based on the Nature of Resources

A firm is defined by the dynamic interaction of resources combined to achieve the objectives. If a firm plans to go from a Present Position to a desired Target Position, it has to:

- Decide a path (Strategy)
- Chose and organise resources (Tactics)
- Put resources to work (Execution)

We can categorize the resources involved in each step:

- Strategic resources (external)
  - Environment
  - Geopolitics
  - Society and regulations
  - Economy
  - Infrastructures and Technology
- Tactical Resources (external or related to the organisation of internal resources)
  - Competitive environment
  - Processes (how internal resources interact)
  - Portfolios of resources, assets etc (how internal resources are allocated)
- Execution resources
  - Human (Employees, Traders, IT people, etc)
  - Technical (Systems, Buildings, Products, Models, etc.)
  - Informational (Customer data, IP, etc.)
  - Partner (Suppliers, Brokers, etc.)
  - Financial (Financial Assets)

The strategic resources listed here are borrowed from the Global Risk Report of the World Economic Forum[2], which identifies trends in major risks such as: Changing Climate, Rising Cyber dependency, Increasing national sentiment, and so on. These trends correspond to major potential events such as social instability, unemployment, fiscal crises, water crises, interstate conflicts. Any of these events would strike one of the five strategic resources named previously.

The taxonomy of execution resources is proposed in particular in the Associate in Risk Management reference (The Institutes)[3]. We propose the tactical resources as intermediate resources between strategy and execution: they define the result of the resource selection and organisation.

From this categorization of resources, we can identify three broad types of risks. Risks impacting Strategic resources can be considered as Strategic risks, as they shake the foundations on which any strategy is built. Risk impacting tactical resources can be called Tactical risks and risk impacting execution resources can be called Execution risks.

It is important to note that according to this taxonomy, financial risk is a particular instance of execution risk. Credit risk for instance is the risk of default for one my obligors, considered as

[2]https://www.weforum.org/reports/the-global-risks-report-2018 (accessed 5/10/2018).

[3]https://www.theinstitutes.org/guide/designations/associate-risk-management-armtm (accessed 5/10/2018).

a financial resource used to achieve my objectives. In other words, "credit risk" would be an execution risk on financial resources, while "operational risks" would be an execution risk on all the other types of execution resources (Human, Technical, Informational, Partner).

This taxonomy of resources may look too focused on operational risk, at least using the usual definition, as we have a more detailed view of nonfinancial resources. But this would be mainly the perspective of a financial institution, given the predominance of financial assets as resources contributing to the achievement of the objectives of the financial industry.

To illustrate this point, it can be noted, for example, that the five largest companies in the SP100 are technological (Apple, Amazon, Microsoft, Alphabet, Facebook) and represent 1 trillion financial assets and 3.5 trillion market capitalization. In contrast, the five largest banks in the SP100 (JP Morgan Chase, Bank of America, Wells Fargo, Citigroup, Goldman Sachs) represent nearly 10 trillion financial assets and 1.2 trillion market capitalization. At the top level, finance uses 30 times more financial assets than technology to generate similar value.

It is therefore quite logical that financial assets are the main focus of risk analysis in the financial industry. Furthermore, we believe that this has contributed to improperly define exposure as a dollar amount, whereas it should be defined as the exposed resource. But we will get back to this point in Part IV.

4.1.5 Examples of Taxonomies

Here we will discuss some examples of risk taxonomies, from various sources, to see if they use the axes defined above: nature of uncertainty, nature of objectives, or nature of resources. We will see that in most cases, they use rather a mix of these dimensions.

We used a mix of academic and practical sources (Table 4.1):

- The taxonomy of RIMS
- The taxonomy of AIRMIC
- The taxonomy proposed by Ashley Bacon, Chief Risk Officer of JPMorgan Chase, in an interview to risk.net, in 2017
- A taxonomy proposed by E&Y in a white paper published in 2017
- The World Economic Forum taxonomy, in the Global Risks Report 2018

TABLE 4.1 Comparison of Risk Categorizations

RIMS	AIRMIC	WEF	E&Y	Ashley Bacon
Operational	Financial	Economic	Strategic	Caused by adverse economic conditions
Hazard	Infrastructure	Environmental	Preventable	Internal wrongdoings by employees or suppliers
Strategic	Marketplace	Geopolitical	External	Mistakes
Financial	Reputational	Societal		Regulatory, political or social forces
		Technological		Market dysfunction
				Natural and man-made disasters

FIGURE 4.3 RIMS Risk Taxonomy

The RIMS[4] proposes a simple categorization in risk quadrants (see Figure 4.3), which is also used by The Institutes[5].

These quadrants are broadly defined on the nature of resources, as discussed previously:

- Economy, society
- Financial assets or liabilities
- People, processes, systems, controls
- Property, liability or personnel loss exposures

Although the correspondence is not exact, we can recognize the decomposition into strategic, tactical and execution resources mentioned previously.

In addition, the RIMS categorization introduces the notion of pure and speculative risk. Pure risk is usually considered to have only a downside, while speculative risk can have either a downside or an upside. We generally believe this view is too simplistic. When settling down a technology start-up in the San Francisco Bay Area, earthquake risk is traded with business opportunities. We will go back to this point when discussing operational risk appetite.

It also proposes a risk owner for each category, as we can see in Table 4.2.

Another set of quadrants (see Figure 4.4) is proposed by AIRMIC, ALARM and IRM, in a joint document[6].

TABLE 4.2 Risk Owners of Risk Categories According to RIMS

Risk Owners	*Strategic*	*Operations*	*Financial*	*Hazard*	
	CEO	COO	CFO	General Counsel	CRO

[4]Risk Management Society, www.rims.org.
[5]www.theinstitutes.org.
[6]https://www.theirm.org/media/886062/ISO3100_doc.pdf (accessed 05/10/2018).

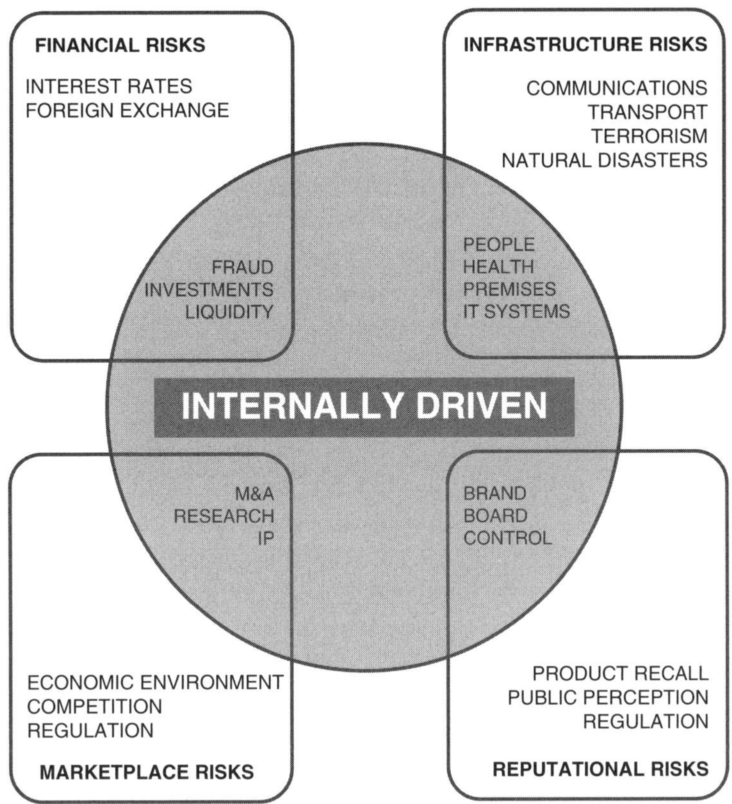

FIGURE 4.4 AIRMIC, ALARM, and IRM Risk Taxonomy

The 4 types of risk considered are:

- Financial
- Infrastructure
- Marketplace
- Reputational

The interesting part of this taxonomy is that, although the four resources broadly match the taxonomy proposed earlier (except for Reputation), there is a "Strategic" and "Execution" dimension in each of the risks discussed.

The taxonomy proposed by the World Economic Forum is of course not an enterprise risk taxonomy. The Global Risk Report defines a global risk as "an uncertain event or condition that, if it occurs, can cause significant negative impact for several countries or industries within the next 10 years."

TABLE 4.3 World Economic Forum Taxonomy of Risks

WEF Risk Categories	WEF Risk Instances
Economic	Asset bubbles Failure of critical infrastructure (e.g., energy) Severe energy price shock
Environmental	Extreme weather events Failure of climate-change mitigation and adaptation
Geopolitical	Failure of national governance Interstate conflict State collapse or crisis
Societal	Large-scale involuntary migration Profound social instability Spread of infectious diseases
Technological	Adverse consequences of technological advances Large-scale cyberattacks Massive incident of data fraud/theft

In Table 4.3, we describe the categories proposed by the World Economic Forum, and some instances of more detailed risks.

Although these categories are clearly not adapted to an enterprise approach, they are certainly the type of stress scenarios considered for instance by financial institutions or regulators when trying to assess the robustness of a firm's balance sheet.

The six categories of risks identified by JP Morgan's CRO, Ashley Bacon[7], are the following:

1. Caused by adverse economic conditions
2. Internal wrongdoings by employees or suppliers
3. Mistakes
4. Regulatory, political or social forces
5. Market dysfunction
6. Natural and man-made disasters

Among these six categories, it is interesting to notice that four can be mapped to the WEF categories in the preceding list.

1. WEF Economic Global Risk: Caused by adverse economic conditions
2. WEF Geopolitical/ Societal Global Risk: Regulatory, political, or social forces
3. WEF Economic Global Risk: Market dysfunction
4. WEF Environmental Global Risk: Natural and man-made disasters

[7] https://www.risk.net/risk-management/5356346/jp-morgans-cro-on-the-banks-six-buckets-of-risk (accessed 5/10/2018).

And the remaining two are operational risks:

1. Internal wrongdoings by employees or suppliers
2. Mistakes

In addition, there is no specific category identified here for market or credit risk. The first category is defined as "everything caused by adverse economic conditions, from interest rate sensitivity to loan losses." But according to this wording, there is no market or credit risk in "normal economic conditions", which means that only stressed situations should be considered as a risk. As Ashley Bacon explains "Banks are in business precisely to take this kind of exposure."

This tends to confirm that the main dichotomy would be between operational and strategic risk.

Finally, the categorization proposed by E&Y is interestingly different, as it considers:

- Strategic risks
- Preventable risks
- External risks

In this document, Strategic risks are defined as related to the implementation of strategic moves: acquisitions, new projects, expansion into new markets. Preventable risks, are, here again and wrongly associated with only a downside, and "should be eliminated". They include misconduct, noncompliance, fraud, and so on. Finally, this report focuses more on External risks, which are decomposed into:

- Political risk, e.g., political instability
- Cybersecurity, e.g., technology dependence
- Social, e.g., social unrest
- Technological, Legal, e.g., changes in tax law
- Economic, e.g., macroeconomic risks
- Environment, e.g., climate change

In our opinion, the way Strategic risks are defined here is closer to Tactical risks, that is, the failure of strategic moves, not the failure of the strategy itself. If a firm decides to expand its business in a given region and fails to do so because the chosen partner was not robust enough, the strategy may still be valid – and a competitor may have succeeded with the same strategy. On the other hand, if the region targeted faces political instability or social unrest, then the strategy needs to be redefined.

To this extent, this taxonomy proposes indeed a decomposition between Strategic risks (which are called External risks here), Tactical risks (which are called Strategic risks here), and Execution risks (which are called Preventable risks here).

The takeaways from this analysis are the following:

- The appropriate dimension to build a taxonomy of risks is the resource exposed.
- Resources are either internally managed or out of the scope of the firm's control.
- Resources are generally associated with type of events.
- Internal resources are typically associated with known unknowns types of events.

- External resources are typically associated with unknown unknowns types of events.
- Internal resources correspond to execution and tactics.
- External resources correspond to strategy.

4.2 DEFINITION OF OPERATIONAL RISK

Having analysed various definitions of operational risk, we can now look at the Basel definition of operational risk, as proposed by the Bank for International Settlements: "*Operational risk is defined as the risk of loss resulting from inadequate or failed internal processes, people and systems or from external events. This definition includes legal risk, but excludes strategic and reputational risk.*"

This definition was further refined into a list of events, proposed in the Loss Data Collection exercise of 2001:

- Internal fraud
- External fraud

TABLE 4.4 Basel Event Types and Associated Resources

Event-Type Category	Definition	Resource Exposed
Internal fraud	Losses due to acts of a type intended to defraud, misappropriate property or circumvent regulations, the law or company policy, excluding diversity/discrimination events, which involves at least one internal party.	Employees
External fraud	Losses due to acts of a type intended to defraud, misappropriate property, or circumvent the law, by a third party	Third parties
Employment practices and workplace safety	Losses arising from acts inconsistent with employment, health or safety laws or agreements, from payment of personal injury claims, or from diversity/discrimination events	Employees, categories of employees
Clients, products, and business practices	Losses arising from an unintentional or negligent failure to meet a professional obligation to specific clients (including fiduciary and suitability requirements), or from the nature or design of a product.	Products Clients
Damage to physical assets	Losses arising from loss or damage to physical assets from natural disaster or other events.	Physical assets
Business disruption and system failures	Losses arising from disruption of business or system failures	Systems
Execution, delivery, and process management	Losses from failed transaction processing or process management, from relations with trade counterparties and vendors	Processes

- Employment practices and workplace safety
- Clients, products, and business practices
- Damage to physical assets
- Business disruption and system failures
- Execution, delivery, and process management

Although based primarily on events (see Table 4.4), the detail of the taxonomy defines the resources exposed.

CHAPTER 5

The Importance of Operational Risk

In this section we will analyse data related to operational risks to support three statements.

The first statement is that operational risk losses are important. This does not mean only that operational risk events did cost a lot in the past – which is true, but also that operational risk is not stable. We will demonstrate this using the example of the 2008 crisis.

The second statement is that operational risk capital is important.

The third statement is that operational risk is related to profit. It is often said that market and credit risks are directly related to the potential profit, but that operational risk is simply a negative risk that could be eliminated at no cost on the business. This is wrong – operational risk taking is directly related to the "speed" of business, and therefore drives profit.

5.1 THE IMPORTANCE OF LOSSES

There is a lot of literature tracing back the origins of creating a specific category for operational risk in banking.

A simple chronology shows that some large operational risk events, real or potential, such as the collapse of Barings Bank after Nick Leeson's rogue trading, the potential Y2K bug, or the terrorist attacks on September 11, 2001, may have reminded the regulators that banks operate in a physical environment, with buildings, systems, and people. Nonfinancial events can have consequences sometimes more serious than credit defaults or market volatility. If we look more carefully at this chronology, and considering that the Basel II reform was already in preparation in the late 1990s, this is probably an a posteriori justification.

Nevertheless, it is interesting to see that the chronology of regulation and events has often coincided, as the Basel III proposal intervenes just after the crisis of 2008 and the collapse of Lehman Brothers. The Basel Committee issued "Principles for Sound Liquidity Risk Management and Supervision" in the same month that Lehman Brothers failed, that is, September 2008.

The same year, the Loss Data Collection Exercise conducted by the Bank of International Settlement, conducted on a panel of 121 banks, showed a cumulated loss amount of approximately €10bn/year, during the years 2002–2007 (see Table 5.1 and the corresponding chart in Figure 5.1). The reporting banks were 50% European, 20% American, 20% Japanese, and 10% countries from other regions of the world.

Ten years later, the ORX association, which collects losses from 85 member banks mainly in the United States and Europe, reports a cumulated loss of €200bn during the years 2011 to 2016, that is, an average of more than €30bn/year (see Table 5.2 and the corresponding chart in Figure 5.2).

Although the reporting banks cannot be matched, there is a clear increase of the total amount of losses reported, taking also into account that ORX uses a €20,000 reporting threshold while more than 80% of the respondents of the BIS LDCE study used thresholds below €10,000.

TABLE 5.1 Loss Data Collection Exercise, 2008

Year	Number of Institutions Reporting	Number of Losses Reported	Total Loss Amount (€ millions)
2002	35	10,216	12,069
2003	55	13,691	4,562
2004	68	22,152	7,212
2005	108	33,216	9,740
2006	115	36,386	7,446
2007	117	36,622	7,875
2008	84	5,582	971

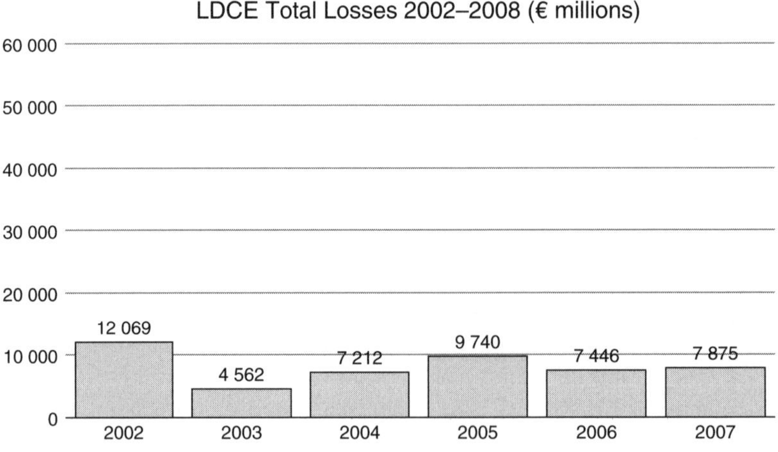

FIGURE 5.1 Results from the 2008 LDCE
Source: Based on data from Bank for International Settlements, July 2009.
The graph is scaled to €60bn maximum for easy comparison with the next graph.

TABLE 5.2 ORX Public Losses Statistics (2017)

Year	Number of Institutions Reporting	Number of Losses Reported	Total Loss Amount (€ millions)
2011	≤85	49 729	56 908
2012	≤85	54 597	34 951
2013	≤85	59 080	26 002
2014	≤85	60 865	34 120
2015	≤85	62 916	27 369
2016	85	60 311	21 312

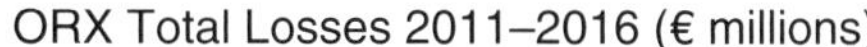

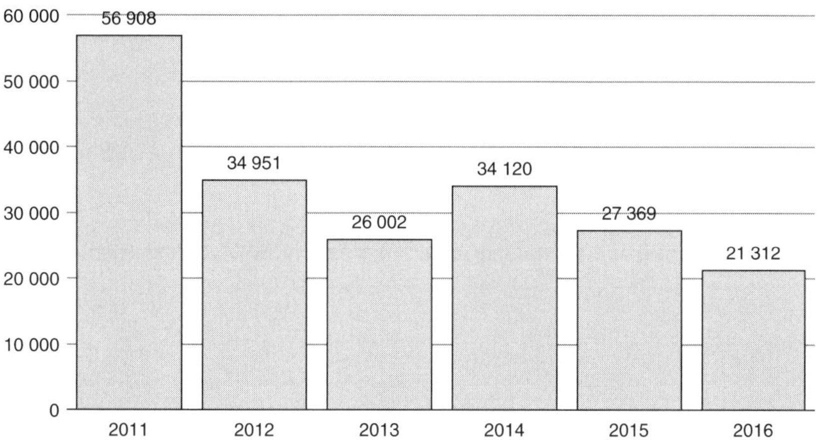

FIGURE 5.2 Operational Risk Loss Data, 2011–2016
Source: Based on data from ORX Public Report, November 2017.

This data is also probably partial, as a study from Harvard Business School in 2016 (see Figure 5.3) reports a cumulated operational risk loss of $540 billion during the years 2008 to 2016, that is, $60 billion, or more than €40 billion/year. This data is based from another ORX Source (ORX News, which uses publicly disclosed events, and hence has a larger scope in number of institutions covered, but is mainly focused on large events).

Finally, our own analysis of legal fines based only on public data total more than $400 billion in the period 2011 to 2016 with two peak years of more than $100 billion (see Figure 5.4). This analysis uses the final settlement date and therefore shows a lag compared to the Harvard report.

Of course, the different sources are not easy to reconcile, because they have different scopes, in time, reporting institutions, thresholds, nature of events, and reporting date, but showing all the sources in a single graph (see Figure 5.5) nevertheless shows two clear conclusions: (1) the operational risk losses has gained an order of magnitude in the past decade, and this is due mainly to legal losses observed after the financial crisis of 2008.

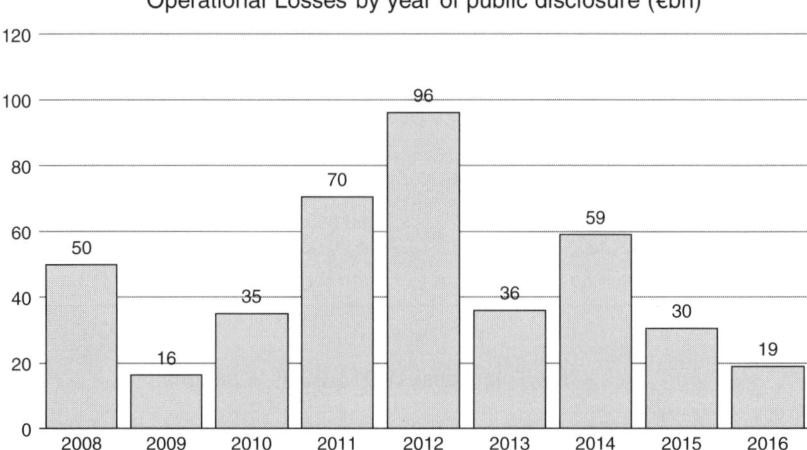

FIGURE 5.3 Operational Losses by Year of Public Disclosure
Source: Based on data from Harvard Business School – Rethinking Operational Risk Capital Requirements, Working Paper, June 2016. Retreated from USD/EUR average yearly exchange rate.

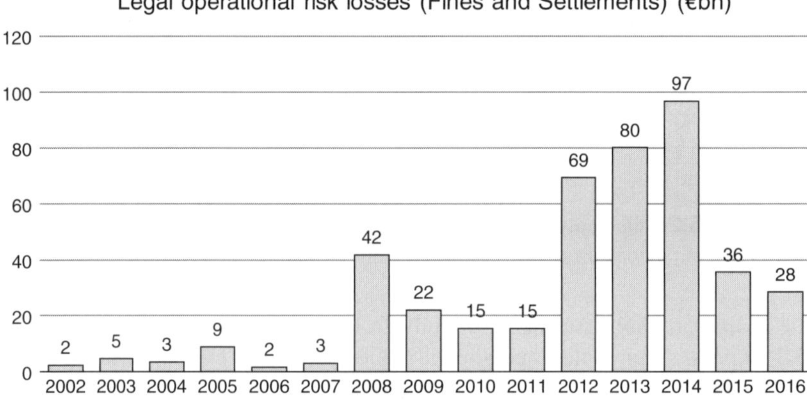

FIGURE 5.4 Legal Operational Risk Losses, 2002–2016
Source: Authors' own analysis. Retreated from USD/EUR average yearly exchange rate.

5.2 THE IMPORTANCE OF OPERATIONAL RISK CAPITAL

The operational risk capital is meant to protect the banks from extreme situations in operational risk losses, that is, the situations having in theory a probability of less than 1 in 1,000 to occur.

The minimum required capital (MRC) related to operational risk has continuously increased during the period from 2011 to 2016.

The Basel III Monitoring Report published by the BIS in September 2017 covers 200 banks including 105 large internationally active banks.

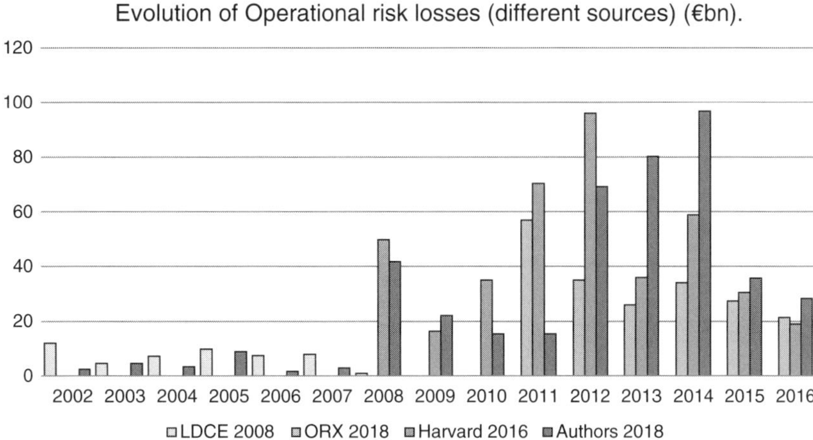

FIGURE 5.5 Evolution of Operational Risk Losses, 2002–2016

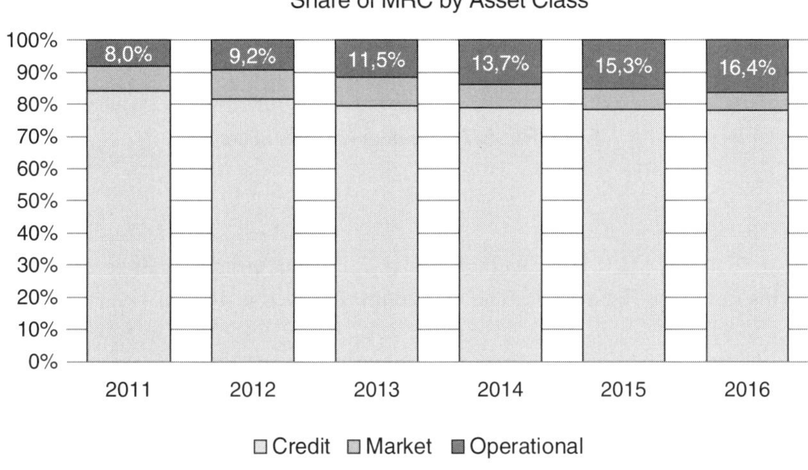

FIGURE 5.6 Share of Minimum Required Capital
Source: Based on data from D416 – Results from the 2017 Basel III Monitoring Report, Bank for International Settlements, September 2017.

From a relative point of view, this report shows that the share of operational risk as a fraction of total MRC has more than doubled from 8.1% in 2011 to 16.4% in 2016 (see Figure 5.6). Once equivalent to the market risk MRC share, the operational risk MRC share is now more than two times bigger. In 2011, operational risk MRC was 10% of the credit risk MRC and is now 25%.

From an absolute point of view, the increase is even more significant. From the same report mentioned above, we observe the numbers shown in Table 5.3.

This data is observed on a group of 92 banks (33 in Europe, 19 in America, and 40 in the rest of the world). This data shows that for this sample of approximately 100 banks, the regulatory capital has increased by almost a factor of three.

TABLE 5.3 Contribution of Operational Risk to Minimum Required Capital

	CET1 Level (€bn)	CET1 Ratio	Operational Risk Share of MRC	Operational Risk MRC
2011	2,136	10.3%	8.1%	€136bn
2016	3,738	12.6%	16.4%	€389bn

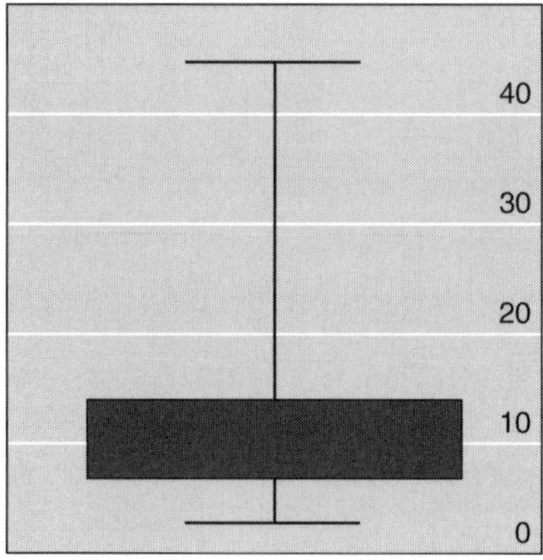

FIGURE 5.7 Operational Risk Share of MRC

The share of 16.4% of MRC is an average, and a significant variance can be observed among banks for this ratio (see Figure 5.7). The maximum observed is 44.7%.

5.3 ADEQUACY OF CAPITAL TO LOSSES

In 2008, if we refer to the document already mentioned (2008 Loss Data Collection Exercise for Operational Risk, Bank for International Settlements, July 2009), we can see that, at that time, the ratio of AMA Regulatory Capital to annualised sum of losses above €20,000 was close to 1:12.

Five years later, in 2012, the annualised losses were around 50 billion euros, with peaks close to 100 billion euros (according to the Harvard Business School Working Paper mentioned earlier) with a cumulated regulatory capital of around €150 billion.

Even at this very simple and aggregate level, we can see that while operational risk capital was an order of magnitude larger that the average losses in the previous decade, this was no longer the case after the 2008 financial crisis: the total regulatory capital for a group of 90 banks was still around €100 billion in 2011, whereas the losses were already close to this level (the average losses in 2011 and 2012, depending on the source used, were around €60 billion). And of course, as this is only an aggregate, it is likely that the regulatory capital was exceeded by losses for some individual banks during this period.

CHAPTER 6

The Need for Measurement

6.1 REGULATORY REQUIREMENTS

6.1.1 Regulatory Capital: The Evolution of the Basel Accord

The general framework of operational risk capital is the set of Basel accords defined by the Basel Committee for Banking Supervision (BCBS).

The Basel Committee was created in 1974 by the central bank Governors of the Group of 10 countries (Belgium, Canada, France, Germany, Italy, Japan, Luxembourg, the Netherlands, Spain, Sweden, Switzerland, United Kingdom, and United States). The Committee is headquartered at the Bank for International Settlements in Basel. It aims at enhancing financial stability by improving the quality of banking supervision worldwide. The Committee membership has now expanded to 45 countries.

The history of the main decisions of the Basel committee can be summarized as follows.

In 1975, a Concordat was published to set out guidelines for co-operation between national authorities in the supervision of banks' foreign establishments. According to BCBS, this accord aimed at avoiding gaps in international supervision so that (1) no banking establishment would escape supervision; and (2) supervision would be adequate and consistent across member jurisdictions.

In 1988, the Basel I accord is mainly focused on credit risk and imposes set a minimum capital to risk-weighted assets of 8%. The principle of this ratio is simple. Assets of a bank were assigned a risk weight (from 0 for cash, claims on central governments, or central banks to 100% for claims on the private sector). For simplicity, only five weights were used: 0, 10%, 20%, 50%, and 100%. The allocation of the assets of the bank allowed to calculate risk weighted assets, and the requirement was that the capital of the banks exceeds 8% of these risk weighted assets. In the Basel I accord, operational risk is not mentioned.

In 2004, the Basel II accord is released. The main evolution of Basel II compared to the previous accord is the introduction of a dialectic between the possibility offered to banks to self-assess their risks using internal models, and the possibility for regulators to control these assessments and models. This balance is introduced through the definition of The First Pillar,

Minimum Capital Requirements, which introduces the use of internal models, and The Second Pillar, Supervisory Review Process. In addition, The Third Pillar, Market Discipline requires banks to disclose information on capital, risk exposures, risk assessment processes, and hence the capital adequacy of the institution. Operational risk assessment appears in this version of this accord, using three proposed approaches: basic (BIA) or standard (TSA), which require no internal model, and advanced (AMA), which requires the development of internal models, subject to regulatory review. The Basel II "deal" was simple and smart: "know your risks, and you will be allowed to reduce your capital". This tradeoff was particularly relevant for operational risks, as identifying, structuring, and assessing operational risks would necessarily result in identifying weaknesses and fixing them.

In practice this deal was probably misinterpreted, as the common and mainstream interpretation of "operational risk modelling" was to model past losses, and to game with the models in order to reduce capital. This probably contributed to the dismissal of AMA (advanced modelling approaches of operational risk) as part of the recent updates to the Basel III accord.

In 2010–2011, the Basel III accord was designed as a response to the 2008 financial crisis, although preparatory works were performed before the default of Lehman Brothers. The new accord strengthens the three pillars established by Basel II, and extends it in several areas, in particular addressing the quality and quantity of regulatory capital, protection against credit cycles, liquidity requirements, and additional requirements for a set of large and international banks considered "systemically important".

After 2011, subsequent changes have been made, and the Basel Committee has completed its postcrisis reforms in 2017. These additional changes can be considered essentially as restrictions to the use of internal models in credit risk and operational risk.

The Basel Committee justifies these changes by noting that (D424in brief):

- *Credibility of the framework*: A range of studies found an unacceptably wide variation in RWAs across banks that cannot be explained solely by differences in the riskiness of banks' portfolios. The unwarranted variation makes it difficult to compare capital ratios across banks and undermines confidence in capital ratios. The reforms will address this to help restore the credibility of the risk-based capital framework.
- *Internal models*: Internal models should allow for more accurate risk measurement than the standardised approaches developed by supervisors. However, incentives exist to minimise risk weights when internal models are used to set minimum capital requirements. In addition, certain types of asset, such as low-default exposures, cannot be modelled reliably or robustly. The reforms introduce constraints on the estimates banks make when they use their internal models for regulatory capital purposes, and, in some cases, remove the use of internal models.

This 2017 reform of the Basel Accord reflects a pendulum swing back on the use of internal models, which had been proposed in the Basel II agreement, and which were meant to allow banks to reduce their capital in exchange for better knowledge of their risks.

6.1.2 Regulatory Capital for Operational Risk

When it was introduced in 2004, the regulatory capital requirement for operational risks could be calculated using four approaches:

1. The Basic Indicator Approach (BIA). In this approach, the capital was equal to a fixed percentage of the average of positive annual gross income over the past three years. The percentage was fixed to 15%.
2. The Standardised Approach (TSA). In this approach, the capital is calculated separately for each business line using a similar approach as for the BIA. The percentage differs depending on the business line, ranging from 12% for the less risky activity (retail banking or brokerage for instance), to 18% for the activities considered the most risky (corporate finance or trading).
3. The Alternative Standardised Approach (ASA) is the same as for the Standard Approach except for two business lines: retail banking and commercial banking. For these business lines, loans and advances replace gross income as the exposure indicator.
4. The Advanced Measurement Approach (AMA): Under the AMA, the regulatory capital requirement will equal the risk measure generated by the bank's internal operational risk measurement system using the quantitative and qualitative criteria for the AMA discussed below. The use of the AMA is subject to supervisory approval.

In the September 2017 version of the Basel III Monitoring report, the Bank for International Settlements notes that almost 70% of large banks use AMA. This proportion is observed on a sample of 81 Group 1 banks which are defined as those that have Tier 1 capital of more than €3 billion and are internationally active. All other banks are considered Group 2 banks.

We will discuss below the mainstream approach that was, and is, still used as part of the AMA, in particular in the United States. This approach is known as Loss Distribution Approach, or LDA.

As part of the 2017 reform of the Basel Accord, the internal modelling for operational risk, that is, the AMA, has been removed.

Two arguments have been used to justify the removal of AMA:

1. The capital requirements were not enough to cover the losses incurred by some banks during the 2008 crisis.
2. The internal models were not easily comparable.

The four existing approaches are replaced by a single approach called Standardised Measurement Approach (SMA), which proposes to calculate the operational risk capital as the product of two factors:

1. One factor related to the bank income (BIC)
2. One factor related to the bank losses (ILM)

If we look at this evolution at a very broad level, we can consider that the SMA has taken the best of the two worlds:

1. The Standard Approach was based on income only, but two banks with the same revenue breakdown across business lines were treated in an identical way, irrespective of, for instance, the quality of their risk management
2. The AMA, in its dominant LDA implementation, was based only on losses.

The SMA can therefore be seen as a combination of the two approaches – at a very broad level only. As explained in the presentation of the SMA[1]:

> The SMA builds on the assumption that the relationship between the BI and operational loss exposure is stable and similar for banks with similar values of the BI. However, business volume is not the only factor that influences operational loss exposure and, in some cases, there could be significant differences in operational exposure between banks of similar BI values. These differences may be due to, for example, banks' different business models. The addition of the Loss Component to the BI improves the risk sensitivity of the SMA.

Although the combination of a business volume indicator and of a risk sensitive indicator, our opinion is that the same confusion that led to the usage of LDA is still present in the SMA: losses are not necessarily representative of risks.

As far as timing is concerned, the AMA is still theoretically in force until 2022, when the banks will have to comply to the new SMA approach. As said in the BIS document "Finalising Basel III: In Brief"[2], "Banks have plenty of time to prepare" for the application of the new reform. But this leaves also plenty of time for new events, and new changes in regulations. For instance, a working paper of the Federal Reserve Board proposes to include a forward-looking component[3] as part of the risk sensitive indicator: this means that the risk component of this model will not only be based on past losses, but also on the bank projections of its risks. A mechanism is included to penalize underestimation of risks.

6.1.3 Supervisory Review

The Basel II accord introduced the Pillar II or Supervisory review, as a balancing requirement to the Pillar I allowance for internal model calculations. According to the BCBS107, "Bank management continues to bear responsibility for ensuring that the bank has adequate capital to support its risks beyond the core minimum requirements".

For operational risk, "the supervisor should consider whether the capital requirement generated by the Pillar I calculation gives a consistent picture of the individual bank's operational risk exposure". This statement opens the possibility for the supervisors to impose capital add-ons,

[1]Bank for International Settlements, Consultative Paper D355, Standard Measurement Approach for operational risk, https://www.bis.org/bcbs/publ/d355.pdf (accessed 05/10/2018).
[2]Bank for International Settlements, Finalising Basel III: In Brief, https://www.bis.org/bcbs/publ/d424_inbrief.pdf (accessed 05/10/2018).
[3]Migueis, Marco, Forward-Looking and Incentive-Compatible Operational Risk Capital Framework (April 23, 2018). Available at SSRN: https://ssrn.com/abstract=3159608 or http://dx.doi.org/10.2139/ssrn.3159608

if they believe that the Pillar I number does not reflect the operational risk overall exposure of the bank. The rationale for add-ons has been in particular explained in BCBS107[4], as "Gross income, used in the Basic Indicator and Standardised Approaches for operational risk, is only a proxy for the scale of operational risk exposure of a bank and can in some cases (e.g., for banks with low margins or profitability) underestimate the need for capital for operational risk."

It is worth noticing that the possible inadequacy of capital calculation was only expressed in that case, and not for AMA. Indeed, AMA was supposed to capture in more detail the risk profile of the banks, through the use of the four mandatory elements.

However, when the practice of AMA was mainly LDA, it could have been useful to compare the capital calculation resulting from loss projections with other calculations resulting from an analysis based on risk analyses and projections.

In practice, we have experienced that situation only once, working with a major US bank, when the regulator required that an alternative model was put in place to challenge the LDA.

Under the SMA regime the capital calculation will be standardized again, although with two factors (Business Indicator and Internal Loss Multiplier). This will increase the focus of banks and local regulators on the Pillar II requirements. One could paraphrase the statement of BCBS107 by saying:

> Business Indicator is only a proxy for the scale of operational risk exposure of a bank, and Internal Loss Multiplier is only a proxy of the operational risk profile of a bank, and they can in some cases underestimate the need for capital for operational risk.

It is therefore likely that banks will undertake a significant modelling effort to justify that they are not in the situation where the Standard Measurement would underestimate the risk. This can already be observed as European regulators are raising the bar on expectations on ICAAP (Internal Capital Adequacy Assessment Process).

6.1.4 Stress Testing

The first stress test exercise in the United States was conducted in early 2009 (SCAP or Supervisory Capital Assessment Program), by the Federal Reserve System to determine if the largest US financial organizations had sufficient capital buffers to withstand a recession. The test used two macroeconomic scenarios, one based on baseline conditions and the other with more pessimistic expectations.

After this first exercise, the Federal Reserve issued in March 2011 the Comprehensive Capital Analysis and Review (CCAR). This initial exercise involved the Federal Reserve's forward-looking evaluation of the internal capital planning processes of large, complex bank holding companies and their proposals to undertake capital actions in 2011, such as increasing dividend payments or repurchasing or redeeming stock. The Federal Reserve evaluated these plans across five areas of supervisory consideration, in particular capital distribution policy, in relation to the ability to absorb losses under several scenarios.

The 19 bank holding companies participating in the 2011 CCAR are: Ally Financial, American Express Company, Bank of America, Bank of New York Mellon, BB&T, Capital One,

[4]Bank for International Settlements, "International Convergence of Capital Measurement and Capital Standards," https://www.bis.org/publ/bcbs107.pdf (accessed 5/10/2018).

Financial Corporation, Citigroup, Fifth Third Bancorp, Goldman Sachs, JP Morgan Chase & Co., Keycorp, MetLife, Morgan Stanley, PNC, Regions Financial Corporation, State Street, SunTrust, US Bancorp, and Wells Fargo. These 19 firms also participated in the 2009 SCAP.

While the first CCAR exercise in 2011 required banks to describe their strategies for managing their capital over a 24-month, forward-planning horizon, it has been extended to a nine-quarter period from 2012 onwards. The first exercise considered only a baseline and adverse scenario, which has later been extended to baseline, adverse, and severely adverse.

Projected losses pertaining to operational risks were included in the CCAR exercise from the first year in 2011, as the capital adequacy was in particular appreciated "to the extent to which the capital plans were supported by a stress scenario analysis framework that considered a range of economic, financial market, and operational events and outcomes".

As the stress-testing exercise is by definition the simulation of a bank balance sheet under adverse economic circumstances (as of 2018, the Federal Reserve scenarios consider 28 variables, such as gross domestic product, unemployment rate, stock market prices, interest rates, etc.), the question of sensitivity of operational risk losses to macroeconomic factors soon arises. In other words, should banks try to capture operational losses conditional to adverse macroeconomic scenarios, or simply adverse operational losses?

The supervisory letter SR15-18 issued on December 18, 2015, gives a reasonable guidance on this point. The risk identification process should include "the firm's particular vulnerabilities", "the firm's own loss history", and "large loss events experienced by industry peers with similar business mix and overall operational risk profiles".

The projection of operational losses should be based on "both quantitative analysis and expert judgment", and the firm "should not rely on unstable or unintuitive correlations to project operational losses", while "Scenario analysis should be a core component of the firm's operational loss projection approaches."

This implies in particular that a mix of approaches need to be used to project losses.

- Recurrent losses, such as errors, individual frauds, individual litigations, and so on can be sensitive on macroeconomic conditions, and loss projections can use regression analyses.
- Large legal matters that are already known and provisioned by the firm can be addressed using stress on provisions.
- All other large losses can be addressed using scenario analysis.

6.2 NONREGULATORY REQUIREMENTS

The preceding discussion demonstrates the regulatory need for operational risk measurement. Before addressing the particular challenges of risk measurement, we will now discuss the need for measurement from an internal, nonregulatory standpoint.

The definition of a risk appetite framework is not a regulatory requirement per se, but more a regulatory expectation, or even strong expectation. In November 2013, the FSB produced "Principles for an Effective Risk Appetite Framework", which standardizes the language and components of the risk appetite framework, establishes regulatory expectations for how it should be operated, and sets senior management and board roles. For instance, the Prudential

Regulation Authority has set its expectations in its Supervisory Statement SS5/16 "Corporate governance: Board responsibilities":

> The business strategy should be supported by a well-articulated and measurable statement of risk appetite (expressed in terms that can be readily understood by employees throughout the business), which is clearly owned by the board, integral to the strategy the board has signed off on, and actively used by them to monitor and control actual and prospective risks and to inform key business decisions. All the directors should have the time and opportunity to contribute to the development of the risk appetite, and to provide appropriate challenge, before final approval by the board.The PRA will expect to see evidence of this active oversight of risks according to the risk appetite. The risk control framework should flow from the board's risk appetite.

The Office of Comptroller of the Currency has expressed its expectation for a risk appetite statement in September 2014: "A covered bank should have a comprehensive written statement outlining its risk appetite that serves as the basis for the risk governance framework. It should contain qualitative components that define a safe and sound risk culture and how the covered bank will assess and accept risks and quantitative limits that include sound stress testing processes and address earnings, capital, and liquidity."

6.2.1 Risk Appetite

In this section, we illustrate why the definition of a risk appetite statement in operational risk requires quantification and modelling.

The rationale of the discussion is as follows:

1. A risk appetite is a risk limit. A risk limit cannot be a maximum amount an organisation accepts to lose, but a maximum amount at a certain level of probability
2. If some assumptions can reasonably be made on the distribution of potential losses, for instance a normal distribution, then the risk appetite can be defined by a parameter of this distribution (for instance, the standard deviation). Otherwise, the limit must be defined at several levels of probabilities. This is the case for operational risk.
3. A risk appetite implicitly defines an associate reward, and this holds also for operational risk.
4. The definition of a risk appetite framework implies an allocation of limits – or appetites, across the different businesses. This definition also implies to define a breach of appetite. This is not self-evident as a single event does not necessarily constitutes a breach of a distribution

For operational risk:

- We will show that there exists an implicit appetite for this type of risk, as increasing operational risk taking may increase speed and productivity, and hence increase profit.
- Operational risk does not follow a normal distribution, and therefore, the definition of appetite needs to be performed at various levels of probabilities. Setting a limit at only a level of probability corresponding to frequent events could mean setting a much higher appetite than intended for more remote events.

6.2.1.1 Definition According to the ISO 31000 vocabulary, risk appetite is defined as the "amount and type of risk that an organization is willing to pursue or retain".

The definition of "amount of risk" poses two problems that we are going to discuss:

1. Can we define a "risk amount"?
2. Why would an organisation "pursue a risk amount"?

The amount of risk cannot be only a monetary amount, that is, how much I accept to lose, as the only upper bound of what I am exposed to lose is my assets. For an organization, the only hard risk limit is bankruptcy. So, this cannot be a proper definition of a risk appetite, and we need to introduce a probability level. This means that the amount of risk, if by this we mean the amount of potential losses, should be defined at, for instance, a 99% or 99.9% probability level. In that case, we would reformulate the definition as "the potential losses at a 99% probability level".

This approach is consistent with the ISO 31000 definition of risk. As risk is defined as the uncertainty on objectives, risk is defined as a distribution, and not as a number. In other words, a risk appetite statement would be a set of loss limits at different levels of probabilities.

If we assume that the risk, or the uncertainty of objectives follows a normal distribution, then the potential losses at different levels of probability are related to each other, as they are all defined in relation to the standard deviation of the risk distribution, or, more precisely, the standard deviation of the objectives that is induced by the risk.

In Figure 6.1, we assume a normally distributed risk, for which the potential loss at a 90% probability level is normalized to 1. Then, setting a risk appetite of 2 at a 90% probability level will ensure that the risk remains within limits at any probability level.

However, if the distribution is not normal, and generally unknown, we need to define the risk appetite at different levels of probability. Otherwise, setting the appetite at a given level of probability may result in a breach of appetite at a more extreme level.

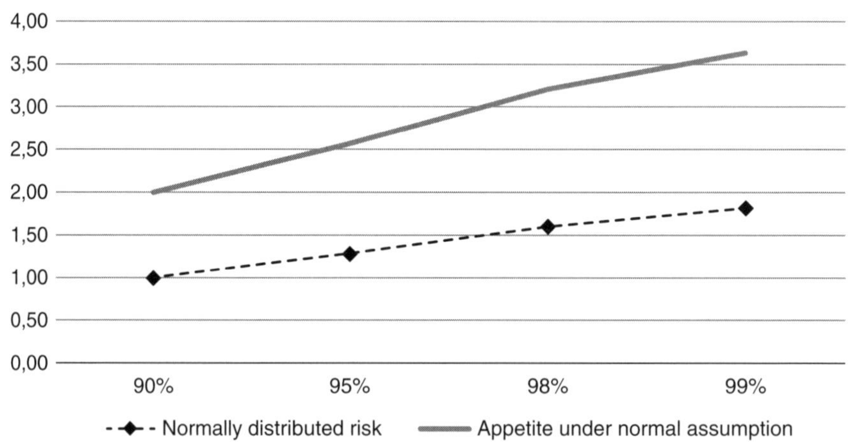

FIGURE 6.1 Risk Appetite Matches Risk Distribution

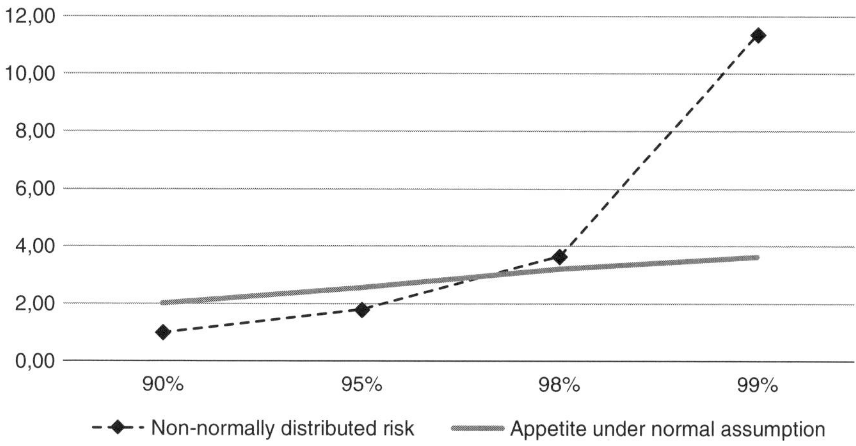

FIGURE 6.2 Risk Appetite Does Not Match Risk Distribution

This other graph (Figure 6.2) shows that if a risk limit is set under a normal assumption, a risk might seem within the firm's appetite for the probability level of 90% and 95%, but exceed by far the limit at the probability level of 99%. The risk distribution used here corresponds to an actual risk scenario of Unauthorized or Rogue Trading. In that particular case, ensuring that the risk remains within limits at a 99% level would require a much lower limit at a 90% level, that is, probably enhanced controls.

If we summarize, we can say that risk can be defined by a single number only if the shape of the distribution is known. For a normal distribution, the standard deviation fully defines the risk, and hence, a risk limit can be expressed this way. If this is not the case, we are left with qualitative statements of risk limits, or we need to define risk levels at different levels of probability.

The second imperfection of this definition is to consider the risk independently of the associated reward. An individual or an organisation will pursue or retain a certain level of risk only if there is an implicit reward associated with this risk. In addition, the appetite for risk is not necessarily constant and independent of the associated level of expected return.

The modern portfolio theory proposed by Markowitz in the simplest framework in which these two problems disappear:

1. As the efficient frontier (Figure 6.3) defines the implicit level of risk you accept by trying to achieve a given level of return, an appetite for risk is equivalent to an appetite for return.
2. Finally, combining the efficient frontier with a utility function makes it possible to define a risk appetite which depends on the expected return.

6.2.1.2 Usage in a Framework If the risk appetite at a firmwide level only, this would imply that potential breaches of risk appetite can be detected only when the aggregated picture of risks is known.

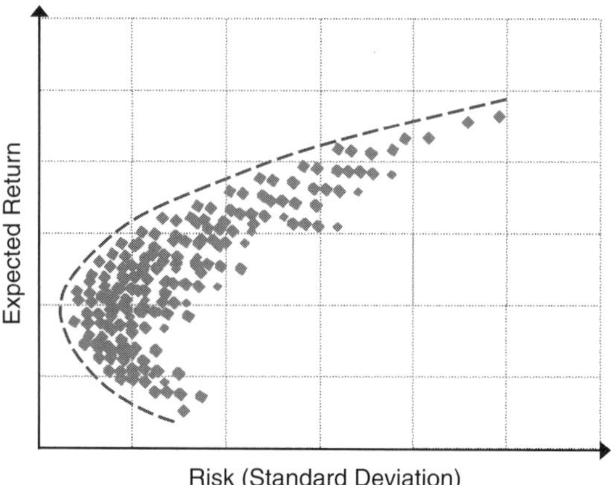

FIGURE 6.3 Efficient Frontier

For this reason, it is obviously a good practice to set risk limits for individual business units, by allocating a fraction of risk appetite to each of these units, exactly as objectives can be allocated to business units. Of course, doing so may be suboptimal but is necessary in a real organization.

The question of the detection of breaches of appetite is also not easy to address.

In the ideal case of portfolio theory, the risk appetite is defined by choosing a combination of assets, which individual risks is considered to be known. As long as the asset allocation corresponds to a given level of risk, even a significant dropdown of my portfolio value is, in theory at least, not a breach of appetite. A normal distribution with a given standard deviation allows the occurrence of any loss, and the observation of a large loss does not violate the assumption of the standard deviation. To avoid this problem, it is possible to use a breach criterion based on losses, considering that a loss that would be very unlikely under the current appetite, is indeed a breach of appetite.

6.2.1.3 Operational Risk Appetite Let us discuss first a statement often heard among operational risk practitioners: "There is no appetite for operational risk, as operational risk has no upside".

To illustrate that this statement is false, let us consider the GDPR, the European General Data Protection Regulation, which will be enforced on May 25, 2018, and in its first months of implementation at the time this book will be printed.

The GDPR will affect data science practice in three areas[5]. First, GDPR imposes limits on data processing and consumer profiling. Second, for organizations that use automated decision-making, GDPR creates a "right to an explanation" for consumers. Third, GDPR holds firms accountable for bias and discrimination in automated decisions.

[5]https://vision.cloudera.com/general-data-protection-regulation-gdpr-and-data-science/ (accessed 05/10/2018).

This implies that GDPR will increase the cost of some now usual data processing actions, or even make them impossible. If these actions were profitable, this means that the enforcement of GDPR will represent of loss of revenue or profit. Therefore, there exists by definition an appetite to breach the GDPR. However, the cost of this breach is probably, but not necessarily, beyond this appetite.

The cost of the breach has been defined by the regulator as a fine up to €20 million or up to 4% of the annual worldwide turnover, whichever is greater. This type of fine is typically beyond appetite, but it could be within appetite in the following (theoretical) situation:

- A firm has created a data processing method that trims down its costs so that its profit is 20% of its turnover, based on this method.
- There is a way to redesign the data processing method in a way that complies with the GDPR, but this will require a significant increase of manpower, thus resulting in a profit to revenue ratio of 12% only.
- By breaching the GDPR, the firm exposes itself to a fine of 4% of its revenue, without certainty, however.

Indeed, some companies have had to change their business due to the new GDPR regulations, and even interrupt it like a French startup that stopped operating because the GDPR would have required a complete change of its software product.

This shows, if it was needed, that operational constraints could make a business impossible to sustain, and therefore, that there could exist an appetite to circumvent rules.

The analysis above is simple to understand because GDPR is a new regulation, and we can see that it has a direct and new impact on business cost. But think about Financial Crime or Sanctions regulations: the need to monitor and process a huge number of transactions and detect suspicious patterns will necessarily slow down the business and make it more expensive. This applies also for MIFID II, and all regulations that impact the speed of business.

Of course, no firm will explicitly express any appetite to breach the law – but this is not a hard limit. All provisions of the GDPR are subject to interpretation and this holds also for Financial Crime or sanctions regulations, or, more simply for Tax regulations. And the recent cases of significant and even egregious breaches of such regulations, show an appetite to at least interpret them in a favorable way.

In simple words, the appetite for operational risk can be seen as the appetite for speed and productivity against safety and compliance.

An even simpler example can be proposed to show that there is an appetite for operational risk: for several years, EMV smart cards have not been used in the United States, leading to payment card fraud rates on an order of magnitude higher than in Europe. This was the price of a higher throughput at supermarket checkouts. Even in France, perhaps the inventor of the smart card, motorway toll payments used a fallback method with the magnetic stripe of the card, because it was considered that the use of the chip would slow down the traffic.

Having said that, how can we define an operational risk appetite framework and detect a breach of risk appetite?

Operational risk, as we discussed earlier, and as it generally admitted, can be described by fat tails distributions. This does not mean that there exists a distribution that properly represents operational risk, just as the normal distribution may represent market risk. This statement simply holds empirically.

Therefore, using a distributional assumption to qualify operational risk and to set an appetite according to this distribution, will generally result in misstatements, as illustrated above for the Rogue Trading case: Setting the appetite at the 90% or 95% probability level, for instance, does not guarantee that the risk will remain within appetite at higher levels.

For the same reason, detecting a breach of appetite in operational risk is also very difficult, in particular if we rely only on losses.

6.2.1.4 Conclusion Risk appetite can be schematically represented by an efficient frontier which represents how the risk and return evolve as the allocation of resources evolves:

- For market risk, risk and return evolve as we change the composition of a portfolio in asset classes (Figure 6.4)
- For credit risk, risk and return evolve as we change the composition of the portfolio of borrowers (Figure 6.5)
- For operational risk, risk and return evolve as we change the organisation of resources and in particular the mix of production and control (Figure 6.6)

Although in practice it is not possible to exhibit the efficient frontier establishing the relation between the expected return of a firm, expressed as a function of its strategy and of the operational implementation of this strategy and the possible negative outcomes, this concept can still be used to think in a more rational way about risk appetite.

The non-normal nature of the distribution of operational risk, as well as the failure of distributional assumptions, requires a better understanding and measurement of operational risk to allow a sound definition of risk appetite for operational risk, which goes beyond qualitative statements, such as “We have low appetite for fines”.

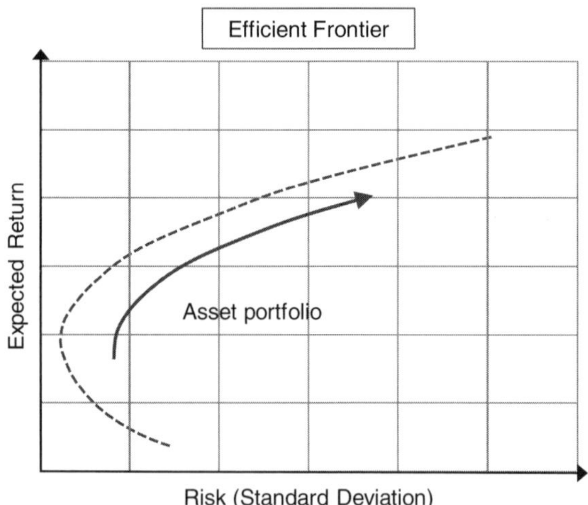

FIGURE 6.4 Market Risk Efficient Frontier
Return and risk evolve as the structure of the portfolio evolves.

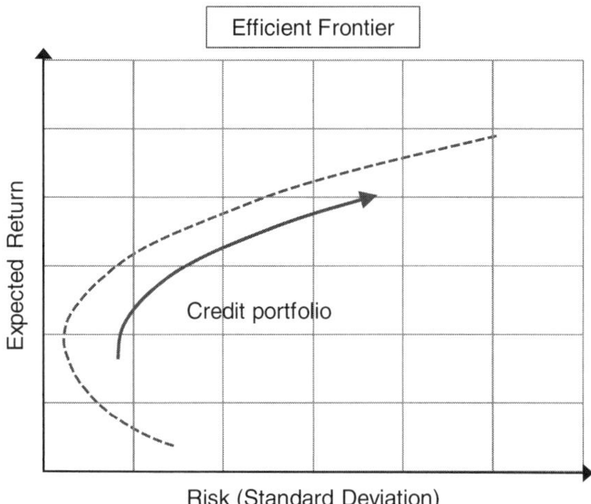

FIGURE 6.5 Credit Risk Efficient Frontier
Return and risk evolve as the structure of the credit portfolio evolves.

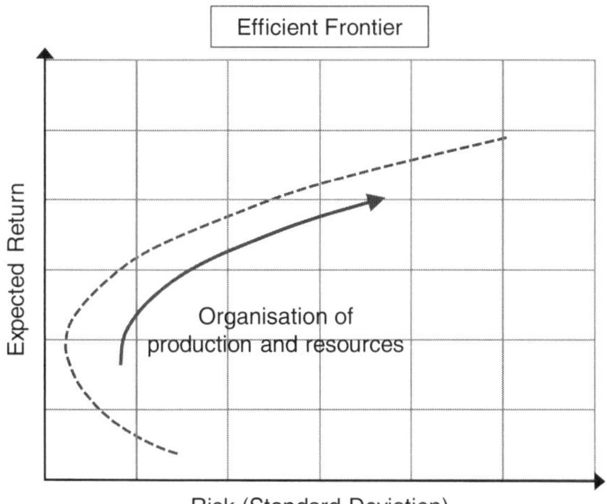

FIGURE 6.6 Operational Risk Efficient Frontier
Return and risk evolve as the organisation of production resources evolves.

6.2.2 Risk Management

Let us begin the discussion with an interesting paradox related to operational risk management at the "micro" and "macro" levels in finance and industry.

For nonfinancial sectors, since credit and market risks are generally marginal, or at least far from the importance they have in the financial sector, operational risk management is indeed close to the full scope of risk management.

In life critical industries, such as energy, transport, chemicals, pharmaceuticals, and others, risk assessment at the micro level cannot rely on Red-Amber-Green assessments. And almost by construction, and fortunately, there is very few loss data that can be used for statistics for risk analysis in life-critical industries. Indeed, these sectors have designed the Probabilistic Risk Assessment tools, such as fault-tree analysis, or bowtie methods. Using these methods, micro-level assessments are analytical and structured, and inferred by decomposing the system at risk into units.

However, when it comes to assessing enterprise risks of one of these life-critical companies, assessments now rely almost exclusively on qualitative approaches.

On the other hand, in the financial sector, the use of probabilistic techniques is, in our experience, absent from the micro-level operational risk assessment. We have never seen a bowtie risk assessment or a fault-tree analysis of a lending process, or even of a critical IT system. Qualitative risk and control assessment are widely used, as we discuss in the RCSA Chapter of Part III.

And when it comes to the evaluation of operational risk at a macro level, this involves distributions, correlations, copulas, and a lot of sophisticated tools to assess a regulatory or economic capital (see Table 6.1).

This perspective shows the major issue of enterprise level risk management in both industry and finance: Management is disconnected from measurement.

Thus, Peter Drucker's corporate mantra "You can't manage what you can't measure" is respected in appearance, but only in appearance. Risk managers in finance measure something they don't really manage, and risk managers in industry manage something other than what they actually measure.

Going back to finance, let us think for a moment about what risk quantification could bring to their management, and how current practice is far from it.

As we discussed earlier, the dominant approach in operational risk measurement is based on loss data. The rationale for this approach is that losses are an expression of the firm's risk profile, and arguably the only objective expression.

The causal graph (see Figure 6.7) that is implicitly implemented in banks today for operational risk management is represented below:

- Risk management is performed at the risk profile level, through RCSA and controls, and therefore, the risk profile of the firm depends on management decisions.

TABLE 6.1 Micro and Macro Level Risk Assessment in Industry and Finance

	Industry	**Finance**
Micro-level assessment	**Quantitative** Fault-tree analysis, bow-tie, and others	**Qualitative** RCSA
Macro-level assessment	**Qualitative** Red-Amber-Green matrices	**Quantitative** Loss distributions, correlations, copulas, and so on

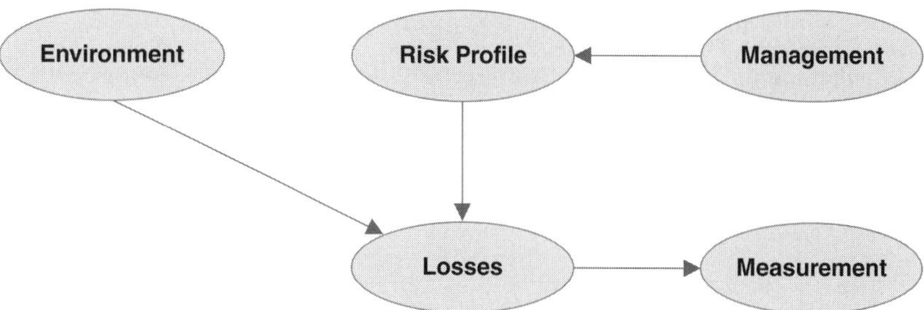

FIGURE 6.7 Risk Management Causal Graph

- Losses are caused by the risk profile of the firm, and external causes beyond the firm's control.
- Risk measurement is performed at the losses level, which implies that the risk measure is dependent on past losses.

From this causal graph, it is clear that the measurement partly depends on management, as we can see a causal path from management to measurement.

However, we can see at least two issues in using this method:

1. The causal links are delayed: losses can be the expression of the risk profile that was in effect several years ago (think for example of legal risks)
2. The causal links are blurred by external causes

This reminds us of the distinction used in machine learning between supervised learning and reinforcement learning[6]. To put it very simply:

- In supervised learning, the machine is told at each step what its result should have been. By comparing it with the result it has obtained, it can thus modify its strategy.
- In reinforcement learning, the machine is only told whether the result it obtained was good or bad. The indication is therefore much less informative, and the learning time can be longer.

Here is how Andrew Barto[7], one of the pioneers of reinforcement learning, simply explains reinforcement learning:

> Mobile phone users sometimes resort to the following procedure to obtain good reception in a new locale where coverage is poor. We move around with the phone while monitoring its signal strength indicator or by repeating "Do you hear me now?" and carefully listening to the reply. We keep doing this until we either find a place with an adequate signal or until we find the best place we can under the circumstances, at which point we either try to complete the call or give up. Here, the information

[6] Richard S. Sutton and Andrew G. Barto. *Reinforcement Learning: An Introduction*. Boston: MIT Press, 2018.
[7] Andrew G. Barto and Thomas G. Dietterich, "Reinforcement Learning and Its Relationship to Supervised Learning." In J. Si, A. Barto, W. Powell, and D. Wunsch II (Eds.), Handbook of Learning and Approximate Dynamic Programming (John Wiley & Sons, 2004), 47–64.

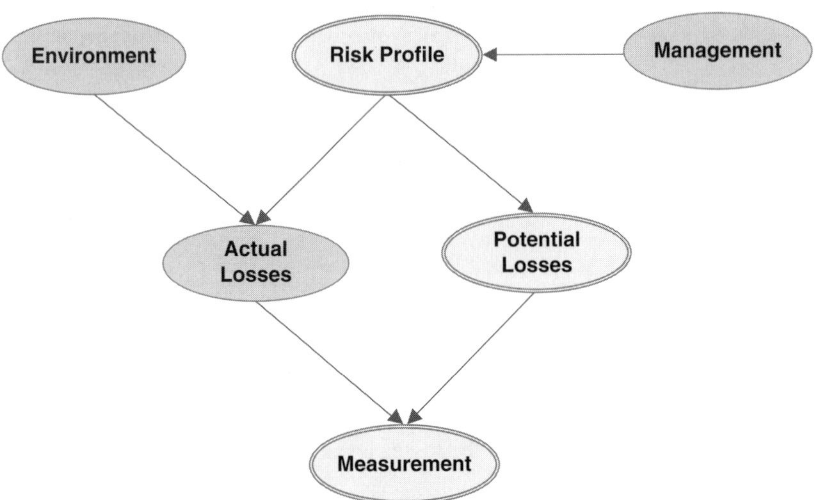

FIGURE 6.8 Risk Management Using Risk Measurement

we receive is not directly telling us where we should go to obtain good reception. Nor is each reading telling us in which direction we should move next. Each reading simply allows us to evaluate the goodness of our current situation. We have to move around – explore – in order to decide where we should go. We are not given examples of correct behavior.

Real life is certainly driven by reinforcement learning rather than supervised learning. But the nature of the reinforcement signal should be thought of carefully. We cannot afford a weak reinforcement signal for risk management of nuclear power plants, such as "Did the plant explode?" We also should not allow the use of weak reinforcement signals in operational risk, such as the 2008 crisis.

Although there is no certainty that the detailed analysis of risks will always prevent severe losses and systemic crises, we believe that the measurement of risk should include the information on risk profile.

We will discuss this further in the next section, but this simply implies that risk measurement is risk-sensitive.

This could be done by implementing an enhanced causal graph such as the one shown in Figure 6.8.

This new graph implies that:

- The risk profile is defined in such a way that it allows to infer potential losses. This excludes de facto purely qualitative assessments.
- The measurement is based on actual losses and on potential losses. This creates a direct and nondelayed path from management to measurement.

CHAPTER 7

The Challenges of Measurement

7.1 INTRODUCTION

In the previous chapters, we have shown the need for operational risk measurement that results from regulatory requirements and nonregulatory needs. We will now discuss the challenges of measurement of operational risk.

7.2 MEASURING RISK OR MEASURING RISKS?

If risk is defined as the effect of uncertainty on objectives, measuring risk is measuring uncertainty. Measuring uncertainty is possible only if the type of uncertainty considered is of the nature of "known unknowns", or possibly "unknown knowns", but exclude unknown unknowns. This limit means in practice there will always remain an error on the measure of uncertainty. As our risk management professor Jean-Paul Louisot used to say "Risk measurement is about drawing knowledge alleys in a cloud of uncertainty".

In practice, if we forget for a while about our quantitative or risk management background, what really is risk measurement?

There are essentially two ways to approach the assessment of uncertainty about the achievement of objectives. The first method is analytical, and the second is global.

The analytical method tries to identify all the possible events that could interfere with the objectives, and to assess the likelihood and the impact of these events. When applicable, the global method considers that the set of possible events is impossible to enumerate and prefers to observe the variance of reaching the objectives in similar situations.

We can compare these two methods in the context of project risk. When starting a new construction or IT project, three objectives can be defined: deliver on time, deliver within budget, and deliver what is expected. Focusing for instance on the timely delivery, we may either:

- Consider all events that can affect the different tasks of the project – such as supplier failure, inadequate technology, key personnel loss – and evaluate their probability and impact on the project critical path.

- Use a database of similar projects and evaluate the statistical distribution of delays on the delivery date.

The second approach is indeed useful for obtaining a reasonable delivery date, and can be used by a manager of a portfolio of projects that is not in direct contact with each of the projects. However, this method is not directly usable for managing the risks of individual projects. In order to effectively manage those risks, one needs to identify them specifically, and to consider mitigation actions: backup suppliers, additional resources and so on.

This simple analysis can be connected with market risk analysis and is more profound that it may appear.

In 1900, Louis Bachelier based his PhD dissertation, "Theory of Speculation," on the central assumption that the stock price returns are unpredictable, due to the uncountable factors that influence the investors' opinions. From this very simple belief (which anyone can understand and discuss), Louis Bachelier derives mathematically one of the most important ideas in the world of finance, that is, that price returns are normally distributed (which most non-mathematicians would find mysterious). This work was indeed rediscovered in the 1950s and Eugene Fama published in 1965 "The Behavior of Stock Market Prices", which introduced the "Efficient Market Hypothesis" (EMH). The EMH, in its strongest form, asserts that all information (past market prices, fundamental information, and even insider information) is fully reflected in securities prices. In other words, price returns are unpredictable.

These two examples demonstrate the tradeoff between the analytic and the global approaches. In market risks, the factors influencing the change of stock prices are impossible to enumerate and quantify, but they are, at a broad level, similar for different securities.

Therefore, a portfolio manager does not understand what is driving the price movements of the individual stocks in his portfolio, but this does not prevent him from managing the risks of his portfolio by optimizing his allocation. This is similar to the approach of a project portfolio manager who does not have control over individual projects and addresses the risk of each one in a statistical way, while trying to control the overall risk of his portfolio.

But in both cases, the manager of a particular project has to manage the identified risks of his project, and the CEO of a listed company needs to manage the risks that may affect its market value.

An intermediate conclusion here is that a purely statistical measurement approach if the risk is measured for an entity considered to be beyond the control of the risk manager. When the risk manager effectively manages the risks – of a company, a project, a portfolio of assets, or a portfolio of projects, the appropriate approach is the analytical one.

The analytical approach of risks is usually decomposed in several steps, as for instance proposed in the ISO 31000 norm (Figure 7.1):

- Risk identification
- Risk analysis
- Risk evaluation
- Risk treatment

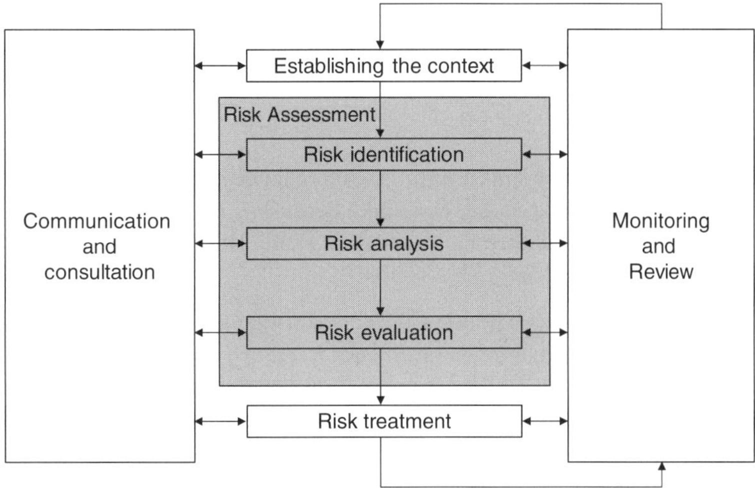

FIGURE 7.1 Risk Assessment in the Evaluation Process (ISO)

In this process, risks should no longer be thought of as "uncertainty on objectives" but rather as "events" that can impact the achievement of objectives.

When we try to enumerate and analyse them, risks are hypothetical future events. They do not exist yet, and therefore cannot be measured. Only the perception or the materialization of a risk are measurable. After the occurrence of the risk ... it's too late: the materialization of a risk is a loss, and no longer a risk. The only thing we can effectively measure ex-ante are perceptions of risks. Any perception of a risk is therefore a model of its potential materialization. This model can be theoretical, empirical, statistical, expert-based, and so on.

This should reconcile both the proponents of the quantitative approach and the advocates of an expert-driven approach: any risk assessment is always a model, and it is always a model for risk perception, not an objective measure.

7.3 REQUIREMENTS OF A RISK MEASUREMENT METHOD

In July 2013, the Basel Committee released a discussion paper called "The regulatory framework: balancing risk sensitivity, simplicity and comparability". This document introduces important concepts and adopts a balanced approach – as far as regulatory risk measurement is concerned at least.

The concepts introduced are simplicity, risk sensitivity and comparability, and the relation between them can be summarized as: the risk sensitivity of the measurement is an important objective, but it is often sought at the expense of simplicity and comparability.

This argument precisely reflects the discussion we just had about the global and analytic methods. Managing the risks for a group of enterprises or projects requires that:

- The portfolio of enterprises or projects should be risk managed using an analytic method.

- The risk of each individual enterprise or project should be measured at a global level, that is, without trying to enumerate the individual events the enterprise is exposed to.
- However, each individual enterprise or project should be encouraged to measure its own risks in an analytical way.

We believe this is exactly the point of view of the regulator in this document: the regulatory measurement should be simple and comparable, because it is meant to be used at the portfolio level, the portfolio being here the financial system. This does not prevent the internal measurements to be analytical and risk sensitive.

There is however a second level of relationship between regulatory requirements and risk measurement. A risk sensitive measurement also tends to reduce risks: when the potential events are identified and analysed, mitigation actions will automatically be identified. When the regulation imposes a risk sensitive measurement, and that this measurement is used to define the regulatory capital, the regulation encourages risk reduction. However, as the Basel Committee notices it, analysing risks for a regulatory purpose may render this analysis inoperant according to Goodhart's law ("When a measure becomes a target, it ceases to be a good measure.").

Let us discuss these concepts in more details.

7.3.1 Risk Sensitivity

It may seem very paradoxical to discuss the fact that a risk measurement should be sensitive to risk. It sounds like saying that a measurement of length should be sensitive to length. However, this illustrates clearly the specificity of risk. As the BIS discussion paper mentioned above states it: "Risk is of course, unobservable".

The BIS paper distinguishes between ex-ante and ex-post risk sensitivity. In a regulatory framework, a measure is ex-post risk sensitive if "it can distinguish with reasonable accuracy between sound banks and those that are likely to fail".

This definition of risk sensitivity may be suitable for a regulator but is probably too binary for a firm. In addition, this definition expresses the sensitivity of risk measurement to "risk". The proposed definition of ex-ante sensitivity to risk is probably more suitable from an enterprise point of view. The BIS considers that a measure is ex-ante risk sensitive if the measure is different for banks with different exposures.

If we connect this definition to the discussion above on the analytical and global approach, an ex-post sensitive measure of risk is related to a global approach of risks. For instance, the Merton model can be considered as ex-post measure of risk, in the sense that it relates the probability of default to a distance measurement.

On the other hand, an ex-ante sensitive measure of risk is related to an analytical approach of risks. To this extent, an ex-ante risk sensitive measure must be sensitive to *risks*, that is, to potential events that may occur and unfold.

Again, it may look a little specious to distinguish "a risk measurement should be sensitive to risks" rather than "a risk measurement should be sensitive to risk". As we discussed above, "risk" in general is not something we can perceive directly, while "risks" can be identified and a perception model can be built for an identified risk event.

A measurement is risk sensitive if the measurement changes according to changes in assumptions or perceptions of risk:

- Change of exposure, or more precisely change of resources exposed to risk. This include in particular mergers and acquisitions; exiting or downsizing a business.
- Change of potential events. In an analytical risk management process, some new risks may be identified and assessed, some risks can disappear, and so on.
- Change of controls, both preventative and protective.

As the BIS points it out, impediments to ex ante risk sensitivity include the multidimensional nature of risk in complex banking organisations, which makes comprehensive risk assessment extremely challenging.

7.3.2 Comparability

When trying to define a risk measurement framework that ensures comparability, the BIS mentions that "two banks with portfolios having identical risk profiles apply the framework's rules and arrive at the same amount of risk-weighted assets and two banks with different risk profiles should produce risk numbers that are different proportionally to the differences in risk."

Why then is comparability different from risk sensitivity? After all, risk sensitivity is about comparing the measure of risk for two different states of the same firm, while comparability is about comparing the risk measure for two different firms.

If we acknowledge this distinction, this means that two firms using the same measurement method, which is presumed to be risk-sensitive, and carrying out exactly the same activities, could nevertheless have different risk measures.

The difference may come from the degree of freedom in the application of the measurement method. Therefore, a risk measurement method will ensure comparability only if it leaves little room for interpretation.

In the discussion paper "The Regulatory Framework: Balancing Risk Sensitivity, Simplicity and Comparability", the following impediments to comparability are listed: computational complexity, which makes it harder to understand the drivers of changes in risk-weighted assets; choices given to banks (e.g., choices between advanced and standardised approaches, and modelling choices within the advanced approaches); differences in interpretation of information and differences in the level of conservatism applied by banks (e.g., value adjustments/provisions, rating grades).

7.3.3 Conclusion

To contribute to effective risk management, risk measurements should be risk sensitive. But risk sensitivity adds complexity and room to interpretation, and thus hinders simplicity and comparability. On the other hand, simplicity often means giving up a detailed risk inventory and analysis, and hence does not contribute to risk mitigation.

If we can't have both, then the regulator, considering a portfolio of institutions, should privilege simplicity and comparability. But the regulator should also encourage the internal use of risk-sensitive and forward-looking measurements. To this extent, we believe that the use of the SMA (Standardised Measurement Approach) together with ICAAP processes is a balanced combination.

7.4 RISK MEASUREMENT PRACTICES

We will now focus on analytical methods for risk measurement. Again, these methods differ from global methods in that they attempt to have a granular and enumerated approach to risks, rather than an overall statistical method.

This type of method can theoretically be used for regulatory purposes or for internal measures, although the trends in regulatory measurement are simplicity and standardization, as discussed at length earlier.

We will briefly analyse the type of risk measurements used for credit risk and market risk and show that they differ in nature from the mainstream method in operational risk measurement, that is, the Loss Distribution Approach. We will also review the methods recommended for individual risk assessment in other industries.

7.4.1 Credit Risk Measurement

Describing the credit risk quantification methods is beyond the scope of this book. However, the principles used in credit risk assessment can inform our discussion on operational risk.

Credit risk, the risk of loss due to a borrower being unable to repay a debt in full or in part, accounts for the bulk of most banks' risk-taking activities and regulatory capital requirements. A bank is exposed to credit risk when it lends money, for example, to individual customers (including mortgages, credit cards, and personal loans), small and medium-sized businesses, and large companies, and from derivatives contracts.

If we define a single credit exposure as the total amount extended to a single counterparty by the bank, most methods used in credit risk assessment are based on:

- An exposure or a pool of exposures (EAD)
- A probability of financial default for the considered borrower or shared among the pool of borrowers (PD)
- The fraction of the exposure that would be lost in case of default, which depends on the characteristics of the loan, in particular the presence of a collateral (LGD, or Loss Given Default).

The fundamental approach to credit risk assessment is to therefore to organise the set of exposure into consistent segments of borrowers and to assess the probability of default and loss given default of each of these segments.

A typical first level of decomposition is:

- Sovereigns
- Central banks

- Banks and other financial institutions
- Corporates
- Residential loans
- Commercial real estate loans
- Credit cards and personal lending

These segments can be further decomposed, using for instance a sector decomposition for corporates, or of course down to assessing the risk of a single large exposure individually.

Assuming that, for each considered segment, we know the fraction of obligors that will default during the next year, the expected loss for this segment is the product EAD.PD.LGD, and the total expected loss is the sum of the products EAD.PD.LGD, over all the segments. Strictly speaking, this loss is not a risk, as it is expected and included in the purchase price for the contracted loan. The risk is the deviation from this "objective", that is, the possibility to face larger proportions of defaults in one or more segments. The standard deviation from the expected credit losses can be calculated provided some additional assumptions are made, in particular on the correlations between defaults.

Now, whatever the sophistication of methods used to calculate this distribution of potential losses, the risk assessment method used for credit risk pertains to the portfolio approach discussed above. This means that:

- The risk for individual borrowers and their potential correlations are assessed statistically, using either internal or external sources, but without performing a detailed enumeration and analysis of the potential events that may lead to the default of the borrower.
- The risk of the overall portfolio depends on its allocation, in particular through correlations, and of the anticipations of the economy, that may impact the probabilities of default and the correlations.

To this extent, the credit risk measurement is risk sensitive:

- It is sensitive to the change of exposure, as the change of portfolio structure will change the result.
- It is sensitive to the change of controls, for instance through a better management of collaterals or more reactive derisking when a borrower is downgraded.
- It is sensitive to the change of potential events. For credit risk, this is usually done through stress testing that will impact the probabilities of default and the correlations.

It is also comparable – at least when the banks do not use internal ratings, and this is precisely the recent trend of regulation. Finally, credit risk measurement is at least partly forward-looking, as it includes the present portfolio of loans, and anticipated economic conditions.

7.4.2 Market Risk Measurement

As with credit risk, it would be well beyond the scope of this book to describe in detail the extensive literature on market risk measurement. Our discussion will focus on whether the approach used differs in nature from the loss distribution approach used for operational risk.

TABLE 7.1 Mapping of Positions and Market Variables in Market Risk

Market Variable / Position	**Stock Market Index**	**FX Rate**	**...**	**Interest Rates**
Simple (e.g., spot position)			Linear dependency	
Complex (e.g., future)			Nonlinear dependency	

Market risk measurement has probably contributed to define and anchor some notions which are now of common use in risk measurement, such as value at risk (VaR). It is usually admitted that the method originated when the chairman of JPMorgan, Sir Dennis Weatherstone, asked his staff to give him a daily one-page report indicating risk and potential losses over the next 24 hours, across the bank's entire trading portfolio.

The VaR method was simply based on the following observations.

A portfolio is a set of positions, such as:

- Fixed income: bonds, swaps, interest rate futures, and so on
- FX: spot positions, forward FX exchange positions, currency swaps
- Equities: spot positions in local or foreign currencies, equity derivatives
- Commodities: future contracts, swaps, and so on

Each position is related to an underlying security, and the position value changes when the value of the underlying security changes. Simple, spot positions react linearly to change in security prices, but futures or derivatives react nonlinearly.

Having established the full mapping (see Table 7.1) between the positions and the underlying securities or market variables, such as FX rates, commodities prices, interest rates, and so on, and assuming that the joint distribution of the set of market variables is known, then we can infer the distribution of the portfolio value, either through mathematical calculation or through Monte-Carlo simulation when the dependencies are too complex.

Although quite simple in theory, the full development of a VaR framework requires defining and building all the tools associated with the theory: historical data sets, statistical assumptions, computerized procedures to calculate volatilities and correlations, and so on. This work was done by JPMorgan in the 1990s and resulted in the RiskMetrics method, which later become a spin-off of the bank.

From this very basic description, we can get an answer to our question. Market risk measurement is, as credit risk measurement, based on a portfolio approach.

This means that:

- The driving forces of the risk (movements of the market variables) are assessed statistically, and from external sources, taking of course the correlations into account,
- The firm market risk is calculated by combining the portfolio positions with the risk driving forces.

The VaR method is now of current use in most banks. One benefit of the portfolio approach is that it can of course be used for stress-testing in a straightforward manner. If a stress is defined as a set of anticipated values for some market variables, then (1) the conditional distribution of the remaining variables can be inferred using the correlations matrices, and (2) the reaction of the portfolio to this stress can be calculated.

7.4.3 Operational Risk Measurement

We have already mentioned that the mainstream method used for operational risk measurement was based on losses, and called the Loss Distribution Approach (LDA). We will discuss this method in full detail in the Part 3 of this book.

For now, let us just notice that the LDA is based on a statistical fitting of the number of operational losses observed and on the statistical fitting of the amount of the losses observed.

To contemplate very simply why this is not a risk measurement method, let us just say that:

- If it was used for credit risk, the Loss Distribution Approach would require banks to create a statistical model of their loan write-offs, and use this model to anticipate future losses, irrespective of their current credit portfolio and of their effort to derisk it.
- If it was used for market risk, the Loss Distribution Approach would imply collecting past market losses observed, as positions are closed, for instance because the latent loss breaches a limit. Then, these past losses would be modelled statistically to anticipate potential future losses, irrespective of the current trading book.

7.4.4 Risk Measurement Methods in the Industry

It is interesting to compare the risk assessment approaches in finance and in other domains.

The ISO31000 "Risk Assessment Techniques" document mentions 31 risk assessment techniques:

1. Brainstorming
2. Structured or semi-structured interviews
3. Delphi
4. Checklists
5. Primary hazard analysis
6. Hazard and operability studies (HAZOP)
7. Hazard Analysis and Critical Control Points (HACCP)
8. Environmental risk assessment
9. Structure "What if?" (SWIFT)
10. Scenario analysis
11. Business impact analysis
12. Root cause analysis
13. Failure mode effect analysis
14. Fault tree analysis
15. Event tree analysis
16. Cause and consequence analysis

17. Cause-and-effect analysis
18. Layer protection analysis (LOPA)
19. Decision tree
20. Human reliability analysis
21. Bow tie analysis
22. Reliability-centred maintenance
23. Sneak circuit analysis
24. Markov analysis
25. Monte Carlo simulation
26. Bayesian statistics and Bayes Nets
27. FN curves
28. Risk indices
29. Consequence/probability matrix
30. Cost/benefit analysis
31. Multi-criteria decision analysis (MCDA)

Among these techniques, 10 are considered as "Strongly Applicable" for risk evaluation:

1. Hazard analysis and critical control points (HACCP)
2. Environmental risk assessment
3. Structure: What if?" (SWIFT)
4. Root cause analysis
5. Failure mode effect analysis
6. Reliability centred maintenance
7. Monte Carlo simulation
8. Bayesian statistics and Bayes Nets
9. FN curves
10. Risk indices

Although loss analysis is certainly a key input in risk identification and in understanding possible failures, loss distribution is not mentioned as an applicable technique for risk evaluation.

PART
Three

The Practice of Operational Risk Management

CHAPTER 8

Risk and Control Self-Assessment

8.1 INTRODUCTION

The Risk and Control Self-Assessment (RCSA) is the process of identifying risks and associated controls. The result of the RCSA is sometimes called the risk register, the heat map, or simply the RCSA. In the remainder of this section, we will refer indifferently to the process or its result by the acronym RCSA.

In the first version of the document "Sound Practices for the Management and Supervision of Operational Risk"[1], the Basel Committee has stated that "Risk identification is paramount for the subsequent development of a viable operational risk monitoring and control system."

The risks facing an organization are not known a priori; they cannot be obtained from the outside. They depend on the objective of the organization, of its environment, and therefore evolve over time. Finally, and most important, risks are only perceptions, and so they depend on the people who have identified them.

Risk identification is always a trade-off between creativity and systematic process. Creative thinking is a good method to identify new vulnerabilities but is subject to various biases that can result in missing some major risks. On the other hand, systematic approaches can rapidly become extremely administrative, boring, and are not exempt from missing new risks, as well.

In the 2011 version of the document[2], under Principle 6, "Identification and Assessment", the Basel Committee provides examples of tools that can be used to identify operational risks:

- Audit findings, insofar as they are based on the identification of control weaknesses
- Internal loss data, as they reveal by definition existing, or past, vulnerabilities
- External loss data, as they can help identifying additional vulnerabilities

[1]Basel Committee on Banking Supervision, "Sound Practices for the Management and Supervision of Operational Risk", February 2003, https://www.bis.org/publ/bcbs96.pdf (accessed 5/10/2018).

[2]Basel Committee on Banking Supervision, "Principles for the Sound Management of Operational Risk", June 2011, https://www.bis.org/publ/bcbs195.pdf (accessed 5/10/2018).

- Risk Self-Assessment (RSA), or Risk and Control Self-Assessment (RCSA)
- Business Process Mapping
- Risk and Performance Indicators
- Scenario Analysis
- Measurement
- Comparative analysis, which "consists of comparing the results of the various assessment tools"

This set of tools may seem a little bit confusing as some items seem to logically come after risk identification, as they depend on identified risks.

For instance, risk and performance indicators, according to the Basel Committee, "are used to monitor the main drivers of exposure associated with key risks". So, they require that these key risks are identified. Scenario analysis can only build on identified and named risks, for which a more detailed assessment will be performed. Obviously, measurement also requires that the risks are defined.

However, this apparent contradiction clearly illustrates the difficulty of risk identification mentioned earlier. There is no perfect method to identify risks, and therefore it is always important to keep in mind, at least in theory, that any activity related to risk (identification, management, measurement, mitigation) can also trigger the identification of other risks.

In practice, our experience shows a certain dominance of systematic approaches over creative ones, at least as far as allocated resources are concerned.

The implementation of a systematic approach is outlined in the Basel Committee document mentioned earlier: "a bank assesses the processes underlying its operations against a library of potential threats and vulnerabilities and considers their potential impact"; "Business process mappings identify the key steps in business processes, activities and organisational functions. They also identify the key risk points in the overall business process".

The recommended approach implicitly focuses on processes, rather than on resources contributing to processes. However, the same document also introduces another requirement in "Principle 7", according to which "Senior management should ensure that there is an approval process for all new products, activities, processes, and systems that fully assesses operational risk." There might be a slight contradiction here, as the unit of risk assessment is different from the unit of approval.

However, these requirements clearly indicate an approach for systematic identification: creating a matrix crossing a list of resources, or a list of processes, with a list of risk events. This, in turn, implies having a proper definition and granularity of processes, or resources, and of risk events.

We will now review the different aspects of creating in practice an RCSA:

- The categorisation of risks, which implies a taxonomy of processes or resources, and a taxonomy of events
- The practice of risk assessment, and in particular the use of risk scores
- The practice of control assessment, and the discussion of inherent and residual risks

To avoid any confusion, we would like to distinguish:

- *The risk taxonomy*, which is the set of risks to which a company can theoretically be exposed. It is defined by the cartesian product of the event taxonomy and of the resource taxonomy.
- *The risk register*, which is a subset of risks belonging to the risk taxonomy, which the firm considered could actually happen. When risk ratings have been added to the risk register, the result will sometimes be called a risk map, or risk matrix.

We will go through these topics, keeping in mind that the RCSA is not a stand-alone piece of knowledge but also a key contributor to further risk analysis, risk reporting, and risk quantification.

8.2 RISK AND CONTROL IDENTIFICATION

The risk register is a list of risks identified by the firm. Since a risk is the potential occurrence of an event on a resource of the firm, the risk register is organized in a two-dimensional matrix. The first dimension is the type of resource, the second is the type of event.

Before identifying the risks and the controls, the taxonomy of the resources and the taxonomy of the event types have to be defined by the firm. This requirement naturally raises a typical "chicken or egg" problem. Indeed, how to be sure that the event categories are relevant if the risks have not been identified? This circularity only highlights the dynamic and iterative nature of the RCSA process. The taxonomies are used to record the risks but they might be updated if new risks are identified that don't match the existing categories.

However, operational risk frameworks have been in place for nearly 10 years in financial institutions and some fairly stable taxonomies have been shared in the industry, at least for the events.

8.2.1 Resource Taxonomy

8.2.1.1 Definition A resource taxonomy is a tree that defines how resources that contribute, directly or indirectly, to the company's activity are organized.

The tree structure of the resource taxonomy is a prerequisite to ensure that the aggregation is possible between one level and the level above.

In general, there are two approaches to defining the taxonomy of resources. The first is based on business processes, the second is based on business units.

The business process approach aims at modelling all the processes that contribute to generating revenues or avoiding losses for the firm (Figure 8.1). Business process mapping method clearly identifies all the steps and stakeholders of every process and describes, in an algorithm-like style, their interactions, to achieve the objectives defined by the firm. One of the main benefits of this approach is to capture the collaborative nature of an organization where many business units might be involved in the same process. Actually, by going through every process and

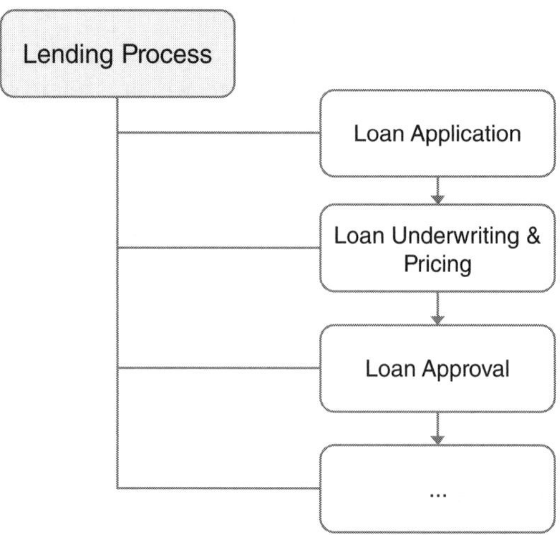

FIGURE 8.1 Example of a Simple Business Process View in Retail Banking

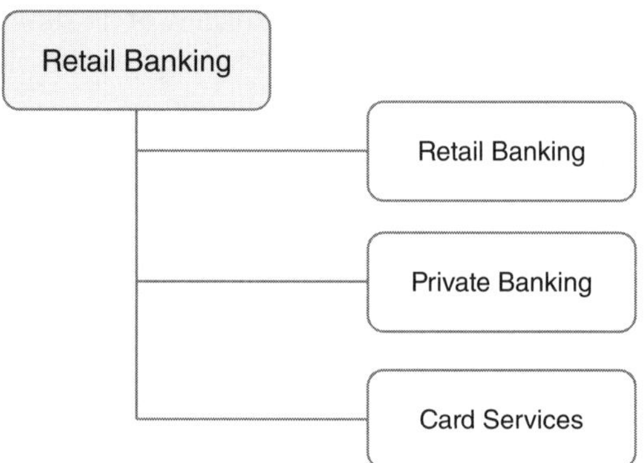

FIGURE 8.2 Example of Business Line Decomposition for Retail Banking

digging into every subprocess, one could theoretically have a deep understanding of all the paths that could fail and generate a loss.

On the other hand, the business line approach (Figure 8.2) is a more siloed decomposition of the firm resources aligned with the functional areas. In a sense, this decomposition can be considered as a refinement of the business structure, as presented in the annual report of a company. The transversal functions must be included in the breakdown – IT, Finance, Legal and so on. – as they may have their own risks.

8.2.1.2 Challenges None of the two approaches is perfect. The three main challenges facing both approaches are related to coverage, knowledge collection, and risk reporting.

Theoretically, processes are supposed to embrace the full scope without overlapping. This is not the case for the business lines decomposition where the support functions like IT might overlap with the business they are serving. For instance, if we consider the risk of trading algorithm runaway, it could be caused by an IT failure or by a human error. When it comes to assigning a risk to a resource category, a choice will have to be made between IT and the process or business line that designs and uses trading algorithms.

The best decomposition for knowledge collection is the one that is more consistent with the organizational chart, because knowledge is owned by people and people can be identified through the organizational chart. Therefore, if a business mapping process has succeeded in aligning the firm's organization with the processes, the business process-based decomposition might be well suited, otherwise, it is likely that a mix of the business line–based and business process–based breakdown should be considered instead. We have experienced this kind of mix in many institutions.

In a hybrid view (Figure 8.3), the firm is broken down into business lines (one or two levels) and then each business line is decomposed into processes. The processes are either assigned to the single business line that owns them or are shared by all the business lines that contribute to the process.

As far as reporting is concerned, although it is recommended to use a categorization that easily matches with the most common regulatory reporting, no breakdown can perfectly match with

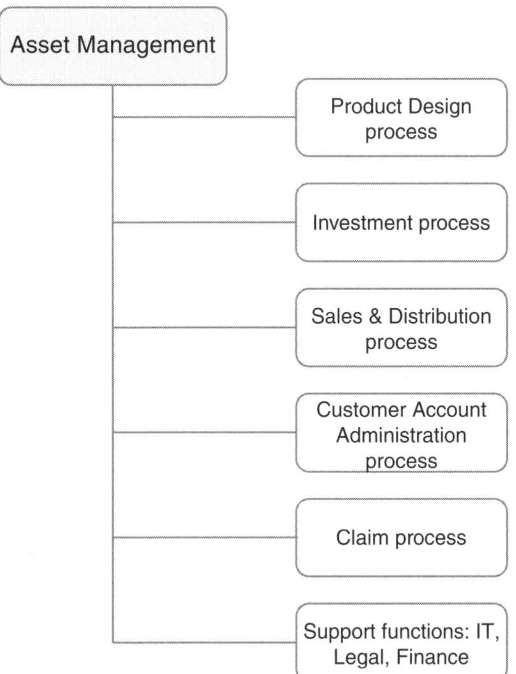

FIGURE 8.3 Example of Hybrid Decomposition for Asset Management

all the types of reporting the firm has to publish. A specific table can be needed to map the cells of the RCSA onto and the cells of the reporting matrix.

For international institutions or institutions with many business units, an additional problem should be thought of when defining the taxonomy of resources: the granularity problem. Depending on the importance of a resource within a business unit, it might be relevant to adjust the granularity of the decomposition under this resource to better capture the risks of the business unit. The adjustment of the granularity to the stakes helps optimizing the allocation of the workload across the entities.

8.2.2 Event Taxonomy

The taxonomy of events is a tree that defines all the potential operational risk events that could strike the firm (see example in Figure 8.4). As of today, most of the event typologies are derived from the loss event type classification defined by the Basel Committee on Banking Supervision in the "International Convergence of Capital Measurement and Capital Standards" document published in 2004[3].

The granularity of the classification is captured through the depth of the tree and might depend on the activities run by the institution. In May 2015, Lloyd Blankfein, then CEO of Goldman Sachs, stated: "We are a technology company". A few months later, Marianne Lake, JPMorgan CFO, said pretty much the same. This shift toward technology, which is likely to impact the entire financial sector, brings new risks, and increases some existing ones. The IT-related event categories – "External Fraud", "Business Disruption and System Failures", "Execution, Delivery & Process Management" – will probably need some refinement to better capture a new risk profile that is more sensitive to cyber risks, technology disruption, and errors.

We have commented on the issues faced when defining the names of the event categories and encourage the reader to refer to Part I, "Lessons Learned in 10 Years of Practice".

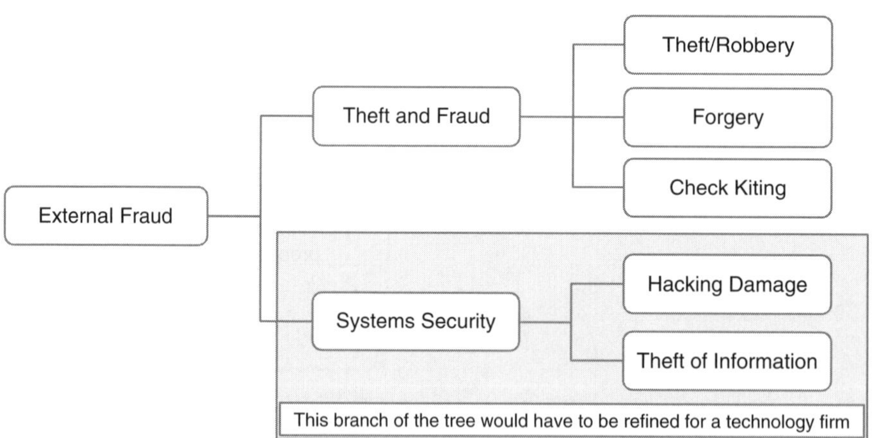

FIGURE 8.4 Example of Decomposition for External Fraud Event Category

[3]See Basel Committee on Banking Supervision, "International Convergence of Capital Measurement and Capital Standards: A Revised framework", June 2004, Annex 7: Detailed Loss Event Type Classification.

8.2.3 Risk Identification

8.2.3.1 Definitions A risk is defined by the four followings items (see example in Figure 8.5):

1. Title: Ideally, this title should contain the name of the adverse event and the name of the resource: "building destruction", "datacenter disruption", "data theft", "misselling of investment products", and so on.
2. Description: A short narrative that aims at describing in a very precise way how the risk is unfolding and which resources are impacted.
3. Event category: Category of the adverse event covered by this risk, defined at the lowest level of the event category tree.
4. Resource category: Category of the resource that is impacted, defined at the lowest level of the resource category tree.

8.2.3.2 Repetition of Risks The very simple definition introduced above raises several issues on the structure of the RCSA.

We can easily understand that many different risks can be assigned to the same *Resource×Event* cell of the RCSA. For instance, a "Denial of service" risk and a "Credit card compromise" risk could be assigned to the same *Information System×Piracy* cell.

Conversely, is it possible that the same risk is assigned to several cells of the RCSA? This is theoretically possible if the decomposition of the resources induces repetitions. For instance, if a firm has chosen to include in the tree of resource categories a level that relates to the business units, and if several business units are running the same operations, then a risk might have to be repeated for each business unit.

Therefore, it is recommended to avoid this repetition by defining a taxonomy of resource categories that is generic enough not to include the actual business units that run the operations.

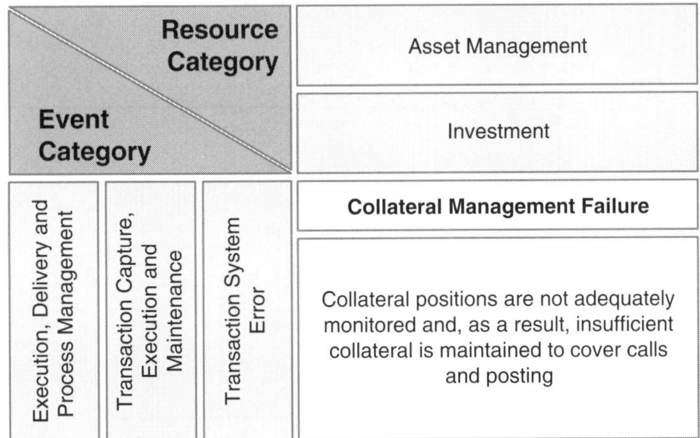

FIGURE 8.5 Example of an Asset Management Related Risk in the RCSA

For example, the same taxonomy should be used by the US units of a bank and by the Asian or European ones.

This is possible if a better distinction between risk identification and risk assessment is made.

The result of the identification process is a list of risks, each risk being assigned to a cell in the RCSA. The table of risks contains one row per risk, a set of columns for the resource category, and a set of columns for the event category. During the risk assessment phase, the business units have to assess all the risks that concern the resources they rely on. For example, a "datacenter disruption" risk would be assessed by US, UK, and APAC business units if these units rely on datacenters. A table must be dedicated to the assessments, with one row per assessment, each row recording the identifier of the risk being assessed, the business unit that is assessing the risk, and the results of the assessment (Figure 8.6).

However, if it is not possible to implement this distinction between identification and assessment, then the definition above should be slightly modified to account for the assignment of a risk to multiple cells of the RCSA.

8.2.3.3 Consistency of the Risk Register

One of the major challenges that a company faces when establishing a risk register is its consistency.

The first potential problem is the naming of risks. Risks that are identified separately by different people in different business units need to be centrally reviewed by the risk team to ensure

Risk Identification Table

Risk	Event	Resource
R1	EVT#1	RES#1
R2	EVT#2	RES#2
...	...	...

Risk	Assessment	Frequency	Impact
...	...	...	...
R2	US	2	3
R2	UK	1	4
R2	APAC	2	1
...	...	...	...

Risk Assessment Table

FIGURE 8.6 Distinction between Risk Identification and Risk Assessment
One table for risks organized around event categories and resources categories, one table for the assessments organized around business units.

that the final risk register doesn't contain multiple versions of the same risk with slightly different definitions.

The second one is related to transversal functions, like IT. A risk that comes from IT could be identified both in IT and in business lines that rely on IT services. In this case, uniqueness of the risk is not desired because it would result in a loss of information on the nature of the risk. But at least it should be made clear that the same risk has been identified by several business lines in the RCSA.

In any case, any proposal for a new risk has to be validated and possibly edited by a moderator, part or the risk team, to build a consistent risk register.

8.2.4 Control Identification

A control is an action or a set of actions that have been taken by the firm to mitigate one or several risks. Two types of controls can be considered: the preventive controls that reduce the likelihood of a risk and the protective controls that reduce the impact of a risk should this risk occur.

A control may mitigate several risks and a risk might be mitigated by different controls.

From a data model perspective, this means that, within the RCSA, controls are defined with two tables. The first table contains the list of controls with a title and a narrative that describes the purpose of the control. The second table contains a list of {control, risk} pairs, each pair representing a control being applied to a risk. An example of such a pair is described in Figure 8.7 for cyber-risk mitigation.

8.3 RISK AND CONTROL ASSESSMENT

After identification, risk and controls are assessed. The likelihood and severity of risks as well as the efficiency of the controls are given a score.

All the business units that contain the resource category involved in a risk have to assess the risk (see Figure 8.8). In the following, the business unit in charge of the assessment will also be called an assessment unit.

RISK R436: Hacking of information systems

The risk of information system hacking can come from outside or from the inside.
Examples:

- Execution of market transactions (takeover of the position of a trader)
- Theft / destruction / modification of data

Some potential weaknesses in the logical security could be exploited:

- Late deactivation of logins in case of transfer or departure of an employee
- No change of passwords to access the posts or the teleconferences
- Absence of automatic standby of posts, without user awareness policy
- Lack of encryption on certain sensitive files (wages, etc.)

CONTROL C029: Encryption of sensitive files

The files XXXX, YYYY, ZZZZ are encrypted

FIGURE 8.7 Example of Control Defined for a Cyber Risk

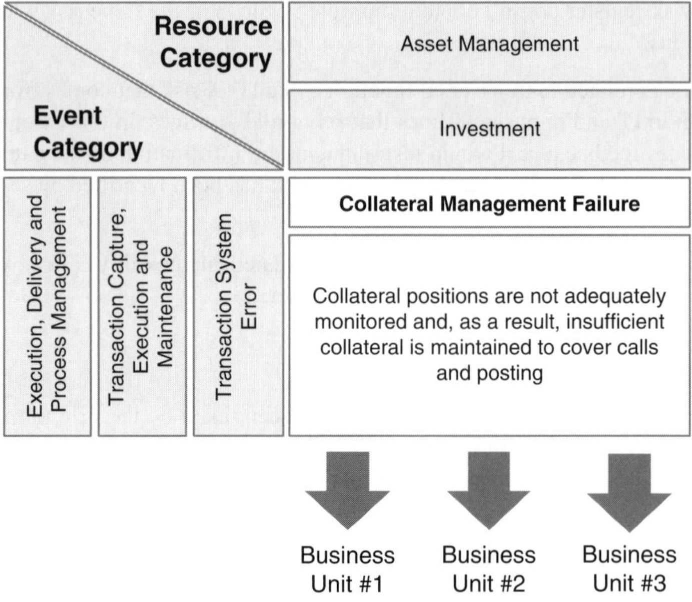

FIGURE 8.8 Assessment of One Risk in Three Business Units

8.3.1 Risk Scoring

8.3.1.1 Definitions Risk scoring consists in rating the frequency[4] and impact[5] of a risk within the context of the assessment unit.

The frequency is the average number of events that are expected for the risk over the next exercise. The impact is the financial consequence of the occurrence of the risk on the firm. Two metrics are considered for the impact: the average impact and the maximum impact.

The impact can be split into several components:

- *Direct losses*: Legal costs, damage cost, fraud costs, loss of revenue, and so on.
- *Indirect losses*: Remediation cost, opportunity cost, and so on.

Strictly speaking, reputational cost is not in the scope of operational risk quantification but it may be assessed as well.

The rating is a score based on a scale defined by the firm. The scale of scores can be purely qualitative and subjective or it can be semi-quantitative. Tables 8.1–8.2 below illustrate the two types of scales.

[4]"Likelihood" and "Frequency" are used indifferently to represent the expected number of events over a period of time.

[5]"Impact" and "Severity" are used indifferently to represent the financial consequence of an operational risk event.

TABLE 8.1 A Qualitative Scale

Frequency	Impact
1 – Very rare	1 – Low
2 – Rare	2 – Medium
3 – Likely	3 – High
4 – Frequent	4 – Major
5 – Very frequent	

TABLE 8.2 A Semi-quantitative Scale

Frequency	Impact
Very rare	Low
Less than 1 in 5 years	*Less than $1,000*
Rare	Moderate
Less 1 in a year	*Multiple of $1,000*
Likely	Medium
Several times a year	*Multiple of $10,000*
Frequent	High
Several times a month	*Multiple of $100,000*
Very frequent	Major
Several times a week	*Multiple of $1,000,000*
Continuous	Critical
Several times a day	*Multiple of $10,000,000*

8.3.1.2 Challenges Four quality criterions can be defined for a scale in the context of operational risk assessment:

1. *Accuracy*: The scale should provide a full range of risk levels for the firm with a reasonable granularity. Each level should be clearly defined and should not lead to any misinterpretation.
2. *Simplicity*: The scale should be simple to use, it should lead to few hesitations to select the right level that matches with a risk.
3. *Comparability*: The risks can be compared within the same business units or between different business units.
4. *Aggregability:* The assessments of several risks can be aggregated. Frequencies can be added; average impacts can be averaged.

Accuracy is important for further risk analysis. Simplicity ensures that the rating is workable. Comparability is critical to prioritize the risks and the mitigation plans. As for aggregability, it is core to two types of applications: reporting and filtering. For reporting, it is necessary to aggregate the risks that belong to a set of cells in the RCSA. For filtering, in order to draw a line between the material and the nonmaterial risks, a prerequisite is to assess each risk at the firmwide level by aggregating the different assessments that have been proposed by the business units.

We now describe the potential difficulties in meeting these quality criteria.

8.3.1.3 Trade-off Between Accuracy and Simplicity The more descriptive the scale, the easier it is to interpret and the more consistent its use. There is a trade-off between the accuracy of the rating scale and its simplicity. Scales above six levels are too difficult to apply, as assessors will waste a lot of time trying to differentiate between the different levels. In addition, this type of scale gives the company a false sense of precision that is not required in this type of exercise. On the other hand, scales with less than three levels are too coarse and likely to provide little information for further risk analysis.

8.3.1.4 Comparison of Risks Is Not Possible for Subjective Scales When a scale does not provide a clear indication of the quantification of its levels, it is impossible to compare the assessments made by different business units for the same risk because the meaning of each level depends on the interpretation of the person assessing the risk. Subjectivity leads to implicit scaling according to the size of the business unit and the assessor. Rescaling the assessment made in one business unit to come up with an "absolute" score is not possible without a quantitative interpretation of the scale.

8.3.1.5 Aggregation of Risks Is Not Possible for Subjective Scales Even if the rescaling problem was fixed, there is no known method to properly aggregate qualitative scores.

As an example, let us examine out how we could aggregate the three assessments of a risk made by different business units (Table 8.3) of a risk made by different business units:

With pure quantitative assessments, we simply would add the frequencies and average the impacts weighted by the frequencies.

Doing the same arithmetic calculation with ordinal numbers is meaningless. It would lead to 9 for frequency and 1.78 for the average impact. Should the frequency be interpreted as "4 – Frequent" or "5 – Very Frequent"? Should the impact be interpreted as "1 – Low" or "2 – Medium"? There is no possible answer without a quantitative interpretation of the scale levels.

8.3.2 Control Scoring

8.3.2.1 Definitions A control is defined for one or several risks. A risk can be applied to several controls. Therefore, the efficiency of a control must be assessed separately for every risk the control is mitigating.

A control can be preventative if it reduces the likelihood of a risk, protective if it reduces the impact should the risk occur, or both. Thus, the efficiency of a control must be assessed with respect to its effect on the frequency or on the impact of the risk.

TABLE 8.3 Averaging Qualitative Assessments

Assessment	Frequency	Average Impact
#1	3 – Likely	2 – Medium
#2	4 – Frequent	1 – Low
#3	2 – Rare	3 – High

TABLE 8.4 A Semi-quantitative Scale for Controls

Control
Inefficient *Less than 25% of losses avoided*
Insufficient *25% to 50% of losses avoided*
Medium *50% to 75% of losses avoided*
Efficient *75% of losses avoided*

Assessment can be risk-centric or it can be made at the level of a [control, risk] pair.

Risk-centric assessment aims at providing a score for the overall efficiency of all the controls that apply to one risk instead of focusing on the efficiency of one control on one single risk.

Moreover, assessment of controls can be made either at the decomposed level of frequency and impact or at the aggregated level. At the decomposed level, the assessor is asked to which extent the control is reducing the frequency and/or the impact. At the aggregated level, the assessor is requested to estimate the effect of the control on the overall cost of the risk.

As with risks, the assessment is made relying on a rating scale (see example in Table 8.4) that describes the different levels of efficiency. The whole discussion about risk rating scales is still valid for controls.

8.3.2.2 Challenges Whatever the type of assessment, assessing controls is challenging because it implies that the situation without controls is known and can be measured.

This condition is only fulfilled in very specific situations where the effects of a control can be predicted or observed or tested.

For instance, if a firm has decided to restrict the access of IT people to sensitive files with credit card data and removed the access rights to 30% of them, the likelihood of a card data theft to occur can reasonably be decreased by 30%. In this case, removing the control in imagination is easy.

On the other side, encrypting the files will probably reduce the impact of an unintentional data loss to zero, but it is hard to estimate the effect of this action on the risk of a credit card compromise, although intuition suggests that it is better to encrypt. This shows that it would be easy to imagine removing the encryption for the first risk ("unintentional data loss"), but it would not be easy for the second one ("credit card compromise").

It could be argued that one should refer to the situation before the firm had implemented the control to know the effect of the control. This is correct, but only for frequent risks, as it is theoretically possible, if nothing else has changed, to observe the frequency and average impact before and after the implementation of the control. Unfortunately, for risks with low frequency, and that category includes most of the major risks, this kind of observation is not available.

The difficulties are enhanced when multiple controls are applied to the same risks, as it is impossible to account for interdependencies between controls. The assessment of the overall efficiency is an attempt to circumvent this potential issue, but then it is even more difficult to define a situation "before" and a situation "after".

Except in very particular situations, assessments of controls are highly judgmental and should be used with caution. In general, no accuracy should be targeted. In our view, this exercise is primarily an opportunity to get aware of what the firm knows about its controls. To this end, it should be clearly indicated for each control whether the assessment is very subjective or is supported by evidence, such as observation, simulation exercises results, or research.

8.3.3 Inherent and Residual Risk

8.3.3.1 Definitions Risks must be assessed on an inherent and residual basis. Inherent risk is defined as the risk prior to the application of controls, while residual risk is defined as the risk after the application of controls.

Before we go any further, let us discuss these definitions. If the inherent risk is the risk before the controls are applied, it should be specified which controls are being considered. Should all controls implemented be included in the scope, or only those implemented in the last year or, why not, only those future controls that should be implemented in the next year?

Since the RCSA is intended to contain a forward-looking assessment of the risks, it is worth considering whether the firm should assess its risks with future controls or with existing controls. This can radically change the interpretation of inherent and residual risk and, consequently, the objective of control assessment.

If we assume that the residual risk is the risk remaining after the application of the future controls to the inherent risk, the inherent risk can be interpreted as the risk based on the current state of the control environment.

On the other hand, if the residual risk is considered to be the risk after the application of existing controls, then the residual risk can be interpreted as the risk based on the current state of the control environment.

With the first option, assessing the inherent risk is easier, because it corresponds to the firm's current environment, but assessing the residual risk requires some form of projection. With the second option, the inherent risk cannot be observed in the current state of the firm and its evaluation requires the existing controls to be removed by thought, which is by no mean an easy task. In contrast, the residual risk reflects the current state of the risk profile.

In practice, the second interpretation prevails: residual risk is the risk after the application of all existing controls. Based on this definition, two methods can be applied to assess inherent and residual risks (see Figure 8.9). The first method is to assess the inherent risk and then assess the mitigating effect of the controls and deduce the residual risk. The second method uses an inverted chain. It begins by assessing the residual risk, and then eliminates the mitigating effect of controls to assess the inherent risk.

8.3.3.2 Challenges What are the major challenges posed by these two methods?

First, arithmetic rules don't work for ordinal numbers: an inherent risk with a frequency rated "4 – Frequent" mitigated by a control rated "3 – Medium" doesn't result in residual risk

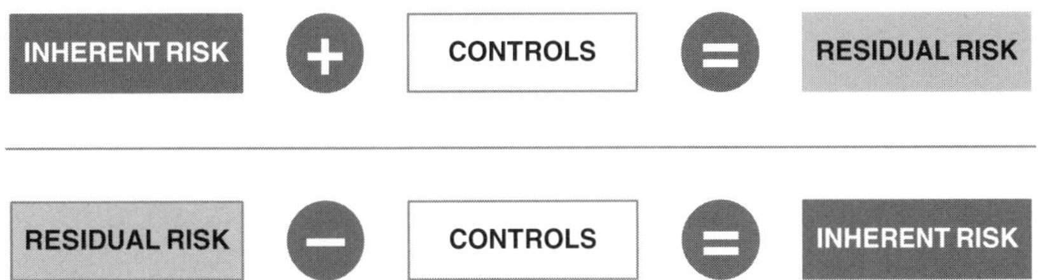

FIGURE 8.9 Two Methods to Assess the Inherent and Residual Risks

with frequency rated "1 – Rare". To overcome this shortcoming, either the firm is relying on semi-quantitative scales or it has to define a set of rules to combine the ratings of risks and controls.

Second, assessing the inherent risk poses the same type of problem as assessing the efficiency of controls. The "No control" situation must be created through imagination. This means that a risk assessment will be carried out on a hypothetical firm – a very difficult exercise that is likely to generate very uncertain assessments.

As practitioners, we recommend the second method because it is more robust and, most important, because it starts by addressing the main problem, which is the assessment of the risks for the firm, not the assessment of risks for a hypothetical firm.

CHAPTER 9
Losses Modelling

Losses modelling can be considered in two ways:

1. Loss Distribution Approach: This consists of modelling the observed distribution of losses, in order to predict the range of potential future losses. This was the most common approach used for calculating the operational risk capital.
2. Loss Regression: This consists of modelling the dependency of losses to other variables, either internal to the bank such as management, or external such as macro-economic conditions. This method is less developed, in particular because of the lack of data, but is relevant for stress testing.

As we discuss in Part II, we believe that the Loss Distribution Approach cannot be considered as a valid risk measurement method, at least not as an internal risk measurement method. Indeed, considering that past losses are representative of risk implicitly means that risk cannot be managed, or, at the very least creates the conditions of a silo approach between risk management and risk measurement.

As people in charge of risk measurement use observed losses, while people in charge of risk management rely on risk and control self-assessment, there is no surprise that the communication between the two teams is limited, if it does exist.

In the Federal Reserve Bulletin of June 30, 2014[1], a very clear statement of the role of the four elements of AMA is made, which, in principle does not gives full precedence to data:

> The AMA does not prescribe any specific approach for operational risk quantification systems, and provides the flexibility for banking organizations to use the four data elements in the most effective way when estimating operational risk exposure on a forward-looking basis. All four elements are critical, required components of a banking organization's operational risk quantification process. Internal operational loss event data often indicate a banking organization's historical operational risk exposure and can provide a foundation for the forward-looking estimation of operational risk

[1] https://www.federalreserve.gov/bankinforeg/basel/files/bcc1401.pdf (accessed 5/10/2018).

> exposure. Depending, however, on a banking organization's specific circumstances (e.g., limited internal data or a significant change in a banking organization's business mix), it may be appropriate to increase the weight given to scenario analysis, BEICFs, or external data for a more informed, forward-looking estimate of risk exposure.

However, this approach has been the most commonly used approach in the past 10 years, in particular because it was implicitly considered as mandatory for US banks, possibly also because an implicit recommendation in the same Federal Reserve bulletin of 2014: "Although not required, many banking organizations use the loss distribution approach (LDA) as a core modelling technique in their AMA quantification processes".

If past losses were a good predictor of future exposure, it could be a good benchmarking method, even if disconnected from actual risk management. A recent 2017 study by the Federal Reserve Bank of Richmond shows that the past losses of a bank are reasonably predictive of future losses[2], and remarks that "the ability of past losses to predict exposure, particularly tail exposure, has not been thoroughly examined in the literature". This study concludes that "Metrics associated with loss frequency and particularly the volume of small loss events prove the most robust in forecasting exposure", whereas "Loss metrics that are significantly affected by large loss events, such as average total annual losses, average loss severity, and the 95th quantile of the operational loss distribution measured from past losses, have an inconsistent relation with future losses." The authors conclude that "these findings are particularly problematic for the use of LDA models to forecast exposure".

We will now discuss the Loss Distribution Approach and Loss Regression in more detail.

9.1 LOSS DISTRIBUTION APPROACH

9.1.1 Foundations

The Loss Distribution Approach has been introduced in operational risk measurement in the early 2000 years, possibly thanks to a paper by Frachot, Georges, and Roncalli in 2001[3]. This method is inspired from actuarial science, in particular in the context of computing the accumulated claim in an insurance company, as developed by Hans Bühlmann in his book *Mathematical Methods in Risk Theory*[4]. In this actuarial work, the question of interest was to be able to infer the total claim an insurance company will face in the future, knowing the total observed to date. The assumptions made were generally weaker than the ones used in operational risk literature.

We mentioned this already, but it is worth contemplating this once again: The theory used borrows from insurance and actuarial science. When modelling accumulated claims, it is reasonable that an insurer considers the claim-generating process as random, as it is not within its

[2]Filippo Curti and Marco Migueis, "Predicting Operational Loss Exposure Using Past Losses" (December 13, 2017). Available at SSRN: https://ssrn.com/abstract=2775427.

[3]Antoine Frachot, Pierre Georges, and Thierry Roncalli, "Loss Distribution Approach for Operational Risk" (March 30, 2001). Available at SSRN: https://ssrn.com/abstract=1032523 (accessed 5/10/2018).

[4]Hans Buhlmann, *Mathematical Methods in Risk Theory*. (Berlin-Heidelberg: Springer-Verlag, 1970).

control. This is not the case when a firm tries to model its own operational losses. By definition, these losses are within the control of the firm, at least partially.

In addition, actuarial science is generally designed for frequency risks, whereas the usage intended for operational risk is to capture the tail risk. Although this borrowing to insurance seemed a clever idea, it also contained the seeds of future problems in operational risk modelling: the gap between management and measurement and the failure to capture tail events.

9.1.2 Description

The loss distribution approach starts from a quite self-evident statement: the total loss one organisation is exposed to is equal to the sum of the amount of individual losses.

The mathematical translation of this statement is simply:

$$L = \sum_{k=1}^{n} l_i$$

In order to make this approach applicable to risk measurement, some assumptions are needed.

A first level of assumptions is required to make this formula capable of inferring the distribution of potential future losses:

- The *number of losses* is a random variable, which follows a particular probability distribution.
- The *amount of each loss* is a random variable, which follows a particular probability distribution.

Using these first and basic assumptions, it becomes possible, in theory, to combine the probability distributions of the number of losses and of the amount of each loss, to calculate the distribution of the total loss (Figure 9.1).

From a mathematical standpoint, the ideal solution would be to be able to calculate as a closed formula the distribution of the sum of the loss amounts, assuming that the distribution of the number of losses and the distribution of each loss are known.

As far as we know, there are no theoretical results that can be used to calculate such a closed formula.

In a more empirical way, this calculation can be considered simply in the form of a simulation. Each run of the simulation would consist of:

- Sampling the future number of losses according to its probability distribution
- Sampling each loss amount according to its probability distribution
- Adding up the loss amounts

Now in order for this computation to be tractable, some additional assumptions are generally made. The assumptions made in the operational risk literature are stronger than the assumptions proposed in Bühlmann's work, who considered only that the future development of claims depends only on the total of the claims incurred up to now, irrespective of how

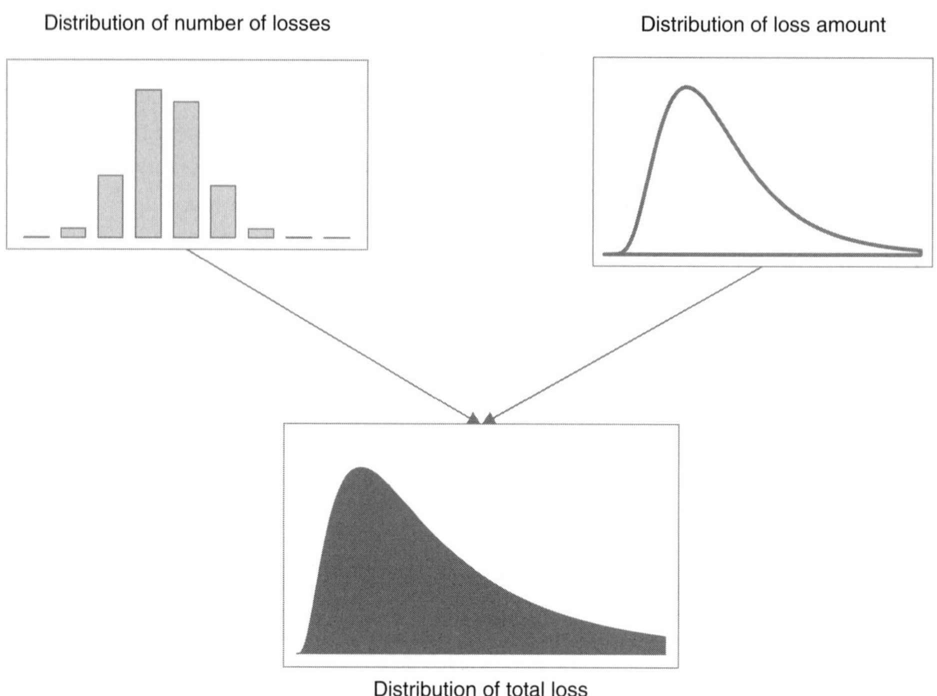

FIGURE 9.1 Principle of the Loss Distribution Approach

they were arranged in the past (in mathematical terms, the accumulated claim process is a Markov process).

In the use of LDA for operational risk, the following assumptions are generally made:

- The amount of each individual losses follows the same distribution and the losses are independent of each other.
- The distribution of the amount of a loss is independent of the distribution of the number of losses.

Using the above assumptions, the core of the LDA algorithm looks as follows:

Repeat $i = 1, Q$

- Draw a number of losses N_i from the frequency distribution F
- Draw N_i times a sample $L_{i,k}$ from the severity distribution, S
- Sum the losses to obtain $A_i = \sum L_{i,k}$, the estimate of annual loss.

Observe the distribution of the total loss.

9.1.3 Application to Operational Risk

With these assumptions, the application of the LDA to operational risk then comes down to proposing two distributions:

1. The mathematical distribution describing the number of future losses
2. The mathematical distribution describing the amount of each loss

The first idea, and possibly the simplest distributions to use, would be to use the observed empirical distributions.

In order to illustrate this simple approach with real data, let us use the ORX source of operational risk losses. Using the public document "Beyond the Headlines – Banking" from ORX, we can observe the following frequency (Figure 9.2) and loss amounts distributions (Figure 9.3).

Now, as the number of banks reporting to ORX is approximately 100, we can imagine an average bank that would represent 1% of the loss data reported:

- The number of losses of this bank would be between 500 and 600 per year.
- The amount of each loss would be distributed according to the histogram shown in Figure 9.3.

In order to be able to run an actual simulation based on these assumptions, there is a small problem we need to fix. The last interval reported by ORX is "€10 million and more". We need to decide an upper bound for this interval. Of course, in practice, this is not something we would need to decide, but that we would observe from actual data.

Depending on whether the upper bound of the interval is set at €50m or to €100m, the average loss would change from €260k to €340k (i.e., an increase of 30%), and we observe the following distributions of the cumulated loss (Figure 9.4).

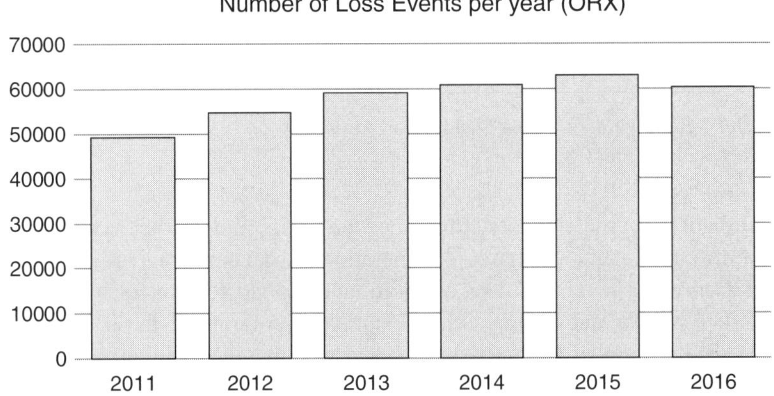

FIGURE 9.2 Number of Operational Risk Loss Events for the Banking Industry
Source: Based on data from ORX.

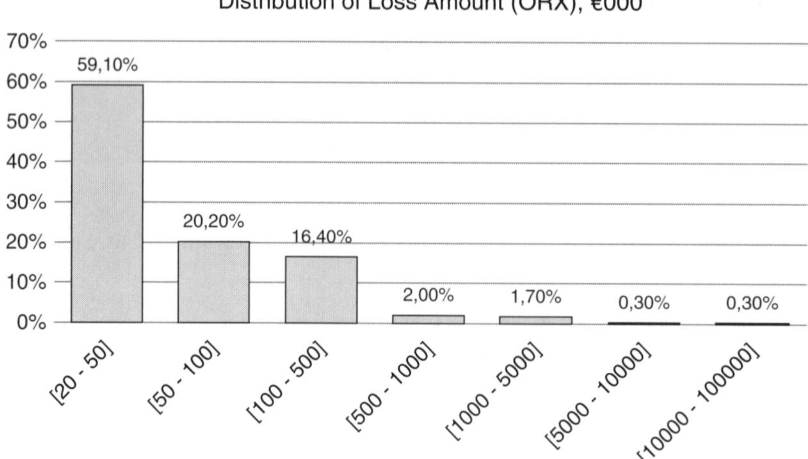

FIGURE 9.3 Distribution of Operational Risk Losses for the Banking Industry
Source: Based on data from ORX.

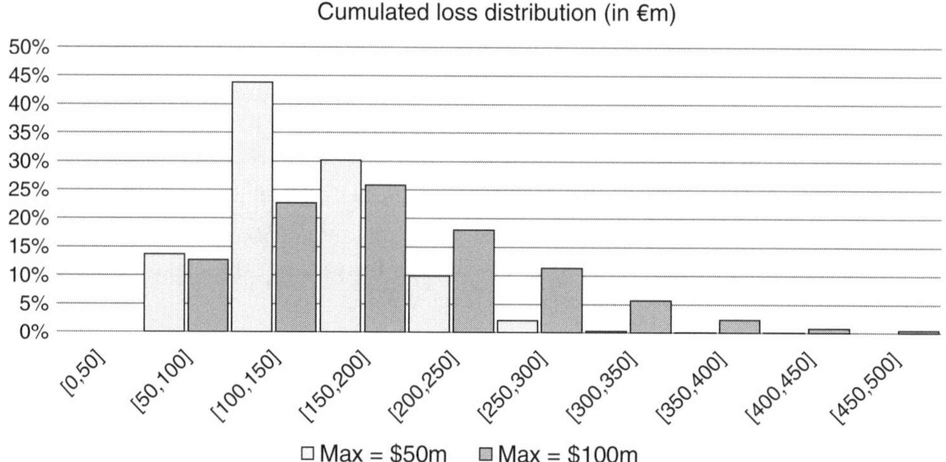

FIGURE 9.4 Simulation of a Loss Distribution Approach
Source: Based on data from ORX.

The distribution of the cumulated loss is driven by the assumption on the maximum. The 99.9% percentile of the cumulated loss, that is, the operational risk capital, according to Basel would be around €300m for a maximum loss at €50m, and around €500m for a maximum loss at €100m. In other words, and in this simple example, the range of the 0.3% biggest losses increases the capital number by more than 60%, twice as much as their contribution to the average loss.

Of course, this is a very simple example, but it illustrates the main challenge of the LDA, which is the sensitivity of the capital to the tail of the individual loss distribution.

9.1.4 Theoretical Challenges

9.1.4.1 Choice of Distributions The choice of a distribution for the number of losses and for the amount of each loss is the first challenge of LDA.

The simple example that we have just built would not convince a regulator of the robustness of a model, as using only the number of losses observed in the recent years, and the empirical observed distribution of their amount does not seem very conservative. We would need to be able to demonstrate that we cannot observe more than 600 losses, and that the amount of a loss cannot exceed €50m, or even €100m.

The typical answer to this challenge is to choose distributions with infinite support, that is, distributions that could grow to infinity.

The typical choice of distribution used in operational risk is the Poisson law for the number of losses, and the Lognormal distribution for the amount of losses.

In most cases, empirical sciences justify the choice of a distribution by (1) a theoretical analysis supporting the fact that the phenomenon modelled can be described by the selected law (2) a parameter fitting. In the situation where the parameter fitting fails, the theory needs to be revised.

The Poisson law has been defined by the French mathematician Denis Poisson in 1838, in a research on probabilities of jury decisions in criminal matters. Although his conclusions were not well received at this time, he proposed a mathematical law which is now of common use. The Poisson distribution provides the probabilities of observing a certain number of events within a certain period of time, given that we know the average number of events occurring during a reference time interval. The main assumption is that the events are independent from each other.

This assumption is reasonably acceptable in the case of operational risk, if we consider for instance the "error" event type. We can assume that any transaction is exposed to an error, with a common probability rate. If we process n transactions per year, and if we assume that errors occur at random with a given probability p, we will observe on average $n.p$ errors. If we want to calculate the probability of observing any number of errors, and if we assume that each transaction is exposed independently to an error, the probability of observing k errors is equal to:

$$\binom{n}{k} \cdot p^k \cdot (1-p)^{(n-k)}$$

This result is a simple combinatorial calculation, assuming the independence of each transaction with respect to the occurrence of an error, and the resulting law is called the binomial distribution.

A binomial distribution can be approximated with good precision by a Poisson distribution of mean $n.p$. As an illustration, the values of the binomial distribution compared with the Poisson distribution for $n = 10{,}000$, $p = 0.1\%$, and k, ranging from 0 to 20, are shown in Table 9.1.

The discussion above shows how the choice of the Poisson distribution could be theoretically justified to represent the number of events for operational risk, at least for a situation where loss events are independent from each other. This assumption is reasonable for errors on transactions, some type of external frauds,and so on.

TABLE 9.1 Comparison of Binomial and Poisson Distributions

k	**Binomial**	**Poisson**
0	0,00005	0,00005
1	0,00045	0,00045
2	0,00226	0,00227
3	0,00755	0,00757
4	0,01889	0,01892
5	0,03780	0,03783
6	0,06302	0,06306
7	0,09007	0,09008
8	0,11262	0,11260
9	0,12516	0,12511
10	0,12517	0,12511
11	0,11379	0,11374
12	0,09482	0,09478
13	0,07292	0,07291
14	0,05207	0,05208
15	0,03470	0,03472
16	0,02168	0,02170
17	0,01274	0,01276
18	0,00707	0,00709
19	0,00372	0,00373
20	0,00186	0,00187

When the discussion turns to severity distribution, there is one simple question that remains unaddressed in the literature: Why use a particular type of distribution? For instance, why use a lognormal distribution? Ideally, the choice of a distribution should be rooted in some theoretical analysis, even a simple one.

For instance, the discussion we just had about the frequency of errors is a simple theoretical analysis. If each transaction is subject to an error with a given probability, and if errors are independent of each other, then the distribution of the number of errors follows approximately a Poisson distribution.

In market finance, the normal shape of the distribution of returns is the consequence of the theoretical assumption of efficient markets[5].

In hydrodynamics, the distribution of the heights of the waves follows a Rayleigh distribution. This is predicted by the linear theory: a superposition of a large number of independent sine waves results in a Gaussian distribution for the elevation of the surface, which corresponds to a Rayleigh distribution for the wave heights[6].

[5]L. Bachelier (1900), "Théorie de la spéculation", Annales Scientifiques de l'École Normale Supérieure.

[6]M. S. Longuet-Higgins (1952), "On the Statistical Distribution of the Heights of Sea Waves." *Journal of Marine Research* XI, 3, pp. 245–226.

In reliability theory, the use of Weibull law has been derived by the probability of failure of the weakest link in a chain of links[7]. The distribution of the weakest link failure is one particular case of application of the Fisher-Tippet theorem. This result of extreme value theory proves that the maximum of a sample of independent and identically distributed random variables can only converge in distribution to either the Gumbel distribution, the Fréchet distribution, or the Weibull distribution.

In most of the cases described above, the distribution derived theoretically partially fails to explain the observed data: the normality of the distribution of market returns fails to explain the frequency of market crashes; the number of high waves is higher than what is predicted by the linear theory. However, these theories can be used as references.

There is no such derivation in operational risk. There is no consensual theory stating that an operational loss is the sum, the maximum, the limit, or any combination of random variables that could justify the use of one particular distribution.

9.1.4.2 Independence Assumption The use of LDA assumes (1) the independence of the distribution of individual loss amounts, and (2) the independence of the distribution of the loss amounts and of the frequency.

These assumptions can be violated in several situations.

When several losses are related to the same cause, such as a major fraud scheme generating multiple losses, this will result in correlated loss amounts. This is of course also true for conduct losses, such as retail mis-selling cases. The PPI (payment protection insurance) case in UK generated millions of complaints, and a refund of more than £30bn to customers, from around 20 banks[8]. All the individual refunds cannot of course be considered as independent and need to be aggregated as a single loss.

In a Basel Coordination Committee bulletin (BCC14-1) already cited, the Federal Reserve states clearly that:

> A fundamental assumption of the LDA is that loss events ... are independent and identically distributed. Sometimes, however, individual losses have a common underlying trigger or instigating factor or a clear relationship to each other. In such situations, a generally acceptable approach is to aggregate losses having a common trigger or instigating factor, or a clear relationship to each other, and treat these related losses as a single event.

The aggregation of several minor losses (fraud, mis-selling) into a larger loss sounds reasonable, as the event in that case is the occurrence of the fraud or of the mis-selling, and the individual cases are consequences of the main event. This applies also when considering the aggregation of fines or settlements imposed by different regulatory agencies for a single event. This was the case for the mortgage settlement case in the United States after the financial crisis.

---

[7]W. Weibull (1951), "A Statistical Distribution Function of Wide Applicability." *Journal of Applied Mechanics* 18, 293–297.

[8]Financial Conduct Authority: https://www.fca.org.uk/news/ppi-monthly-refunds-compensation (accessed 5/10/2018).

For instance, Bank of America had to face more than 20 settlements from different agencies ranging from $20 million to $7 billion. These 20 settlements are of course not independent, and should be considered as one single event.

The independence assumption can also be considered as violated when the losses originated in multiple institutions that were merged or purchased, although this is more questionable. This is for instance the case of JPMorgan, which was fined $13bn in 2013 for the mortgage settlement, most of this amount being attributable to Bear Stearns and Washington Mutual, two firms that JPMorgan purchased in 2008.

9.1.5 Practical Challenges

The use of LDA faces also a lot of practical challenges which are mostly related to distribution fitting.

9.1.5.1 Frequency Distribution Fitting In practice, the Poisson distribution will typically not account for the observed variance of the number of losses.

For instance, the ORX reported number of events mentioned earlier is shown in Table 9.2.

This results in an average number of 57,841 events per year. If for each bank, we assume a Poisson distribution of the number of events, and that these distributions are independent, the total number of events also follow a Poisson distribution, of mean 57,841. This distribution has a close to 0 probability of observing less than 55,000 losses or more than 60,000 losses. We can also consider that the underlying Poisson distributions for each bank are not independent, but rather fully correlated, as the number of losses for all banks may be driven on the economic context of each year. Even in that case, a Poisson distribution would not explain the observed variance of the number of losses of a bank reporting 1% of the total, as shown in Table 9.3.

This would result in a Poisson distribution of mean 578, for which the probability of observing a year with less than 500 events is 0,04%.

In practice, the use of a Poisson distribution does not fit in general on the observed number of losses through time, in particular if there exists a trend in the number of losses. However, one can still use a Poisson law based on a projected frequency to account for some variance around the trend.

TABLE 9.2 ORX Reported Number of Events, 2011–2016

Year	Events
2011	49,279
2012	54,597
2013	59,080
2014	60,865
2015	62,916
2016	60,311

Source: Based on data from ORX.

TABLE 9.3 Number of Events for an Average Bank

Year	Events
2011	493
2012	546
2013	591
2014	609
2015	629
2016	603

The 2009 Range of Practice paper from the Bank of International Settlements[9] reports that more than 90% of banks use the Poisson distribution for modelling frequency of events.

9.1.5.2 Severity Distribution Fitting In the preceding discussion, we have discussed the two main characteristics of the loss distribution approach:

1. The value at risk calculated by using a LDA is highly dependent on the tail of the individual loss amount distribution.
2. There is no commonly accepted theory justifying the choice of a given distribution.

Therefore, there are two drivers for distribution selection:

1. The goodness-of-fit, that is, how well the distribution fits on observed data
2. The conservativeness of the tail, with of course different point of views for the regulators and for the banks

In the absence of theoretical guidance, this results in a large combinatorial potential.

The first degree of freedom in modelling losses is the choice of severity distributions. Several distributions have been considered by researchers and practitioners, in particular in the early years of LDA usage. For instance, a systematic research conducted by the Federal Reserve of Boston in 2007 considered the Exponential, Weibull, Gamma, Lognormal, LogLogistic, and Generalized Pareto distributions. This study has eliminated the "thin tail" distributions (Exponential, Gamma and Weibull), as these distributions would not fit the tails of observed data.

In practice, the use of Lognormal distribution is the most common. A 2015 study in the insurance sector shows that more than 70% of insurance firms use the Lognormal distribution to model severity in operational risk. The 2009 Range of Practice paper from the Bank of International Settlements also reports that the lognormal distribution is the most commonly used in banking, although to a lesser extent (33%).

[9]BCBS160b: Observed Range of Practice in Key Elements of Advanced Measurement Approaches (AMA), https://www.bis.org/publ/bcbs160b.pdf (accessed 5/10/2018).

The second degree of freedom is related to data itself. When distributions do not fit, it becomes tempting to split the data into subsets, with the expectation that the resulting clusters would be more "homogenous" and easier to model. Indeed, the use of LDA does not imply that one unique severity distribution is used for all losses. Several "Unit of Modelling" distributions can be used, following the Basel matrix, or using a different decomposition. The choice of these UOMs is of course driven both by consistency (type of events, business lines), but also by the goodness of fit.

An important issue exists when trying to model the loss amount: the reporting thresholds. Banks usually use a threshold ($10,000 for instance) below which the losses are not reported.

Fitting a law to truncated data is incorrect if truncation is not taken into account in the fitting. In Figure 9.5, we try to minimise the distance between the complete law and the histogram: The bulk of the law concentrates on the observed data, which distorts it considerably.

On the other hand, when considering the fact that data is truncated, we try to minimise the distance between the right part of the theoretical distribution (above the threshold) and the histogram (Figure 9.6).

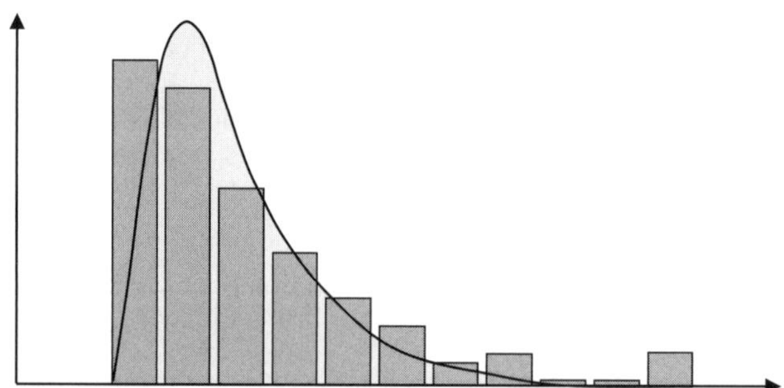

FIGURE 9.5 Fitting a Distribution on Truncated Data with No Collection Threshold

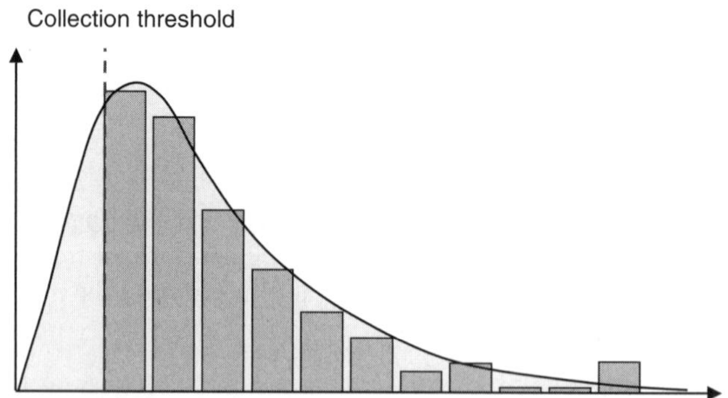

FIGURE 9.6 Fitting a Distribution on Truncated Data Using a Collection Threshold

There exist algorithms based on conditional likelihood calculation, allowing to stabilize the distribution while considering the data truncation.

9.1.6 Single Loss Approximation

One interesting result from 2006 is the Single Loss Approximation (SLA) of the LDA. According to this paper[10], the value at risk obtained using a Monte Carlo simulation as explained above, can be approximated using a simple formula.

The formula just follows but let us explain this very simply.

Assuming for instance a lognormal shape for the distribution of loss amounts, we can observe the α percentile of this distribution. Let us call this number $S(1-\alpha)$. For instance, the 99.9% percentile would be noted $S(0.1\%)$. If the number of losses is fixed and equal to 1:

- There is 0.1% chance that the unique loss is higher than $S(0.1\%)$.
- Therefore, the 99.9% percentile of the cumulated distribution is equal to the 99.9% percentile of the single loss distribution, that is, $S(0.1\%)$.

If the number of losses is fixed and equal to 2:

- There is 0.05% chance that the first loss is above $S(0.0.5\%)$
- There is 0.05% chance that the second loss is above $S(0.0.5\%)$
- This results in approximately 0.1% chances of having at least one loss higher than $S(0.0.5\%)$
- As we have another loss to add, there is more than 0.1% chance that the cumulated loss is higher than $S(0.0.5\%)$.
- If we neglect the contribution of the second loss, we can consider that $S(0.0.5\%)$ is a good approximation of the 99.9% percentile of the cumulated distribution.

If we continue the same reasoning with a number of losses equal to N, we can use $S(0.1\%/N)$ as a lower bound, or as an approximation of the 99.9% percentile of the cumulated distribution.

This is exactly the result proposed in the paper above:

$$C_\alpha \approx F^{-1}\left(1 - \frac{1-\alpha}{\lambda}\right) + (\lambda - 1).\mu$$

This approximation has been studied in detail and its quality is generally good although better approximations exist.

9.1.7 The LDA Paradox

This brief review of the LDA illustrates the paradox of the method. The use of LDA requires a very important effort to collect and organize the losses, considering aggregated events, reporting thresholds,and so on.

---

[10]Klaus Böcker and Claudia Kluppelberg. "Operational VaR: A Closed-Form Approximation." *Risk* 18, no. 12 (2005): 90.

But as far as capital is concerned, everything is based on the tail of the distribution:

- The theoretical loss distribution will strongly depend on the large losses, that is, the tail of the observed distribution
- The capital will strongly depend on the tail of the theoretical loss distribution as, for instance, the Single Loss Approximation shows it.

And while everything depends on the tail, the industry is striving to statistically model this tail, instead of analysing it.

9.2 LOSS REGRESSION

In order to answer the regulatory requirements relative to stress-testing, it is actually worthwhile to explore the correlations between macroeconomic conditions and operational losses, at least for some types of operational losses.

Intuitively, one can propose some mechanisms to support the assumption of a dependency.

Some of these mechanisms have been discussed in an academic paper by Imad Moosa[11]. This paper and others, proposes some prior relations for specific types of risks, which can be summarized in the causal graph shown in Figure 9.7.

We have tried to summarize the commonsense assumptions that could be tested:

Lines represent a causal dependency from a variable to another one. A positive relationship is represented with a solid line, and a negative dependency with a dotted line.

For instance:

- A strong economy has a negative relationship with bankruptcies, unemployment, and possibly regulatory scrutiny – at least a weak economy is expected to generate more scrutiny,

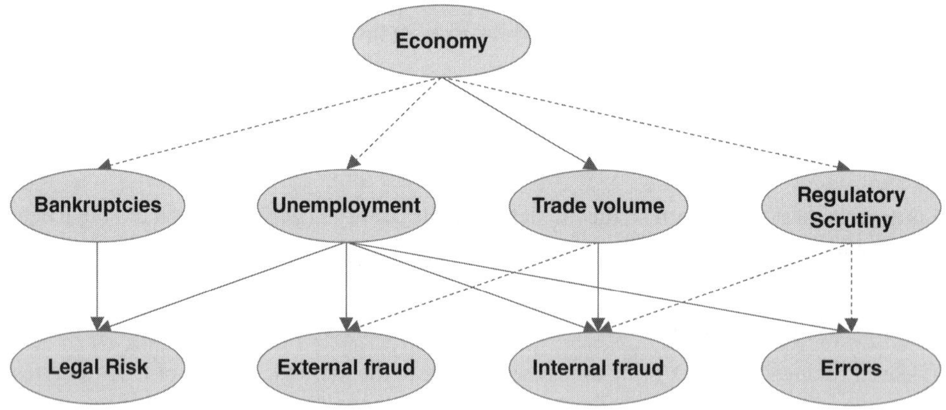

FIGURE 9.7 Dependencies between the State of the Economy and Operational Risk

[11] Imad Moosa, "Operational Risk as a Function of the State of the Economy". *Economic Modelling* 28, no. 5 (2011), 2137–2142.

- External fraud may react both positively and negatively to the state of the economy: a weak economy drives unemployment, which may increase the risk of external fraud, but, conversely, a strong economy increases the volume of trades, and the consumer spending, which offers more opportunities to fraudsters.

If we look at this graph, we see that all types of operational risks considered here receive both a solid and a dotted line. This means that these risks could, through different paths, react positively or negatively to an economic downturn.

Legal risk is an exception, but the delayed observation of litigations and of settlements makes the search for a dependency more complex.

In practice, the academic research on this topic was largely inconclusive, but, as reported in an opinion paper from Oliver Wyman[12], this may well be due to the use of public databases.

In our experience, individual banks are sometimes in position to exhibit reasonably good correlations between macroeconomic variables and some types of losses. This is necessary in the context where the SR15-18 explicitly mentions that the firm "should not rely on unstable or unintuitive correlations to project operational losses".

To conclude on this point, we believe that the use of regression models between certain macroeconomic variables and certain types of operational risk losses is quite legitimate, provided, of course, that the relationship is justified and observable on the data.

[12]"Operational Risk Stress Testing: Emerging Best Practices." https://www.oliverwyman.com/our-expertise/insights/2015/nov/operational-risk-stress-testing.html (accessed 5/10/2018).

CHAPTER 10
Scenario Analysis

10.1 SCOPE OF SCENARIO ANALYSIS

Most of us, as ordinary individuals, have heard of scenarios that could affect all of humanity, whether they address the environment, geopolitics, or the economy. Most of us use scenario analysis in our daily lives without even acknowledging it: planning a wedding or a vacation, choosing a route, and so on. In our professional life, scenarios are everywhere, even if they are rarely formalized: strategic planning, project management, risk management, and so on. Scenario analysis is an essential part of the toolbox that any financial institution should use to assess its capital or conduct stress tests.

It sounds as though the range of scenario analysis applications is very wide and patchy. As mentioned in Part I, we observed that, even in the case of operational risk, the scenario concept could encompass many different realities. Before addressing the very practical issues of their identification and assessment in the area of operational risk, it is worth taking a step back to provide an overview of the scenario analysis landscape. This will be useful to help the reader better understand the rationale, benefits, and limitations of scenario-based approaches to operational risk.

10.1.1 A Few Examples

10.1.1.1 The IPCC Emissions Scenarios You do not need to be a climate expert to be aware of the work of the Intergovernmental Panel on Climate Change. Climate change issues are at the centre of all political debates and are becoming a concern for any citizen who is directly or indirectly affected by increasingly frequent extreme weather events. As stated in their presentation[1]:

> The Intergovernmental Panel on Climate Change (IPCC) is the international body for assessing the science related to climate change. The IPCC was set up in 1988 by the World Meteorological Organization (WMO) and United Nations Environment Programme (UNEP) to provide policymakers with regular assessments of the scientific basis of climate change, its impacts and future risks, and options for adaptation and mitigation.

[1] See "IPCC Factsheet: What is the IPCC?", https://www.ipcc.ch/ (accessed 4/10/2018).

In 2000, the PICC published their well-known Special Report on Emissions Scenarios[2] for policymakers. This report aimed at providing several assumptions about the future level of emissions of greenhouses gases for the period 2000–2100.

More specifically, four narrative storylines were developed to describe the relationship between a set of demographical, social, economic, and technological variables. Forty scenarios were built using state of the art knowledge to cover these four storylines. Each scenario represents a specific quantitative interpretation of one storyline. Within the same family[3] of scenarios, the scenarios might differ both on the assumptions about the drivers as well as on the models used to calculate the gas emissions from the drivers. Thus, for each storyline, a range of driving forces and a range of models are tested that make it possible to propose a range of possible outcomes for gas emissions (see Table 10.1).

In this research, a scenario can be defined by:

- A set of driving variables: demographic, social, economic, technological, environmental.
- An assumption about the evolution profile of each variable over the 2020–2100 period. This profile can be represented by a line, as only one value is assumed for each period of time (see Figure 10.1, and the corresponding data in Tables 10.2–10.3).
- A model that can compute the level of gas emissions from the above assumptions.

As reminded in their report "Scenarios are images of the future, or alternative futures. They are neither predictions nor forecasts. Rather, each scenario is one alternative image of how the future might unfold". None of the scenarios should be considered as more likely or less likely, preferred or desired; they should be considered all together with equal importance to provide a plausible image of what could happen in the future. The future is better represented by a combination of these scenarios rather than by one of them.

This type of scenario consistently integrates qualitative knowledge within a narrative about the future, quantitative interpretation of the narrative, and quantitative models that capture the complex interactions between the driving forces and the gas emissions. It helps in addressing the uncertainties about drivers' assessment and scientific knowledge. Actually, these uncertainties can be considered as the main justification for the use of scenario analysis for future gas emissions assessment.

TABLE 10.1 The A1 Storyline Defined by the IPCC

The A1 storyline and scenario family describes a future world of very rapid economic growth, global population that peaks in mid century and declines thereafter, and the rapid introduction of new and more efficient technologies. Major underlying themes are convergence among regions, capacity building, and increased cultural and social interactions, with a substantial reduction in regional differences in per capita income.

Source: Extract from IPCC, "IPCC Special Report, Emissions Scenarios", 2000, Summary for Policymakers, p. 4.

[2]See IPCC, "IPCC Special Report, Emissions Scenarios", 2000, Summary for Policymakers.

[3]A family of scenarios is defined by the storyline they are quantifying.

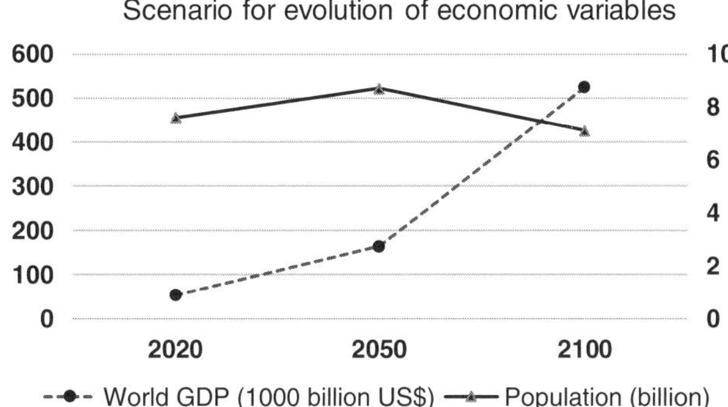

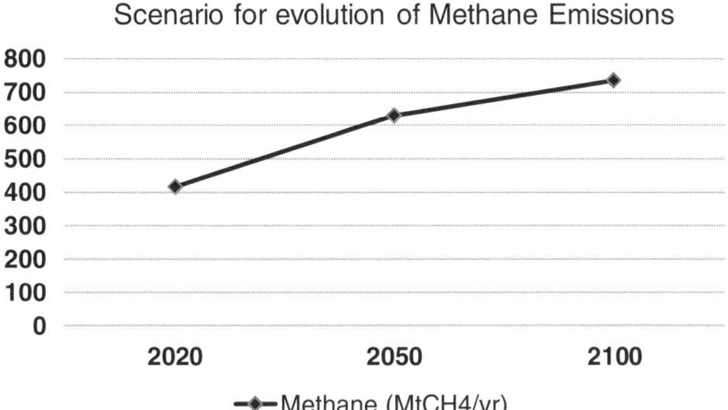

FIGURE 10.1 Extract of One of the IPCC Scenarios for Gas Emissions

TABLE 10.2 Population and World GDP Evolution

Year	2020	2050	2100
Population (billion)	7.6	8.7	7.1
World GDP (10^{12} US$)	53	164	525

Source: Adapted from IPCC (2000, SRES, Table 1b).

TABLE 10.3 Methane Emissions

Year	2020	2050	2100
Methane (MtCH4/yr)	416	630	735

Source: Adapted from IPCC (2000, SRES, Table 3a).

As far as the scenario-building process is concerned, these scenarios are based on state-of-the-art scientific knowledge and involve a wide participation and feedback from several scientific communities within an "open process", to include multiple models. This open and collaborative process should be considered as a typical-ideal for any scenario analysis process.

10.1.1.2 The National Intelligence Council Global Trends Scenarios As indicated on their website[4], the National Intelligence is the center for long-term strategic analysis for the US Intelligence Community. Every four years, the NIC carries out an assessment of the forces and choices that will shape the future of the world over the next two decades. On January 2017, they have completed their sixth exercise and published an unclassified report, "Global Trends, Paradox of Progress", which describes three possible scenarios for the future, depending on major driving forces and political decisions.

This report provides a map of the future that helps the policymakers to figure out the issues they will have to face. It gives the foreign policy departments a better understanding of how the future could unfold depending on the strategic choices made by their government and the other countries, and, as such, this scenario analysis could ultimately influence decisions.

This scenario analysis is a widescale research that involved fieldwork and interviews in more than 35 countries and an academic work with experts in many fields to identify and assess the major trends. Although the assumptions may be supported by quantitative analysis, the outcome of the scenario analysis is mainly qualitative and narrative.

Three scenarios for the future were established following an approach that we can summarize as follows:

1. Seven key trends (see Table 10.4) that are transforming the global landscape were identified based on demographic, economic, social and strategic research.
2. Given these global trends, three key drivers (see Table 10.5) were identified that could shape the future depending on the choices of the policymakers: (1) Dynamics within countries, (2) Dynamics between countries, and (3) Long-term, short-term trade-offs.
3. Three scenarios were developed that postulate different choices about these key drivers and lead to different storylines: (1) "Islands", which describes a world where all countries adopt protectionist policies; (2) "Orbits", where major powers with spheres of influence are attempting to maintain stability at home; (3) "Communities", where local governments and private actors have an increasing role.

Beyond the difference of topic, the geo strategic scenarios by the NIC are quite different from the gas emission scenarios by the IPCC. First, the IPCC scenarios are quantitative interpretations of qualitative narratives while NIC scenarios are purely qualitative. An IPCC scenario is easily described by a set of [variable, value] pairs whereas NIC scenarios rely on complex stories about the key drivers. NIC scenarios encompass a wider range of possible futures than IPCC scenarios, and could lead to a range of quantitative interpretations. This statement is naturally reflected by the number of scenarios: 40 gas emissions scenarios versus three geo strategic scenarios.

[4]https://www.dni.gov/index.php/who-we-are/organizations/nic/nic-who-we-are (accessed 5/10/2018).

TABLE 10.4 Key NIC Trends

The rich are aging, the poor are not. Working-age populations are shrinking in wealthy countries, China, and Russia but growing in developing, poorer countries, particularly in Africa and South Asia, increasing economic, employment, urbanization, and welfare pressures and spurring migration. Training and continuing education will be crucial in developed and developing countries alike.
The global economy is shifting. Weak economic growth will persist in the near term. Major economies will confront shrinking workforces and diminishing productivity gains while recovering from the 2008–2009 financial crisis with high debt, weak demand, and doubts about globalization. China will attempt to shift to a consumer-driven economy from its longstanding export and investment focus. Lower growth will threaten poverty reduction in developing countries.
Technology is accelerating progress but causing discontinuities. Rapid technological advancements will increase the pace of change and create new opportunities, but will aggravate divisions between winners and losers. Automation and artificial intelligence threaten to change industries faster than economies can adjust, potentially displacing workers and limiting the usual route for poor countries to develop. Biotechnologies such as genome editing will revolutionize medicine and other fields, while sharpening moral differences.
Ideas and Identities are driving a wave of exclusion. Growing global connectivity amid weak growth will increase tensions within and between societies. Populism will increase on the right and the left, threatening liberalism. Some leaders will use nationalism to shore up control. Religious influence will be increasingly consequential and more authoritative than many governments. Nearly all countries will see economic forces boost women's status and leadership roles, but backlash also will occur.
Governing is getting harder. Publics will demand governments deliver security and prosperity, but flat revenues, distrust, polarization, and a growing list of emerging issues will hamper government performance. Technology will expand the range of players who can block or circumvent political action. Managing global issues will become harder as actors multiply—to include NGOs, corporations, and empowered individuals—resulting in more ad hoc, fewer encompassing efforts.
The nature of conflict is changing. The risk of conflict will increase due to diverging interests among major powers, an expanding terror threat, continued instability in weak states, and the spread of lethal, disruptive technologies. Disrupting societies will become more common, with long-range precision weapons, cyber, and robotic systems to target infrastructure from afar, and more accessible technology to create weapons of mass destruction.
Climate change, environment, and health issues will demand attention. A range of global hazards pose imminent and longer-term threats that will require collective action to address—even as cooperation becomes harder. More extreme weather, water and soil stress, and food insecurity will disrupt societies. Sea-level rise, ocean acidification, glacial melt, and pollution will change living patterns. Tensions over climate change will grow. Increased travel and poor health infrastructure will make infectious diseases harder to manage.

Source: NIC report "Global Trends: Paradox of Progress", p. 5.

TABLE 10.5 Key NIC Drivers

Dynamics within countries. How governments and publics renegotiate their expectations of one another and create political order in an era of heightened change, marked by empowered individuals and a rapidly changing economy.
Dynamics between countries. How the major powers, along with select groups and individuals, work out patterns of competition and cooperation.
Long-term, short-term tradeoffs. To what extent will states and other actors prepare in the near-term for complex global issues like climate change and transformative technologies.

Source: NIC report "Global Trends: Paradox of Progress", p. 47.

10.1.1.3 The Federal Reserve Supervisory Scenarios for Stress Testing

On June 21, 2018, one could read in the *New York Times* the following good news for the US financial system:

> Biggest Banks Pass Fed's Stress Tests. The nation's biggest banks are strong enough to continue lending if the economy plunges into a severe downturn, an assessment by the Federal Reserve on Thursday that could fuel Wall Street's calls to further relax financial regulations.[5]

In the aftermath of the 2008 financial crisis, financial regulations have been strengthened to ensure that the largest financial institutions would be able to continue their operations in case of a major economic or financial downturn. The FED[6] stress tests are one of the tools that were put in place by the US regulator to test the resilience of the financial system to possible adverse economic and financial developments.

Every year since 2009, the Board of Governors of the Federal Reserve System has to conduct an annual stress-testing exercise for US bank holding companies (BHCs). Since 2017, this exercise also includes foreign banks that hold a significant amount of assets in the United States[7]. The banks have to assess the impact of a set of assumptions on the economic and financial variables on their balance sheet over the next nine quarters.

Strictly speaking, we could consider there are two scenario analysis processes to be carried out: one by the FED, to build some reasonable assumptions on the economy over the next nine quarters; the other by the bank, to propagate the FED assumptions.

How the banks are propagating the scenarios defined by the regulator is beyond the scope of this discussion. But whatever the method, the bank must answer some questions like: What would be the impact of a drop by $x\%$ of the GDP[8] on the revenue of the bank? What would be the impact of a EURO/USD exchange rate reaching y on the losses of the bank?

[5] Matt Phillips and Jim Tankersley, "Biggest Banks Pass Fed's Stress Tests," *New York Times*, 21 June 2018.

[6] The FED is the abbreviation for Federal Reserve. The FED is the central bank of the United States.

[7] To put it simply, Foreign Banking Organizations with more than $50 billion in nonbranch assets should establish an Intermediate Holding Company (IHC). The IHC will be subject to US Basel III, capital planning, Dodd-Frank stress testing, liquidity, risk management requirements and other US Federal Reserve's Dodd-Frank enhanced prudential standards on a consolidated basis.

[8] Gross Domestic Product.

Actually, the question they need to answer is a little bit more complex, because the what-if analysis involves several variables simultaneously. More specifically, the FED defines three scenarios:

1. The *baseline scenario* corresponds to a moderate economic expansion.
2. The *adverse scenario* captures a moderate recession for the US economy.
3. The *severely adverse scenario* reflects a severe global recession (Table 10.6).

As of 2018, each scenario is defined by the projections of 28 variables that describe the United States and international economic conditions over the next nine quarters. Figure 10.2 depicts the evolution of 11 domestic variables through the projection period.

TABLE 10.6 Storyline for the Severely Adverse Scenario[9]

Severely Adverse Scenario. The severely adverse scenario is characterized by a severe global recession that is accompanied by a global aversion to long-term fixed-income assets. As a result, long-term rates do not fall and yield curves steepen in the United States and the four countries/country blocks in the scenario. In turn, these developments lead to a broad-based and deep correction in asset prices – including in the corporate bond and real estate markets. It is important to note that this is a hypothetical scenario designed to assess the strength of banking organizations and their resilience to unfavorable economic conditions. This scenario does not represent a forecast of the Federal Reserve.

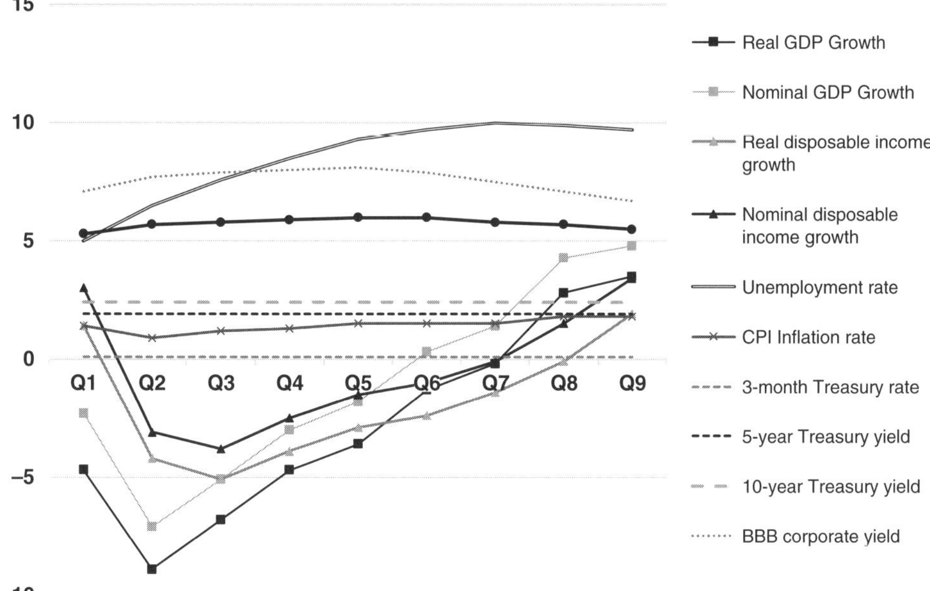

FIGURE 10.2 Severely Adverse Scenario for 11 of the Domestic Variables
Horizontal axis is the time, vertical axis is in percent.[10]

[9]See Board of Governors of the Federal Reserve System, "2018 Supervisory Scenarios for Annual Stress Tests Required under the Dodd-Frank Act Stress Testing Rules and the Capital Plan Rule", February 2018.

[10]See Board of Governors of the Federal Reserve System, "2018 Supervisory Scenarios for Annual Stress Tests Required under the Dodd-Frank Act Stress Testing Rules and the Capital Plan Rule", February 2018, Table 4.A.

None of these scenarios represent a forecast made by the FED. The baseline scenario is built as an average of the projections made by economic forecasters. Depending on the size and business of the firm, some additional components can be included in the adverse and severely adverse scenarios: global market shock for companies with significant trading activities, default of the largest counterparty for companies with substantial custodian business.

The adverse and severely adverse scenarios are not intended to represent the range of possible futures but rather provide the bank with two possible situations they must resist. Unlike the climate or strategic scenarios described in the previous sections, the main goal of these scenarios is not to figure out the whole range of future states of the world but to initiate some specific what-if analyses.

10.1.2 Typology of Scenario Analysis Methods

The examples above illustrate the kind of scenario that almost everyone, as a citizen, has heard about in recent years in the newspapers. They may differ in the scope, use, or level of uncertainty they capture, but they share some common features that characterize the large family of scenario analysis methods.

In this chapter, we will present a short survey of scenario analysis methods, first to give the practitioner some methodological background in order to justify or support the choices that might have been done by his or her firm; and, second, to help the reader understand the scenario methods that are presented in this book and especially the Exposure, Occurrence, Impact method, which will be detailed in the followiong chapters.

This overview of scenario analysis methods seems all the more useful to us because the concept of scenario analysis often seems to us to be interpreted too restrictively in the field of operational risk. In our experience, the dominant view, as far as quantification is concerned, is that scenario analysis is a method to build some additional loss data that will be modelled through a classical distribution fitting process. This practice was already highlighted by the Basel Committee on Banking Supervision in its June 2011 publication, "Operational Risk: Supervisory Guidelines for the Advanced Measurement Approaches", as illustrated by the following statement[11,12]:

> Many observed SBA models do not apply statistical inference to raw scenario data. Very often the SBA-model curves are predetermined and the scenario data are used only to estimate the parameters of those distributions (usually by percentile matching).

To establish a typology of scenario analysis methods, we will use the very good article published in 2008 by the German Development Institute, one of the leading think tanks on global development policy[13]. Although not recent, this state of the art is still relevant; it proposes a complete review of scenario analysis methods, whatever their field of application[14].

[11] See Basel Committee on Banking Supervision, "Operational Risk – Supervisory Guidelines for the Advanced Measurement Approaches", June 2011, para. 209.

[12] SBA stands for Scenario-Based Approaches.

[13] www.die-gdi.de/en/ (accessed 5 October 2018).

[14] See H, Kosow and R. Gaßner (2008), *Methods of Future and Scenario Analysis: Overview, Assessment, and Selection Criteria*, Deutschland.

10.1.2.1 A Simple Definition All the examples that we have been going through are characterized by a large uncertainty. Uncertainties exist about the environment, whether it is economic, demographic, geostrategic, climatic, and so on. Uncertainties also exist about the decisions that will be taken to influence changes in the environment. Scenario analysis is irrelevant when there is no uncertainty about the future. The fundamental assumption that justifies the use of scenarios is that several different futures are possible, not only one single inevitable future.

Scenarios are not predictions or prognosis about the future. The question they try to answer is not "What will happen over the next period of time?" but "What could happen over the next period of time?". The objective is to capture a set of possible futures. Simply, a scenario can be defined as (1) a description of a possible future states of the world and (2) a time path that could lead to this future state.

This definition is perfectly in line with the illustrative scenarios we have presented (see Table 10.7). For instance, an IPCC scenario on climate change proposes a possible future situation[15] in 2010, with a population of 7.1 billion people and a time path from the current population to 7.6 billion in 2020 and 8.7 billion in 2050 before decreasing again to 7.1 billion in 2100.

It should be noticed that even when addressing a short-term future, as in the case of operational risks, the second component of the scenario, that is, the path toward the future, although very narrow and sometimes implicit, is not void. When analyzing a Trading Error scenario over the next year, one has to consider the volume of trading orders that will be executed over the next year. Typically, for this purpose, certain assumptions will be made about how the trading business will grow. These assumptions can be considered as the path toward the future.

10.1.2.2 Use of Scenarios Four main uses or functions are identified for the scenarios by the researchers from the German Development Institute, which we summarize in the following paragraphs, and adapt to our operational risk context.

TABLE 10.7 Application of the General Definition of a Scenario to Three Examples

Scenario	Future State of the World	Path to the Future
IPCC	Date: 2100 Population (billion): 7.1 World GDP (billion US$): 525 000	Date: 2020, 2050 Population (billion): 7.6, 8.7 World GDP (billion US$): 53 000, 164 000
NIC	Date: 2035 "Island": All countries adopt protectionist policies	The path to the future state is a narrative based on quantitative and qualitative research. A prospective analysis over the next five years is provided by region
FED	Date: Present + 9Q Unemployment rate: 9.7% Nominal GDP Growth: 4.8%	Date: Q1, Q2 … Q8 Unemployment rate: 5%, 6.5%, 9.9% Nominal GDP Growth: −2.3%, −7.1%, 4.3%

For IPCC and FED examples, a subset of the variables has been selected for the purpose of illustration.

[15]The scenario is defined by several variables, but for sake of simplicity we illustrate with only one of them.

The first function of scenario analysis is *exploration* of the possible futures. It helps to discover new paths that would not otherwise have been thought of. More important, every day, decisions are made based on our beliefs about the future. Scenario analysis helps to make these beliefs explicit and consistent, and therefore reduces the risk of taking decisions based on flawed assumptions. It is not easy to ensure consistency between explicit assumptions, but it is definitely impossible between implicit assumptions. When it comes to major operational risk events, it is impossible to ensure that all risks are identified. Exhaustivity is out of reach. However, scenario analysis provides us with a powerful tool to expand our knowledge of future risks.

The second function of scenario is *goal-setting*. Instead of exploring the potential futures, one possible future is defined as a target and one should imagine the possible developments that could lead to the target situation from the current situation. Goal setting helps to focus on one objective by exploring the multiple paths to this objective. In the field of operational risks, reverse stress tests can be considered as a typical illustration of goal-setting. As defined by the European Banking Authority[16]: "Reverse stress testing consists in identifying a significant negative outcome and then identifying the causes and consequences that could led to such an outcome". For instance, as an operational risk officer for Investment Banking business, you might want to analyze the situations that could lead to a Rogue Trading fraud larger than US$1 billion. For this purpose, you would need to imagine different scenarios that account for varied possible combinations of desk, market, trading position, time to detection, and so on.

The third function of scenario is *decision-making*. As each scenario is defined by a set of driving assumptions, it is possible to embed within the scenario the potential consequences of actions. From a baseline scenario without actions, multiple scenarios can be derived, each of them would reflect the impact of a particular action plan. In risk management, scenarios are all the more justified as one has to assess the potential efficiency of controls and mitigation actions. Even in a bank where the privileged methods for risk assessment are backward-looking or loss-data-driven, mitigation actions effects can't be captured through approaches that try to extrapolate from the past. A decision is definitely a disruptive event that introduces new paths toward the future. Creative and consistent thinking with scenarios is the appropriate tool to discuss how a decision could shape the future of a firm.

A fourth and nonetheless important function of scenario is *knowledge management*. Scenario analysis, since it is not intended to construct predictions, is not hindered by the risk of not formulating the right opinion about the future. Therefore, two opinions that may seem conflicting could be addressed by two different scenarios, provided that they are supported by consistent assumptions. Ideally, scenario analysis encourages people to share and explain their beliefs about a risk, resulting in more robust and consensual decisions.

The lack of stakeholder commitment to forecasting should be a strong argument for using scenario analysis in legal or regulatory risk assessment. Indeed, when assessing this category of risks, which includes, for example, antitrust regulation breaches, market manipulation, mis-selling or financial crime, the legal team may be reluctant to provide information that could be considered by a regulator as implicit acknowledgment that something is wrong with the current business practices of their firm. Using scenario analysis, they are not expected to give their

[16]See Committee of European Bank Supervisor, "Guidelines on Stress Testing (GL32)", 2010.

prognosis about what will happen in the next year and, therefore, there is no risk that they are held liable for implicitly accepting improper practices.

10.1.2.3 The Four Steps of Scenario Analysis

Despite the multiplicity of approaches, the scenario analysis process can be divided into four main phases, which we now describe in the context of operational risk.

The first phase is the *identification of the scope of the scenario.* This identification implies that two questions are addressed. The first question is about the general purpose of the scenario. Actually, this question is much ahead of the identification of the scope because it is more related to the very justification of the exercise. The purpose of a scenario for operational risk can typically be any of the following: regulatory capital assessment, economic capital assessment, regulatory stress testing exercise, risk management decision making. The second question concerns the area the scenario is applied to.

Basically, for operational risk, this means defining the operational risk event and the business lines that may be affected. Do we speak about conduct risk, cyber risk, or error risk? Are we considering investment banking, retail banking, or card issuer business? The identification of the scope could be very granular or high level, depending on the purpose of the exercise. It could be sufficient to cover the cyber risk as a whole to provide a general assessment, or it could be necessary to identify more specific situations – cyber-attacks on cloud suppliers, data breach, and so on – to better understand the causes and take steps to mitigate the risk. However, regardless of the granularity of the scope identification, the outcome of this process doesn't reflect a single potential path to the future, but rather a set of paths. If we return to the example of the IPCC scenarios, although they represent different paths to the future, they can be considered to be linked to the same scope.

The second phase is the *identification of the key factors*. These factors are the variables which define the future state of the world. For the IPCC scenarios, these factors are the main economic, demographic, social, technological, or environmental drivers identified by the researchers. For the NIC scenarios, three qualitative factors were identified – dynamics within countries, dynamics between countries, and long-term and short-term trade-offs. Finally, for the FED stress scenarios, 28 variables were selected to describe the situation in the US and world economy. This phase should help to refine and structure the narrative about the scenario and, for operational risks, to understand the drivers of the frequency and the severity. As an example, for the Financial Crime risk, these factors could include business volume in foreign countries or the regulatory environment.

This phase should be informed by all the possible knowledge: internal business experts, internal research, external surveys or research and, for operational risks, analysis of material loss data related to the scope under study. This could involve many workshops with different subject matter experts and could be important work.

The third phase is the *analysis of the key factors*. This step aims at providing the potential options for each key factor. This analysis can result in either qualitative assessments, as in the NIC scenarios, or quantitative assessments, as in the IPCC or FED scenarios. Each factor can have multiple evolutions over time that must be described before a set of scenarios can be constructed. Each evolution is a possible future of the factor considered and, as such, can contribute to several scenarios. When analyzing the risk of a material trading error, it is essential to estimate a reasonable range of future market volatility or future trading volume to determine whether the risk is material and to have an idea of the possible severity of the situation.

The fourth phase is *scenario generation*. The previous stage focuses on individual factors and doesn't ensure consistency between the assessments provided for each factor. It is precisely the objective of this fourth phase to propose coherent combinations of the key factors that will lead to coherent scenarios. Some dependencies may exist between the factors that reduce the possible combinations. This phase can rely on quantitative research to shed light on a possible correlation between drivers, but for us, it is mainly a matter of expertise. Experts should decide which combination could exist in a possible future and which combination makes no sense. The outcome of this step is a set of consistent scenarios.

10.1.2.4 The Different Types of Approaches The multiple approaches used to perform scenario analysis can be classified according to three features.

A first boundary can be drawn between *explorative and normative* scenarios. Explorative scenarios are the result of a creative thinking process and should typically reflect what could happen without preconceptions or goals. Most of the scenarios built for operational risk fall into this category. When it comes to assessing the regulatory capital or imagining the appropriate risk mitigation actions, it is necessary to have scenarios that can capture all the plausible situations the experts are able to think about. Normative scenarios aim at capturing goals or preferences defined by the firm and as such constitute a benchmark for thinking about the future. In operational risk, they could be used to define medium-severity situations and as such would be probably considered as one of the possible explorative scenarios. Reverse stress-testing can also rely on scenario analysis to identify the scenario that would lead to predefined situations. But although the objective is defined, it doesn't necessarily reflect a benchmark situation and, furthermore, identifying all the paths that can lead to a stressed situation also requires an exploratory process.

A second distinction can be done between *quantitative and qualitative* scenarios. The quantitative scenarios are based on quantitative research and models, while qualitative scenarios rely on narrative data. Quantitative approaches generally lead to the most formalized scenarios but it should not be considered that qualitative approaches are unstructured and informal. Whether quantitative or qualitative scenario analyses, they must be highly structured to ensure consistency between assumptions. Although scenario analysis is largely based on the subjectivity of many contributors, it should be designed as a rigorous process. Moreover, the boundaries between quantitative and qualitative approaches are sometimes blurred as quantitative and qualitative assumptions are both used for the same scenario. As we will see for the Exposure Occurrence Impact approach used for operational risk modelling, there are some quantitative assumptions about the key drivers, but some of these quantitative assumptions are based on subjective knowledge, and the loss generation mechanism is almost entirely based on subjective expert knowledge.

A third line separates the *baseline scenarios from the decision-making scenarios*. The first category of scenarios assume that no decision is taken to change the course of events as contemplated by the scenario. For a policy-maker, the baseline scenario is a benchmark to explain the potential consequences of the "no-action" option. In operational risks, this type of scenario can help the firm to define a baseline for a cost-benefit analysis meant to decide a risk mitigation plan. But scenarios can also involve certain decisions or actions, as is the case, for example, with some of the IPCC scenarios. Decisions or actions introduce new uncertainties and possible new paths to the future to be explored. Indeed, once a decision is taken, the events could unfold in many different ways. This exploration is essential as it can help to avoid the implementation of false good ideas.

A very good example of such bogus good ideas is described in the book *Managing the Unexpected* by Weick and Sutcliffe[17]. The authors explain how the teams of a nuclear aircraft carrier have addressed some so-called near-misses that happened during aircraft landings and take-offs. Their belief was that the three-people teams in charge of these operations on the carrier deck lacked attention because of very long working days. Based on this conviction, they decided to shorten the workday. The result of this risk mitigation action was quite unexpected: the number of errors increased. After analyzing this counterintuitive consequence, the experts discovered that by reducing the workday, they also increased team rotation, which alters the quality of communication between the three team members. Yet, the good synchronization between the team members is a major driver for the efficiency of operations on the deck. Reducing the workday was therefore a bad idea that might have been avoided by considering several scenarios for the decision.

10.1.2.5 Quality Criteria for Scenarios As discussed above, a scenario is not a forecast and, as such, it makes no sense to try to back-test a scenario against reality. Being a little provocative, we could even say that a scenario that has crystallized is not better than a scenario that has not occurred. Furthermore, since a scenario analysis process generally generates several scenarios, most of them will not materialize in the future. It would be illogical and fully inconsistent with the explorative function of the scenarios to define the realization of the scenario as a quality criterion. Therefore, strictly speaking, scenario analysis is not a science, because its validation through reality check is generally not possible. The validation of scenario as forecasting models is not possible, since at most one path will materialize, and back-testing of scenarios is only possible under the very restrictive assumption that the same scenarios would have been designed in the past.

However, the scenario analysis process should, in many respects, satisfy the rigor of a scientific approach. This is all the more important for the credibility of scenarios as they largely rely on subjective assumptions that can be challenged and ultimately give the impression that a scenario is only a collection of gut feelings, and is therefore, not appropriate to support real decisions or risk assessment. The researchers of the DIE[18] identified five criteria, which we have merged into four, and which we think are relevant for operational risks.

1. *Plausibility* is the first requirement for any scenario. This criterion means that each assumption of a scenario is not purely theoretical, but reflects a possible development. To achieve plausibility, the process needs to involve subject matter experts and, ideally, conduct some research to support reasonable assumptions. This is the reason why, for operational risk, the scenario-based approaches consume more resources than purely data-driven approaches. When addressing a cyber risk scenario, the central risk management team needs to involve the IT people to discuss the exposures as well as the business

[17] K. E. Weick and K. M. Sutcliffe (2001), *Managing the Unexpected: Resilient Performance in an Age of Uncertainty* (San Francisco: Jossey-Bass).

[18] Deusche Institut für Entwicklungspolitik, www.die-gdi.de/en/ (accessed 5 October 2018).

people to assess the potential areas of impact, but it should rely on external research[19] to verify whether internal assessments are consistent with industry-based assessments.

2. *Consistency* means that assumptions must to be consistent with each other. Ensuring consistency requires a very good knowledge of the subject. For each scenario provided by the FED, assumptions regarding GDP, interest rates, unemployment, and so on, must be consistent with economic theories and empirical data. In a more limited scenario, when assessing the drivers of a Wire Transfer Error operational risk, it should be ensured that the probability of an error depends on the amount of the transfer, reflecting the fact that controls are more important on high-value transfers.
3. *Distinctness* between the scenarios is necessary if we want to cover the entire scope defined for the scenario analysis. For qualitative scenarios, this means that two scenarios must capture two images of the future that can be easily distinguished. This property is fairly easy to ensure for qualitative scenarios (e.g., NIC scenarios) as the scenarios have a small number of key drivers with very distinct states. For quantitative scenarios where each assumption may be represented by a continuum of values (e.g., range for the amount of a wire transfer), the distinctness can only be required between the extreme scenarios.
4. *Transparency* might be the most important criterion, as it drives the improvement of the assumptions over time and is the condition for validating scenario assumptions. Transparency means that all assumptions must be clearly explained, documented, and sourced. This quality is definitely required for operational risk assessment, because the scenario analysis process is iterative and generally doesn't involve all stakeholders at the same time in large firms. Traceability of the iterations and clear documentation is key to make sure that the assumptions are appropriately reflecting the views from all SMEs.

10.1.3 Scenario Analysis in Operational Risk

While all of the above characteristics of scenario analysis also apply to operational risk, the vocabulary may differ and the process may contain some specific features. In the following sections, we deal with the two steps usually applied when building a set of scenarios that capture the most severe operational risks of a firm: (1) scenario identification and (2) scenario assessment.

With regard to scenario evaluation, we will discuss here the usual practice of most companies, rather than the structured approach proposed by the XOI method (Figure 10.3). This method will be described in detail in Part IV of the book.

10.2 SCENARIO IDENTIFICATION

The objective of scenario identification is to establish a list of events that could lead to material losses for the firm. Focusing on large potential losses is not a constraint, as scenarios could also capture small and medium potential losses. Theoretically, one could use scenario-based approaches to address frequent risks but it is not recommended, as other types of methods like statistical models might be more appropriate and less resource consuming.

[19]See for example the research conducted by the Ponemon Institute on the cost of data breaches, https://www.ponemon.org/ (accessed 5 October 2018).

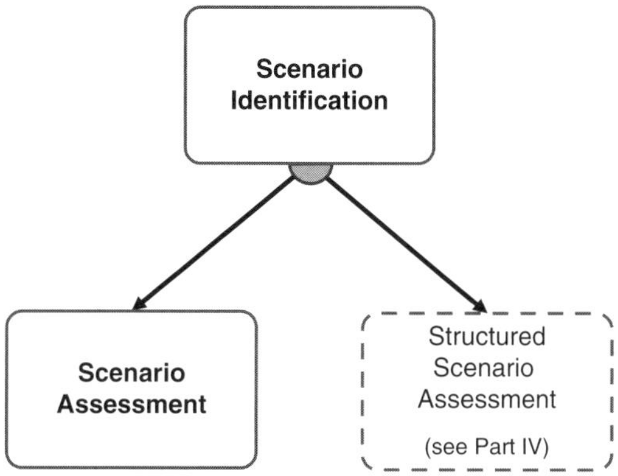

FIGURE 10.3 Scenario Analysis Process in Operational Risk
The Structured Scenario Assessment is described in Part IV.

In this chapter, a scenario should be considered as a set of adverse situations based on the same underlying mechanism, rather than a single situation, as was previously the case. To identify the operational risk scenarios that could arise in the future, a firm should analyze:

- *What has already happened in the past to the firm*, because, without any change in the environment or the controls, this could happen again in the future. This information is contained in the internal loss data.
- *What the business is believing about future possible events*. The risk register, as a result of the RCSA, should reflect this forward-looking view of the firm operational risk profile.
- *What has already happened in the past to the industry* could also happen to the firm, given that, without any further analysis, it is reasonable to assume that all the firms in the same industry bear the same risks. This information can be retrieved from external loss data.
- *What external actors think about the future operational risk landscape*. The main sources to go through are the surveys conducted by consulting firms or research laboratories.
- *Senior management's opinion about emerging risks*. This view, elicited during workshops, will complement the business' view because it is more strategic, more forward looking, and more transversal.

With the exception of senior management contribution, theoretically, the scenario identification process should have only one input: the risk register, that is, the result of the Risk and Control Self-Assessment process.

Indeed, this risk register should contain all the risks identified in the firm, and each risk should be assigned a frequency and impact rating, summarizing all relevant information: internal losses, external losses, review of external surveys and research, and SMEs knowledge.

But as we explain in detail in Part I, this perfect situation cannot exist in the real world. Even if the RCSA process is perfect and integrates all sources of information, each iteration requires some time to be completed. And new events and information generally become available between the beginning of an RCSA iteration and the beginning of scenario identification process. This justifies considering the RCSA at the same time as the other elements of knowledge to carry out the scenario identification (see Figure 10.4).

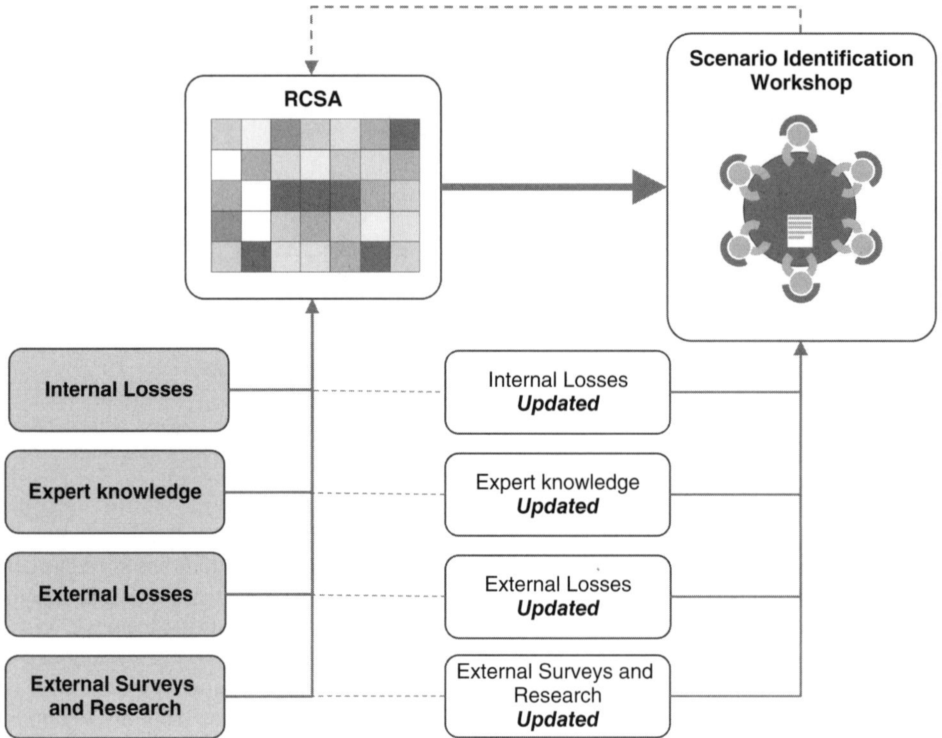

FIGURE 10.4 Scenario Identification
The RCSA is the main source for scenario identification, as all knowledge should be reflected in the RCSA. However, as new information may be available, it should be used for scenario identification. Any gap should be fed back into the RCSA.

10.2.1 Risk Register Filtering

The risk register is the first element to be considered, as it normally contains all the risks identified by the business along with a first qualitative assessment of them. The risk register is intended to reflect a forward-looking view of the firm operational risk profile as perceived by business.

It should be recalled here that a distinction is made between the *risk taxonomy*, which is the combination of a hierarchical list of events and a hierarchical list of activities, and the *risk register*, which is a set of risks defined according to this taxonomy,

The risk taxonomy reflects the granularity of the risk analysis conducted by the firm and should serve as a common reference matrix for organizing the risks, the internal losses, and the external losses. The Basel matrix is an example of a risk taxonomy. The risk taxonomy covers the full range of operational risks.

Each risk is assigned a frequency and severity rating by the business units that deem it relevant. It is recommended that a gravity measurement should be able to capture potential extreme events. This means that the average severity is not the right measure, as it can be low, even if the loss can be very high. This is particularly true for events that are very frequent but could also result in very large losses like trading errors[20] or wire transfer errors[21]. The maximum plausible severity is a better metric.

In theory, it would be preferable to use the inherent risk rather than the residual risk, as major events often occur after control failures. However, as discussed in Part I, it is in most cases impossible to properly assess the inherent risk. Indeed, as discussed in Part I, this would mean being able to remove all the controls by thought.

The ratings recorded in the risk register are supposed to be comparable between the different lines of business. This means that, even if at some point in the RCSA process, the scoring was relative to the size of the business, a scaling should have been applied to ensures *comparability*.

Provided a score has been selected and an aggregation operator[22] has been defined, a risk register can be represented as a matrix where the rows represent the loss event categories, the columns represent the business lines, and the cells contain an aggregate score. For instance, if the aggregation operator is simply "MAX", each cell contains the maximum of the observed scores for the risks belonging to that cell (Figure 10.5).

For scenario identification, a score that reflects the maximum severity should be preferred. This matrix representation is a very convenient way to locate cells that contain potential scenarios.

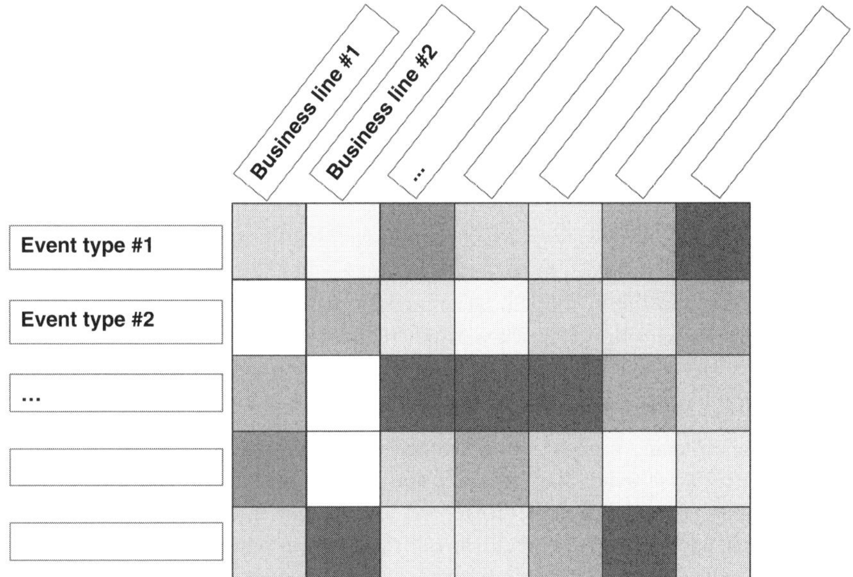

FIGURE 10.5 Matrix Representation of a Risk Register
Darker cells represent more severe risks.

[20]As an example, in 2015, a BNP Paribas error – the bank late cancelled a sale of certificates at an incorrect price – resulted in a loss of approximately €160 million. Source: lesechos.fr, 2017/03/11 (accessed 5 October 2018).
[21]In April 2018, Deutsche Bank sent an erroneous $35 billion wire transfer. The error was promptly corrected and did not lead to any loss, but this example illustrates that errors can also occur on huge amounts. Source: money.cnn.com, 2018/04/19 (accessed 5 October 2018).
[22]MAX() is a simple aggregation operator consistent with the identification of extreme events.

Indeed, if low scores are represented by light grey cells and high scores by dark grey cells, a quick glance at the matrix would identify risks that may require scenario analysis.

When a row contains several dark grey cells, this may indicate a transversal risk, that is, an event that can strike several lines of business. Damage to premises or outages of shared resources (building destruction, data center outage, etc.) are typical examples of such transversal risks. When a row only contains one dark cell, this may indicate an event that specifically targets one line of business. Rogue trading, credit card compromise are examples of specific business risks.

The reality is not always as simple as the graph above. For an illustration we present a real risk register of a major financial institution in Figure 10.6. It is shown in transposed format, that is, lines are business activities and columns are risk events. We clearly see some regions of concentration of dark cells, mostly vertical, as the matrix is transposed. These dark columns may indicate transverse risks.

The risk management team should define a threshold to filter out cells and related risks that could lead to potential large losses and, as such, would require scenario assessment. If we switch from the event category/business line representation to the usual severity/frequency matrix, the rule for identifying the scenarios is materialized with a vertical line. Risks to the right of the vertical line have a severity above the threshold and should therefore be selected as potential scenarios (see Figure 10.7).

A practical rule is to consider that potential losses greater than 0.1% of the total revenue are worth being covered by a scenario. For a bank with an annual revenue of $20 billion, this would mean that losses above $20 million must be addressed by a scenario. This rule of thumb can help define the score threshold, provided that the severity score can be converted into a dollar amount.

Any firm could certainly use its own selection criteria to identify the scenarios from the RCSA. Here, we recommend a simple rule based on the maximum severity score, as it focuses on extreme events only, but this rule could be refined by including the frequency score in order to prioritize the risks with the highest expected frequency. However, we do not recommend building complex scores that combine frequency and severity, as their interpretation might be very tricky and could raise some issues when comparing the risks.

At the end of this filtering process, we still need additional work to get a list of scenarios. Two situations may arise depending on the granularity of the risk register. If the risk register is very granular, that is, if the risks focus on clearly defined loss generation mechanisms, then there is no need to further investigate the risks to discover potential scenarios. On the contrary, some risks with similar loss generation mechanisms may need to be covered by the same scenario. A typical situation is that of risk registers where event categories are broken down by cause. As an illustration, if your risk register makes the distinction between wire transfer delay, wire transfer beneficiary error, wire transfer currency conversion error, and wire transfer amount error, you should consider one single scenario – wire transfer error – to cover these four risks.

On the other hand, if the risk register has a low granularity, each cell of the matrix would cover multiple loss generation mechanisms. To identify the one that could lead to large losses, a deep dive into the cell might be needed. For example, if a risk of trading error has been

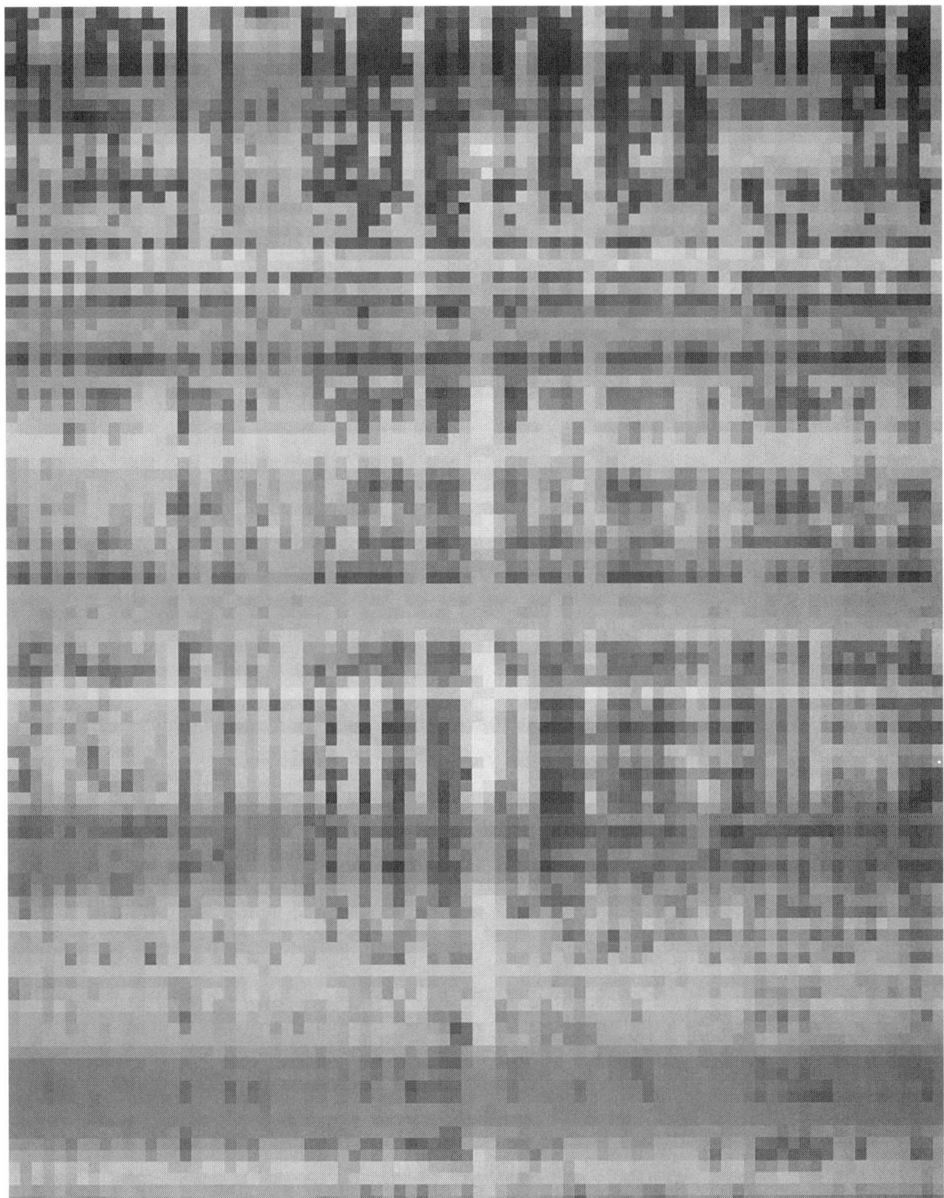

FIGURE 10.6 A Real Risk Register
Lines are business activities, columns are risk events.

identified, it may be relevant to make a clear distinction between the human errors and the trading algorithms errors as the exposure is not the same: a trading order in the first case, an algorithm in the second case.

The outcome of the risk register filtering is a first set of scenarios defined by a label and a brief description. The label should summarize the loss generation mechanism in no more than a

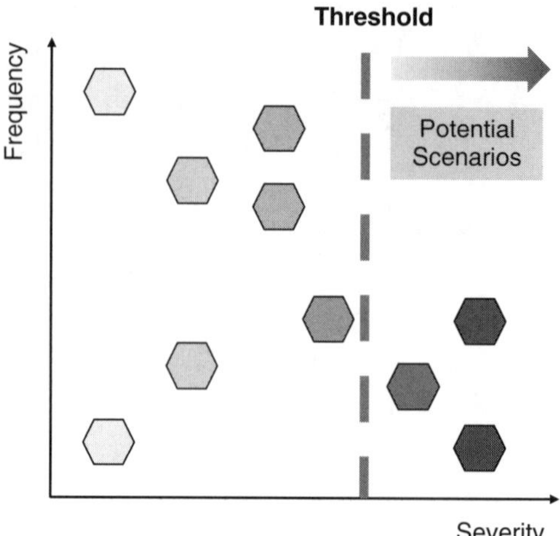

FIGURE 10.7 Scenario Identification Using a Severity Threshold
Risks are represented by hexagons in the Severity-Frequency space. All risks above severity threshold should be considered as potential scenarios.

short sentence. Each scenario can cover one or multiple risks, each scenario can either belong to a cell Event Category × Business Line or be defined across several cells.

10.2.2 Internal Losses Analysis

Any event that has already occurred to the firm in the past can occur again in the future if the business and control environment is the same. For this reason, a large internal loss can be considered, before any additional analysis, as the realization of a scenario.

The problem here is (1) to identify new scenarios that were not identified from risk register and (2) to identify the losses that can be assigned to existing scenarios.

To achieve these two objectives, it is recommended to carry out a three-step process:

1. Selection of large internal losses
2. Mapping of internal losses onto the risk register structure
3. Analysis of each large loss to identify new scenarios

10.2.2.1 Selection of Material Losses First, the firm operational risk team must define a materiality threshold above which losses should be analyzed as potential realizations of scenarios. This threshold should be the same as the one defined for the severity in the risk register, if any. As proposed above, our experience is that 0.1% of the total revenue is a reasonable threshold.

10.2.2.2 Mapping of Material Losses Second, each loss above the materiality threshold must be mapped onto one cell of the risk register structure. Like the risks, the internal losses are organized into a matrix by risk event categories and business lines.

If the internal loss database and the risk register have the same structure, that is, same risk event categories and same business units, then this assignment is straightforward. On the other hand, if the structures are different, three situations may be encountered that are described in Table 10.8.

10.2.2.3 Analysis of Large Losses At this stage, each of the large losses has been assigned to a cell Event Category×Business Line of the risk register structure. From the previous step of risk register filtering, we also know the scenarios associated to each cell of the risk register[23].

TABLE 10.8 Mapping the Risk Register and the Loss Data Register

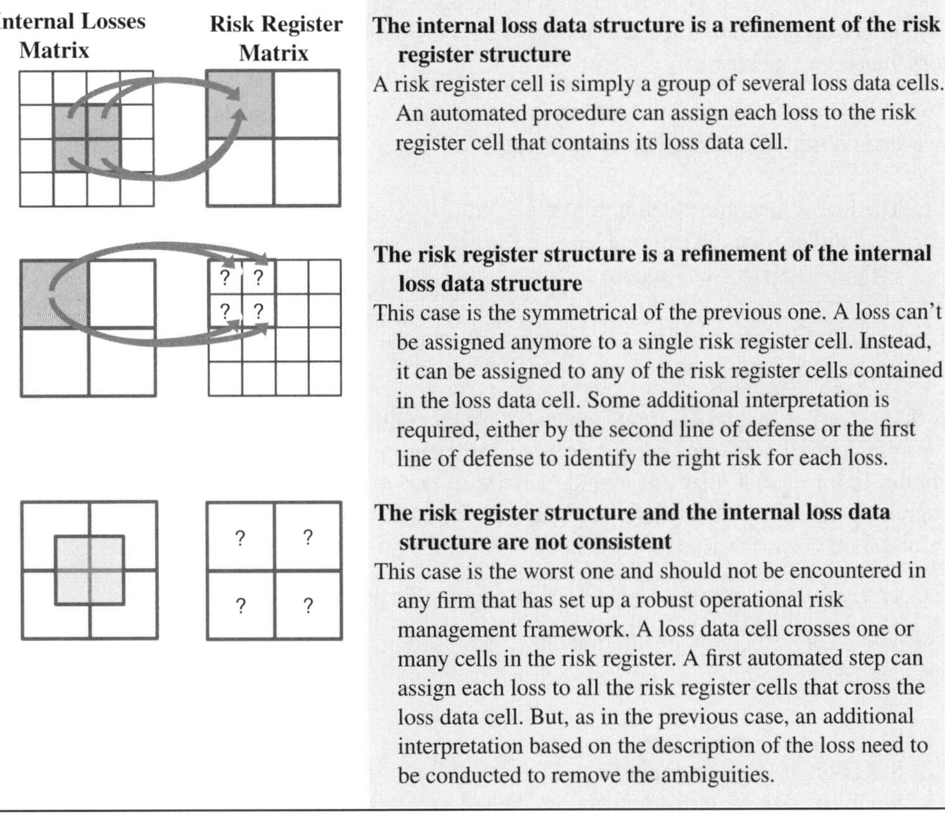

Internal Losses Matrix	Risk Register Matrix	
		The internal loss data structure is a refinement of the risk register structure A risk register cell is simply a group of several loss data cells. An automated procedure can assign each loss to the risk register cell that contains its loss data cell.
	? ? / ? ?	**The risk register structure is a refinement of the internal loss data structure** This case is the symmetrical of the previous one. A loss can't be assigned anymore to a single risk register cell. Instead, it can be assigned to any of the risk register cells contained in the loss data cell. Some additional interpretation is required, either by the second line of defense or the first line of defense to identify the right risk for each loss.
	? ? / ? ?	**The risk register structure and the internal loss data structure are not consistent** This case is the worst one and should not be encountered in any firm that has set up a robust operational risk management framework. A loss data cell crosses one or many cells in the risk register. A first automated step can assign each loss to all the risk register cells that cross the loss data cell. But, as in the previous case, an additional interpretation based on the description of the loss need to be conducted to remove the ambiguities.

[23]Some scenarios may cover several cells.

Therefore, it is now necessary to read the detailed description of the loss to decide whether:

- This kind of loss could not occur anymore because the business environment or the controls have changed.
- It is a realization of a scenario that has already been identified for this cell.
- It would justify the definition of a new scenario, as this loss is the outcome of a loss generation mechanism that has not been captured by any of the scenarios attached to the cell.

If the detailed description does not contain sufficient information, it may be necessary to trace the source of the loss report.

10.2.3 External Losses Analysis

Relevant scenarios can also be inspired by industry loss data. Since activities are similar from one bank to another, it is reasonable to think that what happened to other institutions could also affect the firm, although it could be with a different intensity and even with a different loss generation mechanism.

To some extent, external loss analysis is very similar to the internal loss analysis. However, two main differences should be pointed out:

1. The losses must be scaled before use.
2. It is unlikely that the external loss data structure proposed by the vendor will be consistent with the risk register structure.

The second point means only that mapping of material losses onto the risk register structure will not be straightforward.

A first remark is that an external loss that does not contain a detailed description of the event, for confidentiality reasons cannot be used for scenario identification. The same conclusion applies to a loss that does not include any indication of the size of the business, as this loss cannot be scaled up. Therefore, we must assume that the external loss data include all the information necessary to define the context in which the event occurred.

External loss data can be provided by vendors or collected internally.

The process described for the internal losses analysis should be slightly updated by introducing a scaling step:

1. Scaling of external losses
2. Selection of large external losses
3. Mapping of the external losses onto the risk register structure
4. Analysis of each large loss to identify new scenarios

We have already described the last three steps, so we will focus only on the scaling phase.

Why is scaling necessary? If my bank has a total income of $20 billion, should I consider, as a potential realization of a scenario, an external loss of $10 million that occurred to a bank with

TABLE 10.9 RMBS Cases As of April 2018

Bank	Year	Settlement Amount ($ Million)
JPMorgan Chase & Co	2013	13,000[24]
Bank of America	2014	16,650[25]
Citigroup	2014	7,000[26]
Goldman Sachs	2016	5,000[27]
Morgan Stanley	2016	2,600[28]
Deutsche Bank	2017	7,200[29]
Credit Suisse	2017	5,280[30]
Barclays	2018	2,000[31]

Source: US Department of Justice.

a $90 billion total income? The answer is "no". Any loss should be analyzed in the context of the institution in which it occurred. A large institution, since it has more transactions, more clients and run larger businesses, is likely to incur greater losses than a small institution. It is not surprising that the banks that incurred the largest losses for Residential Mortgage Backed Securities cases are the largest financial institutions in the world (see Table 10.9).

As a consequence, a loss incurred by a firm A should be scaled before being used by a firm B for its scenario identification process.

How to scale an external loss? How could one scale the $6.2 billion trading loss incurred by JPMorgan in 2012 in the so-called "London Whale" scandal[32]. How to scale the Deutsche Bank $7.2 billion fine for mis-selling of RMBS products? The right scaling factor is the metric that is strongly related to the loss. For a trading loss, it sounds reasonable to look at the average market exposure of the bank as a good business metric since, everything else being equal, a trading loss is proportional to the position taken by the bank. On the other hand, for a mis-selling case, the compensation to clients would be related, not necessarily proportional, to the number of

[24] https://www.justice.gov/opa/pr/justice-department-federal-and-state-partners-secure-record-13-billion-global-settlement (accessed 5 October 2018).

[25] https://www.justice.gov/opa/pr/bank-america-pay-1665-billion-historic-justice-department-settlement-financial-fraud-leading (accessed 5 October 2018).

[26] https://www.justice.gov/opa/pr/justice-department-federal-and-state-partners-secure-record-7-billion-global-settlement (accessed 5 October 2018).

[27] https://www.justice.gov/opa/pr/goldman-sachs-agrees-pay-more-5-billion-connection-its-sale-residential-mortgage-backed (accessed 5 October 2018).

[28] https://www.justice.gov/opa/pr/morgan-stanley-agrees-pay-26-billion-penalty-connection-its-sale-residential-mortgage-backed (accessed 5 October 2018).

[29] https://www.justice.gov/opa/pr/deutsche-bank-agrees-pay-72-billion-misleading-investors-its-sale-residential-mortgage-backed (accessed 5 October 2018).

[30] https://www.justice.gov/opa/pr/credit-suisse-agrees-pay-528-billion-connection-its-sale-residential-mortgage-backed (accessed 5 October 2018).

[31] https://www.justice.gov/opa/pr/barclays-agrees-pay-2-billion-civil-penalties-resolve-claims-fraud-sale-residential-mortgage (accessed 5 October 2018).

[32] Although this loss is market related, we consider it is an operational risk event as some violations of securities laws for oversight failure have been admitted by the firm.

clients to whom the product was sold and, therefore, to the total income generated by that product.

Thus, theoretically, the scaling factor should depend on the type of event. But practically, it is not workable to assign each external loss a specific scaling factor because, in most cases, it would not be possible to find a quantitative value for this factor. A typical factor used for scaling is the total operating income[33]. Table 10.10 summarizes the 2017 operating incomes for a sample of the six largest US banks by assets, as extracted from their 2017-12-31 BHCPR report[34].

Based on that table, a $100 million loss for JPMorgan Chase & Co would be equivalent to an approximatively $30 million loss for Goldman Sachs.

Once the scaling factor is defined, another question arises: Which date should be considered to evaluate this factor? Three main dates or periods are generally of interest for a loss.

The *occurrence date* is the date on which the event occurred to the company. For a legal or regulatory event, the occurrence is not the beginning of the misconduct or rules violation, but rather, the date an investigation was initiated or an action filed.

The *payment date* is the date on which the loss is materializing or is made official in the company. For most events, the payment date can be interchangeable with the occurrence date. But for legal or regulatory events, payments could start many years after the occurrence of the event. Especially for complex matters involving many plaintiffs, settlements could be agreed many years after the misconduct has been initiated.

For long-term events, such as legal and regulatory violations, the *relevant period* represents the period during which the misconduct lasted. It is generally not recorded in external loss databases and would require a detailed analysis of the loss to be measured.

For instance, Barclays has just agreed, on March 2018, to pay a $2 billion civil penalty for the sale of RMBS between 2005 and 2007. In that example, we can read that a civil action has

TABLE 10.10 Operating Income of Large US Banks

Bank	**Operating income[35] ($ Billion)**
JPMorgan Chase & Co	102
Bank of America	88
Citigroup	72
Wells Fargo	89
Goldman Sachs	34
Morgan Stanley	38

[33]For a bank, it is the sum of the net interest income and the noninterest income.

[34]Bank Holding Company Performance Report built from data collected by the Federal Reserve System and available at https://www.ffiec.gov/ (accessed 5 October 2018).

[35]Values are rounded to the closest billion unit.

TABLE 10.11 Dates Involved in a Multiyear Loss

Barclays Agrees to Pay $2 Billion in Civil Penalties to Resolve Claims for Fraud in the Sale of Residential Mortgage-Backed Securities
The United States has reached agreement with Barclays Capital, Inc., and several of its affiliates (together, Barclays) to settle a civil action filed in December 2016 in which the United States sought civil penalties for alleged conduct related to Barclays' underwriting and issuance of residential mortgage-backed securities (RMBS) between 2005 and 2007. Barclays will pay the United States two billion dollars ($2,000,000,000) in civil penalties in exchange for dismissal of the Amended Complaint.
Following a three-year investigation, the complaint in the action, *United States v. Barclays Capital, Inc.*, alleged that Barclays caused billions of dollars in losses to investors by engaging in a fraudulent scheme to sell 36 RMBS deals, and that it misled investors about the quality of the mortgage loans backing those deals. It alleged violations of the Financial Institutions Reform, Recovery, and Enforcement Act of 1989 (FIRREA), based on mail fraud, wire fraud, bank fraud, and other misconduct.

Source: Excerpt from the DOJ press release, Thursday March 29, 2018[36].

been filed in December 2016. We could consider this date as the occurrence date, although the misconduct had started in 2005. The payment date is March 2018 as Barclays has officially agreed to pay on this date. The relevant period is from 2005 to 2007 (see Table 10.11).

For a short-lasting event, the annual income of the occurrence year can reasonably be used as a scaling metric. For long-lasting events, especially legal and regulatory ones, theoretically, the average revenue during the relevant period should be considered. In practice, the latter policy could be applied only if the firm processed its external data to identify the relevant period. Otherwise, a simplified policy must be used: since the occurrence year is closer to the relevant period than the payment year, the annual income during the occurrence year could be a good choice, but the payment year could also serve as a reference, because it reflects the date when the firm will pay, and, therefore, the revenue in the payment year can be considered as a reference to establish the penalty.

Let us now describe how we would scale the $2 billion external loss described above for a company of $10 billion annual revenue. We will use the December 2016 occurrence date as the reference date for the revenue. In 2016, the annual revenue generated by Barclays, as reported in its 2016 Annual Report, page 246 is £22,625 million[37]. The average GBP/USD exchange rate during 2016 is 1.36765, with fluctuations between 1.21484 and 1.48691. Using the average rate to convert Barclays revenue in USD, this yields a $30.9 billion revenue. As the $2 billion penalty represents 6.45%[38] of the Barclays revenue it would correspond to a $645 million penalty for an institution with a $10 billion revenue.

After all external losses have been scaled, the selection, mapping and analysis steps can be performed as for internal loss data. However, a precaution must be taken to define the selection threshold. As the scaling process can introduce many uncertainties (choice of the scaling factor, choice of the evaluation period, volatility of the exchange rate), it is recommended to account

[36]See https://www.justice.gov/opa/pr/barclays-agrees-pay-2-billion-civil-penalties-resolve-claims-fraud-sale-residential-mortgage (accessed 5 October 2018).

[37]Barclays PLC, "Annual Report 2016, Building the Bank of the Future", 2017.

[38]6.46% = $2 billion penalty divided by $31 billion revenue.

for a confidence margin as not to miss potential material external losses. For instance, if a materiality threshold of 0.1% for the loss to revenue ratio is targeted, a lower threshold of 0.08% could be used instead.

10.2.4 Review of External Surveys

What external professionals or researchers think about the future operational risk landscape is a valuable source of information to identify emerging or top risks. These prospective studies are generally designed by specialized companies – research laboratories, business press, insurers, IT companies, and so on – through annual surveys.

These surveys can be generalist, such as the Top 10 Operational Risks published each year by the online journal risk.net (see Table 10.12), or very domain-specific, such as the annual Cost of Data Breach Study conducted by the Ponemon Institute and commissioned by IBM. A risk intelligence process must be conducted by the group risk team to identify these studies.

These studies may not reveal anything that is not already known to the firm, but their main interest is to highlight major industry trends. When we read the top 10 2018 published by risk.net, we do not discover any new scenarios, but their ranking remains very interesting. For most risks, this ranking cannot be inferred from the analysis of past losses. Cyber risk, here represented by IT Disruption and Data Compromise, is currently on the top list of concerns for the management of the banks. However, when looking at the internal or external losses, or even at the Ponemon Institute study[39], no real big financial loss has been incurred in financial institutions. Thus, the past losses related to these two risks would not make them possible scenarios.

Regardless of the company's opinion of the results of these external surveys, if the industry is concerned about new threats, they deserve to be subjected to scenario analysis before deciding whether they are important to the firm.

TABLE 10.12 Top 10 Operational Risks for 2018, According to Risk.net

#1: IT Disruption
#2: Data Compromise
#3: Regulatory Risk
#4: Theft and Fraud
#5: Outsourcing
#6: Mis-Selling
#7: Talent risk
#8: Organisational Change
#9: Unauthorized Trading
#10: Model Risk

[39]"2018 Cost of a Data Breach Study: Global Overview", Benchmark research sponsored by IBM Security, Independently conducted by Ponemon Institute LLC, July 2018.

However, these surveys do not generally provide ready-to-use scenarios. Rather, they address risk themes that include several possible scenarios. Therefore, the risk team should investigate the subject further to identify a list of potential scenarios. For instance, starting with the above top 10, we could break down the risk of IT Disruption into a "Cyber Attack on Critical Application"[40] scenario that would cover the cyber-attack related outage and a "Critical Application Outage" scenario that would address the technical failures.

10.2.5 Scenarios Workshops

The analysis of internal and external losses, ensures that a firm does not miss scenarios that have already occurred. The screening of RCSA high severity risks guarantees that the perception of business lines is included. The review of external surveys covers the main threats perceived by the industry.

But all these sources of information are, to some extent, rooted in the past and do not reflect a really prospective view of risks. To take a step back from a retrospective vision, it is necessary to rely on more creative approaches.

To carry out this out-of-the-box thinking process, workshops are an appropriate tool. Their main purpose is to:

- Imagine new loss generation mechanisms, especially transversal ones that might have been missed by too narrow analyses
- Identify the strategic drivers that may change the operational risk profile by increasing the likelihood or the severity of the risks identified, or lead to the emergence of new risks

Ideally, senior executives, strategists, or experts should attend these workshops. Indeed, the sources already used did not really call upon their skills and opinions. Indeed, the sources already used have not really used their skills and opinions, which will have the advantage of having a certain distance from daily activities.

This type of workshop could, for instance, cover topics such as future new regulations and how they could lead to potential large fines, the impact of climate change on the probability or severity of natural catastrophes, the impact of technological breakthroughs, such as the blockchain, on the cyber risks profile.

A series of workshops per business line, one per main topic of interest – legal and regulatory, IT, climate, and so on – with senior executives and domain experts would help to identify new scenarios or, at a minimum, assign new priorities for the assessment of previously identified scenarios.

10.3 SCENARIO ASSESSMENT

The scenario assessment aims to provide an estimate of the average or extreme loss incurred if the scenario occurs.

[40] DDOS-like attack.

The input for the scenario assessment is the list of identified scenarios and, ideally, for each scenario a document that contains:

- The scope of the scenario
- The list of internal losses associated with the scenario
- The list of external losses associated with the scenario

The result of scenario assessment process is a document that contains for each scenario:

- The full storyline of the scenario
- An assessment of the expected loss and of some relevant loss percentiles
- The main drivers of the loss generation mechanism
- A trend analysis for the main drivers

10.3.1 The Storyline

A scenario must tell a story about how some future losses might occur. A coherent scenario covers only one loss generation mechanism subject to different conditions, related to the environment, activity, or controls.

As discussed above in 10.1 Scope of scenario analysis, two important quality criteria are the transparency of each scenario and the distinctness between scenarios. For this reason, the first condition is that the story must be clearly defined.

This means that the *scope and the rationale of the scenario* must be clearly explained and approved by the stakeholders and, ideally, the *loss generation mechanism* should be as detailed as possible.

10.3.1.1 Naming a Scenario A good story begins with a good title. Properly naming the scenario is, in our experience, critical to ensure mutual understanding and an efficient communication within the firm. A good name for a scenario should meet the following criteria:

- It should refer to an event.
- It should not be too broad.
- It should focus on the event rather than the causes.

A simple test to check whether these criteria are met is to consider whether a scenario name could also be the name of a loss in the database.

To illustrate this point, we can review each of the 10 top risks defined in risk.net risks and test the criteria just defined (see Table 10.13).

We note from these examples that the naming of scenarios is not simple, but the good news is that once the right name is chosen, it is likely that the loss generation mechanism will be easy to define. Conversely, in our experience, a poorly defined name will always lead to misunderstandings with all stakeholders, including regulators.

[41] Whether this assessment is driven by the regulation (e.g., risk-weighted assets for Basel regulation reporting) or not.

TABLE 10.13 Review of Top 10 Operational Risks

#1: IT Disruption	**Too broad**. Too many types of events are addressed: Data center disruption, critical application disruption, external IT infrastructure outage, and so on.
#2: Data Compromise	**OK**. This name contains a resource ("Data") and an event ("Compromise"). However, it might be split into several subscenarios, depending on where the data is stored. A merchant data compromise could be distinguished from the internal data compromise for example.
#3: Regulatory Risk	**Cause**. Change in regulation is not an operational risk but it could be the cause of new breaches and subsequent fines. Without a breach, a change in regulation could not directly result in a loss that would be reported in the internal loss database.
#4: Theft and Fraud	**Too broad**. This name refers to a risk theme, not a potential loss. All external and internal fraud events are covered. This theme intersects the "Data Compromise" scenario the "Rogue Trading" scenario.
#5: Outsourcing	**Not an event**. Outsourcing in itself is a practice, not a risk. Supplier failure would be a better name actually.
#6: Mis-Selling	**OK**. Although this risk could be split into several sub scenarios depending on the type of product that are mis-sold, this name is meaningful.
#7: Talent Risk	**Ambiguous**. This name is unclear about the scope of the risk. It could refer to shortage of talents, which is not an operational risk but rather a driver for other operational risks (i.e., frauds, errors). It could also relate to loss of key staff which is a valid scenario. The name "Loss of Key Staff" would therefore be preferred.
#8: Organisational Change	**Cause**. Organisational change is not a risk but a driver that could increase the likelihood or severity of other risks.
#9: Unauthorized Trading	**OK**. Although it should be clarified within the storyline whether this name also includes "Rogue Trading", this name is a good one as it is self-explanatory and could certainly be the name of a loss in the database.
#10: Model Risk	**Too broad**. Many operations or reporting are relying on models. In a financial institution, models are everywhere: to price the financial products, to assess the risks of the firm[41], and so on. At minimum, the category of models should be defined in the name.

10.3.1.2 Building a Storyline In its simplest form, the storyline is a detailed description of the scope of the scenario. In more advanced versions this is a description of the loss generation mechanism. Defining the scope of the scenario is part of the identification step, but is a prerequisite for any assessment. Where this scope is not sufficiently precise, it will be discussed and refined in sessions devoted to scenario evaluation.

The way the storyline is written depends on the source of the scenario identification. When the scenario has been identified from internal or external losses, the storyline can be established by stylizing the loss narrative.

Stylization is the process of extracting key points from the script. This process, which should be led by an expert, trims all the particularities read in the loss narrative and only selects those characteristics that can be generalized.

Let us illustrate how stylizing would work on the example of the $2 billion fine imposed by the Department of Justice to Barclays for the mis-selling of RMBS products. In the description, we have highlighted the important features in grey (see Table 10.14). Each highlighted element could be replaced by a variable to create a generic narrative.

The matching between specific information and generic variables is described in Table 10.15.

The result of this first stylisation step would be a generalized story for the loss, as shown for instance in Table 10.16.

Actually, this generalized story is not the storyline of a scenario, but it highlights its main features. In this case, the scenario would address the mis-selling of investment products. Following the discovery of the breach, the amount of the penalty would depend on the rules that were breached, the duration of the misconduct and the subsequent number of harmed investors.

This story should be generalized to include any type of action against the firm for improper sales of investment products. The following storyline (Table 10.17) is a realistic and very simple option for this scenario. It clearly defines in a few sentences the scope of the scenario.

A more structured version of this storyline (Table 10.18) would include a description of the loss generation mechanism with the exposure, the event and the consequences.

It is necessary to know the loss generation mechanism to assess the probability and potential severity of the scenario, as it details the main drivers of potential losses for the coming year.

We explained how a storyline for a scenario could be built by stylizing a past internal or external loss. If the scenario is identified from another source – RCSA, external survey or workshops – and has never happened in the past, neither in the firm nor in the other institutions, stylization is not the appropriate method to establish the storyline but the target remains the same. The scope and, as far as possible, the loss generation mechanism should be described.

TABLE 10.14 First Step of Scenario Stylisation

Barclays Agrees to Pay $2 Billion in Civil Penalties to Resolve Claims for Fraud in the Sale of Residential Mortgage-Backed Securities
The United States has reached agreement with Barclays Capital, Inc., and several of its affiliates (together, Barclays) to settle a civil action filed in December 2016 in which the United States sought civil penalties for alleged conduct related to Barclays' underwriting and issuance of residential mortgage-backed securities (RMBS) between 2005 and 2007. Barclays will pay the United States two billion dollars ($2,000,000,000) in civil penalties in exchange for dismissal of the Amended Complaint. Following a three-year investigation, the complaint in the action, *United States v. Barclays Capital, Inc.*, alleged that Barclays caused billions of dollars in losses to investors by engaging in a fraudulent scheme to sell 36 RMBS deals, and that it misled investors about the quality of the mortgage loans backing those deals. It alleged violations of the Financial Institutions Reform, Recovery, and Enforcement Act of 1989 (FIRREA), based on mail fraud, wire fraud, bank fraud, and other misconduct.

Source: Excerpt of the DOJ press release, March 29, 2018.

TABLE 10.15 Second Step of Scenario Stylisation

Selection from Narrative	Corresponding Variable	Explanation
"Barclays Capital, Inc. and several of its affiliates "	THE FIRM	This type of loss could happen in the firm conducting the scenario analysis.
"$2 Billion"	PENALTY	The amount of the penalty depends on the number of mis-sold investors.
"Residential Mortgage-Backed Securities"/"36 RMBS deals"	INVESTMENT PRODUCT	This case is related to RMBS sales but could happen for a different investment product
"The United States"	THE PLAINTIFF	The firm could be sued by any regulator, authority or class of investors.
"2005 and 2007"	RELEVANT PERIOD	This information is not necessary for a basic storyline but might be relevant to refine the loss generation mechanism.
"The Financial Institutions Reform, Recovery, and Enforcement Act of 1989"	THE RULES	Regulations and rules that are breached in a mis-selling case depend on the case and on the country.
"Billions of dollars"	DETRIMENT	The harm caused to the investors depends on the volume of products that were sold to the investors.

TABLE 10.16 Stylised Storyline

<THE FIRM> Agrees to Pay <PENALTY> in Civil Penalties to Resolve Claims for Fraud in the Sale of <INVESTMENT PRODUCTS>.

<THE PLAINTIFF> has reached agreement with <THE FIRM> to settle a civil action in which <THE PLAINTIFF> sought civil penalties for alleged conduct related to <THE FIRM>'s underwriting and issuance of <INVESTMENT PRODUCTS> during <THE RELEVANT PERIOD>. <THE FIRM> will pay <THE PLAINTIFF> <PENALTY> in civil penalties in exchange for dismissal of the Amended Complaint.

The complaint in the action alleged that <THE FIRM> caused <DETRIMENT> in losses to investors by engaging in a fraudulent scheme to sell <INVESTMENT PRODUCTS>, and that it misled investors about the quality of the <INVESTMENT PRODUCTS>. It alleged violations of <THE RULES>.

TABLE 10.17 Mis-Selling Scenario Summary

The scenario covers the situation where the firm has allegedly misrepresented or omitted material facts about a product that was sold to many clients, or a high-value product sold to a few wholesale clients. It also considers situations where the product sold does not meet the clients' needs and requirements. This scenario focuses on investment banking business.

TABLE 10.18 Mis-Selling Scenario Loss Generation Mechanism

The exposure: As part of its investment bank business, the firm is underwriting and or selling some investment products. Some of those products have raised massive investments.

The event: On one of the products, the firm is sued for having misrepresented or omitted material facts about the product or for having sold the product to clients whose needs or requirements did not match with the product's risk profile.

The consequences: As a consequence, the firm may incur the following financial penalties:

- Disgorgement of all the undue profits generated by the product. The generated profits depend on the total amount of money invested in the product.
- Compensation to investors who have incurred investment losses. The compensation depends on the fraction of clients who are claiming and on the financial losses incurred by the investors on the market.
- Regulatory fine imposed by the authorities to deter further similar practices. This fine depends on the seriousness of the case, that is, on the duration of the misconduct, on the harm caused to the investors, on the causes of the misconduct and on the level of cooperation with the regulator.

For scenarios coming from RCSA, engaging subject matter experts through workshops led by the risk management team is the usual method to define a storyline accepted by all stakeholders. For scenarios identified from external survey, an initial version of the storyline is generally described in the survey and may need to be refined by SMEs. When scenarios are identified through creative thinking workshops, defining the scope and the loss generation mechanism should be done in session during the workshops.

10.3.2 Assessment Methods

In this chapter, we discuss the typical methods used by practitioners to evaluate scenarios. The XOI approach will be described in Part IV. Although these methods are intended to provide an assessment of the potential loss, they cannot be considered as quantitative methods because they generally do not follow a rigorous methodological process. Their result is usually an informed estimate.

Depending on the intended use for the scenario, two types of assessments are usually performed by the firms:

1. The assessment of the expected loss through the assessment of likelihood and average severity
2. The assessment of percentiles of potential losses

10.3.2.1 Assessment of the Expected Loss From a mathematical standpoint, "Expected Loss" has a precise meaning. It is the expected value of the distribution of future losses. The assessment of this expected loss cannot be done empirically, as there is generally not enough data to build a robust estimate. Since the assessment process is rather qualitative, the firms often deviate from the mathematical definition of expected loss and assess something that is closer to a plausible or typical loss. A general practice is to consider the most common situation covered by the scenario and try to assess its probability and severity.

Therefore, the expected loss generally does not integrate all the potential losses that could occur but focuses on the occurrence of a particular situation. Both likelihood and severity assessment are expert-based. However, the quality of the assessment depends on the quality of the description of the loss generation mechanism. The best case is when an equation with simple drivers can be established for likelihood and severity based on the loss generation mechanism. Then the expected loss can be evaluated from the estimation of simple drivers.

As an illustration, let us consider the assessment of the outage of an application processing automatic payments and debits, some of which are regulated and result in a high penalty rate. The figures are fictitious but the equations are real. The typical situation used to assess the expected severity[42] was a full-day interruption of the application during one of the five monthly peak days. The impact of this outage was estimated at one day of interest to be paid to the clients as compensation. The formula for estimating this impact could be expressed as:

$$\begin{aligned}&(\text{Average Monthly Volume of Regulated Payments and Debits})/5\\&\quad\times \text{Daily Penalty Rate}\\&\quad\times \text{Outage Duration}\end{aligned}$$

Where:

Average Monthly Volume of Regulated Payments and Debits	= \$2 Billion
Daily Penalty Rate	= 10%
Outage duration	= 1 day

The resulting estimate for the average impact would be \$40 Million. To assess the likelihood, that is, the frequency of this "average" situation, we can use an educated guess based on historical data and SME opinion. The frequency is estimated at 25% (1 in 4 years), and the corresponding expected loss is therefore equal to \$10 Million.

It should be noted that this expected loss is not in the nature of a mathematical expectation. Indeed, the assumption for the outage duration is one possible case rather than an average duration. However, by changing the assumptions on the drivers in the equation, especially the duration of the outage, we could consider different situations.

This example illustrates the most structured way to assess the expected loss, but if we want to give an overview of possible approaches, we can list three methods in ascending order of structuration:

10.3.2.1.1 Direct Assessment of Expected Loss The SMEs try to provide directly an amount for the total average loss related to the scenario over a period of time. This is not the approach we recommend, as it generally leads to poorly justified estimates that can be challenged easily.

[42]As explained above, "expected severity" must not be thought of as the mathematical expectation of the severity distribution.

10.3.2.1.2 Assessment of Frequency and Average Severity The SMEs must assess the two usual metrics that quantitatively define a risk. This approach is better than the previous one because it simplifies the assessment process and provides more knowledge about the scenario. For frequency, the use of internal historical data, if available, could lead to a first estimate. When no internal losses are available, using the number of external losses that occurred into similar institutions (same type of business lines and same level of revenue) is possible. When no data are available, a conservative estimate could be calculated as follows: if no event has occurred in the last N years, a 1/N frequency would be considered as conservative as it would implicitly assume that an event could occur every N years. For the impact, the average of past internal losses could serve as a benchmark. If no internal data are available, averaging scaled external loss data could be a relevant solution, provided that the scaling factor has been chosen appropriately. If no internal and external loss data are available, a pure expert assessment is necessary.

10.3.2.1.3 Driver-Based Assessment of Frequency and Average Severity This approach has been illustrated above. A simple equation is established for severity and less often for frequency. SMEs are asked to assess the drivers of the equation. This method is the more demanding because it involves a deeper analysis of the loss generation mechanism. But it is also the more consistent, as it ensures the continuity between expert knowledge and outcomes of the assessment.

10.3.2.2 Assessment of the Percentiles When scenario analysis is used to complement quantitative methods in order to provide estimates for potential extreme losses, assessment of the percentiles of the loss distribution is required.

Mathematically, the 99% percentile[43] of the loss distribution is the amount that has less 1% probability to be exceeded. If a company estimates its 99% loss percentile for mis-selling over the next year at $150 million, it means that it estimates that it could suffer a loss of $150 million with less than a 1% probability over the next year. This does not mean that the company could not incur fines of $1 billion, but these higher losses would have probabilities of less than 1% to occur.

Obviously, SMEs and risk management cannot be asked to give accurate estimates of percentiles, as this would imply being able to establish at least a partial loss distribution which is not possible for a human expert. Therefore, the kind of question that is generally asked to the SMEs and risk management is to determine the event that could happen once every 10 years, the loss that could happen once every 100 years, and so on.

They are asked to build extreme point estimates, that is, the most severe situations at different levels of probability, rather than assessing actual percentiles. The difference between the two can be easily understood through a simple example. When an expert has to build a story for an event that he believes could happen once in 100 years, he will use his experience to think of an exceptional situation. For example, he will consider a large number of mis-sold customers for a particular product and propose this case as having a probability of 1%.

[43] 99% is used for illustration purpose only.

TABLE 10.19 Frequency Assessment

Situation	Typical Probability	Comment
Frequent	1 in 2 years	Loss events should be observed in the internal loss database.
Unusual	1 in 10 years	A couple of loss events could be observed in the internal loss database.
Extreme	1 in 100 years or less	Internal loss database would generally not contain such losses but external loss databases could.

But there are probably other cases, with slightly different assumptions, that would also have a 1% probability. For example, a similar case for a different product. This means that a case with a 1% probability is not the 1% percentile, which is generally higher.

It is impossible to be accurate when estimating these points as percentiles. At least, point estimates need to be consistent together, that is, the higher the probability level the larger the loss, but also consistent with the observed past external and internal losses. Each firm can define the probability levels that are aligned with its objectives and the context of the scenario analysis, but the typical practice is to cover three kind of situations:

1. Frequent situation that an employee is expected to experience many times in a carreer
2. Unusual situations that the firm may typically experience one or two times in a decade
3. Extreme situations that the firm may have experienced during its history or that the other firms in the same industry have experienced a few times over the past years

Typical frequencies for each of these situations are summarized in Table 10.19.

More situations can be assessed by the firm and different typical probability levels can be used, but when the probability levels are defined, two methods can be considered to estimate the related percentiles[44]: the benchmark method and the driver-based method.

10.3.2.2.1 Benchmark Method The benchmark method is based on the historical data, internal and external. It is a pure backward-looking estimation and should be used only to challenge the final estimates or to provide some initial guess before the driver-based method is applied.

The benchmark method follows the steps described and illustrated in Table 10.20.

Note that for extreme percentiles, this method may not work because the number of banks and the years of losses observed are not sufficient. Indeed, if, for instance, the loss data covers 100 companies and 8 years, the size of the table in step 4 would be 800. We can consider that the 1 in 100 years point can be estimated with this sample that contains 800 potential years, but assuming that the 1 in 1,000 years point can be estimated from 800 years is more challengeable. In this case, the maximum of the sample can be used as a benchmark but will likely underestimate of the extreme percentile.

[44]While we are aware that this is an abuse of language since point estimates of adverse situations are not strictly equivalent to mathematical percentiles, we use the word percentile for simplicity.

TABLE 10.20 Assessment of Scenario Percentiles Using a Benchmark Method

Bank	Year	Loss ($M)
MyBank	2010	150
Bank1	2011	320
Bank1	2011	2000
Bank1	2017	800
Bank2	2014	50

① Collect all internal losses and external losses related to the scenario under assessment.
The firm may decide the starting date and the companies to be included in the sample.

Denote by C the total number of companies and by N the number of years covered by the loss history.

In the example, "MyBank", that is conducting the scenario analysis, suffered a $150 millions loss in 2010, while "Bank1" incurred two losses in 2011, a $320 million loss and a $2 billion loss.

Bank	Year	Loss ($M)	Scaling Factor	Scaled Loss ($M)
MyBank	2010	150	100%	150
Bank1	2011	320	20%	64
Bank1	2011	2000	20%	400
Bank1	2017	800	22%	178
Bank2	2014	50	200%	100

② Scale external losses using the revenue of the firm as a scaling factor.

Each external loss is multiplied by the ratio between the revenue of the firm and the revenue of the company that incurred the loss. Both revenues are evaluated at the year of loss occurrence.

"Bank1" has a revenue that is 5 times that of "MyBank" revenue in 2011, thus its $2 billion loss is equivalent to a $400 million loss for "MyBank".

Bank	Year	Scaled Loss ($M)
MyBank	2010	150
MyBank	2011	0
MyBank	...	...
MyBank	2017	0
Bank1	2010	0
Bank1	2011	464
Bank1	...	...
Bank2	2017	178
...		

③ Aggregate the individual losses per year and company.

For each company, for each year[45], sum up the losses that occurred to the company during the year.

Years without any loss are represented with a 0 loss. Every row in the resulting table represents a potential year of loss for the firm.

Index	Bank	Year	Scaled Loss ($M)
1	MyBank	2011	0
2	MyBank	2017	0
...			
792	Bank1	2011	464
...			
800	Bank8	204	520

④ Calculate the empirical percentiles by sorting the previous table in ascending loss amount order and retrieve the rows that correspond to the desired levels of probability.

If the loss database covers C companies and N years, the P percentile is the loss that corresponds to the row which number is $INT(P \times C \times N)$.

The 99% percentile is reached on the 792th row for a $464 million annual loss as the loss database covers 8 years and 100 companies: $792 = 99\% \times 100 \times 8$

[45]For illustration purposes, we assume a one-year exercise, but this could be generalized to any periodicity.

10.3.2.2.2 Driver-Based Method This method uses the storyline and the loss generation mechanism described for the scenario. The idea is (1) to identify the main drivers of the loss generation mechanism, (2) to propose some assumptions on the values of these drivers at different levels of probability, (3) to estimate the resulting components of the loss depending on these drivers.

This process may use some simple equations for severity, but it is mainly a qualitative process based on expert judgements. Let us illustrate this method on an example inspired from a real scenario analysis run by an insurance company. For confidentiality purpose, the storyline and the data have been modified from the original documentation.

The scenario addressed in this example is a "Data Theft" scenario. This scenario covers the intentional theft or unintentional loss of customers' data by an employee. As a consequence, the firm could incur fines, compensation costs to redress the clients, fraud costs, and remediation costs. The cost of the loss is mainly driven by the number and the type of data that were stolen.

Four situations[46] corresponding to four levels of probability were described and assessed. We summarize the situations in Table 10.21.

In this assessment, probability levels must be considered qualitatively and are reflecting what should be considered as a frequent loss event, a likely loss event, an extreme loss event, and a remote loss event. From a methodological point of view, this assessment can be compared to the IPCC and FED scenario analyses presented at the beginning of this chapter. Each situation is defined by a narrative and a set of drivers quantified at each level of probability. Table 10.22 summarizes all the assumptions for each situation.

With this example, we have highlighted that operational risk scenario assessment, although it is a highly qualitative process, helps the firm to better understand its major risks and how it could mitigate them. In the original assessment conducted by the firm, the narrative also included a full analysis of the postevent mitigation actions. We didn't report this analysis as it relates to the firm specific controls, but the result of these mitigation actions is captured through the assessment of the drivers.

We must not be misled by the apparent accuracy of the objective. The probability levels should be considered as labels more than numbers. It is certainly impossible to provide expert-based assessment of actual percentiles and these percentiles only indicate that experts are being asked to go through different levels of likelihood. In practice, there is no difference in nature between the meaning of the baseline, adverse and severely adverse scenarios of the FED scenarios and the 1 in 2, 1 in 10, and 1 in 50 scenarios presented above. Providing certain levels of probability as targets only helps us to determine to what extent a scenario should be more severe than another.

[46] Strictly speaking, each situation is a scenario as defined at the beginning of this chapter, but in operational risk practice, a scenario is more a range of situations than a specific one.

TABLE 10.21 Assessment of Scenario Percentiles Using a Driver Method

1 in 2 years: $0 Million
An employee accidently leaves their USB stick on the tube. This stick contains a small number of individual customer's data (less than 20). No passwords are left with the stick. Business protection rules applied by the employee ensure that the data will destroy themselves if the incorrect password is entered more than 10 times.
No financial loss is expected for the firm.
1 in 10 years: $10.5 Million
A rogue employee, as part of their job, has access to customer data and downloads 250,000 individual customer data with the full name, the date of birth, and the policy numbers. This employee intends to sell this file to criminal gangs that can use this data to commit identity theft or gain access to the firm policies.
The costs arising from the event would be:
Compensation to customers: $7.5 million
As a result of the error and of the media coverage, 10% of the customer would claim for compensation (this 10% number is consistent with external data for similar cases) and accept the $300 individual compensation offered by the firm.
Fines: $2 million
Two fines would be imposed by the relevant authorities: a $500,000 fine for failing to protect customers data and a $1.5 million fine for system and control failing.
Remediation cost: $1 million
Overhaul of security system would require a $1 million investment.
1 in 50 years: $91 Million
A rogue employee, as part of their job, has access to the customer database, and downloads 500,000 individual customer data with the full name, the date of birth, the address, the policy numbers, and the bank accounts. This employee intends to sell this file to criminal gangs which can use this data to commit identity theft or gain access to the firm policies or to bank accounts.
The costs arising from the event would be:
Compensation to customers: $85 million
As a result of the error and of the media coverage, 30% of the customer would claim for compensation and accept the $300 individual compensation offered by the firm. This compensation would amount to $45 million.
Moreover, all the customers would be offered a one-year identity theft cover worth $50/year, which would result in additional cost of $25 million.
0.1% of the customers had their policy fraudulently surrendered and will be reimbursed. Based on business data, the average amount of a fraud is estimated to $30,000. This would represent a total $15 million amount.
Fines: $3.5 million
Two fines would be imposed by the relevant authorities: a $500,000 fine for failing to protect customers data and a $3 million fine for system and control failing.
Remediation cost: $1 million
Overhaul of security system would require a $1 million investment.
Claim processing cost: $1.5 million
150,000 complaints must be processed. On the basis of two complaints per hour, 75,000 hours would be necessary, 20$ each.

TABLE 10.21 (*Continued*)

1 in 200 years: $241.5 Million
A rogue employee, as part of their job, has access to the customer database and downloads 1,000,000 individual customer data with the full name, the date of birth, the address, the policy numbers, and the bank accounts. This employee intends to sell this file to criminal gangs which can use this data to commit identity theft or gain access to the firm policies or to bank accounts.
The costs arising from the event would be:
<u>Compensation to customers: $230 million</u>
As a result of the error and of the media coverage, 50% of the customers would claim for compensation and accept the $300 individual compensation offered by the firm. This compensation would amount to $150 million.
Moreover, all the customers would be offered a one-year identity theft cover worth $50/year which would result in additional cost of $50 million.
0.1% of the customers had their policy fraudulently surrendered and will be reimbursed. Based on business data, the average amount of a fraud is estimated to $30,000. This would represent a total $30 million amount.
<u>Fines: $5.5 million</u>
Two fines would be imposed by the relevant authorities: a $500,000 fine for failing to protect customers data and a $5 million fine for system and control failing.
<u>Remediation cost: $1 million</u>
Overhaul of security system would require a $1 million investment.
<u>Claim processing cost: $5 million</u>
500,000 complaints must be processed. On the basis of two complaints per hour, 250,000 hours would be necessary, $20 each.

TABLE 10.22 Drivers Assumptions for Different Situations

	1 in 2	1 in 10	1 in 50	1 in 200
Volume of compromised data	<20	250,000	500,000	1,000,000
Type of data	Encrypted	Not encrypted	Not encrypted	Not encrypted
Full name		Yes	Yes	Yes
Date of birth		Yes	Yes	Yes
Policy number		Yes	Yes	Yes
Bank accounts		No	Yes	Yes
Claim rate	0%	10%	30%	50%
Individual compensation	–	$300	$300	$300
Identity theft cover price	–	Not proposed	$50/year	$50/year
Percentage of defrauded customers	0%	0%	0.1%	0.1%
Average cost of a fraud	–	–	$30,000	$30,000
Fines	0	$2 million	$3.5 million	$5.5 million
Number of claims processed per hour	–	2	2	2
Hourly wage cost for claim processing	–	$20	$20	$20

PART Four

The Exposure, Occurrence, Impact Method

CHAPTER 11

An Exposure-Based Model

Operational risk is generally not considered an exposure-based risk. This is the first usual misconception, and when businesses miss this dimension, they can be overwhelmed by the variety of events, which can seem difficult to identify and to structure. In addition, they are likely to mix up hazards, causes, and events.

But, if one thinks about operational risk with a fresh mind, one will find that it is in fact very clearly exposure-based. Working with employees exposes a firm to fraud; working with traders exposes a firm to rogue trading; selling products exposes a firm to mis-selling; having competitors exposes a firm to cartels; and operating in buildings exposes a firm to natural disasters or terrorist attack. When looked at this way, no single operational risk is not exposure-based.

The single difference is that exposure is not a dollar amount, whereas exposure to credit risk and to market risk is a money amount. One lends a certain amount or takes a position, and this amount of money is exposed to a risk of default or to the volatility of the markets. This "money" exposure may have hidden from banks the true definition of "exposure at risk" – that it is a resource. A firm combines resources to achieve its objectives and any event that may harm a key resource will endanger the achievement of objectives: this is the definition of risk. In the case of banks, customers' money is certainly a resource. But employees, products, suppliers, and so on, are also resources, and these resources are exposed to operational risk.

The exposure is the number of objects that may be hit by a risk event, and other industries have identified this notion. In airline safety, for example, the exposure is the number of flights. Each time a plane takes off, it is exposed to a risk. The exposure in this case is certainly not a dollar amount, nor the number of passenger miles, nor the number of aircraft. A plane on the ground is not exposed to the risk of an accident.

11.1 A TSUNAMI IS NOT AN UNEXPECTEDLY BIG WAVE

The second misconception concerns potential loss forecasting. It is clear from internal or shared loss databases that operational risk losses show at least an 80–20 Pareto distribution. In reality, 5% of major losses explain 95% of the total loss amount. So, the major risks or scenarios drive operational risk costs.

The loss distribution approach, commonly in use in Europe and North America for more than 10 years, is based on the idea that potential large losses can be extrapolated from recurring losses. This idea is simply wrong. There is no logic in extrapolating repeated individual credit card frauds into a large merchant or payment processor compromise, such as the recent Target data breach. There is no logic in extrapolating individual lawsuits into a major class action. The underlying mechanisms and, in most cases, the resources at risk are not the same.

Using the loss distribution approach (LDA) is in reality extrapolating waves to predict a tsunami. But waves are produced by wind, and tsunamis by seismic activity – a tsunami is not an unexpectedly big wave.

11.2 USING AVAILABLE KNOWLEDGE TO INFORM RISK ANALYSIS

Let us identify which data or knowledge is available to model operational risk.

On one hand we have all the data/knowledge related to operational risk losses or events: internal losses, external losses that could be obtained from consortia and scenarios. For now, let us define scenarios as the analysis of particular situations that could generate large operational losses, and the unfolding of these situations.

On the other hand, we have information on the firm: its business, measured by various indicators, business variables that express the exposures of the firm, and macroeconomic variables and correlations that potentially express the context and how operational risks might be sensitive to this context.

This is the overall picture that needs to be considered to determine how to model operational risk. Two ways of organising this data and knowledge can be considered.

Those following the data-driven point of view try to create an operational risk model as a statistical law, represented by some parameters and inferred from data. All the sources are considered as contributors to the constitution of a loss database. In addition to observed losses, other sources are used to complement the loss database when no event has been observed, in particular potentially extreme events. For instance, these additional data points are generated using scaling or expert scenario assessment. The paradox is that most of the mathematical effort is spent in distribution fitting, while the distribution itself is strongly driven by potentially extreme events assessed qualitatively. One can now start to see the problem created with the LDA – it is almost as if the industry knew the qualitative assessment of the extreme events was critical to the quantification, but decided it was imperative to have a complex statistical model focused on the rest of the information to model the risk.

On the other hand, the scenario-driven point of view is precisely focused on the potential large future losses. Building scenarios means analysing the loss-generating mechanism, which is a forward-looking approach. In the near future, banks will need to consider possible attacks on blockchain as a major operational risk. How will this be addressed? By using statistical data? By extrapolating existing cyber-attacks on centralised architectures? We need to understand the possible attacks, how they can unfold and how they can be stopped. In this approach, all information and knowledge is used to inform the loss-generation mechanism.

There is also a key difference in the way the two approaches can be challenged. The data-driven approach can only be challenged by backtesting. The scenario-driven approach can certainly be backtested, but can also be challenged in the details of the mechanism, and scenarios can also be challenged by other experts, by external events, and so on.

11.3 STRUCTURED SCENARIOS ASSESSMENT

If we abandon the second misconception of extrapolating losses, we can focus on scenarios, each of which is defined by a particular exposure. Abandoning the first misconception as well – that operational risk is not exposure-based – we can arrive at something we call "structured scenario assessment".

This approach can be observed in a rogue-trading scenario, which is a good example of a loss-generation mechanism being described and later turned into a structured scenario. A trader builds and conceals a large directional and unprotected position – naked trading without adequate hedging positions – with the aim of creating large profits once the market moves in favor of the position. The position is detected a few weeks later during a control with a counterparty. However, unwinding the position generates a large loss as the market has moved against the position.

As discussed at the beginning of this article, the exposure to this risk is the number of traders working at the firm. Any of these traders can 'go rogue', thereby exposing the firm to such a loss. The impact will of course depend on the magnitude of the limit breaches and of the duration of the fraud.

The scenario can be broken down into three dimensions:

1. Exposure – the traders
2. Occurrence – going rogue
3. Impact – the market loss when the position is finally discovered and unwound.

Business indicators can be used to assess the number of traders in a position to perpetrate fraud, and internal and external data can be used to assess the probability of a trader going rogue. The size of the position that can be built and the time to detection can be assessed based on existing controls, both internal and external – relations with counterparties or clearing houses, for instance. Finally, the loss will be dependent on the market movements when the position is unwound, which can be assessed using market data.

Such a structure can also be used for all of the following purposes:

- It can be used to generate a distribution of potential losses according to the loss mechanism. Monte Carlo simulation of all the drivers involved in the model is used, that is, each of the variables driving exposure, occurrence, or impact. Once the distribution is built, the percentiles can be observed and used for capital calculation. This can be very different from extrapolating loss data or asking experts to directly assess the 1/20, 1/50, and 1/100 events.

- Stress testing can be performed on drivers, rather than relying on external correlations. If we consider an adverse scenario, we can explicitly stress one or more of the scenario variables. For example, if a rogue-trading event occurs in a highly volatile market, the losses might be higher, but some controls such as margin call monitoring could also be less efficient.
- Risk management can be directly represented in the loss-generation mechanism. Again, assuming that a stronger and more systematic control of positions with counterparties would detect a concealed position sooner, one might consider the benefit of this control on the cost of the risk.
- Capital allocation is straightforward. Most of the time this is performed through the allocation of the exposure units. But it can be also reflected in stronger or weaker controls, depending on the line of business or legal entities.
- Finally, the scenario challenge is certainly more robust. When using a purely expert approach, the challenge meetings are usually boring: too high, too low, and so on. In that case it is very easy to identify weaknesses in the scenario: incomplete exposure, missing key driver, and so on.

11.4 THE XOI APPROACH: EXPOSURE, OCCURRENCE, AND IMPACT

The XOI approach is the quantified version of the risk exposure as defined by a combination (resource, event, consequence). A risk exposure is the possibility that a tangible or intangible resource of the organisation is hit by an event, with certain consequences.

Table 11.1 presents a few examples of risk exposures as combinations or resource, event and consequences.

TABLE 11.1 Exposure, Occurrence, and Impact for Usual Risk Events

Risk Type	Exposure	Occurrence	Impact
Business disruption	Buildings, datacentres	Natural disaster, industrial disaster, terrorism	Cost of building Loss of revenue
IT disruption	Systems	System failure	Customer compensation Loss of revenue
Internal fraud	Employees	Fraud	Funds misappropriation
Reporting error	Reporting (e.g., tax reports)	Regulator prosecution	Fine and redress
Supplier failure	Supplier	Financial default or technical disruption	Switching cost Loss of dependent revenue
Breach of regulation	Jurisdictions	Regulator prosecution	Fine and settlement
Mis-selling	Products	Class action	Fine and settlement

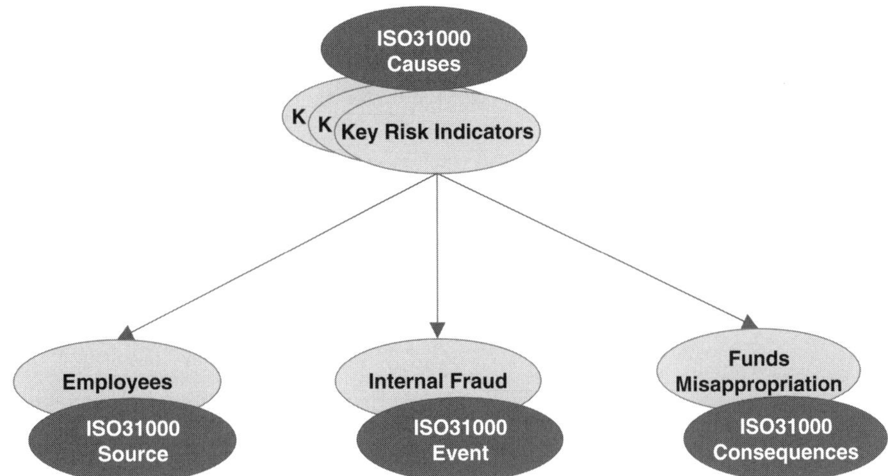

FIGURE 11.1 The XOI Method and ISO31000

This structured approach to risk assessment is compatible (see Figure 11.1) with the ISO 31000 concept of risk description: *a structured statement of risk usually containing four elements: sources, events, causes and consequences.*

CHAPTER 12
Introduction to Bayesian Networks

12.1 A BIT OF HISTORY

In his landmark essay ("Essay Towards Solving a Problem in the Doctrine of Chances," 1763), Thomas Bayes introduced two essential notions in the theory of decision.

On one hand, he defines probability as a notion related to what is nowadays called utility. According to Bayes, the price P that I am willing to pay to be able to benefit from the R gain that the occurrence of an uncertain event would offer me, *defines* the probability of this event, as P/R.

On the other hand, he defines the notion of conditional probability, highlighting the fact that the probability of a future and uncertain event depends on the level of information available to the person trying to assess this probability. This notion is fundamental because it expresses the fact that the uncertainty is specific to one person, and depends on her level of knowledge, and is thus closer to a belief than to a frequency.

By formalizing the intuitive link between information and probability, or in other words the dialectic between knowledge and uncertainty, Bayes has laid the groundwork for any theory of decision. The rational decision is one that searches for all available information. This is what "make an informed decision" means.

During the 1970s, and until the early 1980s, artificial intelligence was essentially represented by expert systems. Expert systems are characterized by a formal approach to knowledge. In expert systems, knowledge is seen as some specific sort of data, manipulated by a logical deduction tool, the inference engine. Expert systems rely on formal logic, of order 0 or 1, but always characterized by deterministic causality. From data (known facts P) and rules (If P then Q), they can deduce new facts (Q) by essentially using the syllogism as inference rule: if P is true (fact or premise) and if we know that P implies Q (rule) then, Q is true (new fact or conclusion). In the early 1990s, the use of expert systems quickly began to decline. In our opinion, the reason for this decline is the difficulty of collecting expertise under deterministic constraints. In other words, and for having practiced it for a long time, it is very difficult, if not illusory, to compel an expert to formulate a deterministic rule. Indeed, the rules expressed by experts are often valid in a limited field. In other words, they tolerate exceptions. The experts are then put in a very uncomfortable situation. Indeed, they either express false rules because they have a limited scope – but an expert system cannot take this into account. Or they must identify all the exceptions so that their rules are fully accurate, which is practically impossible.

In the late 1980s, Judea Pearl, a researcher at UCLA, proposed a probabilistic approach to artificial intelligence, called "Bayesian networks". This approach was aimed precisely at going beyond the limits of expert systems, and their inability to take into account uncertainty in reasoning. This approach integrates into a very simple formalism the Bayesian approach of probabilities – the probability of an event depends on the level of knowledge of its context, and a representation of causality.

The road to true artificial intelligence is difficult and far from complete, but it is likely that Bayesian networks will be a significant milestone.

12.2 A BIT OF THEORY

Bayesian networks are probabilistic causal models. The graph represents the structure of a domain knowledge, and probabilities represent the uncertain part of this domain.

Let's explain this idea with a very simple example in industrial safety.

An operator working on a machine may be injured if he misuses it. This risk depends on the experience of the operator and the complexity of the machine. "Experience" and "Complexity" are two determining factors of this risk (Figure 12.1).

Of course, these factors do not make it possible to create a deterministic model. Even if the operator is experienced, and the machine simple, this does not guarantee that there will be no accident. Other factors may be involved: the operator may be tired, disturbed,, and so on. The event remains random, but its probability of occurrence depends on the factors identified.

The diagram shown in Figure 12.1 represents the causal structure of this model[1] (graph).

This graph can be supplemented by probability tables. The most important table is the one that expresses the dependence of the accident on the operator's experience and the complexity of the machine (Table 12.1).

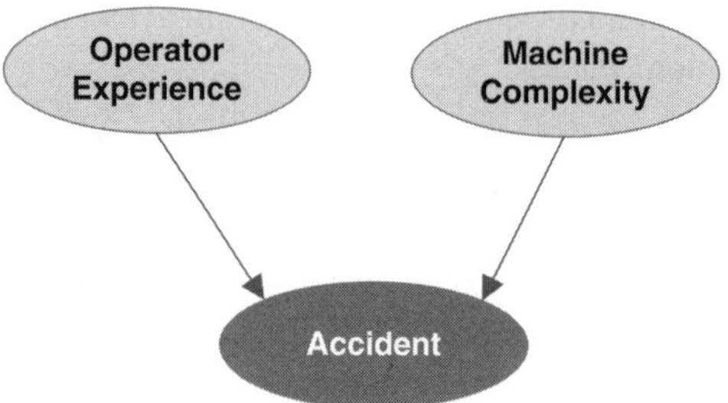

FIGURE 12.1 A Simple Causal Graph for Risk

[1]For the attentive – and French-speaking – reader who will have noticed that this example is very similar to the one proposed in the French Wikipedia page on Bayesian networks, no surprise: we have contributed to the writing of this page (https://fr.wikipedia.org/wiki/R%C3%A9seau_bay%C3%A9sien).

TABLE 12.1 Probability Table for the Worker Accident Risk

Complexity	Low			Medium			High		
Experience	**Low**	**Medium**	**High**	**Low**	**Medium**	**High**	**Low**	**Medium**	**High**
Accident	1.0	0.5	0.1	1.5	1.0	0.6	2.0	1.6	1.1
No accident	99.0	99.5	99.9	98.5	99.0	99.4	98.0	98.4	98.9

It is clear here that knowledge is not complete. If the user is experienced and the machine is simple, there will probably be no accident (0.1% chance in the example above). But maintaining a residual probability acknowledges the fact that not all risk factors are considered in this model.

The Bayesian network therefore represents both knowledge and uncertainty of the domain. What is known is represented by the causal structure (the graph). What is not known is materialized by probabilities.

The Bayesian network ultimately expresses that the experience of the operator and the complexity of the machine influence the probability of an accident. This is precisely the meaning of Thomas Bayes' approach: the probability depends on context.

12.3 INFLUENCE DIAGRAMS AND DECISION THEORY

We can go a little further with the model above, to make it a decision support tool. We can introduce two other "variables" into the graph: the decision to set up an operator training programme, and the choice of a machine supplier. These two decisions would have a direct influence on risk factors, as shown in Figure 12.2.

Let us define the total cost of risk as the sum of the costs of decisions and of the costs of accidents. We can see from the augmented graph that this cost can be studied with a Bayesian network.

For instance, we can try to minimize the mathematical expectation of this cost, considered as a negative "utility". The resulting Bayesian network has oval nodes, which are random variables, rectangular nodes, which are decisions, and diamond nodes embodying a utility. Such a network is called an influence diagram. It allows us to directly calculate the "utilities" of the different decisions.

In this example, the calculation of average utility would show for instance that the decision to choose a better machine supplier would reduce the cost of risk more than simply upskilling the employees through a training program. However, a closer analysis would show in this example that the choice to implement the two mitigation actions would reduce significantly the probability of a severe accident.

12.4 INTRODUCTION TO INFERENCE IN BAYESIAN NETWORKS

The first use of Bayesian networks is that of a "conditional probability calculator". Given a model, assumed to be constructed by an expert, the use of a Bayesian network amounts to calculating the probability of a nonobserved variable conditionally to the observed variables.

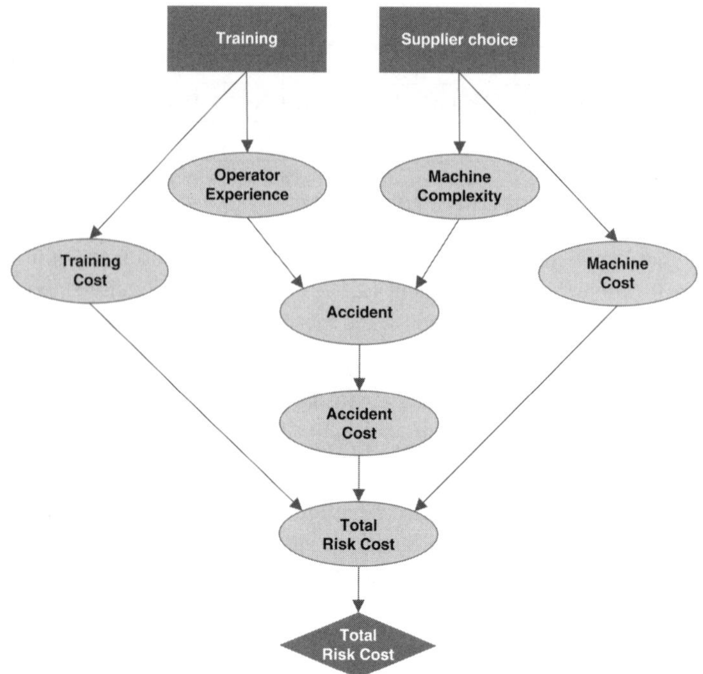

FIGURE 12.2 An Influence Diagram Based on a Simple Risk Model

This usage is called "belief update". The reader familiar with the calculation of conditional probabilities will recognize that this calculation can quickly become very heavy if the graph is complex. The question is in fact to what extent a variable observed at a point of the graph must be taken into account in the calculation of the probability of the variable of interest.

In the context of a medical diagnostic application, the general form of the network used will be as shown in Figure 12.3. Note that this is an abstract model representing a set of variables in the form of a single node, such as "Personal and Family Medical Background".

In the presence of a set of symptoms, the practitioner can sometimes establish her diagnosis with sufficient certainty. This is the case if the conditional probability of one of the pathologies comes off quite clearly:

$$P\ (Pathology \mid Context, Symptoms, Background)$$

If this is not the case, the practitioner may have to ask additional questions about the patient (recent trips, etc.) or have additional tests done. The theory makes it possible to characterize the questions that are not relevant, that is to say those that would not change the calculated probability. These questions are those for which already known data block the flow of information between them and the diagnosis. This blocking situation is expressed graphically by the notion of *d*-separation, which is one of the foundations of the graphical part of Bayesian networks. The computational algorithms used in Bayesian networks combine graph theory and probability theory. The graph theory part is undoubtedly the most complex. The normalization

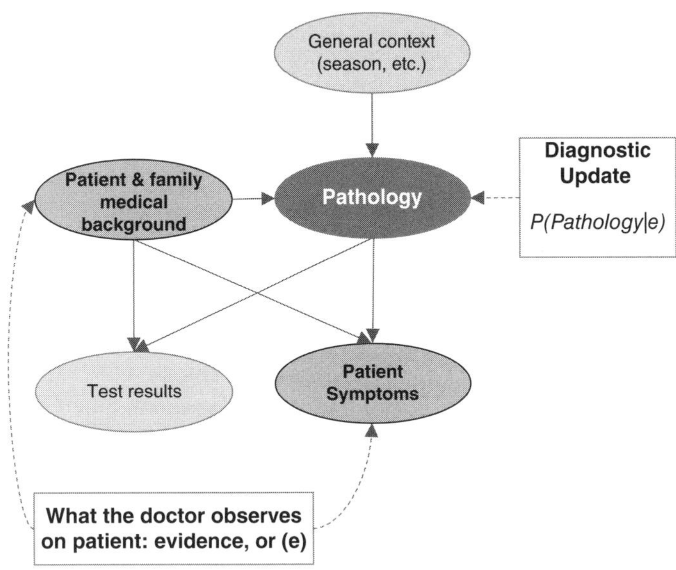

FIGURE 12.3 Inference in Bayesian Networks

of a graph representing a field of knowledge is the necessary condition for inference. This standardization can be very complex for some networks. The resolution of this problem, or at least the search for efficient solutions in the absence of an optimal solution, mobilized domain researchers for several years. The solutions are now stabilized but remain relatively difficult to access.

12.5 INTRODUCTION TO LEARNING IN BAYESIAN NETWORKS

A second domain of research for Bayesian networks is the automatic construction of models. This is a fascinating subject. Indeed, if we think about it, the notion of conditional probability also applies to models. From this point of view, Bayesian theory offers an answer to one of the most critical aspects of empirical modeling, which is the dialectic between observations and the model.

In the empirical approach, a model is inferred by a scientist from a theoretical perspective validated by observations, either numerous or well chosen. If, in a particular situation, an observation contradicts the model, we are invariably led to one or the other of the following conclusions: either the observation is rejected as insufficiently reliable, or the model is questioned (see Figure 12.4).

Since Bayesian networks are not deterministic but probabilistic, they tolerate "error". A Bayesian network does not usually provide a decision, but only a likely conclusion. If the facts contradict it, there is no reason to reject the model since the opposite conclusion was also possible, but simply less likely. However, if the model goes wrong too often, i.e. if the most probable output provided by the model almost never matches the observation, the model can be challenged. Bayesian theory applies perfectly here, simply saying that the model becomes less likely, compared to competing models.

FIGURE 12.4 Bayesian Learning in Bayesian Networks
Using Bayes' rule to infer the most likely model from observations.

"Reality" can be modeled in different ways. For a given model, observations are more or less likely. The accumulation of observations makes it possible to select the most likely model, transforming machine learning into an inference problem.

$$P\ (Model \mid Observations) = k \cdot P\ (Model) \cdot P\ (Observations \mid Model)$$

CHAPTER 13

Bayesian Networks for Risk Measurement

13.1 AN EXAMPLE IN CAR FLEET MANAGEMENT

We will use a nonfinancial example to illustrate the application of Bayesian networks for risk management. We consider a risk manager addressing the road accident risk for the company's truck fleet. He wants to represent the three parameters (exposure, occurrence, and impact) of this risk using a Bayesian network.

For this particular risk, the appropriate *exposure* measurement is the distance covered by the fleet during one period of time. Each kilometer covered by a truck is exposed to the occurrence of a road accident. The number of trucks would not be an appropriate measurement for exposure, since buying a new truck does not increase the risk of accident until the truck is on the road. Similarly, a driver contributes to the risk exposure only when he is at the wheel.

This measure of exposure is generally used by national authorities, such as the *Observatoire national interministériel de sécurité routière*[1] in France.

The number of kilometers covered per year for the considered company is the selected measurement for exposure. In a prospective risk management point of view, this is clearly a random variable since we cannot know in advance the number of kilometers that would be covered next year.

Using the distance covered as a measure of exposure is only acceptable because we will analyse further the risk for each individual kilometer. We will examine whether this kilometer is covered by an experienced driver, on a freeway or on a minor road,, and so on.

This means that the probability of accident occurrence will be calculated "individually" for each kilometer, or at least for typical clusters of kilometers.

The drivers of the total distance covered during one year are mainly of a commercial nature: if we consider that the company will not change the structure of its activity next year, the

[1] National Observatory of Road Transportation Safety.

exposure will be increased by a factor of growth – say 3–10%, depending on the market growth, the policy of the company, the policy of competitors, and so on. On the other hand, a change of structure of activity – for instance focusing on long distance transport, may have a more radical impact.

The probability of *occurrence* of an accident can be considered as dependent of various factors, among which the most significant would probably be:

- Truck driver qualification
- Truck driver condition
- Road used (freeway, urban motorway, minor road)
- Speed

Similarly, the severity of the accident, when it happens, will increase with speed, and possibly with the nature of the freight.

Since we try to build a simple introductory example, let us assume the simplified model:

- Exposure depends only of activity growth – no change in activity structure or competition.
- Probability of occurrence depends only of truck driver qualification, road used, and speed. Obviously, speed depends also on the type of road used.
- Severity depends only on speed.

We could use a Bayesian network to represent the risk of accident for one unit of exposure, that is, for one kilometer covered by a truck. Given the actual probability of accident (the order of magnitude being around 10 accidents for 100 million of km), we will rather consider a unit of 1million kilometers.

The graph in Figure 13.1 above proposes a structure for the car accident risk, and can be read as follows.

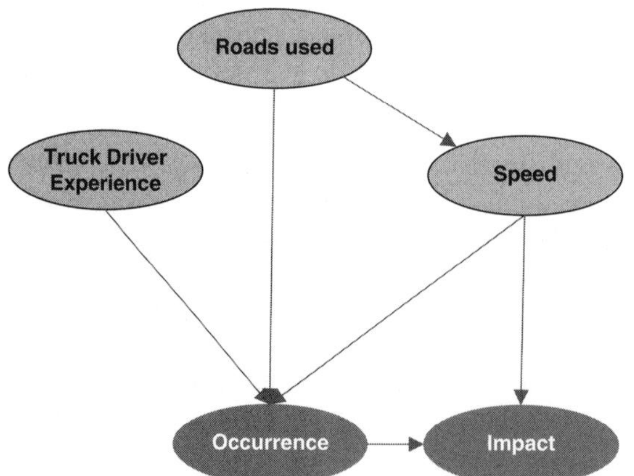

FIGURE 13.1 A Bayesian Network for Car Accident Risk

Each kilometer covered by a given truck is exposed to the risk of an accident. *The probability of occurrence of an accident* depends on:

- The qualification of the truck driver at the wheel during this particular kilometer
- The type of road on which this kilometer is covered
- The speed at which this kilometer is covered

If an accident does occur, *the cost (or impact) of the accident* will depend on the speed at that time. It is clear that these dependencies are not deterministic: for instance, an accident can sometimes be serious at low or moderate speed, while in "lucky" situations a high-speed accident may be benign[2]. The Speed → Impact dependency expresses that *on average* an accident would be more severe if it occurs at a high speed.

13.1.1 Nodes and Variables

In a Bayesian network, each node represents a discrete random variable, that is, a variable with at least two possible outcomes.

Bayesian networks can in principle deal with continuous variables, but discrete nodes are more usual. Furthermore, using continuous variables in Bayesian networks imposes restrictions for architecture and usable algorithms. In practice, as far as prospective risk analysis is concerned, the use of discrete or discretized variables would be generally appropriate and even recommended for a better communication of the models.

The road transport fleet risk management variables can be described as in Table 13.1.

TABLE 13.1 Variables of the Car Fleet Management Model

Variable	Possible Outcomes	Comments
Truck Driver Qualification	Low Medium High	This variable represents the level of qualification of the driver at the wheel for the exposure unit considered (i.e., one km).
Road Used	Freeway Urban motorway Minor road	This variable represents the type of road on which the kilometer is covered.
Speed	Low Moderate High	This variable represents the speed at which this kilometer is covered.
Occurrence	0 1	This variable represents the occurrence of an accident under specific conditions.
Impact	0–10 10–100 100–1,000	This variable represents the cost of an accident, measured in some specific unit.

[2]The fact that dependencies are not deterministic has been discussed earlier. This simply means that other drivers exist, but cannot be captured, such as traffic density.

13.1.2 Probabilities

Since each variable is considered random, its distribution must be defined. This means that the probabilities of the different outcomes must be defined.

In our example, it is easy to specify the probability of the two "root" variables: truck driver qualification and road used.

Provided the company has detailed information on its drivers, it can rapidly establish that:

- 10% of the truck drivers have not yet taken the training programme and can be considered as poorly qualified.
- 60% of the truck drivers have taken the training programme and have 3 to 5 years of experience.
- 30% of the truck drivers have taken the training programme and have 6 to 15 years experience.

If we assume that drivers cover approximately the same mileage regardless of their qualification, this repartition can be extended to kilometers covered.

If we assume further that the company has detailed reports on its activity, the repartition of kilometers covered can be computed as follows:

- 70% of the kilometers are covered on freeways.
- 10% of the kilometers are covered on urban motorways.
- 20% of the kilometers are covered on minor roads.

Therefore, if we consider a "random kilometer" for this company, we can reasonably assume that the expected outcomes for Qualification and Road Used would be as shown in Table 13.2.

This would not hold if the company had a specific driver assignation policy. For instance, is the company assigns only experienced drivers to missions where a significant mileage is covered on minor roads, this would introduce a dependency between the "Road Used" and the "Truck Driver Qualification", as shown in Figure 13.2.

In this case, the repartition of kilometers covered per type of road would still be of interest, but would not be enough to quantify the network: the probabilities of "Road Used" conditional to "Truck Driver Qualification" would be required.

Note that this could be again easily computed from activity reports and would look like the Table 13.3.

TABLE 13.2 Distribution of Driver and Road Variables

Truck Driver Qualification	Low	10%
	Medium	60%
	High	30%
Road Used	Freeway	70%
	Urban motorway	10%
	Minor road	20%

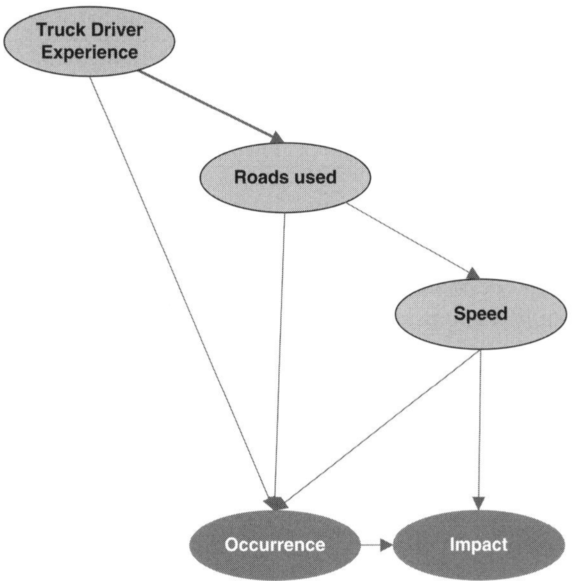

FIGURE 13.2 Car Accident Risk: Introducing a New Dependency to Reduce Risk

TABLE 13.3 Distribution of Road Conditional to Driver

Road Used \ Driver Qualification	Low	Medium	High
Freeway	90%	77%	50%
Urban motorway	2%	6%	20%
Minor road	8%	17%	30%

TABLE 13.4 Distribution of Speed Conditional to Road

Speed \ Type of Road	Freeway	Urban Motorway	Minor Road
Low	20.0	33.3	50.0
Moderate	30.0	33.3	30.0
High	50.0	33.3	20.0

Now we need to analyse the speed on each type of road (Table 13.4).

In this simple example, we have used three qualitative modalities of speed: low, moderate, and high. In practice, these indicators may be some ratio between the actual speed and the speed limit per type of road.

The last required information is relative to accident occurrence and accident cost. First you need to express how the three drivers (truck driver qualification, road used, and speed)

influence the probability of an accident, and then how the speed will increase the severity of an accident.

Hopefully you will not have enough statistics in your activity reports to have a reliable belief on this question. You may collect national statistics, or discuss with experts.

Finally, you come out with these tables, which express your present "belief" about the question, based either on national statistics, or on expert interviews.

For the probability of accident given the different conditioning variables (truck driver qualification, speed, and type of road), we will use Table 13.5, showing a differentiated accident probability for one million kilometers.

The two extremes are "Experienced truck driver at a relatively low speed on a freeway": around one accident for 100 million kilometers, and "Unexperienced truck driver at a relatively high speed on a minor road": around seven accidents for 100 million kilometers.

Similarly the distribution of accident severity depends on speed and is represented in Table 13.6.

TABLE 13.5 Conditional Probability of Accident

Speed	Truck Driver	Road Used	No Accident	Accident
Low	Low	Freeway	97	3
Low	Low	Urban motorway	96	4
Low	Low	Minor road	95	5
Low	Medium	Freeway	98	2
Low	Medium	Urban motorway	97	3
Low	Medium	Minor road	96	4
Low	**High**	**Freeway**	**99**	**1**
Low	High	Urban motorway	98	2
Low	High	Minor road	97	3
Moderate	Low	Freeway	96	4
Moderate	Low	Urban motorway	95	5
Moderate	Low	Minor road	94	6
Moderate	Medium	Freeway	97	3
Moderate	Medium	Urban motorway	96	4
Moderate	Medium	Minor road	95	5
Moderate	High	Freeway	98	2
Moderate	High	Urban motorway	97	3
Moderate	High	Minor road	96	4
High	Low	Freeway	95	5
High	Low	Urban motorway	94	6
High	**Low**	**Minor road**	**93**	**7**
High	Medium	Freeway	96	4
High	Medium	Urban motorway	95	5
High	Medium	Minor road	94	6
High	High	Freeway	97	3
High	High	Urban motorway	96	4
High	High	Minor road	95	5

TABLE 13.6 Conditional Cost of Accident

Severity \ Speed	Low	Medium	High
0–10	70%	20%	20%
10–100	20%	60%	20%
100–1000	10%	40%	60%

Table 13.6 expresses that, when an accident occurs at low speed, the cost of this accident is less than 10 in 70% of situations, between 10 and 100 in 20% of situations, and above 100 in 10% of situations. This distribution is changed as the speed increases, for instance 60% of the accidents that occur at high speed cost between 100 and 1000.

13.1.3 Dependencies

A link in a Bayesian network is intepreted as a causal relationship, that is, A→B means that A is one of the causes of B. In other words, if A and B are uncertain variables, and the causal relation A→B holds, then the distribution on B will be different for different outcomes of A.

This is exactly what we showed just above by introducing the dependency between the "Truck Driver Qualification" and the "Road Used" nodes.

Introducing a dependency in a Bayesian network should be considered only if you can quantify it. Introducing a dependency requires more explicit knowledge and has a certain cost. In some situations, you may be positive about a qualitative dependency, but unable to quantify it. In other situations, you may have evidence supporting a dependency, but no way to use it in your application. For instance, even if it is established that driving on drugs increases the probability of an accident, it would be extremely difficult to get statistics on how many kilometers are covered by drivers who are on drugs for your fleet.

Adding a cause to a node is also expensive in terms of statistical analysis, or expert interview: for instance the distribution of "Occurrence" has 27 lines, each of them representing the probability of an accident for 1 million of kilometers, given the values of the three causes identified. Adding another cause to "Occurrence", would have multiplied by three the volume of this table, if this new cause had three possible outcomes.

13.1.4 Inference

A Bayesian network represents the dependency structure of a knowledge domain.

Once the graph has been created and the probability tables defined, a Bayesian network software will calculate the overall distribution of the set of variables, as shown for instance in Figure 13.3.

The graph above shows the Bayesian network for the truck fleet risk, augmented with "monitor windows", that is, distribution windows. This means that each variable is shown with its actual distribution:

- The distribution of "Truck Driver Qualification" corresponds to what we have initially defined (this is the actual repartition of our drivers).

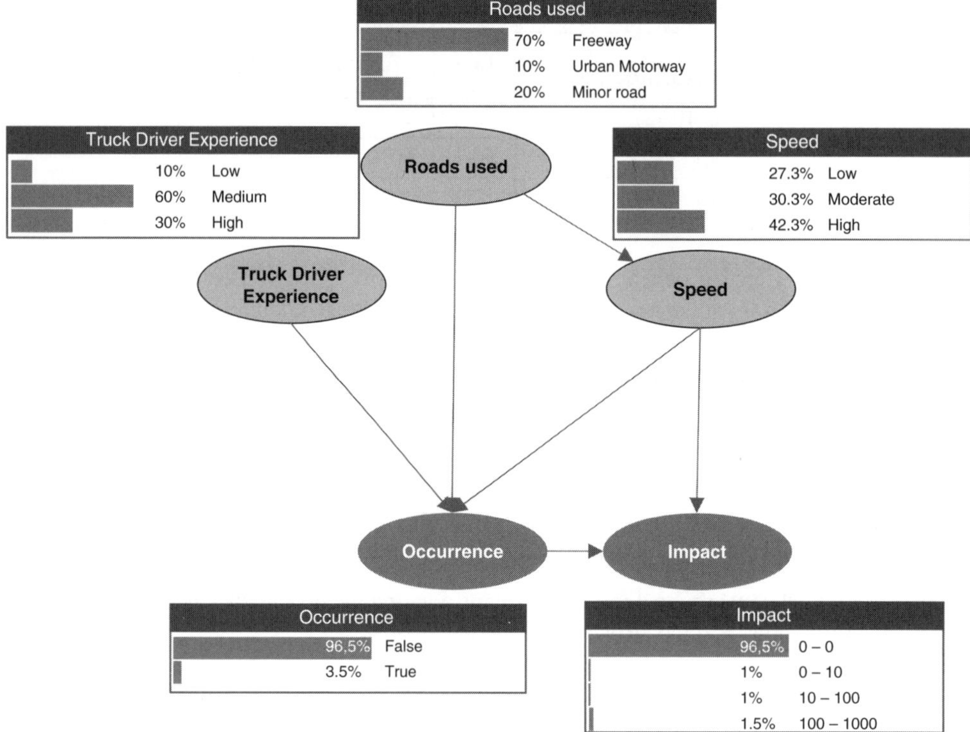

FIGURE 13.3 Marginal Distributions in the Car Accident Risk Bayesian Network

- The distribution of "Road Used" corresponds also to what we have initially defined (this is the actual statistics of the mileage of the company)
- The distribution of the "Speed" does not look familiar: Actually it has been computed by the inference engine the Hugin tool from the distribution of "Road Used", and the conditional distribution of "Speed" given "Road Used". We will go back to this calculation further on.
- The distribution of "Occurrence" shows that altogether the probability of an accident for 1 million of kilometers is 3.45%.
- The distribution of "Impact" shows again that in 96.55% of cases, the cost incurred for 1 million of kilometers will be 0 (no accident). This is consistent with the previous node. This node shows also that for around 1% of cases, a cost of 0 to 10 will be incurred. For another 1% of cases, a cost of 10 to 100 is incurred. Finally, for around 1.5% of situations, a cost of 100 to 1,000 is incurred.

The first result that we get from defining our model and entering the data in the tool is the actual distribution of the costs incurred for one unit exposed (here one million kilometers).

How is this calculation performed?

We will illustrate this on a simple example: the calculation of "Speed" distribution.

We start from the two initial tables (Table 13.7).

TABLE 13.7 Table of Road Types usage

Road Used	Freeway	70%
	Urban motorway	10%
	Minor road	20%

TABLE 13.8 Table of Distribution of Speed Conditional to Road Type

Speed \ Type of Road	Freeway	Urban Motorway	Minor Road
Low	20.0	33.3	50.0
Moderate	30.0	33.3	30.0
High	50.0	33.3	20.0

The "Speed" distribution is computed as a simple product (Table 13.8) of the two tables above:

$$70\% \times \begin{bmatrix} 20.0 \\ 30.0 \\ 50.0 \end{bmatrix} + 10\% \times \begin{bmatrix} 33.0 \\ 33.0 \\ 33.0 \end{bmatrix} + 20\% \times \begin{bmatrix} 50.0 \\ 30.0 \\ 20.0 \end{bmatrix} = \begin{bmatrix} 27.33 \\ 30.33 \\ 42.33 \end{bmatrix}$$

What is exactly this table product? It is simply the application of the "total probability theorem" version of Bayes theorem:

$$P\,(Speed) = P\,(Speed \mid Type\ Of\ Road) \cdot P\,(Speed)$$

Now we come to inference per se. Inference in a Bayesian network is simply using the Bayes theorem. Consider the "accident" situation. This means that we would like to calculate the distribution of the other variables *given that we know that an accident has occurred.*

In a Bayesian network tool, this is done simply by entering a piece of evidence. In Figure 13.4, we have entered "True" in the "Occurrence" node.

Now we see that the distributions of most variables have changed compared to the initial, unconditional situation:

- First the distribution of "Impact" has changed: obviously, since we assume now that an accident has occurred, the cost cannot be 0. We can see that 29.5% of the accidents cost between 0 and 10, and so on. Note that these figures could have been simply deduced from the initial distribution.
- More interesting, we see that the profiles of other variables have changed. The qualification of drivers has changed from Low: 10 – Medium: 60 – High: 30 to Low: 13.5 – Medium: 63.5 – High: 23. This seems intuitive since highly qualified drivers have less chance to have an accident.
- Similarly, assuming that an accident increases the probability of "Minor Road" and "High Speed".

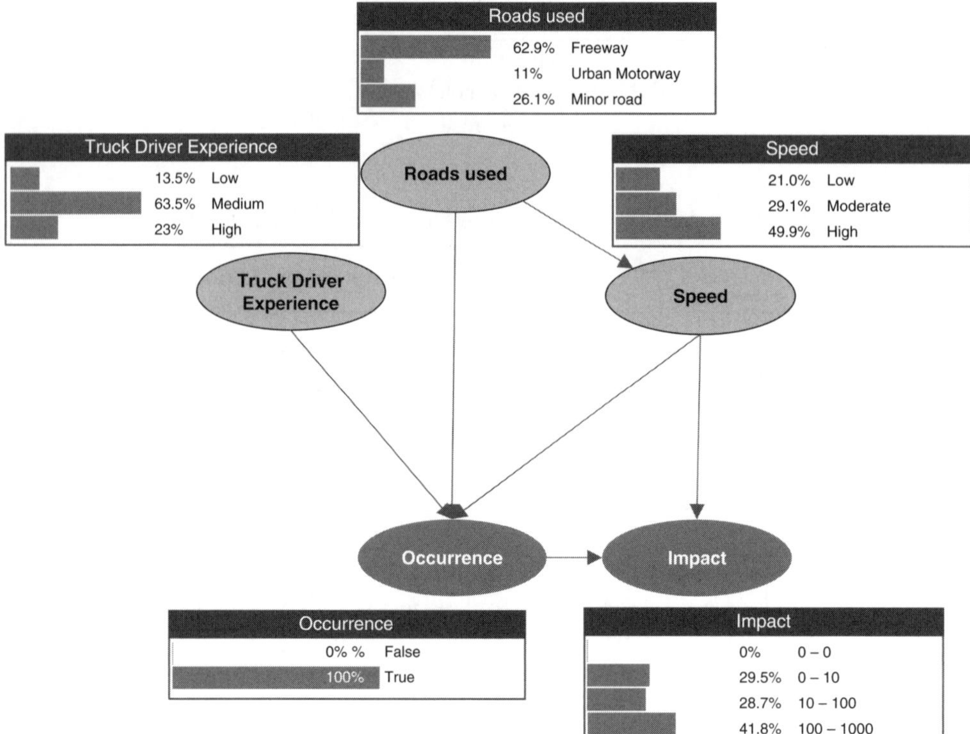

FIGURE 13.4 Inference in a Bayesian Network (1)
Observations of distribution of causes conditional to the occurrence of an accident.

Now we can try to understand the "typical" severe accident. For this, we will now select "100–1,000" in the "Impact" node, as shown in Figure 13.5 below.

The results are quite intuitive: the typical severe accident would take place at a high speed, and on a freeway. The driver profile is not changed.

13.1.5 Learning

A Bayesian network contains knowledge in two different "forms":

1. The causal structure of the graph
2. The probability tables

We already discussed the fact that knowledge can be generally obtained from two sources: either empirically, that is, from data, or from domain experts.

This holds also for a Bayesian network, at least in theory. In practice, experts will help building the causal structure of the model, and the quantitative part of the model (probability tables) will be inferred from statistical data.

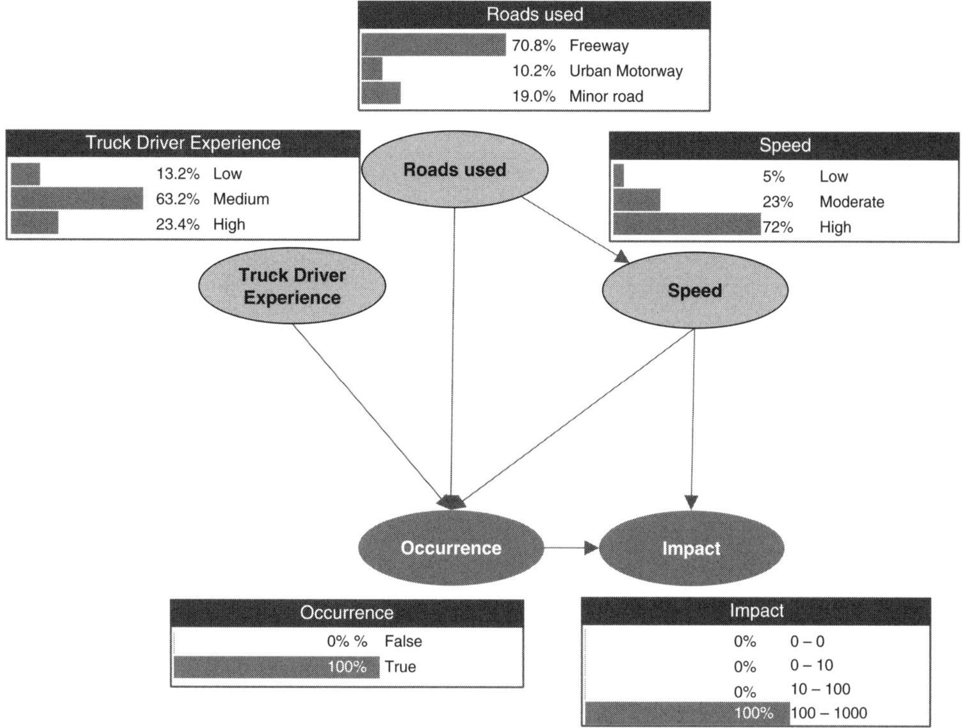

FIGURE 13.5 Inference in a Bayesian Network (2)
Observations of distribution of causes conditional to the occurrence of a severe accident.

This is exactly what we did in the simple example above: the fact that speed increases both the probability and the severity of an accident can be assessed by an expert, but statistical data are required to assess precisely to which extent.

In theory, it could have been possible to derive the causal structure directly from data. Specific learning algorithms can be used for that purpose. However, building the model structure directly from data is usually not feasible because no statistical database would be available where all useful variables are simultaneously present.

Let us go back to the truck fleet example:

- Assessing the conditional probability of impact given speed requires a national accident database
- Assessing the probability of accident given road used and driver qualification requires company records

Building the whole model directly from data would require a global database where all fields would be simultaneously present. But most probably, no national database will have any information regarding the driver qualification, and no company records will be large enough to be representative of accident rate.

TABLE 13.9 Learning from Experts or from Data

	Expert Assessment	Learning from Data
Causal Structure	Usual	Difficult, requires large amount of data
Probability Tables	Difficult, reserve to rare events	Usual

Table 13.9 summarises the usual practices for knowledge acquisition in Bayesian networks. Although learning structure from data may be appropriate for some specific applications, such as data mining, we believe that these recommendations are valid for most risk management applications.

CHAPTER 14
The XOI Methodology

The XOI, or Exposure, Occurrence, and Impact method, is a generalisation of the approach described in the Chapter 13's example of car fleet management.

14.1 STRUCTURE DESIGN

14.1.1 Choice of the Exposed Object

Two essential conditions must be met to ensure that the calculations obtained from the model are valid:

1. Exposure units must be exposed independently to the risk.
2. Each exposure unit should only be hit once in the year.

These conditions have an impact on the choice of the exposure definition:

- The fact that an exposed unit is hit by the risk should not increase the probability of another also being hit.
- If a unit can be struck several times in the year, it must be broken down into several units with a shorter time interval.

In most cases, perfect independence is impossible, for at least one reason: the occurrence of an event with a severe impact in a firm will trigger immediate corrective actions, which should reduce the occurrence probability of other similar type events, at least in the short term.

Even if it is clear that no exposure measure choice can guarantee perfect independence, it is important to ensure that an obvious dependence does not exist.

A scenario describes the occurrence of a conjunction of events that leads to a loss. But what is the risk exposed object precisely? For example, let us consider an internal fraud on transfers. An employee issues and processes fraudulent transfers. What is the exposed object? The transfer? The employee? The beneficiary of the transfer?

A way of answering this question is to consider doubling the exposure.

All things being equal, for which hypothesis do we consider that the risk will be increased?

- If we double the number of transfers
- If we double the number of employees
- If we double the number of clients

Even if we consider that increasing the activity or the number of transfers or clients can, marginally, encourage the employees to commit fraud, the correct answer is clearly the second one.

Are employees independently exposed to this risk? Yes, if we consider that the employee's fraud motivations are strictly personal (gambling debts, lifestyle incompatible with his/her salary, etc.) and as such are not contagious: the fact that an employee is a fraudster does not increase in an obvious manner the probability of another member of his or her team engaging in fraudulent activities.

Can an employee also be hit several times in the year? No, if we consider that the impact of the loss is the sum of all his or her fraudulent activity.

Under these conditions, the employee is the object effectively exposed to the fraud risk. This verifies the above conditions:

- The exposure units are exposed independently of the risk.
- Each exposure unit cannot be hit more than once a year.

The second exposure choice rule sometimes raises practical difficulties.

The conditions that can guarantee the uniqueness of the loss impacting an object are the following:

- It is a transitional object, and the loss is of the same essence as the object: for example, a data entry error on a transaction. A transaction that is issued is, or is not, correct. Once issued, it disappears, and it makes therefore no sense to consider that it could be hit twice. Similarly, the definitive judgment relating to a lawsuit is only pronounced once.
- It is a physical object which is destroyed by the loss: a building hit by a fire for example.
- The considered loss can take place only once per year at the most: for example, a fine on an inexact fiscal reporting can happen only during a control, and thus once a year at the most.

However, some scenarios do not always fall into one of these situations.

For instance, a server breakdown can happen several times in the year. A customer's confidential data can be stolen – notably on the internet – several times in the year. A building can, in theory, be flooded twice in one year, and maybe even more often.

Two methods are proposed to bypass this difficulty:

1. Changing the exposed object. For example, in the case of a data theft on the internet, it can be preferable to use the session as an exposure unit, rather than the customer. A session can be hacked only once.

2. Using "time slices". For example, a server is exposed 365 days a year, and can in theory break down once every day. If we take a look at failures with a significant length (from 3 to 24 hours), only one of these failures can happen each day. Therefore, we can consider that the appropriate exposure unit is the "server.day". The number of these units, somehow artificial, is equal to 365 times the number of servers. Each of these units only has a limited life time – one day – and can be hit by an unavailability only once.

This approach is a pragmatic implementation of the mathematically rigorous approach which would consist in considering an "instantaneous peril" and in defining the probability of an object being hit during an infinitesimal period, in other words dp/dt.

14.1.2 Choice of the Key Risk Indicators (KRIs)

The Key Risk Indicators are the drivers having an influence on one of the three risk variables: exposure, occurrence, and impact.

The process for selecting indicators is straightforward. We outline it hereafter, and we will give more details further for specific drivers of exposure, occurrence, and impact.

First of all, only a variable with a *causal*–type of influence on one of the risk variables can be selected as a risk indicator.

The KRI notion used in the literature sometimes describes a different reality: KRIs are often seen as an *indication* of a risk increase, without this link being necessarily causal. An indicator is then a parameter that can serve as a clue on the state of one of the nonmeasurable risk causes, but which is not in itself a driver of the risk.

Let us consider, for example, the "fat finger" risk, that is, the risk of error in data entry: the occurrence probability of this risk increases if the workload of the operator increases. A heavier work load will also tend to increase the operation process time span. Thereby, the underlying causal model is as follows:

- The workload is a cause of errors.
- The workload is a cause of slowdown.

In these conditions, an increase in the processing time can be a clue of an increased work load, and, consequently, of an increased risk. But the processing time cannot be considered as a risk driver. This kind of indicator is not considered in our approach.

Once the choice of the indicators is effectively limited to the causes of exposure, occurrence or impact, we can distinguish four indicator types:

1. Nonmeasurable indicators
2. Measurable indicators
3. Predictable indicators
4. Controllable indicators

Nonmeasurable indicators have links with one of the risk factors, yet it is not easy to measure them either by expert assessment, or objectively. For example, agents' workload, training level, and so on, will often be mentioned as risk causes in error risks, but are indeed difficult to quantify. This type of indicator is most often involved when modelling the occurrence probability.

We can establish a distribution for *measurable indicators*, even if we cannot predict them. For example, the market variation – stock markets or currencies – often plays a role in the evaluation of the impact of a risk of error involving market operations. Such variation is of course very difficult to forecast. And even if we had reliable forecasting models, they would be of no use as the moment of occurrence of a loss cannot be foreseen. However, the distribution of this variation, or in other words its range, gives information on the variability of the modelled risk. Even if the loss happens in a totally unforeseeable way, we can probabilise the market variation on the day of its occurrence: we thus can quantify the probability of a sharp variation causing a significant loss. This type of indicator intervenes most often to model the impact.

Predictable indicators are those for which a forecast, at least by expert assessment, can be established. They are generally exposure indicators, as long as the exposure is related to activity and activity forecasts can be established.

Controllable indicators are those for which a prior decision can modify the distribution. They are essential indicators, since they offer a possibility of action on the risk, and therefore of mitigation. Most often, exposure and impact indicators are controllable, more rarely probability indicators. At the most general level there are three types of reduction measures: Avoidance (exposure reduction), Prevention (occurrence probability reduction), and Protection (impact reduction). Reducing the number of persons who have access to sensitive data is a reduction action which can be made: it has a direct impact on the fraud risk cost, and this impact can be evaluated. Reducing the cap of certain operations directly reduces the impact, which can also be evaluated. On the other hand, the effect of a prevention measure – for example implementing an additional control – is difficult to evaluate. This discussion should be considered with the section further on, "Taking into Account the Existing Mitigation Systems".

14.1.3 Modelling and Conditioning the Exposure

14.1.3.1 Principles The fact that the exposure is a random variable may not be obvious. It seems that the number of exposed objects, once the appropriate measure is defined, is an indicator, and not a variable.

It is important to remember that the evaluation of operational risks, as any risk management activity, is a forecasting activity: risks must be quantified for the forthcoming year. The quantification of the exposure must then be a forecast.

This forecast can be relatively simple for stable activities, but more uncertain for fast-growing activities (in the case of a possible merger, for example).

The drivers that may cause exposure to change are of two types: external factors, for example, macroeconomic; or internal factors, notably strategic or commercial decisions.

In practice, we will generally consider expert based forecast assessments. In particular assessments based on commercial action plans are recommended as they contribute to express the link between risk and return.

It is important to remember that the growth forecasts cannot be considered as independent from one activity to another. This will induce a correlation between two scenarios for which the exposure is linked to the activity growth.

14.1.3.2 Practice In practice, we recommend using the following approach for the exposure conditioning.

The exposure planned for year N+1 is equal to its value for year N, multiplied by a growth factor. This growth factor is evaluated by expert assessment, by formulating three hypotheses:

1. A low hypothesis
2. A medium hypothesis
3. A high hypothesis

These three hypotheses are assumed to have a probability of 25%, 50%, and 25%, respectively.

In certain particular cases, and notably concerning fraud risks, the exposure measure could be a fixed quantity, which takes into account the planned workforce reorganisation.

Every exposure indicator being the object of hypotheses is examined in its relation with general firm activity growth forecasts.

14.1.3.3 Modelling and Conditioning the Occurrence Occurrence modelling is generally the most difficult task.

To be coherent with the exposure definition, the occurrence must be defined as the following random variable:

> The event hits the exposed object during the next period (year).

The occurrence of an event will then always be a random Bernoulli variable, that is, which can only take the values "True" or "False". By assumption, the exposure unit is chosen to guarantee that an exposed object cannot be hit several times.

The minimum occurrence modelling consists in evaluating a probability: that the considered peril effectively hits the exposed object during the next period.

Three methods are possible for this evaluation:

1. Empirical evaluation
2. Theoretical evaluation
3. Subjective evaluation

Empirical and theoretical evaluations should be preferred when applicable.

14.1.3.3.1 Empirical Evaluation This evaluation is obtained simply by dividing the number of losses effectively observed in the past by the number of exposed objects in the past. If we have p years of observation, we consider that the loss probability is equal to the number of losses observed over these p years, divided by the sum of the number of objects exposed during these q years.

14.1.3.3.2 Theoretical Evaluation The theoretical evaluation of the loss probability, if it is unconditional, amounts to using an external evaluation. This type of evaluation is only applicable in the cases where the considered event is not specific to the firm, and where an external study can be used to evaluate this probability (health issues, logistics, and in certain legal cases).

This evaluation can be based upon:

- External experts, for instance government health experts, consulting firms specialising on fraud or data thefts,, and so on.
- An empirical evaluation over an external scope (for instance ORX)
- A causal analysis of the event

The last approach, namely the causal analysis, draws inspiration from industrial safety methods, such as causal trees. According to this approach, an event occurs only when several unfavourable conditions are observed simultaneously. If it is possible to identify these multiple causes, an empirical evaluation of the probability of each of the causes can be used.

14.1.3.3.3 Subjective Evaluation In case none of the preceding approaches can be used, we can use a subjective evaluation, that is, an expert assessment. This is notably the case if the available risk event data, with or without loss, is not representative of the activity or of the risk management system in place.

14.1.3.3.4 Occurrence Conditioning The conditioning of the occurrence, that is, the identification of the occurrence drivers, can be:

- A structural form, when the occurrence is analysed as the simultaneous occurrence of several events: causal analysis within the framework of a theoretical evaluation of the occurrence probability.
- A probabilistic form, when the probability of the occurrence, or of one of its causes, depends on the exposed object, or on external circumstances.

14.1.3.3.5 Practice In practice, the most common occurrence modelling approaches are in descending order:

- Empirical evaluation.
- Theoretical evaluation, decomposing occurrence into the conjunction of several drivers.
- Evaluation by expert assessment.

14.1.3.4 Modelling and Conditioning the Impact The third step in scenario modelling is modelling its impact.

It is important at this stage to consider a situation in which the loss has already taken place, and to try to identify the variables which could modify its impact: these variables can be linked to the exposed object or to the conditions in which the loss takes place.

In practical terms, the use of a simple "impact equation" is recommended. This equation expresses the fact that the loss impact is, for example, the sum of two terms, the product of an amount by a rate,, and so on. This breaking down is iterative: each of the drivers used in the equation can be in turn broken down into several other terms, and so on.

14.1.3.4.1 Suggested Cost Breakdown An initial breakdown to be considered is:

- Restitution/compensation costs
- Fraud/theft costs
- Loss/damage to physical assets
- Additional staff costs (overtime)
- Fines/penalties

14.1.3.4.2 Loss of Business Loss of business is not a direct cost, but the firm should be in position to face the loss of revenue when a major scenario occurs. In order to reflect the impact of a scenario on business, we suggest using the *loss of revenue on expected business*. This is a short-term measurement, and this choice could be discussed but we believe that loss of expected business should be considered when dealing with operational risk and more generally risk scenarios.

14.1.3.4.3 Impact on Capital Scenarios having an impact on business may have an impact on capital held to secure this business against other types of risk. In other words, when a scenario occurs and reduces the business, then a certain amount of capital can be released.

We do not consider this type of impact in scenarios.

14.1.3.5 Taking into Account the Existing Mitigation Systems The modelling is always carried out considering existing mitigation actions in place.

We consider indeed that it is vain to carry out risk modelling setting aside from these actions, insofar as the risk managers and the experts' knowledge and experience integrate the existence of these controls.

A probabilistic scenario model integrates the mitigation controls in place for year N. It can suggest or evoke certain mitigation measures in subsequent years. Under these conditions, it is possible to evaluate the potential benefit of a new mitigation action.

14.2 QUANTIFICATION

14.2.1 Definition

The quantification of a model is performed through the following operations:

- For every indicator in the model, and without a cause (model root indicators): by establishing their unconditional distribution.
- For every indicator in the model, and determined by one or several causes: by establishing their conditional distribution relatively to their causes.

The quantification is carried out from the following data and knowledge sources:

- Business data from information systems
- Internal loss data
- Expert assessment
- External loss data (such as ORX)

The quantification process is guided by the model graph which defines all the indicators used in the modelling. No indicator must be used in the quantification if it has not been mentioned and explained in the model graph.

14.2.2 Occurrence Quantification

The occurrence probability quantification is carried out according to three modes:

1. Empirical evaluation: comparing the number of losses effectively observed in the past with the number of objects exposed in the past.
2. Theoretical evaluation: in this case, the occurrence is broken down into several indicators, each being the object of a request.
3. Subjective evaluation (by expert assessment).

The empirical evaluation case is the one being discussed here.

To support this evaluation, we can use the following approaches:

- Some losses were observed within the firm during the past 10 years. The number of objects which were exposed during this period is assessed (E1).
- No loss was observed within the firm during the past 10 years, but some losses were observed over the extended scope (E2)
- No loss was observed in the industry during the past 10 years (E3).

The proposed evaluations for the probability of occurrence are detailed in Table 14.1.

14.2.3 Impact Quantification

Impact quantification often uses activity indicators, typically the distribution of certain amounts (claims, transactions, transfers, and so on) or the distribution of external indicators (rating, fines, and so on).

Some models use risk event data to calculate the impact indicators, which does not mean that these models should be considered as loss distribution approach models.

TABLE 14.1 Empirical Assessment of the Probability of Occurrence

Case	Scope	Observed Losses	Reference Exposure	Probability Evaluation	Comment
E1	Firm	k	$\sum X(i)$ Sum of exposures during the years considered for the firm	$k/X(i)$	
E2	Industry	k	$\sum X(i)$ Sum of the exposures over the available history and the industry.	$k/\sum X(i)$	
E3	Industry	0	$\sum X(i)$ Sum of the exposures over the available history and the industry.	$1/\sum X(i)$	One loss is considered conservatively.

For instance, in a scenario involving fines, comparing the fines with a company turnover, allows calculating a distribution of a "fine coefficient". This coefficient is then applied to every business unit, even for those which did not suffer a loss. This is a very different approach than an LDA approach applied to the recorded losses. The same type of approach can be applied to internal fraud, lawsuits, and so on.

With these principles laid out, we can now explain in more detail the rules for the evaluation of impact indicators used in the models. In every case the goal is to forecast: the indicators are supposed to represent the future, not the past.

The rules below therefore enable us to evaluate how to establish such a forecast: can we use recently observed risk event data, or should we on the contrary use the entire available past risk event data? Is the firm data sufficient or should we use outside data?

14.2.4 Indicator Characterisation

Four indicator characteristics, summarized in Table 14.2, will now be analysed.

14.2.4.1 Type of Indicator The indicators that are used in the impact models are of one of the following types:

- Boolean
- Label
- Numbered
- Interval

In most cases, the possible values of the variable (states) are known, and their probabilities must be assessed.

In some cases, the probabilities are predefined (for instance using percentiles) and the states of the variable needs to be assessed.

TABLE 14.2 Indicator Characteristics

Type	• Boolean • Label • Numbered • Interval
Variability	• Object • Context • Circumstances
Predictability	• Stable • Volatile • Tendency
Representativeness	• None • Internal • Sector

TABLE 14.3 Indicator Variability

Type	Example(s)	Data Variability
Object	Trade amount	The indicator is variable for each loss and must be considered with a distribution
Circumstances	Market variation	The indicator is variable for each loss and must be considered with a distribution
Context	Time to detection	The indicator is stable for the simulation year but can be considered with a certain uncertainty (for example a low medium high assumption LMH)

14.2.4.2 Indicator Variability A variable used to calculate the cost of a simulated loss may be related to:

- The specific object hit by the event
- The specific circumstances of the event
- The general context of the firm

The three cases are summarized in Table 14.3. For example, the impact of a data input error on a market trade depends on:

- The amount of the trade: This variable is related to the object
- The variation of the market in the days following the error: This variable is related to the circumstances of the loss
- The number of days before the error is detected: This variable is related to the context of the firm, and in particular the controls in place.

In the previous example, market variations during the days that follow the error depend on the day of the loss: if it happens at a time of high market volatility, it can have serious consequences, whereas if it takes place during a quiet period, the consequences will be less important. On the other hand, the time required to detect the error is related to the firm and is rather stable throughout the year.

14.2.4.3 Indicator Predictability Three cases are considered and summarized in Table 14.4.

TABLE 14.4 Indicator Predictability

Evolution	Predictability	Example(s)	Assessment
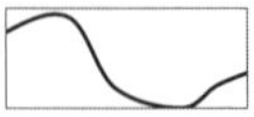	Stable indicator	Average credit card fraud amount	Value of the indicator for the previous year.
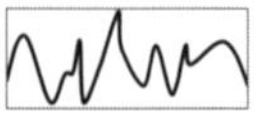	Volatile indicator	Annual return of the stock market	Average value of the indicator over a long period
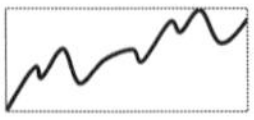	Trend indicator	Number of clients	Linear model

14.2.4.3.1 Stable Indicator The indicator shows some inertia, without any visible trend. The indicator does not vary much from one year to the next, but does over a longer period, without any tendency arising. In this case, the best forecast for year N+1 is the value of year N, if the latter can be assessed in a representative way. If not, we use data over a long period.

14.2.4.3.2 Volatile Indicator The indicator varies a lot from one year to the next, without any visible tendency over a long period. In this case the best forecast for year N+1 is the average indicator over a long period.

14.2.4.3.3 Trend Indicator The indicator shows a linear trend. In this case the best forecast for year N+1 is the one obtained by the trend model.

Other tendency types (cyclical, nonlinear etc.) could be considered, but are generally not, given the considered term of analysis. For a cyclical indicator, either the cycle is short, and in that case the indicator is considered "volatile", or the cycle is long, and the indicator is then considered to be "stable" over a short period.

14.2.4.4 Data Representativeness Once the indicator's predictability has been analysed, we have to determine whether internal data are sufficient, or if external data is necessary.

Three cases are considered, and summarized in Table 14.5.

1. Available internal data are sufficiently representative.
2. Available internal data are not sufficiently representative.
3. No data can be found.

14.2.4.4.1 Representative Internal Data If internal data is representative, then the indicator should be preferably assessed using this data. For example, for the individual amount claimed in a mis-selling action, the number of observed losses can be considered sufficiently important to use business unit data only.

14.2.4.4.2 External Representative Data If the data is observed only over a small number of cases internally, it is best to use external data. For example, if the firm has undergone only a few sanctions by control authorities, assessing the amount of these fines will be more robust if based upon the whole banking industry, or even the whole financial industry including insurance, given the larger scope of the represented situations. In some situations we may even resort to data from general industry – for instance in a "Breach of competition law" scenario.

14.2.4.4.3 No Representative Data This situation can arise if we consider for example a new activity, for which it is difficult to collect any relevant data.

TABLE 14.5 Data Representativeness

Representativeness	Example(s)	Assessment
Internal	Amount claimed in a mis-selling action	Internal data
Sector	Breach of competition law	All sectors data
None	Breach of GDPR regulation	By expert assessment on the basis of comparison with other regulations

TABLE 14.6 KRI Evaluation Based on Empirical Distribution

Interval	Probability	Minimum	Maximum
1	10%	Observed minimum	10% percentile (such that 10% of the KRI samples are below this value).
2	10%	10% percentile	20% percentile (such that 20% of the KRI samples are below this value).
...			
9	10%	80% percentile	90% percentile (such that 90% of the KRI samples are below this value).
10	9%	90% percentile	99% percentile (such that 99% of the KRI samples are below this value).
11	0.9%	99% percentile	99.9% percentile (such that 99.9% of the KRI samples are below this value).
12	0.1%	99.9% percentile	Observed maximum

14.2.4.5 Assessment Once the data characterisation has been performed, it is advisable to collect risk event data on the recommended scope, in order to effectively assess the KRI.

Depending on the situation, the techniques detailed below can be used:

14.2.4.5.1 Expert Assessment As with empirical evaluations, KRI evaluations by expert assessment are as much as possible performed with three assumptions:

1. A low hypothesis, generally favourable
2. A medium hypothesis
3. A high hypothesis, generally adverse

The probabilities for these assumptions are assumed to be 25% for low and high, and 50% for medium. This is useful to encourage experts to consider a range rather than a single assumption.

14.2.4.5.2 Evaluation Based on Empirical Distributions It is advised that KRIs based on empirical data are divided into 12 intervals, as shown in Table 14.6.

The last two intervals are used to avoir an overestimation of extreme events. Indeed, we generally note a change in the order of magnitude between the 90% quantile and the maximum. This change in magnitude generally only concerns very few and rare data points. Under these conditions, using a uniform assumption between the 90% quantile and the maximum would lead to greatly overevaluating the probability of extremes.

14.3 SIMULATION

14.3.1 The Bayesian Network Scenario Model

14.3.1.1 Introduction The last quantification stage of a scenario model is its simulation. The simulation of this model allows the precise evaluation of the variability of the cost of the scenario: the goal of the simulation is to establish the distribution of the potential losses due to the scenario.

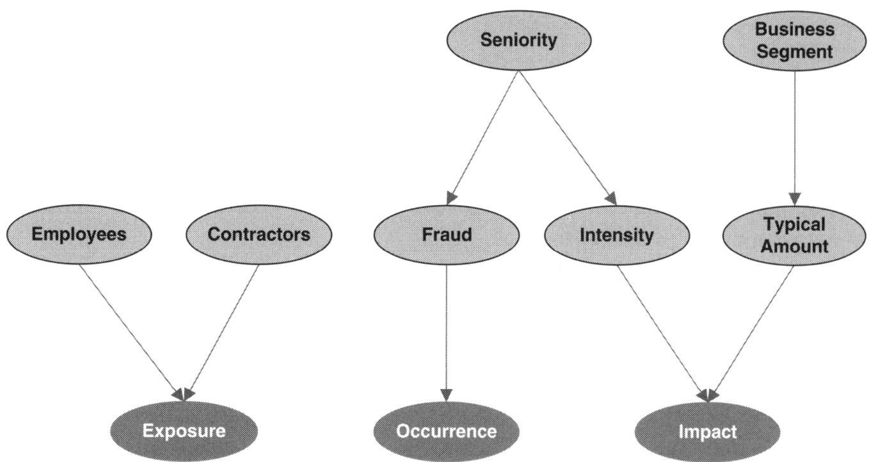

FIGURE 14.1 Representation of a Scenario as a Bayesian Network

The model used in the simulation is automatically generated from the structure and quantification detailed above.

The model expresses the conditional distribution of the three risk variables:

1. Exposure
2. Occurrence
3. Impact

This model is made of two parts:

1. A graph, which is the direct representation of the structure.
2. A set of probability tables, which result directly from the quantification.

14.3.1.2 Representation of a Scenario as a Bayesian Network An example of the representation of a scenario using a Bayesian network is shown in Figure 14.1.

Exposure

The **Exposure** is the sum of the number of employees (**Employees**) and of the number of contractors (**Contractors**).

Occurrence

For each exposed person, the **Occurrence** is equal to the occurrence of a **Fraud**.

The probability of occurrence of a **Fraud** depends on the **Seniority** of the considered employee.

(*Continued*)

Impact

The impact is the product of:

- The typical amount traded in the considered business area (**TypicalAmount**)
- The number of fraudulent transactions the fraudster will be able to issue before being stopped (**FraudIntensity**)

The typical amount (TypicalAmount) traded depends on the considered business area (**BusinessArea**)

The number of fraudulent transactions (FraudIntensity) depends on the seniority of the employee (Seniority).

14.3.2 Bayesian Network Simulation

14.3.2.1 Goal Reminder The simulation aims at building the distribution of the potential cost of the scenario for the year to come, and to observe some metrics based on this distribution:

- The EL (Expected Loss): Mathematical expectation of the cumulated loss over one year.
- The VaR (ValueAtRisk at 99.9%): Annual cumulated loss which can be exceeded with a probability of 1 in 1000.

There are three risk variability factors:

1. The exposure: Next year, the number of exposed objects can change.
2. The occurrence: As each object is exposed to the risk, each of them can suffer a loss. The number of losses varies from 0 to the number of exposed objects.
3. The impact: The amount of the loss can vary depending on the characteristics of the exposed object or the circumstances under which the loss takes place.

14.3.2.2 Simplified Algorithm The simulation principle is therefore very simple, and can be explained as follows:

Repeat the following operations a large number of times (e.g., S = 1 million)
    Sample the exposure*, that is, sample an X_i value from the random variable "Exposure", according to its marginal distribution.*
    For each object *between 1 and* X_i
        Sample the occurrence*, that is, sample the random binary variable "Occurrence" following its marginal probability. In other words, decide whether the exposed object is or is not hit.*
        If there is an occurrence, ***sample the impact*** *of the loss, that is, sample the random variable "Impact" following its marginal probability.*
    Add the costs *of every loss that occurred, and record the cumulated loss* L_i
Organise the cumulated losses L_i *in an array, and deduct an empirical distribution.*

This algorithm gives a flavour of the Monte-Carlo simulation being used, but this is an approximation of the true algorithm. Indeed, in certain models, links can exist between the Exposure and the Occurrence, or the Occurrence and the Impact.

For example, in the internal fraud model example above, we notice that:

- The hierarchical level of the employee drives the Occurrence (in other words, the probability of fraud depends on the hierarchical level of the employee).
- The hierarchical level of the employee also drives the Impact (in other words, the distribution of the fraud amount depends on the hierarchical level of the employee through his or her salary range).

Under such conditions, sampling the Occurrence and the Impact independently would lead to an error.

14.3.2.3 Detailed Algorithm

Repeat a large number of times (N = 1 Million)

  Sample the Exposure

    Identify every node that is a direct or indirect exposure cause.

    For each of these nodes:

      If it has no parent, sample it according to its unconditional distribution.

      If there are one or several parents, wait until every parent is sampled, then sample the node conditionally to the observed values of these parents

    Sample the exposure conditionally to its parents.

  For each exposed object

    Sample the Occurrence

      Identify every node that is a direct or indirect occurrence cause.

      For each of these nodes:

        If it has already been sampled as part of exposure sampling, do not resample it.

        Otherwise:

          If it has no parent, sample it according to its unconditional distribution.

          If it has one or several parents, wait until every parent is sampled, then sample the node conditionally to the observed values of these parents.

      Sample the occurrence conditionally to its parents.

    Sample the Impact

      Identify every node that is a direct or indirect impact cause.

      For each of these nodes:

        If it has already been sampled as part of the exposure or of the occurrence sampling, do not resample it.

        Otherwise

          If it has no parent, sample it according to its unconditional distribution.

If it has one or several parents, wait until every parent is sampled, then sample the node conditionally to the observed values of these parents.

Sample the impact conditionally to its parents.

Add the costs of every loss which took place, and record the total loss L_i.

Sort the cumulated losses L_i in a table, and deduct an empirical distribution.

CHAPTER 15

A Scenario in Internal Fraud

15.1 INTRODUCTION

As the simple example in Chapter 14 illustrates, the exposure measurement for internal fraud is generally the number of employees. Employees having access to specific functions could potentially perpetrate a fraud in their domain.

- Accountants with appropriate credentials could find a way to create fake suppliers in the accounting system and initiate payments.
- Employees having access to large volumes of unencrypted card data could compromise these data and sell them to criminal networks.
- Traders can take unauthorized positions to cover past losses, or even create fictitious positions to accumulate profit. This is the example we will now study in detail.

15.2 XOI MODELLING

15.2.1 Analysis

We will now analyse in more detail the "Rogue Trading" scenario.

The history of Rogue Trading cases goes back to the nineties with the Baring's case, and significant cases are publicly disclosed on a regular basis. Table 15.1 lists the most significant cases from 1995.

The fact that rogue trading activities can also lead to a profit suggests that some major cases may not have been disclosed.

This XOI scenario is a stylized representation of the recent cases of rogue trading (the Goldman Sachs case in 2007, the Société Générale case in 2008, and the UBS case in 2011).

All these cases share a similar mechanism:

- The rogue trader designs a mechanism to conceal a trading position. This mechanism usually involves creating fictitious positions that cancels the market risk of the fraudulent position.

TABLE 15.1 Rogue Trading Cases

Year	Institution	Product	Amount ($ billion)
1995	Barings Bank	Nikkei Futures	1.3
1995	Resona		1.1
1996	Sumimoto	Copper	2.6
2002	Allied Irish Bank	FX Options	0.69
2004	National Australia Bank	FX Options	0.19
2005	China Aviation Oil	Jet Fuel Futures	0.55
2007	Goldman Sachs		0.12
2008	Société Générale	Stock Index futures	6.9
2011	UBS	Stock Index futures	2.3

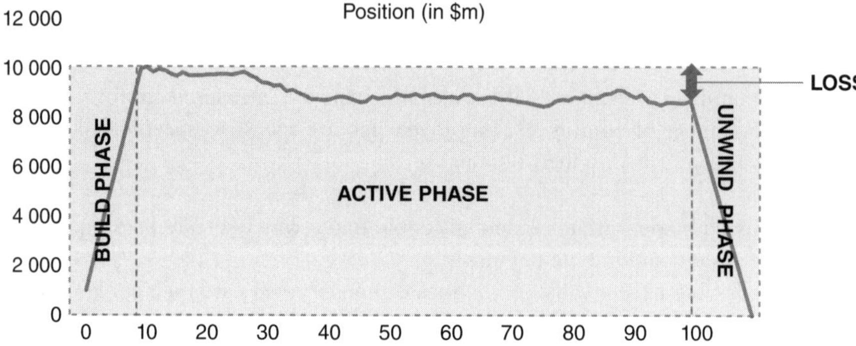

FIGURE 15.1 Daily Evolution of a Concealed Trading Position

- Using this mechanism, the trader builds a large, unhedged direction position, which is kept active for several days or weeks.
- As the market does not move in favour of the trader's bet, the position accumulates latent losses.
- At some point, thanks to internal monitoring systems, reconciliation with third parties, or as a consequence of an error of the trader in his concealment activity, the position is identified and unwound.
- The bank needs to acknowledge the market loss.

The calculation of the potential loss uses some typical market risk assumptions.

First, for simplicity reasons, we do not consider the fact that the position exposed is smaller at the beginning (build phase) and at the end (unwind phase). We consider that the position exposed is constant for the calculations of P&L (see Figure 15.1).

While the position is alive, P&L are recorded every day as the market moves. The market daily change is assumed to follow a normal distribution of mean 0 and of standard deviation σ.

At the end of the active period, either a loss or a gain is observed. The fraction "Cumulated P&L / Position" at the end of the period is follows a normal law of mean 0 and standard deviation $\sigma.\sqrt{T}$. where T is the time during which the position was active. For T days, it means that the

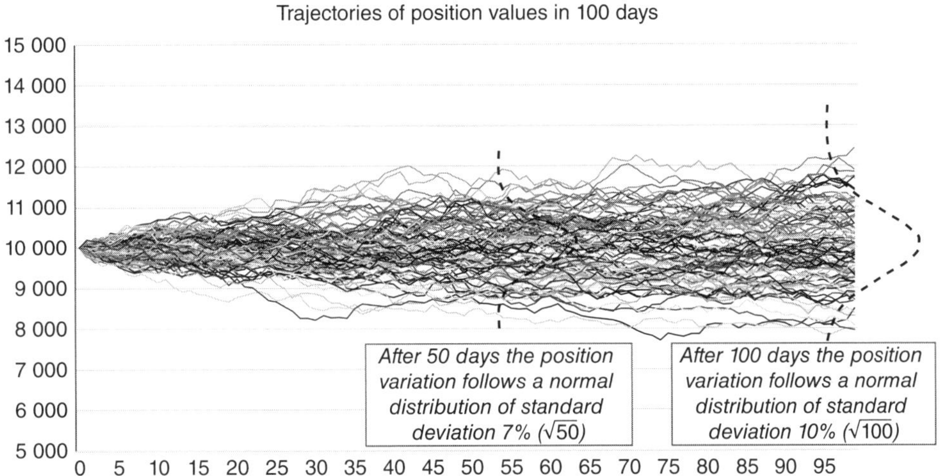

FIGURE 15.2 Variations of a Concealed Trading Position

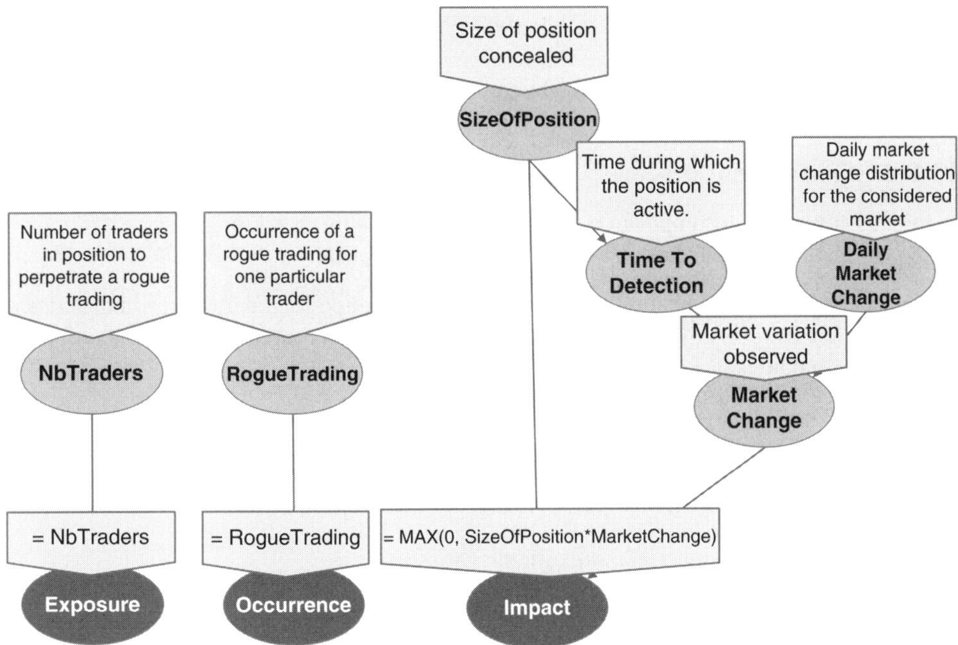

FIGURE 15.3 XOI Model for Rogue Trading Scenario

position at the end will be equal to k times the initial position, where k follows a normal law of mean 0 and standard deviation $\sigma.\sqrt{T}$.

This is illustrated in Figure 15.2, using an assumption of $\sigma = 1\%$.

TABLE 15.2 Quantification of Rogue Trading Drivers

Dimension	Driver	Suggested Quantification Method
Exposure	Number of traders	Observation
Occurrence	Rogue trading	External data, based on the number of observed cases and an estimate of the population of traders
Impact	Size of position	Expert judgement informed by external cases
Impact	Time to detection	Expert judgement informed by external cases
Impact	Daily market change	Observed market variation

15.2.2 Structure

Based on the analysis above, the XOI approach of this scenario can be summarized as follows:

- A trader intentionally and successfully circumvents the controls, and builds a large position. The position is detected and unwound after several weeks.
- The objects exposed to the risk are the traders.
- The scenario occurs if one of these traders go rogue.
- The impact is the size of the position times the market variation observed.

The graph in Figure 15.3 represents the loss generation mechanism above.

15.2.3 Quantification

Using this structured decomposition, the quantification approach is straightforward, although the quantification of some drivers will require expert judgment, as shown in Table 15.2.

The *number of traders* in position to perpetrate a rogue trading can be observed in the considered firm. Usually, it is advised to consider front-office traders trading derivatives on bonds, equities, commodities or FX.

For the purposes of the exercise, let us consider that this number is 500 in the considered firm. However, as they may exist some interrogation about the exact population to consider, and also because the scenario is analysed for the future, it can be useful to consider a range rather than an exact number. We will use the 400-600 range.

The *probability of occurrence* is more difficult to assess.

We will use the case E2 as referenced in the methodology:

- No loss has been observed for the firm.
- Some losses have been observed in the industry.

We need to assess the probability as:

$$\frac{2.\ Number\ of\ Observed\ Rogue\ Trading\ Cases}{20\ years.\ TotalNumberOfExposedTraders}$$

TABLE 15.3 Assessment of Concealed Trading Positions

Assumption	Range	Probability
Low	\$1–3 billion	25%
Medium	\$3–5 billion	50%
High	\$5–10 billion	25%

The number of observed rogue trading cases is 9. As mentioned earlier, it is reasonable to consider that only half of the cases have been publicly disclosed, at least be some rogue traders may have realized profits. This is the explanation for the factor 2 in the formula above. These cases have been observed from 1995 to 2017, which we round to 20 years.

The next question is the number of exposed traders in the industry. This might be more difficult to quantify, but there are a number of studies which evaluate the number of front office FTE[1]. This number has been estimated to around 50,000 in 2017, and has significantly decreased. Assuming that only 20% of this population is trading derivatives on equities, bonds, commodities of FX, this yields a population exposed of approximately10,000 as of today. As this population has decreased, we are conservative is assessing the probability as:

$$\frac{2.10\ cases\ (rounded\ up)}{20\ years.\ 10000\ traders\ (rounded\ down)} = 0.01\%$$

The *size of the concealed position* is more difficult to assess. We know for instance that Kerviel (Société Générale) position was close to €50 billion. The position of Adoboli was around \$12 billion, according to news reporting prosecutor explanations. Similarly, the position of Matthew Taylor (Goldman-Sachs) was reported at \$8.3 billion.

For the purposes of our discussion, we will assume three sizes of positions, summarized in Table 15.3.

This type of assessments will typically be discussed with subject matter experts, considering the size of the market activity of the firm, the controls in place, and so on.

Finally, the *time to detection* also requires expert opinion. Adoboli maintained his fraudulent positions during the summer 2011. The case of Kerviel is more complex. According to the "Mission Green" Report of the General Inspection of the Bank, Kerviel started his fraudulent activities back in 2005. In January 2007, he builds a large short position on DAX futures, which reaches almost €6 billion in March 2007, and €30 billion in July 2007. The position is then cut and rebuilt from September onwards, but all fraudulent positions are zeroed by December 31, 2007.

The huge €50 billion position is built from December 31, 2017, and cut on January 18.

Therefore, although the rogue position was maintained for less than three weeks, various concealed positions have been built, maintained and unwound from at least January 2007.

[1] See, for instance, Coalition (https://www.coalition.com/).

TABLE 15.4 Assessment of Time to Detection

Size of Position	Range	Time to Detection
Low	\$1–3 billion	10 to 30 weeks
Medium	\$3–5 billion	5 to 20 weeks
High	\$5–10 billion	5 to 20 weeks

For the purposes of our discussion, we have assumed that the time to detection was depending on the size of the positions. Larger positions are assumed to be detected sooner as they may generate control activities (as for instance they may generate large margin calls). The assumptions are summarized in Table 15.4.

15.2.4 Simulation

Repeat a large number of times (N = 1 Million)

Sample the Exposure

Identify every node that is a direct or indirect exposure cause:

- *NbTraders*

Sample it according to its unconditional distribution:

Uniform [400–600]

Sample the exposure conditionally to its parents.

Exposure = NbTraders

For each exposed Trader

Sample the Occurrence

Identify every node that is a direct or indirect occurrence cause.

- *RogueTrading*

  Sample it according to its unconditional distribution.

  Binomial with P(True)=0.01%

Sample the occurrence conditionally to its parents.

Occurrence = RogueTrading

Sample the Impact

Identify every node that is a direct or indirect impact cause.

SizeOfPosition

TimeToDetection

DailyMarketChange

MarketChange

For each of these nodes:

Sample in order:

- *Nodes with no parents*
  - *SizeOfPosition*
  - *DailyMarketChange*
- *Node dependent of SizeOfPosition*
  - *TimeToDetection*
- *Formula dependent nodes*
  - *MarketChange*

Sample the impact conditionally to its parents.
SizeOPosition
MarketChange
Add the costs of every loss that took place, and record the total loss L_i.
Sort the cumulated losses L_i ***in a table, and deduct an empirical distribution.***

This simulation[2] yields the results represented in Figure 15.4.

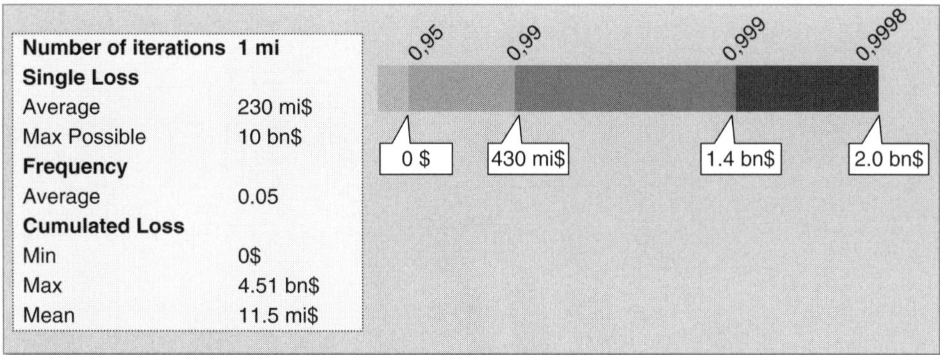

FIGURE 15.4 Simulation of the XOI Model for Rogue Trading
All statistics shown are the result of the combination of the initial assumptions.

[2]The simulations are performed using the MSTAR tool, which is an implementation of the XOI model.

CHAPTER 16
A Scenario in Cyber Risk

16.1 DEFINITION

16.1.1 The First Cyber Attacks: Card Data Breaches

When we started working on operational risk, 10–15 years ago, some of our clients considered IT risk and logistics as a common risk domain. This seemed justified at that time, since these are support functions that are not directly linked to the banking business. Compared to other support functions, such as human resources or accounting, IT and logistics are much more technical and require extensive expert knowledge. The nature of the knowledge involved makes communication between risk analysts, business experts, and technical experts sometimes difficult.

By considering buildings, power supply, telecommunications, and information technology within a broad logistics function, the types of risks considered were implicitly limited to external supply failures or internal errors or failures.

If this seems like a distant past to you, it is worth remembering that in 2001, less than 20% of American households had an online bank account, and only 50% banked online in 2009. An interesting infographic on this topic is available on the Wells Fargo website[1].

The only domain for which the explicit notion of attack was identified was card payment. France, a country considered to be the inventor of the smart card[2], has always been a pioneer in the field of credit card payment. The creation by French banks of an economic interest grouping, "GIE Carte Bancaires"[3], to share the technical infrastructure necessary for card payments, has contributed to the identification of systemic risks associated with cards. Indeed, the fact that a bank could, by managing payments received by its merchant customers (acquiring side), handle card data from customers of other banks (issuing side) highlighted the banks' interdependence with regard to this risk. In addition, other actors a priori less secure than banks, such as major retailers, also had access to large volumes of data.

[1]Wells Fargo, "20 Years of Internet Banking", https://www.wellsfargohistory.com/internet-banking/ (accessed 5/10/2018).

[2]Kevin J. O'Brien, *New York Times,* "Smart Card – Invented Here", https://www.nytimes.com/2005/08/10/world/europe/smart-card-invented-here.html (accessed 5/10/2018).

[3]Cartes Bancaires, http://www.cartes-bancaires.com/ (accessed 5/10/2018).

Finally, credit card data potentially provides access to payments, which naturally made them critical data. Although France had developed and equipped its bank cards with chips that made them almost inviolable, the fact that these cards could be used abroad without the chip being activated further reinforced the systemic nature of risk.

No matter how good the protection system put in place, using sensitive data in an open world made banks vulnerable to attacks, far from their own information systems.

Credit card fraud remains one of the most important and significant risks related to information processing. In the past 10 years, around 10 major cases involving the compromise of more than 5 million records have been observed, with a maximum of at least 130 million records for Heartland compromise in 2009. The Heartland case is estimated to have resulted to $300 million losses for banks in the United States[4].

In 2013, another major card breach was perpetrated in Target, one of the largest US retail chains, by criminals who stole 40 million credit and debit card numbers.

Target has reported data breach costs of $248 million, where other sources estimates range from $240 million to $2.2 billion in fraudulent charges alone[5].

16.1.2 Trending: Customer Data Breaches

The digitalization of most economic exchanges naturally increases the fear of new type of cyber attacks. The recent Federal Reserve paper "Cyber Attacks and the Digital Dilemma" sums it up perfectly: "With the power and convenience of greater connectivity comes more potential for vulnerability to intruders."[6]

Personal information is considered a key type of data, as of course massive volumes of such data are stored in databases and in the cloud.

The question of personal data breaches receives a lot of attention from regulators and from banks, but the consequences for banks remain difficult to assess, except of course if we consider potential regulator fines.

Although the Ponemon Institute proposes a cost of about $7–8 per record for a massive compromise (over 10 million records)[7], this cost does not necessarily seem to be confirmed in reality.

In 2014, JP Morgan Chase reported to the SEC a major data compromise, affecting 76 million homes and 7 million small businesses[8]. This is potentially the largest possible attack on customer data in the United States, although the bank indicated that no specific banking data had been compromised (account number, password, and so on). JP Morgan stated that it was not

[4]US Secret Service, "Sentencing in Largest Data Breach Prosecuted in United States", https://www.secretservice.gov/data/press/releases/2018/18-FEB/GPA_07-18_Drinkman-Smilianets_Sentencing_2.pdf (accessed 5/10/2018).

[5]Congressional Research Service, "The Target and Other Financial Data Breaches", https://fas.org/sgp/crs/misc/R43496.pdf (accessed 5/10/2018).

[6]The Federal Reserve of Richmond, "Cyberattacks and the Digital Dilemma", https://www.richmondfed.org/-/media/richmondfedorg/publications/research/econ_focus/2017/q3/cover_story.pdf (accessed 5/10/2018).

[7]IBM, "Ponemon Institute's 2017 Cost of Data Breach Study", https://www-01.ibm.com/common/ssi/cgi-bin/ssialias (accessed 5/10/2018).

[8]US SEC. JPMorgan Chase & Co Form 8K, October 2, 2014, https://www.documentcloud.org/documents/1308629-jpmorgan-on-cyberattack.html (accessed 5/10/2018).

seeing any "unusual fraud activity" resulting from the breach meaning that the hackers have not used the information they obtained for fraudulent purposes.

The hidden cost of data breaches is a common topic of discussion in scenario analysis workshops. The impact on customer loyalty and the impact on share price are regularly discussed in data compromise scenarios, without the experts really proposing any quantification options. As an example, we looked at the consequences of the JP Morgan Chase data breach on its customer loyalty and stock price.

For customer loyalty, the Ponemon Institute reports that the "abnormal churn rate" is on average 3.4% for all industries and 6.1% for financial institutions.

Interestingly, if we look at the total deposits reported by JP Morgan Chase from 2011 to 2017 in their annual report, the only year when we observe a decrease is 2015, after the October 2014 breach.

The total deposits of JP Morgan Chase decreased from $1.36 trillion to $1.28 trillion, that is, exactly 6.1% (see Table 16.1 and the corresponding graph in Figure 16.1). During the same

TABLE 16.1 Evolution of JP Morgan Chase Deposits, 2011–2017

	Deposits ($m)	Growth
2011	1 127 806	–
2012	1 193 593	5,8%
2013	1 287 765	7,9%
2014	1 363 427	5,9%
2015	**1 279 715**	**–6,1%**
2016	1 375 176	7,5%
2017	1 443 982	5,0%

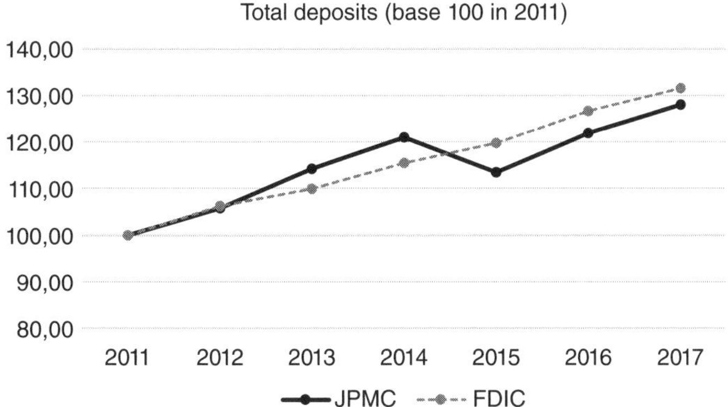

FIGURE 16.1 Evolution of Deposits for JPMorgan Chase and Total FDIC
The charts are scaled to base 100 in 2011. The decrease in 2015 is due to the reduction of nonoperating deposits, and is not related to an impact of the major2014 data-breach on customer loyalty.

periods the total US deposits reported by FDIC grew steadily. But in the 2015 exercise, systemic banks had to implement a new definition of cash[9]: The regulators required that only the cash required to fund a company's upcoming payments would be likely to remain on deposit during a time of stress. For this reason, JPMC reports that they have reduced nonoperating deposits of $200 billion. Therefore, in reality, no effective decrease of deposits have been observed as a consequence of the data breach.

For stock price, several studies, including a specific report from Centrify and the Ponemon Institute, report a drop of share price of approximately 2% for US firms suffering a databreach[10], which is recovered in a couple of months.

It is not clear either if this finding does apply to JP Morgan Chase, as we effectively observe a drop of share price in October 2014 (see Figure 16.2), but the recovery is quite fast and the performance over three years seems stable (see Figure 16.3).

The average daily return of JPM stock is 0.027% during the year before the event, and 0.035% during the event.

Of course, this is just an example. However, given that JP Morgan has probably suffered one of the largest personal data breaches to date, the additional consequences of personal data breaches, on customer loyalty or share price, seem questionable or, at least, can be minimized if managed properly.

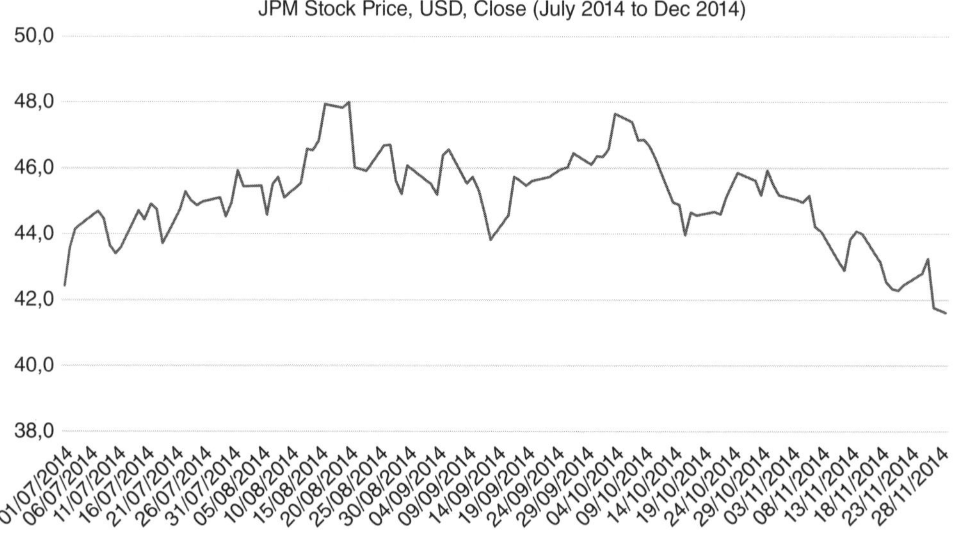

FIGURE 16.2 JPMC Share Price in the Period Before and After the Data Compromise
There is a slight decrease in October 2014, which does not appear significant if we look at a longer period.

---

[9]JPMorgan Chase, "A Defining Moment", https://www.jpmorgan.com/jpmpdf/1320694326138.pdf (accessed 5/10/2018).

[10]Centrify and Ponemon Institute, "The Impact of Data Breaches on Reputation and Share Value", May 2017, https://www.centrify.com/media/4737054/ponemon_data_breach_impact_study.pdf (accessed 5/10/2018).

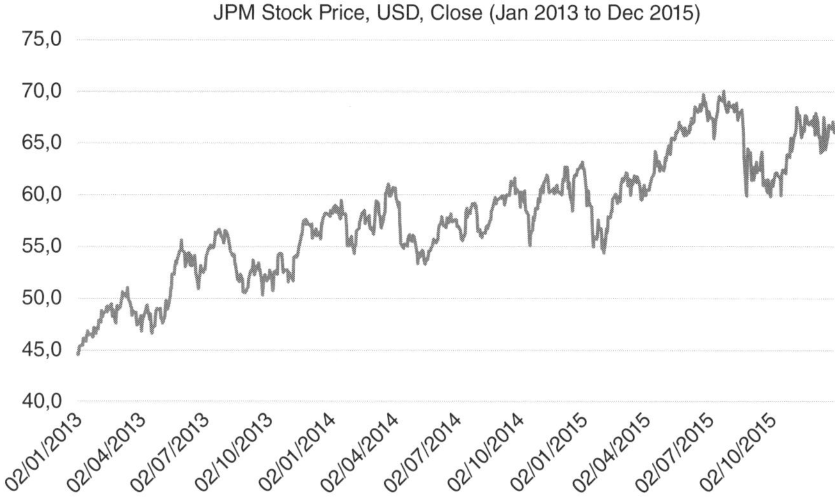

FIGURE 16.3 JPMC Share Price One Year Before and After the Data Compromise
The trend is not impacted.

16.1.3 Generalisation: The Cyber Attack Wheel

There exist several taxonomies of Cyber Risk, one of the most complete being the Carnegie-Mellon CERT taxonomy[11].

The CERT defines "*Operational cyber security risks*" as "*operational risks to information and technology assets that have consequences affecting the confidentiality, availability, or integrity of information or information systems.*"

The CERT taxonomy considers four main classes:

1. Actions of people – action, or lack of action, taken by people either deliberately or accidentally that impact cyber security
2. Systems and technology failures – failure of hardware, software, and information systems
3. Failed internal processes – problems in the internal business processes that impact the ability to implement, manage, and sustain cyber security, such as process design, execution, and control
4. External events – issues often outside the control of the organization, such as disasters, legal issues, business issues, and service provider dependencies.

This definition rightly covers both intentional and nonintentional causes. As the recent MFI report on cyber risk[12] notes: "Cyber risk can be unrelated to cyber-attacks: for example, software updates or natural disasters can lead to the crystallization of cyber risk through business disruptions without any nefarious intent".

[11]CERT, "A Taxonomy of Operational Cyber Security Risks Version 2", https://resources.sei.cmu.edu/asset_files/TechnicalNote/2014_004_001_91026.pdf (accessed 5/10/2018).

[12]International Monetary Fund, "Cyber Risk for the Financial Sector: A Framework for Quantitative Assessment", https://www.imf.org/en/Publications/WP/Issues/2018/06/22/Cyber-Risk-for-the-Financial-Sector-A-Framework-for-Quantitative-Assessment-45924 (accessed 5/10/2018).

In our practice however, we have noticed that banks tend to separate the main classes above in such a way that:

- Action of people is considered as the true "Cyber risk".
- Systems and technology failures are considered as "Technology risk".
- External events are considered as "Supplier failure" or "External disruption".

In the discussion that follows, we will therefore consider mainly "cyber attacks", although we propose a general definition of cyber attacks based on three dimensions of analysis:

1. What is the critical resource that can be accessed through an attack?
2. How can this critical resource be attacked?
3. Who has interest to attack this resource and why?

If we think for instance of the type of attacks being discussed:

- A card data compromise is typically perpetrated by criminal networks as it is possible to monetize card data, and it can be perpetrated through merchants – which is usually the weakest point of the system, or possibly through employees.
- A personal data breach is typically less interesting for criminals as personal data cannot be monetized as easily as card data, but can be of a lot of interest for competitors or political activists

The proposed generalization, which can be of course adapted and enhanced, is based on the categorisation presented in Table 16.2.

This allows us to define the following "Cyber Attack" wheel, represented in Figure 16.4.

The various cyber scenarios are defined by combining three criteria: the attackers, the access and the assets. Who is attacking what and how will define the storyline of the cyber risk scenario.

TABLE 16.2 Cyber Attacks: Attackers, Access, and Assets

Attackers	Criminal networks Political activists Foreign governments Competitors
Access	Internet or specialized networks Third parties Employees
Assets	Card data Customer data Business data Trade secrets Applications Funds

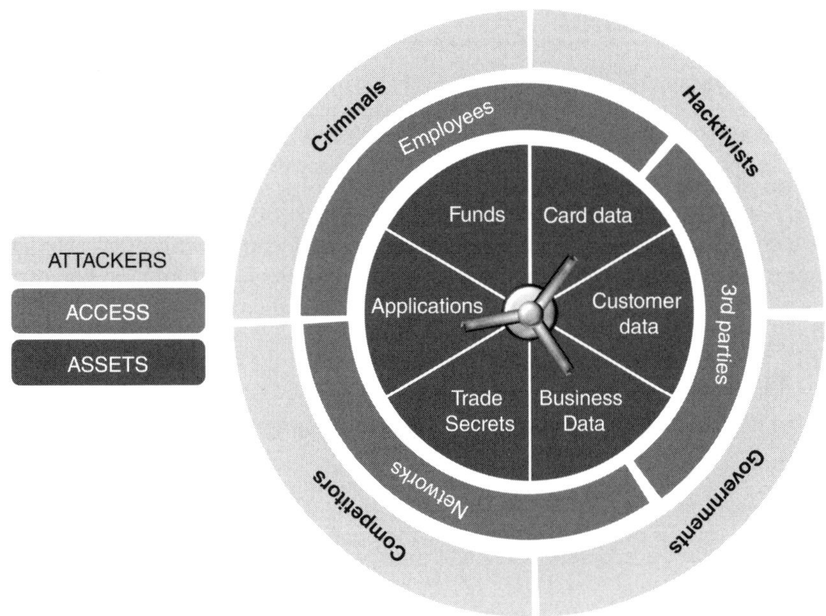

FIGURE 16.4 The Cyber Attack Wheel

16.1.4 On the Magnitude of Cyber Risk

In practice, when evaluating the full range of operational risk for banks, Cyber Risk is generally not very significant compared for instance to Conduct Risk. Our experience is that Cyber Risk contributes at the moment to only 5–10% of the total capital allocation of banks, be it economic or regulatory capital.

However, Cyber Risk receives more attention than Conduct Risk in the news or the specialized conferences. One of the leading conferences of the field has even be renamed into "OpRisk and CyberRisk". We don't see similar attention for Conduct Risk, which importance is probably, at the moment, one order of magnitude bigger.

A first explanation for this could be that it is easier to gather in conferences and discuss external attacks, cyber criminals and activists, rather than discussing the conduct of banks. To some extent, Cyber Risk is a more honorable risk than Conduct Risk.

If this explanation seems too cynical, we can consider another explanation, which is related to the systemic nature of Cyber Risk. This nature is well documented in the aforementioned document from the International Monetary Fund, quoting the DTCC Systemic Risk Barometer[13] – the 2018 edition reports Cyber Risk as the top systemic risk.

To this extent, the interdependency of financial institutions when it comes to cyber risk is not analysed here, and would require some joint effort, which is beyond the scope of this book.

---

[13]DTCC, "Systemic Risk Barometer", 2018, http://www.dtcc.com/~/media/Files/Downloads/Risk-Management/Systemic-Risk-Barometer.pdf (accessed 5/10/2018).

16.2 XOI MODELLING

16.2.1 Analysis

Table 16.3 presents an overview of the XOI decomposition of the main scenarios we consider for cyber risk, as well as their representation on the Cyber Risk Wheel.

Looking at a specific example, the cyber attack critical application, a structured story describes how a potential loss could be generated: "This scenario occurs in case of an external attack that makes a critical application or a group of those unavailable and limit or stop operations. This scenario focuses on significant attacks, either in duration or in magnitude."

16.2.2 Structure

Using the XOI decomposition proposed above, this story can be translated into the graph shown in Figure 16.5.

We can distinguish three types of nodes in Figure 16.5.

The *Exposure, Occurrence, and Impact* nodes (dark grey) are structural and are assessed indirectly through their drivers:

- *Exposure* is equal to the number of applications exposed to an attack. Applications here should be thought of more like services rather than actual internal applications. This level of granularity is compatible with scenario assessment. If the SMEs believe that a denial of service is possible for the whole bank information system, then another unit of exposure "All Services" could be added. This allows to consider attacked targeted against one particular application, as well as a more powerful attack on the bank.

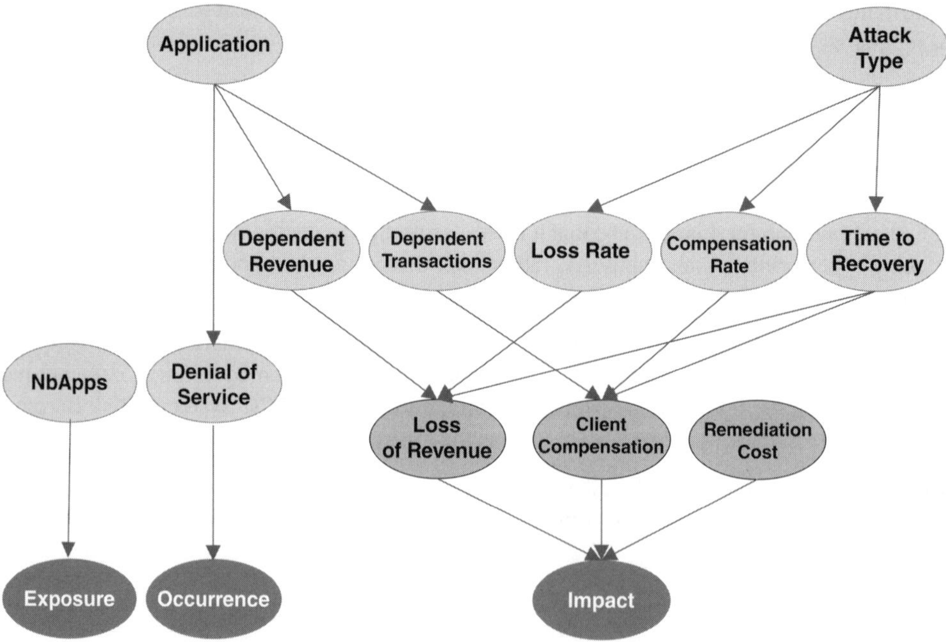

FIGURE 16.5 The XOI Graph for the Scenario Cyberattack on Critical Application

TABLE 16.3 Cyber Risk Scenarios

Scenario	Cyber Risk Wheel	Description	Exposure	Occurrence	Impact
Merchant or Processor Card Compromise	Asset: Card Data Access: Third Party Attacker: Criminal	Theft of customer card data within a large merchant, followed by the subsequent sale of this data to criminal networks.	Merchants or processors handling large volumes of bank card data	Internal fraud or intrusion within merchant or processor	Cost of fraud and cost of cards reissue
Internal Credit Card Compromise	Asset: Card Data Access: Employee Attacker: Criminal	Internal compromise of large volume of credit card data (either from issuer or acquirer systems), followed by the subsequent sale of this data to criminal networks.	Employees having access to large volumes of bank's card data (issuer or acquirer side)	Internal fraud	Cost of fraud and cost of cards reissue
External Credit Card Compromise	Asset: Card Data Access: Networks Attacker: Criminal	External attack of large volume of credit card data (either from issuer or acquirer systems), followed by the subsequent sale of this data to criminal networks.	Systems storing credit cards data	Network Intrusion	Cost of fraud and cost of cards reissue
Internal Customer Data Compromise	Asset: Personal Data Access: Employee Attacker: Activist	Losses due to compromise of customer data (with the exception of credit card data considered in other scenarios).	Employees having access to large volumes of bank's customer data (excluding cards)	Internal fraud	Potential direct losses, client protection, legal, and regulatory costs.
Cyber attack – Customer Data Compromise	Asset: Personal Data Access: Networks Attacker: Activist	Losses due to compromise of customer data (with the exception of credit card data considered in another scenario).	Systems storing large volumes of customer data (excluding cards)	Network Intrusion	Potential direct losses, client protection, legal, and regulatory costs.
Cyber attack – Critical Application Disruption	Asset: Application Access: Networks Attacker: Criminal, Activist	External attack that makes a critical application or a group of those unavailable and limit or stop operations.	Critical business applications.	Denial of service attack	Loss of business and customer detriment
Cyber attack – Fund Misap-propriation	Asset: Application Access: Networks Attacker: Criminal	External attack directly targeting funds misappropriation.	Systems, employees (social engineering)	Network Intrusion	Funds misap-propration
Cyber attack – Data alteration	Asset: Application Access: Networks Attacker: Criminal, Activist	External attack targeting integrity of firm data (sabotage). This affects outcomes of business operations.	Systems, employees (social engineering)	Network Intrusion	Potential direct losses and correction costs

- *Occurrence* is equal to the "Denial of Service", which in turn depends on Application.
- *Impact* is equal to the sum of Loss of Revenue, Client Compensation, and Remediation Cost.

The formula nodes (medium grey) are intermediate nodes, which are calculated using formulas applied to their parent nodes:

- Loss of revenue is calculated as the product of:
  - The daily revenue which depends on the application (Dependent Revenue)
  - The fraction of this revenue that would be lost (Loss Rate)
  - The time to recovery in days (Time to Recovery)
- Client compensation is calculated as the product of
  - The daily amount of transactions which depends on the application (Dependent Transactions)
  - The compensation rate applied to transactions
  - The time to recovery in days (Time to Recovery)
- Remediation cost is assessed as a lump sum

The driver nodes (light grey) need to be assessed individually. This can rely on various data sources: Subject matter experts, external research, internal and external loss data are useful input that allows scaling and assessing the drivers.

16.2.3 Quantification

Table 16.4 presents some hypothetical, but reasonable, ranges of values for each driver.

One driver node requires some specific discussion.

The "Type of Attack" node has been considered in this model to reflect a key finding of an external research. According to Verizon, in its "Databreach Investigation Report"[14], version 2016, "Attacks are either large in magnitude or they are long in duration, but they are typically not both, and many are neither."

This finding has been confirmed in the 2018 version of this report, where it is shown that most DDOS attack durations can be measured in hours rather than days, and that "most companies that do suffer a DDoS normally aren't under attack that long each year – the median is three days."[15]

Considering that banking systems are more robust than the majority of organizations networks, we will consider that 80% of the attacks have a low-level impact, and 20% have a high-level impact.

16.2.4 Simulation

This structure and driver distributions are compiled into a Bayesian Network that is sampled through Monte Carlo simulation to estimate the distribution of the potential losses over the next year.

---

[14] Verizon, 2016, "Data Breaches Investigation Report", http://www.verizonenterprise.com/resources/reports/rp_DBIR_2016_Report_en_xg.pdf (accessed 5/10/2018).

[15] Verizon, 2018, "Data Breaches Investigation Report", https://www.verizonenterprise.com/verizon-insights-lab/dbir/ (accessed 5/10/2018).

TABLE 16.4 Quantification of Cyber Attack Drivers

Driver	Type	Assessment	Source
Number of critical applications	Objective	Five applications: • Cards • Transfers • Trading • Loans • Internet banking	Business data, resiliency team
Type of attack	Subjective	Duration: 80% Magnitude: 20%	External research, (Verizon) reviewed by SMEs.
Denial of service	Subjective	Probability of 5–20% per application	External research, reviewed by SMEs.
Dependent revenue	Objective	Internet banking: $5–10 million Cards, loans: $10–20 million	Business data
Dependent transactions	Objective	Transfers: $70–80 billion Trades: $4–6 billion	Business data

Compensation rate	Subjective	For 1 $m transactions:
		• Transfers: 0–10$.
		• Trades:
		  • Duration of attack: 0–300$
		  • Magnitude of attack: 0–600$
			These ranges can be assessed based on daily interest rates and market variations.

Loss of revenue rate	Subjective	Duration of attack: 20% Magnitude of attack: 100%	SMEs
Time to recovery	Subjective	Duration of attack: 2–12 days Magnitude of attack: 0–2 days	External research, reviewed by Resiliency Team, business impact analysis.

The generic simulation discussed above would be in that case implemented as follows:

Repeat a large number of times (N= 1 Million)

Sample the Exposure

The exposure is constant here and equal to five applications

For each Application

- *Cards*
- *Transfers*
- *Trading*
- *Loans*
- *Internet banking*

Sample the Occurrence

The only parent of Occurrence is "Denial of Service"

Sample "Denial of Service" conditionally to the applicaton

Occurrence is equal to "Denial of Service"

Sample the Impact

Identify every node that is a direct or indirect impact cause.

- *Application*
- *Type of Attack*
- *Dependent Revenue*

- *Dependent Transactions*
- *Compensation Rate*
- *Loss of Revenue Rate*
- *Time to Recovery*
- *Loss of Revenue*
- *Customer Compensation*
- *Remediation Cost*

For each of these nodes:

If it has already been sampled as part of the exposure or of the occurrence sampling, do not resample it.

This is the case for "Application"

Otherwise

Sample in order

- *Nodes with no parents*
  - *Type of Attack*
  - *Remediation Cost*
- *Nodes dependent on Application or Type of Attack*
  - *Dependent Revenue conditional to Application*
  - *Dependent Transactions conditional to Application*
  - *Compensation Rate conditional to Type of Attack*
  - *Loss of Revenue Rate conditional to Type of Attack*
  - *Time to Recovery conditional to Type of Attack*
- *Formula dependent nodes*
  - *Loss of Revenue conditional to Dependent Revenue, Loss of Revenue Rate, Time to Recovery*
  - *Customer Compensation conditional to Dependent Transactions, Compensation Rate, Time to Recovery*

Sample the impact conditionally to its parents.

Add the costs of every loss that took place, and record the total loss L_i.

Sort the cumulated losses L_i in a table, and deduct an empirical distribution.

Using the illustrative assessments proposed above, running the simuation using the MSTAR tool would give the results shown in Figure 16.6.

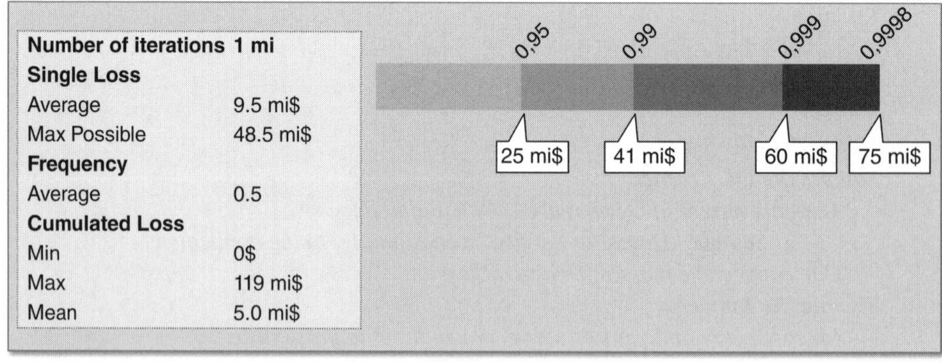

FIGURE 16.6 Simulation of the XOI Model for Cyber Attack

CHAPTER 17

A Scenario in Conduct Risk

17.1 DEFINITION

Most the analysis carried out in Part II of this book, and related to the importance of operational risk, can be explained by the consequences of the subprime mortgage crisis, and the huge fines that resulted from this crisis.

All these fines can be considered as related to conduct risk, as for instance the sales of mortgage-back securities, which are considered as mis-selling case.

According to Thomson-Reuters, financial institutions increasingly tend to adopt a separate working definition of conduct risk, as for instance 70% of G-SIFIs (Global Systemically Important Financial Institutions) have a separate definition of Conduct Risk.

However, among the 10 US and European institutions that paid almost $100 billion in fines and settlements to diverse bodies (DOJ, FDIC, State of New York, and so on) less than 50% explicitly propose a definition of conduct risk in their annual report.

Here is a sample of the definitions proposed:

1. The risk of detriment to customers, clients, market integrity, competition, or [the firm] from the inappropriate supply of financial services, including instances of wilful or negligent misconduct.
2. Conduct risk is the risk that [the firm's] employees or agents may (intentionally or through negligence) harm customers, clients, or the integrity of the markets, and thereby the integrity of the firm.
3. The risk that improper behavior or judgment by our employees may result in a negative financial, nonfinancial or reputational impact to our clients, employees, or the Group or negatively impact the integrity of the financial markets.
4. Conduct risk, a subcategory of operational risk, is the risk that any action or inaction by an employee of the Firm could lead to unfair client/customer outcomes, compromise the Firm's reputation, impact the integrity of the markets in which the Firm operates, or reflect poorly on the Firm's culture.

5. [The risk] from actions (or inactions) of the bank or its employees inconsistent with the Group's Code of Conduct, which may lead to adverse consequences for our stakeholders, or place the bank's sustainability or reputation at risk, including in the long term.
6. Conduct risk is the risk resulting from behavior that does not comply with the Company's values or ethical principles.

All definitions except 1 and 6 focus on employees' behaviour as the cause of conduct risk, rather than on the firm's culture. Definitions 1 and 6 are not specific, and therefore could cover the situation where the culture of the firm drives unethical behaviour.

All definitions except 1, 5, and 6 focus on clients and markets being exposed to the consequences of conduct risk. Definition 1 extends the consequences to competitors, and definition 6 does not specify. Definition 5 is, in a sense, more restrictive, as it focuses on "stakeholders".

The Federal Reserve Bank of New York in a paper called "Misconduct Risk, Culture, and Supervision" stays focused on the role of employees in misconducts, but points out that "the impact of employee misconduct extends beyond the individual and can impact the firm as a whole, as well as the economy and financial markets more broadly"

The European Banking Authority provides a more operative definition, by simply listing the situations the local regulators should focus on.

> Competent authorities should assess the relevance and significance of the institution's exposures to conduct risk as part of the legal risk under the scope of operational risk, and in particular to:
>
> a. Mis-selling of products, in both retail and wholesale markets;
> b. Pushed cross-selling of products to retail customers, such as packaged bank accounts or add-on products customers do not need;
> c. Conflicts of interest in conducting business;
> d. Manipulation of benchmark interest rates, foreign exchange rates or any other financial instruments or indices to enhance the institution's profits;
> e. Barriers to switching financial products during their lifetime and/or to switching financial service providers;
> f. Poorly designed distribution channels that may enable conflicts of interest with false incentives;
> g. Automatic renewals of products or exit penalties; and/or
> h. Unfair processing of customer complaints.

We believe that focusing only on employees as the source of conduct risk cannot always suffice to explain the major misconduct cases that occurred in the recent years, in particular the mortgage-based securities or the PPI case. If the misconduct was the sole responsibility of the employees, it would mean that each employee makes the decision to behave in this way independently. It would therefore become highly unlikely that hundreds or thousands of employees would have decided on their own initiative to sell unsuitable, unnecessary, or too-risky products to their customers. This type of behaviour occurs not because employees do not respect the rules, but because the rules are, explicitly or implicitly, poorly defined. Marketwide misconduct cannot be not attributable to employees only, but rather to a firmwide or market culture of greed.

We also believe that limiting the impact of conduct risk to some direct stakeholders of the bank is not sufficient, because, for instance, it is not questionable that the mis-selling of mortgage-backed securities has harmed the society as a whole, beyond the clients of banks and the financial markets. The same can be said about the recent LIBOR rigging case. Several banks have been accused of misreporting their LIBOR submissions, thus affecting the level of LIBOR. The distortions on LIBOR rates have caused different types of economic harm, such as inflation of interest rates paid on variable-rate mortgages or reduced payments for states or municipalities using LIBOR for floating-rate obligations. Financial crime and terrorism financing, which we believe should be considered as conduct risk cases, have an indirect impact which of course goes far beyond the financial sector.

For these reasons, we suggest to consider a broad definition of conduct risk, such as "the risk that detriment is caused to the bank's customers, an identified group of individuals, the financial markets, or the society as a whole, because of the inappropriate execution of the bank's activities".

It is important to understand that the existence of detriment is the most important dimension of the definition of a risk of misconduct. Misconduct does not necessary imply that the execution of the business activities can be considered inappropriate a priori.

In other words, business practices that do not comply to existing rules are a case of misconduct. But business practices that caused a significant detriment, may finally be considered as misconduct, even though they did not violate any explicit rule at the time they were designed.

Considering the above, two types of causes of misconduct can be identified: negligence and greed:

1. Negligence will allow inappropriate behavior to occur, although strict enforcement of controls could prevent it.
2. Greed, or a culture of profit, will allow the development of unethical practices that will eventually be revealed as harmful.

Negligence is linked to compliance, and greed is linked to culture.

17.2 TYPES OF MISCONDUCT

We have analysed more than 600 cases of fines or settlements resulting from inappropriate conduct in the financial industry in the past 20 years, and we propose a list of the 10 main types of misconduct, summarized in Table 17.1.

We believe the list proposed is reasonably comprehensive as it covers all cases of misconduct listed by EBA, and considers additional situations which are related to the typical activities of the financial sector.

17.2.1 Anticompetitive and Manipulative Practices

Proposed definition: The firm has allegedly engaged in activities that breach the antitrust regulation or that aim at rigging market prices.

TABLE 17.1 Mapping of Misconduct Types to EBA Definition

Proposed Misconduct Type	EBA Misconduct Type
Anticompetitive practices and market manipulation	Manipulation of benchmark interest rates, foreign exchange rates or any other financial instruments or indices to enhance the institution's profits
Financial crime	
Customer tax evasion	
Mis-selling (retail banking)	Mis-selling of products, in both retail and wholesale markets; Pushed cross-selling of products to retail customers, such as packaged bank accounts or add-on products that customers do not need; Barriers to switching financial products during their lifetime and/or to switching financial service providers; Poorly designed distribution channels that may enable conflicts of interest with false incentives
Mis-selling (wholesale banking)	Mis-selling of products, in both retail and wholesale markets
Improper loan management	
Client overcharging	Automatic renewals of products or exit penalties; and/or
Fund improper disclosure	
Counterparty misrepresentation	Conflicts of interest in conducting business
Antibribery and corruption	Conflicts of interest in conducting business

We will now review these cases in more detail.

Antitrust law is the broad category of laws that are meant to keep business operating honest and fairly. Antitrust laws regulate the way companies do business in order to prevent businesses from having too much power. A trust is a large group of businesses that work together or combine in order to form a monopoly or control the market.

A market manipulation occurs when an economically rational actor deliberately injects false or fraudulent information into the market to cause demand or supply to deviate from their economic fundamentals. Market manipulation undermines trust in the prices, that is, "market integrity". For this reason, they can impact the economy even after the manipulative behaviour has stopped.

Market manipulation and anticompetitive practices differ in nature. Simply put, violations of antitrust laws intend to alter the competition in the long run, while market manipulation is characterized by the short-term intent to profit from fraudulent acts or artificial prices.

However, the current legal practice, at least in the United States, is that actions for market manipulations cases are increasingly based on claims brought under the antitrust laws[1].

[1]Shaun D. Ledgerwood and Jeremy A. Verlinda, "The Intersection of Antitrust and Market Manipulation Law", January 31, 2017. Available at SSRN: https://ssrn.com/abstract=2908878 (accessed 9/10/2018).

As mentioned above for the LIBOR case, anticompetitive and manipulative practices are the type of misconduct that potentially has the broader impact: not limited to the financial markets, they can impact the economy as a whole.

The LIBOR case is possibly the most emblematic case of manipulative practices. LIBOR (London Inter-Bank Offered Rate) is a benchmark interest rate based on the rates at which banks lend funds to each other on the London interbank market. The rate is published daily and was administered by the British Bankers' Association (BBA), before the scandal. Many banks worldwide use LIBOR as a base rate for setting interest rates on consumer and corporate loans.

LIBOR is considered to underpin hundreds of trillions of dollars in securities and loans. Barclays[2] and 15 other global financial institutions (notably Citigroup, Crédit Suisse, Deutsche Bank, JP Morgan, Rabobank, Royal Bank of Scotland, Société Générale) were involved in the scandal and fined more than $9 billion in total[3].

17.2.2 Financial Crime

Proposed definition: The firm is sued by a regulatory body or the justice department for having breached the antimoney laundering rules in a country. In the United States, this covers violations of BSA/AML, on one hand, or of Sanctions/IEEPA, on the other hand.

By far the most significant cases in recent past were the cases related to the violation of sanctions. In particular, BNP Paribas[4] was fined almost $9 billion in the United States after pleading guilty of processing billions of dollars of transactions through the US financial system on behalf of Sudanese, Iranian, and Cuban entities subject to US economic sanctions.

17.2.3 Customer Tax Evasion

Proposed definition: The firm is sued for allegedly helping its clients to optimize or evade tax.

In 2014, Crédit Suisse has pleaded guilty to conspiracy to assist US taxpayers in filing false returns[5]. More recently, HSBC agreed to pay €300 million to French authorities to settle allegations that it helped wealthy clients at its Swiss private bank evade taxes[6].

17.2.4 Mis-selling (Retail Banking)

Proposed definition: the firm has allegedly, intentionally or not, misrepresented or omitted material facts about a product that was sold to many clients. It also considers situations where the product sold is not fitted for the client even if not misrepresented.

---

[2]Harvard Business School, "Barclays and the LIBOR Scandal", https://www.hbs.edu/faculty/Pages/item.aspx?num=43888 (accessed 5/10/2018).

[3]*The New York Times*, "Tracking the Libor Scandal", https://www.nytimes.com/interactive/2015/04/23/business/dealbook/db-libor-timeline.html#/#time370_10900 (accessed 5/10/2018).

[4]US Department of Justice, "BNP Paribas Agrees to Plead Guilty and to Pay $8.9 Billion for Illegally Processing Financial Transactions for Countries Subject to US Economic Sanctions", https://www.justice.gov/opa/pr/bnp-paribas-agrees-plead-guilty-and-pay-89-billion-illegally-processing-financial (accessed 5/10/2018).

[5]US Department of Justice, "Credit Suisse Pleads Guilty to Conspiracy to Aid and Assist US Taxpayers in Filing False Returns", https://www.justice.gov/opa/pr/credit-suisse-pleads-guilty-conspiracy-aid-and-assist-us-taxpayers-filing-false-returns (accessed 5/10/2018).

[6]Cour d'Appel de Paris, https://www.economie.gouv.fr/files/files/directions_services/afa/CJIP_HSBC.pdf (accessed 5/10/2018).

Mis-selling is probably the major conduct risk for retail banking. It is consubstantial to a product-oriented type of sales, and could therefore apply to any type of retail product. Selling a comb to a bald man it the archetypal mis-selling, but with less consequences than for financial products. The purchase of financial services such as pensions or mortgages can have life-changing consequences and the most fragile households can suffer dramatic consequences from a mis-selling.

The Payment Protection Insurance in the UK is the largest case of retail mis-selling in the recent history. This insurance was designed to cover repayments in some circumstances such as unemployment, accident, illness, disability, or death. More than 60 million PPI policies have been sold throughout the UK, mainly between 1990 and 2010, for an estimated total amount of £50–80 billion. But it has been shown that in a very large proportion of cases, this insurance was sold to people who did not need it because they would never be able to activate it. As a consequence, banks have repaid a total of nearly £30 billion to their customers to date[7].

17.2.5 Mis-selling (Wholesale Banking)

Proposed definition: the firm has allegedly, intentionally or not, misrepresented or omitted material facts about a product that was sold to many clients (investors) or that was massively sold to a few wholesale clients. This scenario focuses in particular on securities business where many investors could be harmed because of misleading securities.

The sales of securitized residential mortgage-based securities (RMBS) to investors is the largest recent case of mis-selling wholesale, and arguably the largest misconduct event to date.

Subprime mortgages were pooled and organized in tranches, in such a way that the top tranche was presented as a very low-risk asset. Lower tranches were further pooled in CDOs, creating new artificially low risk assets. The development of mortgage securities business was based on an erroneous assumption of independence, which justified an apparent diversification of risk.

The total fines resulting from this case were around $110 billion, an impacted almost half of the largest banks in the world (Ally, Bank of America, Barclays, Citigroup, Credit Suisse, Deutsche Bank, Goldman Sachs, HSBC, JPMorgan Chase, Morgan Stanley, Royal Bank of Scotland, Société Générale, UBS, Wells Fargo)[8].

17.2.6 Improper Loan Management

Proposed definition: the firm is sued for having allegedly mismanaged many loan holders during servicing process.

The National Mortgage Settlement in the United States is the other part of the subprime crisis, when the massive mis-selling of securitized mortgage-based securities is the first part. This major case was also referred to as "the foreclosure crisis" or the "robosigning scandal". The name referred to the practice of having bank employees quickly approve many foreclosures by taking a cursory look at whether all documents are in order.

---

[7]The Financial Conduct Authority, "PPI Explained", https://www.fca.org.uk/ppi/ppi-explained (accessed 5/10/2018).
[8]*Wall Street Journal*, "Where Did the Money Go?", http://graphics.wsj.com/bank-fines-where-did-the-money-go (accessed 5/10/2018).

Large banks in the United States reached a settlement of a total of $9.3 billion with the federal government on alleged abuses of mortgage servicing, and in particular abusive foreclosures[9].

17.2.7 Client Overcharging

Proposed definition: The price of a product is considered abusive in relation to the market price. This differs from mis-selling as in that case the product is considered in line with the customer's needs.

An example is the case of undue overdraft fees. In 2012, Citizens Bank, then owned by agreed to pay $137 million to settled a class action lawsuit for having allegedly charged undue overdraft fees. More specifically, the bank had updated its internal computer systems "to re-sequence the actual order of its customer debit cards and ATM transactions, by posting them in highest-to-lowest dollar amount".[10] This settlement involved other banks in the United States, including Bank of America, PNC, and JP Morgan Chase.

17.2.8 Fund Improper Disclosure

Proposed definition: The firm has allegedly omitted or misrepresented material facts to the investors of the fund or to the fund itself, fraudulently or not. This is a specialized version of the mis-selling scenario for funds.

The Madoff case[11] is an example of fund improper disclosure, as some fund managers included Madoff funds in their own products.

17.2.9 Counterparty Misrepresentation

Proposed definition: the firm has allegedly omitted or misrepresented, intentionally or not, fraudulently or not, some material facts to the investors or clients of a company it is doing business with.

In general, this case occurs when the counterparty defaults and shareholders seek the firm's liability, as an underwriter, lender, CIB service provider, or shareholder. In most cases, the liability is shared with other banks.

According to the Stanford Law School[12], there is an average of 220 securities class actions in the United States per year, among which more than 50% resulted in a settlement. In most litigations, the company remains solvent and compensate the plaintiffs. The situation precisely addressed here is when the company defaults and bank's liability is sought.

The most well-known case of counterparty misrepresentation is the Enron case in 2001, resulting in more than $6 billion settlements for banks, in particular CIBC, JP Morgan, and Citigroup.

---

[9]The US Department of Justice, "The National Mortgage Settlement", https://www.justice.gov/ust/national-mortgage-settlement (accessed 5/10/2018).

[10]US Government Publish Office: 09-2036, In Re: Checking Account Overdraft Litigation, https://www.gpo.gov/fdsys/granule/USCOURTS-flsd-1_09-md-02036/USCOURTS-flsd-1_09-md-02036-2 (accessed 5/10/2018).

[11]The Madoff Recovery Initiative, http://www.madofftrustee.com/recoveries-04.html (accessed 5/10/2018).

[12]Stanford Law School, Securities Class Action Clearinghouse, http://securities.stanford.edu/index.html (accessed 5/10/2018).

17.2.10 Antibribery and Corruption

Proposed definition: The firm is sued for bribery or violation of antibribery and anticorruption laws. Two major regulations are the UK Bribery Act under UK law, and the Foreign Corrupt Practices Act (FCPA) under US law.

In 2016, JP Morgan agreed to pay $264.4 million to the DOJ, SEC, and Federal Reserve to resolve FCPA offenses related to the "Sons & Daughters Program", which the Hong Kong subsidiary of the firm used to gain winning banking deals by awarding prestigious jobs to relatives and friends of Chinese government officials.[13]

17.3 XOI MODELLING

17.3.1 Analysis

Statistical modelling of misconduct is not easy. Indeed, individual losses, such as individual payments to mis-sold customers, cannot be used for this purpose, because:

- Either they are the result of individual behaviour, and are not predictive of a major event.
- Or they are the result of firmwide behaviour and, therefore, they are not independent.

Therefore, extrapolating individual losses to deduct a significant loss is not relevant.

Merging individual cases with large events is not relevant. A case of serious misconduct is not of the same nature as individual misconduct, just as an individual card theft is not of the same nature as a major card data compromise.

We will now discuss how to apply the Exposure, Occurrence, and Impact method to address conduct risk.

17.3.1.1 Exposure The units of exposure for conduct are not:

- The clients, as they are not exposed independently
- The employees, for the same reason

The appropriate unit of exposure depends on the type of misconduct, but generally it is of the nature of a product or a business segment.

Considering the product or the business segment as the unit exposed to conduct risk is straightforward for:

- Anticompetitive practices and market manipulation
- Mis-selling (retail banking)
- Mis-selling (wholesale banking)
- Improper loan management

[13]US Department of Justice, "JPMorgan's Investment Bank in Hong Kong Agrees to Pay $72 Million Penalty for Corrupt Hiring Scheme in China", https://www.justice.gov/opa/pr/jpmorgan-s-investment-bank-hong-kong-agrees-pay-72-million-penalty-corrupt-hiring-scheme (accessed 5/10/2018).

- Client overcharging
- Fund improper disclosure

In each of these cases, it is a product that bears the risk, whether it is abusive sales, overcharging, anticompetitive practices, or improper management.

Products can be reasonably considered as independently exposed because, even if there exists a greed culture in the company, many circumstances are necessary for a product to give rise to a massive case of misconduct.

17.3.1.2 Occurrence The assessment of the riskiness of a product with respect to misconduct will of course depend on the type of scenario.

A truly objective practice would be to analyse the product business metrics, and link them to the existence of a latent misconduct.

For instance, working a with major insurance company, we used the loss ratio[14] as a driver of a potential misconduct: low levels of loss ratios may indicate too high premiums (and potential overcharging) or poor value (and potential mis-selling).

This method was the basis of a survey carried out by the Office of Fair Trade in 2006, reviewing the PPI, years before the first provisions were made by banks.

According to this survey, the loss ratio was, for instance, of 14% for credit card PPI, 16% for secured loan PPI, and 18% for unsecured personal loans, whereas the loss ratio for household insurance is 54%, 80% for medical insurance, and 82% for motor insurance.[15]

In general, a product with exceptional performance that cannot be justified by a clear competitive advantage is a sign of a potential behavioural problem. This must be related to the discussion we had in Part II on operational risk appetite. By definition, there is an appetite for highly profitable products, which can sometimes prove unethical in the long term.

However, we must recognize that it is difficult to implement this type of approach in practice, as designating a priori the riskiest products can turn out to be counterproductive in the case of a future litigation.

The way to address this situation is generally to perform risk analysis at the level of business segments rather than individual products.

17.3.1.3 Impact The consequences of a case of misconduct when it is revealed are potentially of three kinds:

1. Disgorgement of undue revenue or profit
2. Compensation for harmed parties or for the society
3. Deterrence for the company and for other companies

[14]The loss ratio is the ratio of total losses incurred (paid and reserved) in claims plus adjustment expenses divided by the total premiums earned.

[15]Office of Fair Trading Payment protection insurance, "Report on the Market Study and Proposed Decision to Make a Market Investigation Reference", October 2006, https://londoneconomics.co.uk/wp-content/uploads/2011/09/70-Research-into-Payment-Protection-Insurance-in-the-UK.pdf (accessed 5/10/2018).

It is clear that these consequences may be disproportionate to the company's activity and the benefits it has derived from its practices.

Of course, the compensation of customers who are victims of abusive sales will be directly related to the revenue earned with these customers.

But the compensation of the company for negligence in terrorism financing is potentially disproportionate to the savings achieved through less strict monitoring of transactions, or to the profits made by allowing questionable financial flows.

However, the deterrence effect is maximum when severe but not exaggerated: in most cases, a regulator will not take the risk of shutting down a firm for misconduct, as the resulting detriment for the society might even be higher.

From the above, it results that the severity of a misconduct event might be appreciated in relation to specific businesses revenue, for disgorgement or compensation, or in relation with the firm total revenue, for deterrence.

This is confirmed when reviewing the sentencing guidelines of different regulatory bodies.

The European Commission[16] recommends using the relevant revenue to calculate the fine and the total revenue to cap the fine (maximal deterrence):

- The percentage which is applied to the value of the company's relevant sales can be up to 30%, depending on the seriousness of the infringement.
- The fine is limited to 10% of the overall annual turnover of the company.

The FCA[17] also relates the fine to the relevant revenue: "Having determined the relevant revenue, the FCA will decide on the percentage of that revenue that will form the basis of the penalty. In making this determination, the FCA will consider the seriousness of the breach and choose a percentage between 0% and 20%".

On the other hand, the sanctions for Financial Crime under IEEPA can go up to twice the amount of the transactions[18]. This means that a sanction can in theory shutdown a bank. The sanction is therefore adjusted to be in proportion with the revenue of the firm.

17.3.1.4 Statistical Analysis of Conduct Losses Related to Revenue

We have conducted a statistical analysis to support the idea that the fines are related to revenue.

For the identification of matters and the assessment of their total impact, various sources were used and cross-checked:

- Newspapers
- Regulators websites
- DOJ releases
- Academic databases

---

[16]European Commission, "Fines for Breaking EU Competitiion Laws", http://ec.europa.eu/competition/cartels/overview/factsheet_fines_en.pdf (accessed 5/10/2018).

[17]Financial Conduct Authority, FCA handbook 2018, Chapter 6, Penalties, §6.5A.2, https://www.handbook.fca.org.uk/handbook/DEPP/6/5A.pdf (accessed 5/10/2018).

[18]US Department of the Treasury, International Emergency Economic Powers Act https://www.treasury.gov/resource-center/sanctions/Documents/ieepa.pdf (accessed 5/10/2018).

The revenues of the banks were sourced back to annual reports of the banks.

This represents:

- 609 cases totalling $415 billion
- 90 banks
- 20 years of observation

The data were pre-processed as follows:

- Revenues were bucketed according to their magnitude (in logarithm).
- Similarly, losses were bucketed according to their magnitude (in logarithm).

Considered at the bucket level, there is a linear relationship between the average magnitude of the loss and the average magnitude of the revenue (Figure 17.1).

Similarly, there exists a relationship between the dispersion of the loss and the average magnitude of the revenue, if considered at the bucket level (Figure 17.2).

The relation has been found statistically significant and stable through time. The stability has been tested by re-estimating the relation with partial data, up to a given year only.

The conclusion is that the expected conduct loss can be considered to follow a power law (in square root of the total revenue), with a dispersion following a similar law.

These findings are consistent with a recent report of the European Parliament[19] stating that "there are signs that conduct costs (per unit of total assets) have been stronger for small and mid-sized institutions ..."

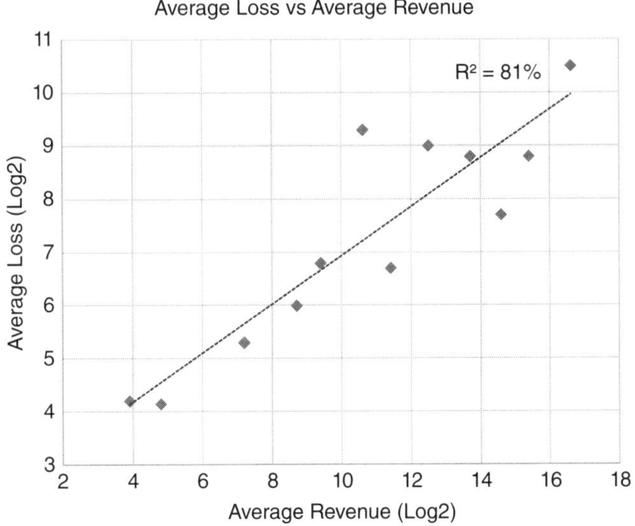

FIGURE 17.1 Average Conduct Loss as a Function of Bank Revenue (log2)

[19]European Parliament, "Fines for Misconduct in the Banking Sector -- What Is the Situation in the EU?", http://www.europarl.europa.eu/RegData/etudes/IDAN/2017/587402/IPOL_IDA(2017)587402_EN.pdf (accessed 5/10/2018).

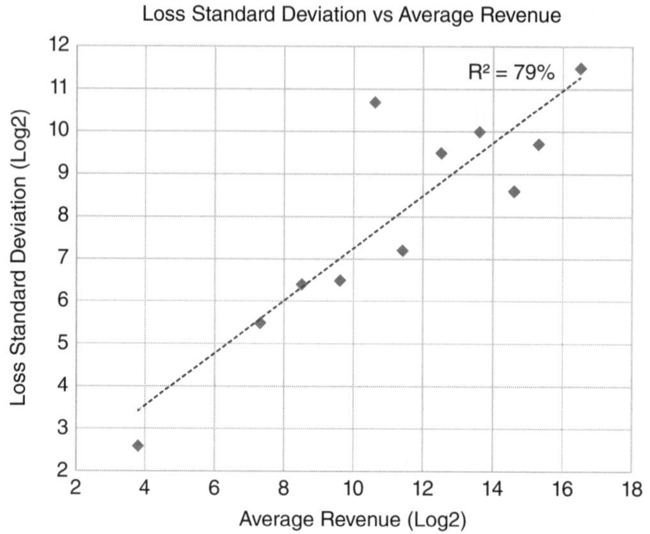

FIGURE 17.2 Dispersion of Conduct Loss as a Function of Bank Revenue (log2)

17.3.2 Structure

From the analysis and discussions above, we suggest a common scenario structure for the Conduct Risk events considered. This structure is shown in Figure 17.3.

Of course, this structure is only a recommendation and can be superseded when a more specific structure could allow a more adapted analysis of the loss generation mechanism.

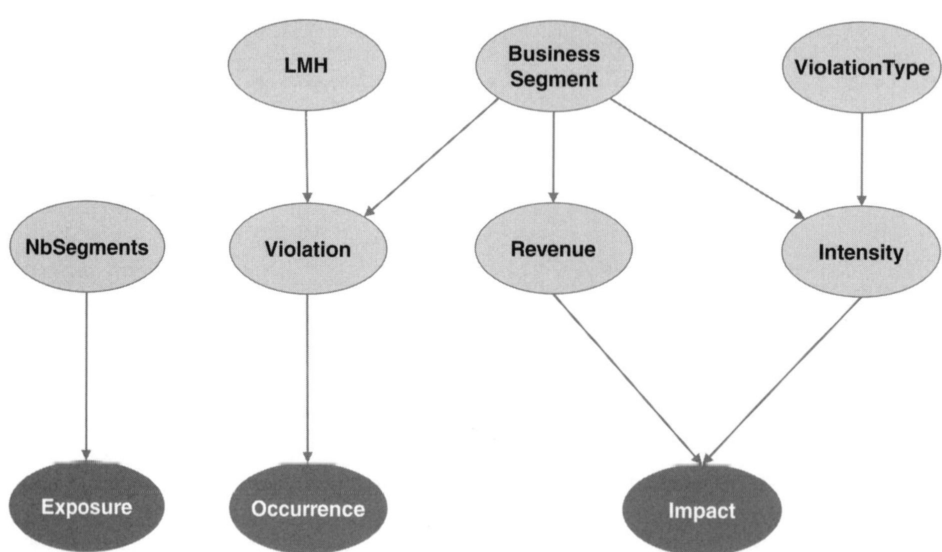

FIGURE 17.3 The Generic XOI Graph for Conduct Scenarios

- The units of Exposure should be some decomposition of the revenue: product, business segment, business segment for a given region, and so on. The appropriate granularity depends on the scenario.
- The probability of Occurrence may depend on the Unit of Exposure, and should be assessed considering observed events, risk scores of the product segments, and forward-looking analysis.
- The Impact is equal to the revenue of the considered unit of exposure, multiplied by an intensity coefficient. The intensity may depend on the particular type of violation considered – if the scenario covers more than one event.

This is the general structure proposed to represent Conduct Risk. Of course, depending on the knowledge available within an institution, a more detailed structure can be put in place. For instance, the Mis-Selling Retail scenario can be represented using the more specific graph shown in Figure 17.4.

The above structure has been enhanced as follows:

- The probability of a mis-selling retail massive litigation occurring has been made dependent of a risk score, assumed to be measured in the firm.
- The intensity of the mis-selling settlement has been decomposed. The intensity is by definition the ratio of the total settlement divided by the relevant revenue. In the above structure, the intensity is expressed as the product of the mis-Selling rate, that is, the fraction of clients mis-sold multiplied by the duration during which the misconduct took place.

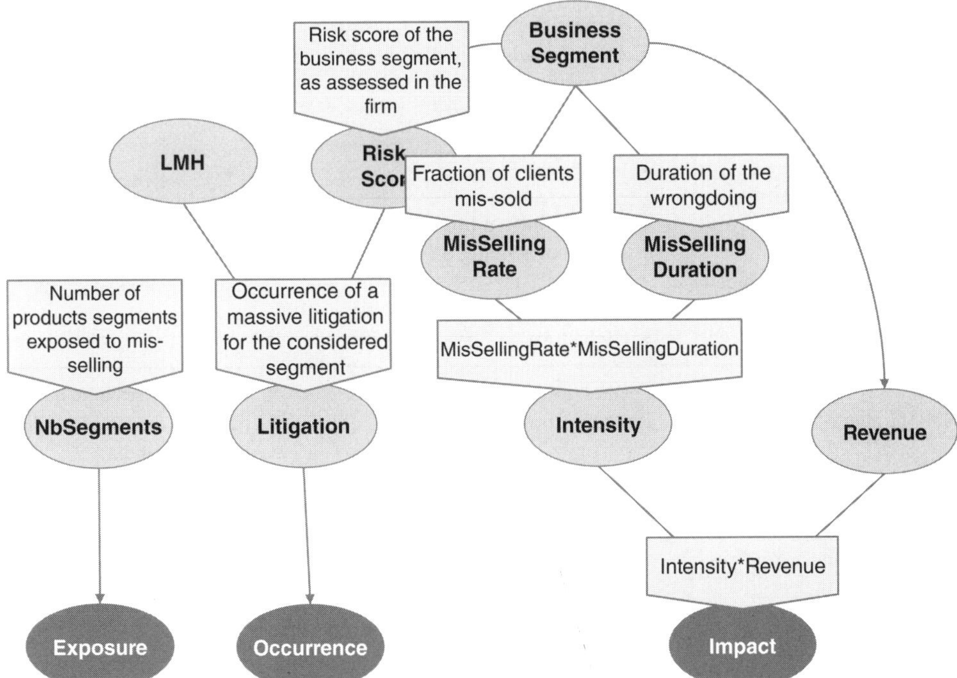

FIGURE 17.4 An XOI Graph for the Mis-Selling Conduct Scenario

17.3.3 Quantification

The quantification of such a scenario is, of course, very dependent on the firm, and in particular on the existence of risk scores for products.

We present a table of hypothetical, but realistic, quantifications for each of the drivers in Table 17.2.

TABLE 17.2 Quantifiction of Mis-selling Drivers

Driver	Type	Assessment	Source
Number of product segments	Objective	We considered seven segments: • Banking and cards • Home financing • Auto financing • Student financing • General insurance • Investment • Life insurance and pensions	Firm business structure
Risk score	Subjective	We used the following scores: Low risk products: • Home financing • General insurance • Life insurance and pensions Medium-risk products: • Auto financing High-risk products: • Banking and cards • Student financing • Investment	Internal risk assessment
Litigation	Subjective	The probability of litigation is estimated depending on the risk score: • Low: 0.5% to 1.5% • Medium: 1% to 2% • High: 1.5% to 2.5%	External cases analysis
Mis-Selling rate	Subjective	Ranging from 0 to 20%.	External cases analysis, business data, and product risk assessment
Duration of mis-Selling	Subjective	The duration is assumed to range from 1 to 10 years, with the following assumptions: • 1 to 3 years in 80% cases • 3 to 5 years in 15% cases • 5 to 10 years in 5% cases	External cases analysis, business data, and product risk assessment.

17.3.4 Simulation

Repeat a large number of times (N = 1 Million)

Sample the Exposure

The exposure is constant here and equal to seven segments

For Each Business Segment

- *Banking and Cards*
- *Home Financing*
- *Auto Financing*
- *Student Financing*
- *General Insurance*
- *Investment*
- *Life Insurance and Pensions*

Sample the Occurrence

Identify every node that is a direct or indirect occurrence cause.

- Business Segment
- LMH
- Risk Score
- Litigation

Sample in order

- Nodes with no parents
  - Business Segment
  - LMH
- Nodes dependent on Business Segment
  - Risk Score conditional to Business Segment
- Nodes dependent on LMH and Risk Score
  - Litigation conditional to LMH and Risk Score

The only parent of Occurrence is "Litigation"

Occurrence is equal to "Litigation"

Sample the Impact

Identify every node that is a direct or indirect impact cause.

- *Business Segment*
- *MisSelling Rate*
- *MisSelling Duration*
- *Intensity*
- *Revenue*

For each of these nodes:

If it has already been sampled as part of the exposure or of the occurrence sampling, do not resample it.

This is the case for "Business Segment"

Otherwise

Sample in order

- *Nodes with no parents*
  - *No such node here*

- *Nodes dependent on Business Segment*
  - *MisSelling Rate conditional to Business Segment*
  - *MisSelling Duration conditional to Business Segment*
  - *Revenue conditional to Business Segment*
- *Formula dependent nodes*
  - *Intensity conditional to MisSelling Rate and MisSelling Duration.*

Sample the impact conditionally to its parents.

Add the costs of every loss that took place, and record the total loss L_i.

Sort the cumulated losses L_i in a table, and deduct an empirical distribution.

Using the illustrative assessments proposed above, running the simuation using the MSTAR tool would give the results shown in Figure 17.5.

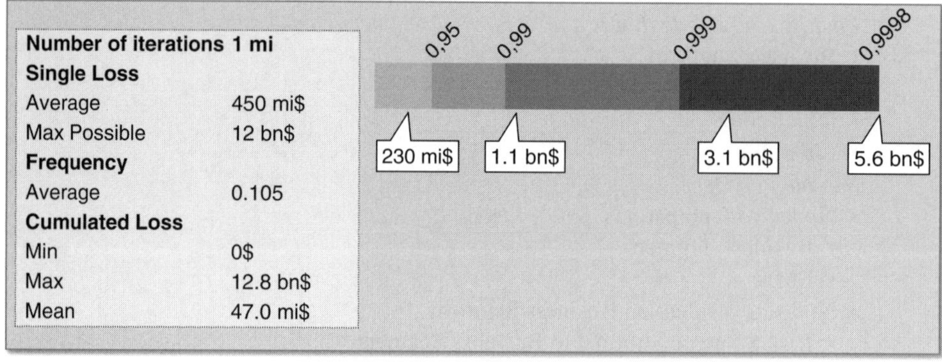

FIGURE 17.5 Simulation of the XOI Model for Mis-selling

CHAPTER 18
Aggregation of Scenarios

18.1 INTRODUCTION

When used for capital calculation, scenarios need to be aggregated. Indeed, not all scenarios will occur the same year, but they cannot either be considered fully independent. As discussed in Part I, the correlation level is one of the main drivers of the final capital number: the typical diversification benefit ranges from 30% to 60% of the sum of the scenario outcomes, when considered at a 1 in 1,000 level.

Correlation assessment is not easy for experts, as the notion of correlation is not always intuitive.

First, what correlation are we talking about? We can think of at least two types of correlations:

1. The occurrences are correlated, that is, the occurrence of A makes the occurrence of B more likely: for instance, a business centre disruption may disorganize temporarily the firm and make the occurrence of fraud more likely.
2. The impacts are correlated, that is, the occurrence of A and B are independent, but should they occur during the same period, their consequences would be correlated, because they are driven by a common factor: for instance, the occurrence of a manual trading error and of an IT disruption may be independent, but their consequences are correlated through market volatility, which drives directly the error loss, and the compensation to corporate clients if the trades are delayed due to IT disruption.

Second, mathematical properties of correlation are not always intuitive. Correlation is not always transitive, that is, the fact that A and B are correlated, and B and C are correlated, does not necessarily imply that A and C are correlated. This holds however when the correlation levels are 100%. Nevertheless, correlations matrix must respect some consistency criterion, that is, they must be positive semi-definite (PSD).

During a specific project, we had the opportunity to examine a significant sample of expert-based correlation assessments. The same operational risk scenarios were assessed independently in at least five different legal entities of the same multinational company, and so were the correlations between the scenarios:

- We observed a significant spread of correlation assessment: the correlations for the same pair of scenarios ranged sometimes from 0 to 100%.

- The situation where A and B, and B and C were 100% correlated, but A and C were considered not correlated, was observed.
- And of course, the resulting matrices were almost never positive semi-definite (PSD).

A simple alternative to expert assessment can be to use a uniform correlation assumption. This is easy to do, easy for regulators to review and benchmark, and leads to positive semi-definite matrices. However, this is not very useful for understanding and managing the risk profile.

We describe here a structured approach that is consistent with the XOI method for scenario assessment. This method is focused on occurrence correlation and is based on the identification of dependency paths through scenarios.

Assessing dependencies between two scenarios is not done directly, but by assessing the causal dependencies assessed between the scenario and a predefined set of seven environment factors (Figure 18.1), considered to be representative of the typical high-level drivers of an operational risk scenario:

1. Corporate strategy
2. Compliance and relations with the regulators
3. Legal and relations with customers
4. Human resources and competence
5. Internal control resources
6. IT and logistic resources
7. Economic environment

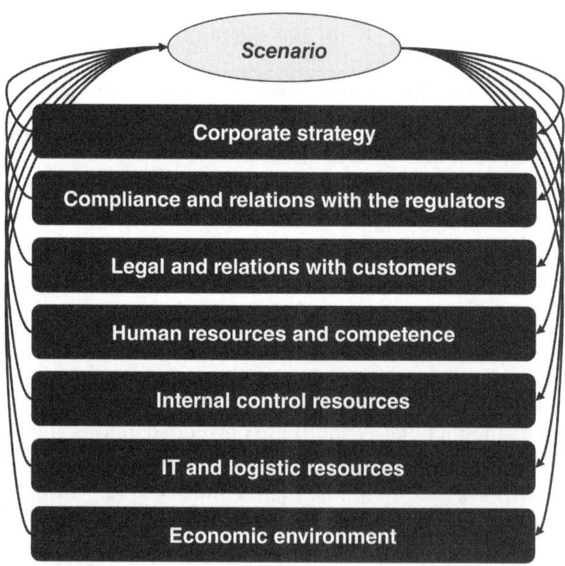

FIGURE 18.1 Factors Used for Scenario Dependency Assessment

These factors can be seen as the main internal and external resources and stakeholders of a firm:

- Internal resources
  - Corporate strategy
  - IT and logistic resources
  - Human resources and competence
  - Internal control resources
- External stakeholders
  - Compliance and relations with the regulators
  - Legal and relations with customers
- General environment
  - Economic environment

This is consistent for instance with the joint AIRMIC, IRM, and ALARM papertitled "A Structured Approach to Enterprise Risk Management and the Requirements of ISO 31000"[1].

This approach has several benefits compared to the usual alternative, that is, expert assessment of correlations:

- The use of Environment Factors gives a structure and rationale to dependency assessment.
- The use of Environment Factors allows assessing dependencies between scenarios without gathering all the scenario owners in the same room. This is not only a practical benefit, but also a way to reduce biases: each scenario owner assesses its own side of the dependency, and the dependencies are calculated, merging all contributions. Since the result is more difficult to predict, this contributes to reducing biases.

The assessment of dependencies between scenarios and environment factors should be performed during the structured assessment workshop.

For each scenario, the experts are invited to consider whether:

- The occurrence of the scenario is made more likely by a deterioration of a factor
- The occurrence of scenario is likely to result in the deterioration of a given factor

18.2 INFLUENCE OF A SCENARIO ON AN ENVIRONMENT FACTOR

From a general standpoint, a scenario is said to have an influence on an environment factor, if the occurrence of the scenario would result in the deterioration of the environment factor during the same year.

[1] A structured approach to Enterprise Risk Management (ERM) and the requirements of ISO 31000, https://www.theirm.org/media/886062/ISO3100_doc.pdf (accessed 5/10/2018).

The second-order effects should not be considered. By second-order effects we mean effects that result in a decision taken by the firm in reaction to the occurrence of a scenario. For instance, if a major IT disruption occurs, it is possible that the firm will allocate more resources to IT. This may deteriorate the balance of human resources in other areas such as internal control. This type of dependency should not be reported here as they are considered second order.

Typical first-order dependencies are the impact of a pandemic on human resources, or the impact of a major IT disruption on IT and logistic resources.

Positive influences, that is, situations where the occurrence of the scenario would result in an improvement of the environment factor, should not be considered, adopting a conservative approach. In general, positive influences would not be spontaneous but would result from a firm reaction, and hence, would be second order.

The influence should be rated as low, medium, or high. As we consider the influence of a scenario on an environment factor for the same year, it is advised to rate the influence:

- As low if the environment factor would most probably revert to its normal state in less than one month after the occurrence of the scenario,
- As medium if the environment factor would most probably revert to its normal state in one to three months after the occurrence of the scenario,
- As high if the environment factor would be durably or permanently affected by the occurrence of the scenario.

This is consistent with the objective in mind, which is to use these influences to assess dependencies between scenarios: if an environment factor is resilient to the occurrence of a particular scenario, it will not significantly contribute to increase the probability of another scenario.

In Tables 18.1 and 18.2, we give some more details on the way to interpret the influences.

18.3 INFLUENCE OF AN ENVIRONMENT FACTOR ON A SCENARIO

An environment factor is said to influence the occurrence of a scenario, if the deterioration of the factor, compared to the present situation, would increase the probability of occurrence of the scenario.

The influence should be rated low, medium, or high. It is advised to rate the influence:

- As low if a deterioration of environment factor would increase the probability of occurrence of the scenario of less than 20%, during the period when this factor is effectively deteriorated
- As medium if a deterioration of environment factor would increase the probability of occurrence of the scenario of 20% to 50%, during the period when this factor is effectively deteriorated,
- As high if a deterioration of environment factor would increase the probability of occurrence of the scenario of more than 50%, during the period when this factor is effectively deteriorated.

Below we give some more details on the way to interpret the influences.

TABLE 18.1 How a Scenario Influences an Environment Factor

A Scenario Is Said to Influence	If ...	How to Assess the Influence
Corporate strategy	The occurrence of this scenario would imply changing or adapting the strategy of the firm, in particular in terms of products – think of a massive customer complaint, or distribution channels.	A change in corporate strategy will generally be a long-term change. Rate high only.
Compliance and relations with the regulators	The occurrence of this scenario is likely to increase attention of the authorities – domestic or foreign on the firm. This would happen, for instance, if some major issue is disclosed to the press.	A change in regulator attention strategy will generally be a long-term change. Rate high only.
Legal and relations with customers	The occurrence of this scenario would probably result in a discontent of customers, which in turn may increase the risk of massive complaints or litigations.	The discontent of customers would depend on the situation considered. For instance, a business disruption is likely to raise a discontent limited in time, while the consequences of a data-theft may me more durable.
Human resources and competence	The occurrence of this scenario is likely to affect the productive human resources of the firm, therefore resulting in more errors, delays, and so on. Internal control resources are dealt with separately.	This will be appreciated as depending on the duration needed to manage the consequences of the scenario.
Internal control resources	The occurrence of this scenario is likely to affect the internal control resources of the firm, therefore resulting in more frauds, non-compliances, and so on.	This will be appreciated as depending on the duration needed to manage the consequences of the scenario.
IT and logistic resources	The occurrence of this scenario is likely to affect the IT system of the firm. This would result in a more manual processing of operations, increasing the risk of errors, delays, frauds, and so on.	This item will generally be influenced by IT disruption or project failure scenarios. IT disruptions would typically have a low/medium impact, while project failures could have long-lasting consequences.
Economic environment	It is generally considered that a firm scenario will not influence the economic environment. Some global operational risk scenarios such as Pandemics are exceptions.	

TABLE 18.2 How a Scenario Is Influenced by an Environment Factor

A Scenario Is Said to Be Influenced by	If ...	How to Assess the Influence
Corporate strategy	A change in corporate strategy – products, distribution channels, and so on – could make the scenario more likely.	
Compliance and relations with the regulators	An increased attention of the regulator, or a deterioration of the relations with the regulation authorities could make the scenario more likely.	Possible failures to comply with the regulation are not dependent of the regulator attention, but their detection might be.
Legal and relations with customers	A deteriorated climate with customers (resulting from any cause such as IT disruption, data compromise, discontent of the service, and so on) could make the scenario more likely.	Technical events may change the sentiment of the public to the firm, and hence increase the probability of some potential scenario to trigger the same year.
Human resources and competence	A reduced workforce or a loss of human competences could make the occurrence of the scenario more likely.	The situation considered here is a general deterioration of human resources or competence. This would typically increase significantly the probability of errors, but only slightly the probability of scenarios depending on very specific resources.
Internal control resources	A reduced internal control resources could make the occurrence of the scenario more likely.	The situation considered here is a general deterioration of internal control resources or competence. This would typically increase significantly the probability of frauds, but more slightly the probability of non-compliance.
IT and logistic resources	An IT disruption, or IT systems not in line with customers or third parties expectations (due for instance to a project failure or delay) could make the occurrence of the scenario more likely.	When IT systems are down and a backup solution is used, increasing the probability of errors, internal and external frauds, and customer discontent.
Economic environment	A degradation of the economic environment could make the occurrence of the scenario more likely.	An economic downturn would increase the probability of internal and external frauds, loss of key teams, and customer discontent in particular as far as investment products are concerned, and so on

18.4 COMBINING THE INFLUENCES

Once the bidirectional influence between scenarios and environment factors have been assessed, the influences need to be transformed into pairwise scenarios influences. There are two ways scenarios A and B could become dependent after the analysis of the information collected:

- Either A influences an environment factor, which in turn influences B (this is called a serial path dependency)
- Or both A and B are influenced by the same environment factor (this is called a divergent path dependency).

In Table 18.3, we propose a simple example of the three scenarios just designed. For simplicity, we have used a Yes/No dependency.

This can be represented in the graph shown in Figure 18.2.

If we want to assess a possible dependency between the scenarios Rogue Trading and Mis-Selling, for instance, we can identify the serial paths shown in Figure 18.3, that is, the paths that go from Rogue Trading to Mis-Selling through an environment factor.

TABLE 18.3 Scenarios and Factors: Mutual Influences

Is the scenario impacted by the environment factor?	**Corporate strategy**	**Relation with Regulators**	**Relation with Customers**	**Human Resources**	**Internal Control Resources**	**IT and Logistic Resources**	**Economic environment**
01. Rogue Trading	✓			✓	✓		✓
02. Cyber Attack on Critical Application	✓						✓
03. Mis-selling (retail business)	✓	✓	✓	✓	✓		✓
Would the scenario impact the environment factor?	**Corporate strategy**	**Relation with Regulators**	**Relation with Customers**	**Human Resources**	**Internal Control Resources**	**IT and Logistic Resources**	**Economic environment**
01. Rogue Trading	✓	✓	✓				
02. Cyber Attack on Critical Application		✓	✓				
03. Mis-selling (retail business)	✓	✓	✓		✓		

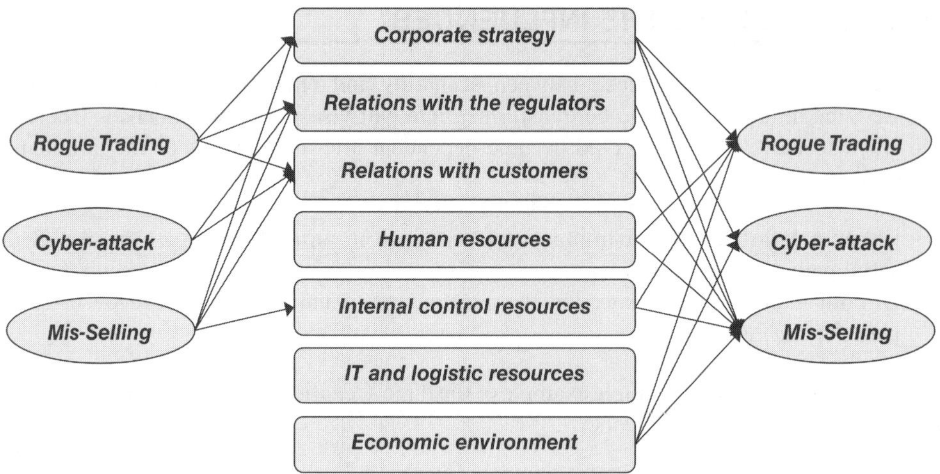

FIGURE 18.2 Scenario Dependencies Paths

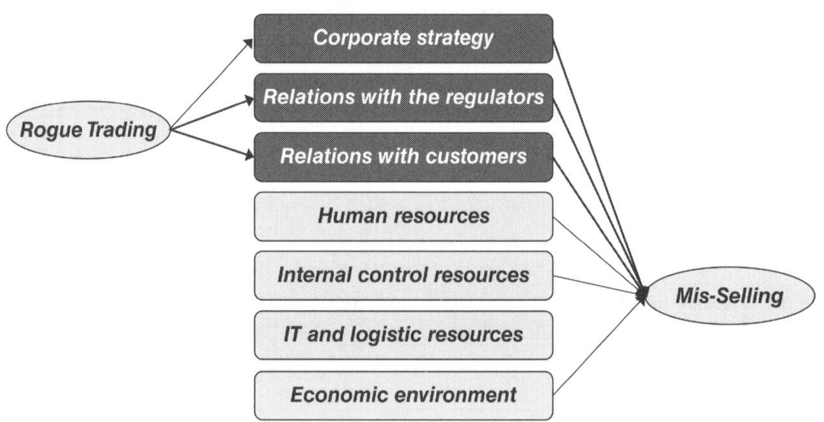

FIGURE 18.3 Serial Paths between Two Scenarios

To identify the divergent paths, we simply have to identify the environment factors that influence both Rogue Trading and Mis-selling, as shown in Figure 18.4.

This results in three serial paths and four divergent paths between the scenarios, that is, seven dependency paths.

18.5 TURNING THE DEPENDENCIES INTO CORRELATIONS

A simple way to use this dependency analysis is to transform the dependency graph into a correlation matrix, with each path between two scenarios being worth one correlation unit.

To be able to assess this elementary correlation, we need to formulate a simple quantitative hypothesis: To what extent would the probability of occurrence be increased if the factor were

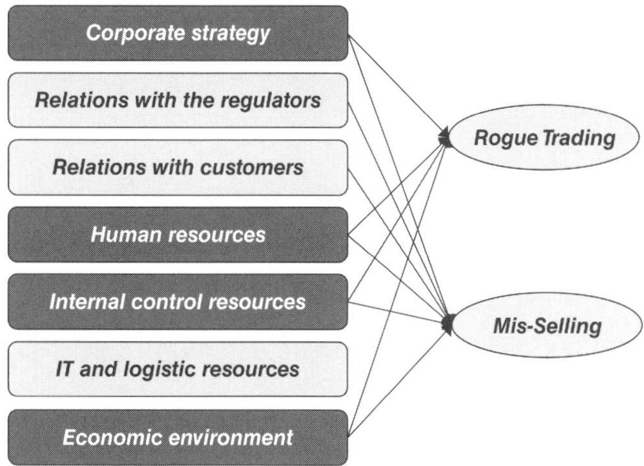

FIGURE 18.4 Divergent Paths between Two Scenarios

to deteriorate? For example, assuming that this increase would be on average 50%, we were able to demonstrate that a conservative correlation assumption for a dependency path would be approximately 2%.

In the above example, this would result in a correlation of about 15% between the scenarios Rogue Trading and Mis-Selling scenarios.

Beyond the practical benefits already mentioned, the mathematical advantage of using this structured method for correlation is that the resulting correlation matrix is PSD.

The calculations to arrive at a correlation weight per path, as well as those to show that the resulting matrix is PSD, are not detailed here because they are too technical.

CHAPTER 19
Applications

19.1 INTRODUCTION

Scenario analysis is a key component of the regulatory frameworks for both operational risk loss projections and risk management. In its 2011 supervisory guidelines for the Advanced Measurement Approach[1], the Basel Committee on Banking Supervision (BCBS) states:

> A robust scenario analysis framework is an important part of the ORMF[2] in order to produce reliable scenario outputs which form part of the input into the AMA model.

At the time of writing, the Advanced Measurement Approach has been abandoned as an appropriate method to calculate the regulatory capital of a bank, but the scenario analysis still remains an essential component of an effective stress-testing framework for the Internal Capital Adequacy Assessment Process (ICAAP). This is clearly indicated in the SR 15-18 letter issued by the US Federal Reserve for large and complex institutions (page 41, Appendix 1):

> The firm should have transparent and well-supported estimation approaches based on both quantitative analysis and expert judgment, and should not rely on unstable or unintuitive correlations to project operational losses. Scenario analysis should be a core component of the firm's operational loss projection approaches.

For the CCAR[3] process, which is the main component of the ICAAP for large US domiciled banks, although banks are not requested to include major operational risk events in the supervisory stress tests as they are considered as idiosyncratic risk events, these events should be included in bank's specific stress tests.

---

[1]See Basel Committee on Banking Supervision, "Operational Risk – Supervisory Guidelines for the Advanced Measurement Approaches", June 2011.

[2]Authors' note: ORMF: Operational Risk Management Framework.

[3]CCAR, "Comprehensive Capital Analysis and Review Process Is a US Federal Reserve Supervisory Program for Large Active Banking Holding Companies (>=$50 billion in total consolidated assets) Domiciled in the United States".

Beyond the regulations mentioned above, it should be kept in mind that an institution is subject to many regulations, international or jurisdiction-specific, and that each of these regulations may have its own requirements for assessing operational risk scenarios. To ensure consistency between all the approaches developed within a firm and avoid ad-hoc responses to each problem, it is recommended to design a multipurpose framework that can be shared by all teams who need to assess operational risk scenarios.

In addition, regulations vary over time to adapt to changes in the environment. New regulations may impose new scenario analysis requirements. For example, corporate exposure to climate risks are a concern for the G20 Financial Stability Board (FSB), which created the Task Force on Climate-Related Financial Disclosures (TCFD) to develop consistent reporting criteria for climate-related financial risks.

By design, the XOI (Exposure, Occurrence Impact) method is independent of the type of application. Since its inception in 2006, this method has enabled its users to meet many regulatory and nonregulatory requirements:

- AMA Operational Risk regulatory capital (Pillar 1, Basel II/III),
- IMA Operational Risk Solvency Capital Requirements (Pillar 1, Solvency II)
- Economic Capital (Pillar 2/ICAAP, Basel III)
- Operational risk stressed capital (CCAR)
- Assessment of controls efficiency
- Assessment of the cost of a new project
- Insurance optimization for a financial institution's real estate portfolio

In the following, we provide an overview of how the XOI approach can be used to address the three main applications to be considered in regulatory or nonregulatory contexts:

1. Projection of operational risk losses
2. Projection of losses related to operational risk under stress
3. Assessment of risk mitigation measures

The boundaries between regulatory and nonregulatory applications are blurred as most regulations foster integrated frameworks in which operational risk models used to estimate capital are also used to support risk management or strategic decisions.

However, we prefer to study these categories independently, since each of them can use specific features of XOI models.

An XOI model is the implementation of the loss generation mechanism for a risk event and relies on three building blocks:

1. A graph, also called "structure", that formalizes the assumptions on the exposure, the occurrence, the impact, and their main drivers
2. A set of quantitative assumptions on the distributions of these drivers
3. A simulation engine that compiles the structure and the quantitative assumptions into a Bayesian network to sample the potential losses related to the risk event

Strictly speaking, the scenario assumptions consist of the structure and all driver distributions. The engine is not part of the scenario assumptions.

The design of XOI models gives them two essential features:

1. Two-sided representation: the structure and quantification assumptions define a unique[4] empirical distribution of potential losses. In other words, building a XOI model implicitly means providing an empirical loss distribution.
2. Sensitivity: When the assumptions on the structure or the drivers are changed, the empirical loss distribution is automatically updated.

We will now describe how we can combine XOI models and take advantage of these two features to meet regulatory and nonregulatory requirements.

19.2 REGULATORY APPLICATIONS

19.2.1 Operational Risk Capital Charge

The capital charge application can be formulated as *defining the required level of capital to cover the operational risk losses at a given confidence level and time horizon.*

The time horizon is generally one year and the confidence level depends on the regulatory requirements. To assess the operational risk regulatory capital with the Advanced Measurement Approach under Basel II/Pillar 1, a 99.9% confidence level is required. To assess Economic Capital as part of the ICAAP process, no confidence level is officially defined: "*banks need to determine an appropriate confidence level for their economic capital models that may vary for different business models*"[5].

This "operational risk capital charge" problem can be translated in a mathematical problem: *Estimate the percentile, at a given level of confidence, of the distribution of the future operational risk losses over a period of time.*

This mathematical translation might need a slight adaptation for economic capital. Depending on its risk profile and the treatment of business-as-usual loss events, a firm could decide that the economic capital should only cover the unexpected losses. As a result, the mathematical expectation, or the most likely loss, should be subtracted from the percentile to obtain the economic capital. Whatever the situation, if we are able to build the overall distribution of the future operational risk losses, it is straightforward to extract any relevant statistics: percentile, mean, most likely value, and so on.

In the fictitious example shown in Figure 19.1, the confidence level for regulatory capital is 99.9% but the firm may consider that this level is too conservative and set its confidence level for economic capital at 95%. The firm could also exclude the BAU risks from the economic capital as they are covered by insurance.

The first step toward the construction of the loss distribution is to decompose the operational risk space into units of measurement (UoM). Two types of UoM are defined: the UoMs relating

---

[4] Although the sampling process based on Monte Carlo simulation has some variance and can lead to variable samples, we refer here to the theoretical distribution to which this process would converge if the sample size were infinite.

[5] See Basel Committee on Banking Supervision, "Range of Practices and Issues in Economic Capital Frameworks", March 2009.

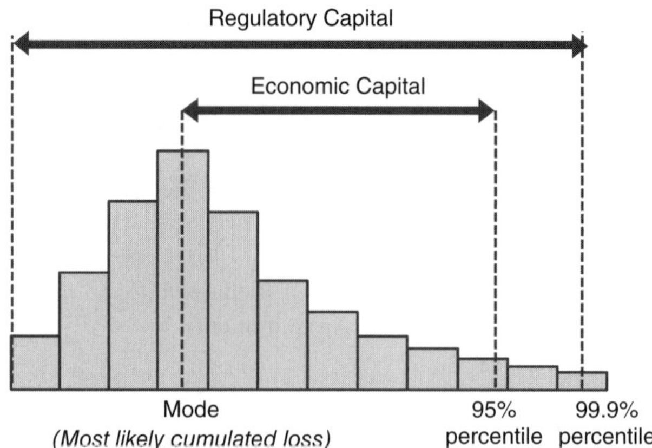

FIGURE 19.1 Inferring Regulatory and Economic Capital from a Loss Distribution

to material risks quantified with scenario-based approaches and the UoMs relating to milder risks that will be modelled through statistical approaches[6].

The process used to segregate high and low severity risks has been discussed in Part III. This process typically relies on the RCSA, supplemented by an expert-based decision. Keep in mind that the main purpose of this process is that extreme risks are analyzed in detail by SMEs and not only addressed with statistics.

The second step is to develop a XOI model or a statistical model for every UoM, depending on its type. It should be noted that, by construction, XOI models will contribute to the tail of the loss distribution since they represent the most material risks while statistical models will contribute to his body since they capture lower severity risks.

The screenshot in Figure 19.2 shows a complete operational risk model with 14 structured scenarios and 3 LDA components, represented in the MSTAR simulation tool.

The third step is to select the copula and define the correlation matrix to represent the joint distribution between the UoM operational risk distributions[7].

We have already discussed the challenges of assessing the correlations between scenarios, and presented a method based on causality analysis. However, in a complete model, we have to also assess the correlations between statistical components; and between statistical components and scenarios.

The assessment of the correlation between moderate events and severe events is an interesting question, and has been the subject of research in safety engineering.

[6]The low frequency and low severity risks are not material, the medium to high frequency but low severity risks can be addressed by statistical models like the Loss Distribution Approach.

[7]The use of a correlation matrix and a copula are not the only methods to represent the dependencies between scenarios. As shown above, it is possible to use a more structural method based on the identification of dependency paths between scenarios. But the correlation matrix/copula is the most common approach and hence the easiest to benchmark for regulators. As the purpose of this chapter is not to compare the potential benefits of the multiple aggregation methods, we illustrate the capital charge calculation with this commonly used method.

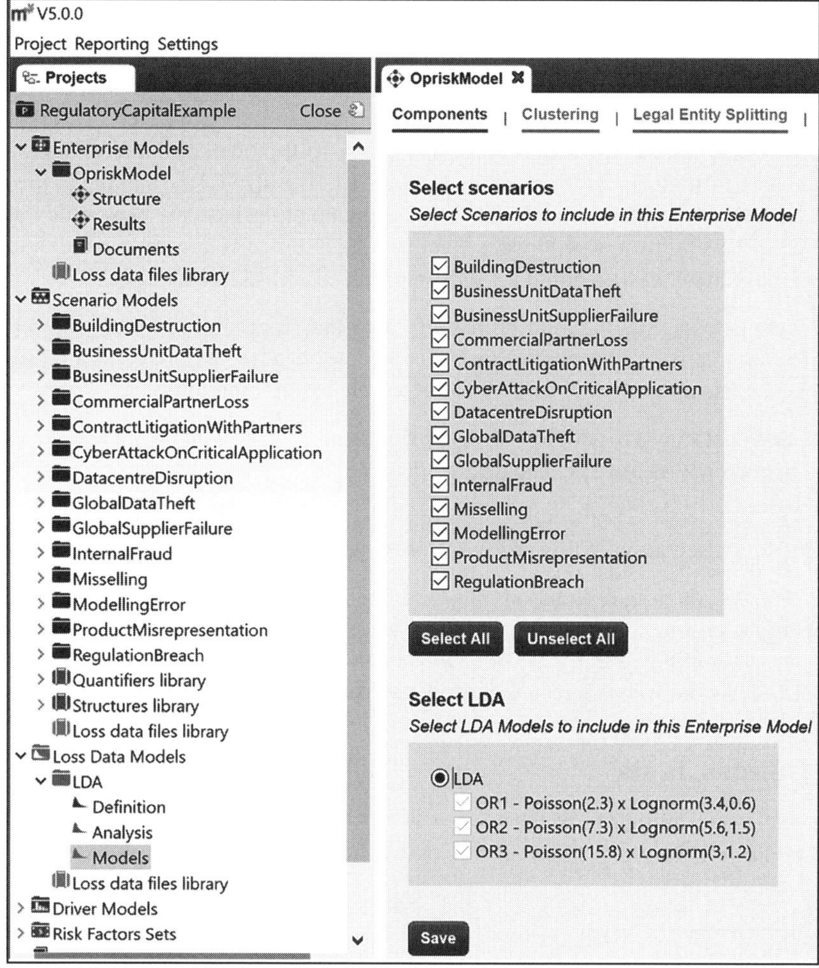

FIGURE 19.2 A Complete Operational Risk Model in MSTAR Tool

In a few words, two points of view can be considered:

1. An increase in the frequency of minor events may indicate a weakening of controls, which could lead to more serious events – provided of course that controls addressing minor events also have an effect on major ones, which we doubt.
2. A decrease in the frequency of minor events reduces the vigilance of the organization, and could also allow important events to occur.

That said, and given that the contribution of statistical UoMs to the tail of the model is expected to be small compared to scenario models, we propose a conservative assumption for capital modelling. This assumption simply considers a 100% correlation rate between LDA components, on the one hand, and between LDA components and scenarios, on the other hand.

This would mean in practice to (1) calculate the aggregate loss distribution for XOI scenario models, and then (2) add the percentiles of each LDA to the percentile of the aggregate scenario loss distribution.

The fourth step is to sample each of the UoM models, independently, to generate a large number of potential future losses. The sampling algorithm for XOI models is detailed in Part IV and the sampling algorithm for LDA is detailed in Part III. The size of the sample is the number of years we need to simulate to achieve a stable estimate of the extreme percentile defined by the confidence level. From experience, a 1 million sample size is generally enough to ensure the stability of the 99.9% percentile for most of the XOI and LDA models[8].

The fifth step is to sample the joint probability distribution according to the selected copula and correlation matrix. As a matter of fact, this process[9] can be interpreted as a reordering of the independent samples in order to reflect the correlation assumptions.

The sixth and final step is to add the reordered UoM samples to calculate the overall sample of potential operational risk losses. The desired percentiles of this aggregated sample must then be extracted.

A simplified representation of this process is presented in Figure 19.3.

In conclusion, the dual representation of XOI models is particularly useful for capital calculation, which is an operation on distribution. The empirical loss distribution aspect of XOI models allows sampling, exactly as for LDA models, but their "loss generation mechanism" aspect also allows more sophisticated dependency structures to be defined.

19.2.2 Stress Tests

The stress-test application can be formulated as follows: define the level of capital that would be required to cover future operational risk losses under stressed conditions over a given time horizon.

What is the difference between this problem and the problem of operational risk capital charge presented above?

Stress tests are one of the tools used by the regulator or the firm itself to assess the robustness of its capital plan. The time horizon imposed by the regulator for this exercise might be longer than one year. For CCAR, the firms are required to submit a detailed plan over a nine-quarter horizon. Changing the time horizon may affect many aspects of the modelling process.

First it could change the scope of the risk events to be considered. The longer the time horizon, the more prospective the identification should be. If a bank has a current plan to move some of its transactions to a blockchain-based process over the next three years, some new

[8]As the LDA used in this context are only meant to cover low severity risks, the severity distribution used should be "thin-tailed". This ensures a swift convergence of the Monte-Carlo simulation process.

[9]If M denotes the number of UoMs, and N denotes the size of the sample, this process generates N M-uplets of probabilities. For every M-uplet of probabilities $\{p_1, \ldots, p_k, \ldots, p_M\}$ picked out from this sample, corresponds to a M-uplet of loss percentiles $\{L_1, \ldots, L_k, \ldots, L_M\}$, where L_k is the ${p_k}^{th}$ percentile in the loss sample generated for the kth UoM during the previous step.

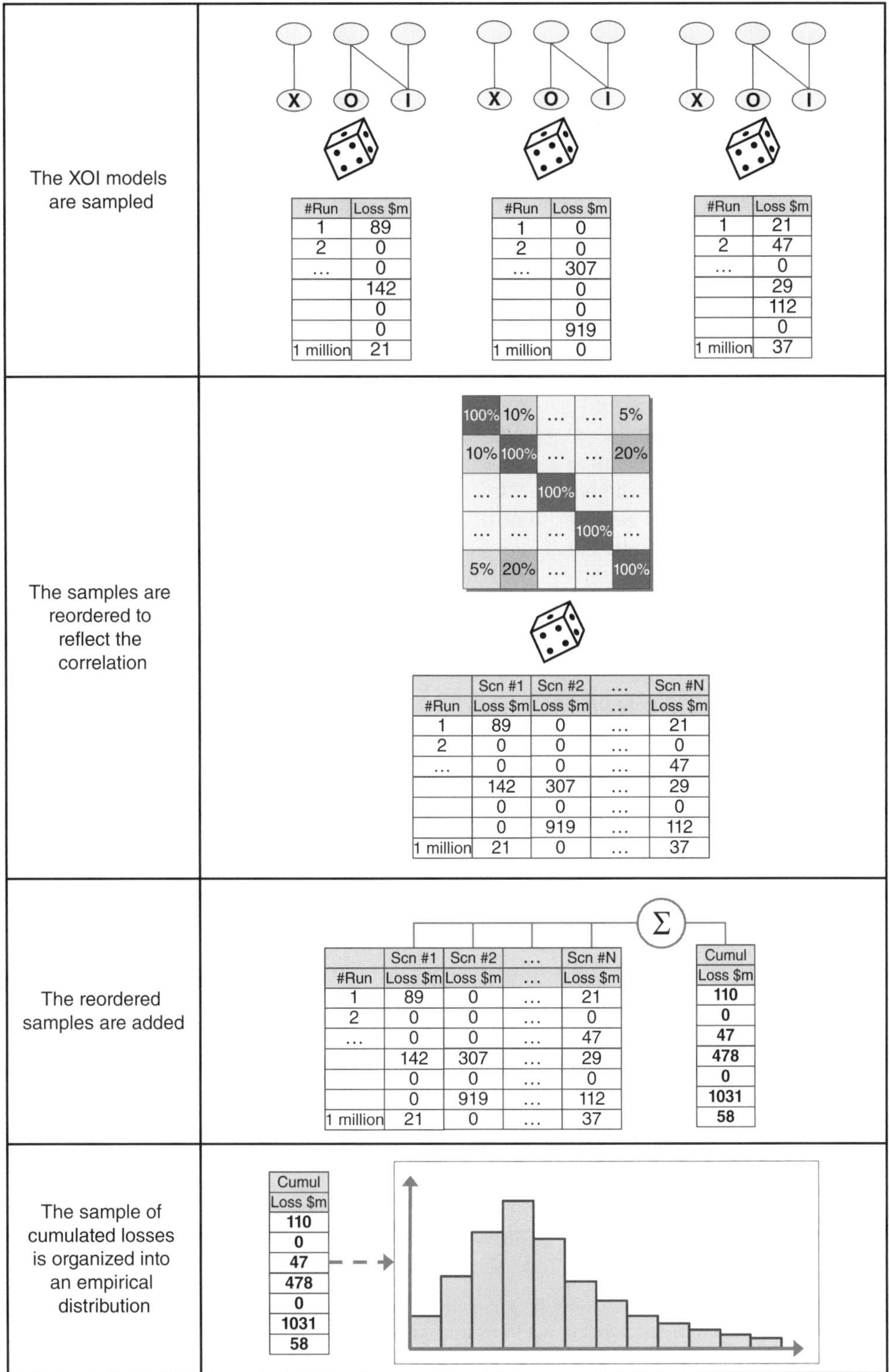

FIGURE 19.3 Building the Potential Loss Distribution Using XOI Models

challenges and risks might be worth being considered: new regulatory risks, technical risks during implementation, and so on.

Not only the risks scope, but also the distribution of the drivers may also depend on the time horizon. First, the probability of an adverse event occurring in a given period increases with the length of that period: this is the first dimension of any risk exposure analysis. The longer you are exposed, the more likely you are to suffer a loss, everything else being kept equal. In addition, a longer time horizon potentially implies that a greater number of situations must be represented in driver distributions.

It seems that even though XOI models may be different, the modeling method does not change when the time horizon changes. But is that really the case? The stress scenarios defined by the FED[10] are quarterly assumptions based on a set of economic indicators. Ideally, therefore, the firm analysis should stick to this schedule and understand how fluctuations in economic indicators could influence risks on a quarterly basis.

In theory, this could mean that an operational risk model is required for each quarter. Fortunately, given that operational risks are either idiosyncratic or loosely related to FED variables, the construction of such a "high frequency" operational risk model is not only intractable but also irrelevant. In the best case, for some of the scenarios, the design of two models could be considered to cover two consecutive one-year periods[11].

However, it is technically possible to cover several periods of time with different risk profile within a single XOI model by applying the following method:

- The exposure is be the product of the number of exposed units by the number of periods of time. For example, in the case of a cyber attack scenario, the economic context drives the revenue, the volume of transactions, and the compensation to the clients in case of higher market volatility.
- A “Period” node is introduced to the graph of the XOI model and conditions the nodes, which distribution is sensitive to the period of time. In the case of the cyber attack scenario, the “Period” node drives the Revenue, the volume of Transactions, and the Compensation rate.

This multiperiod adaptation of the cyber attack scenario is shown in Figure 19.4 above.

Apart from the question of time horizon, which we just explained how to address with an XOI model, how does the evaluation of capital under stress differ from the assessment of capital charge for operational risk?

Assuming that there is no change in the risk profile to be expected over the period, could we reuse the XOI models we designed for regulatory capital assessment, and apply a similar process to estimate a remote percentile that would be considered as a projection of operating losses under stress?

This would be an appealing idea, because it would mean that all we would have to do is assign each level of stress[12] a confidence level, and then follow the same process as for regulatory capital.

---

[10]Refer to the Scenario Analysis chapter in Part III for a description of the FED regulatory scenarios.

[11]Actually, in the context of CCAR, the second model would cover one year and one quarter.

[12]Either defined by the regulator or by the firm

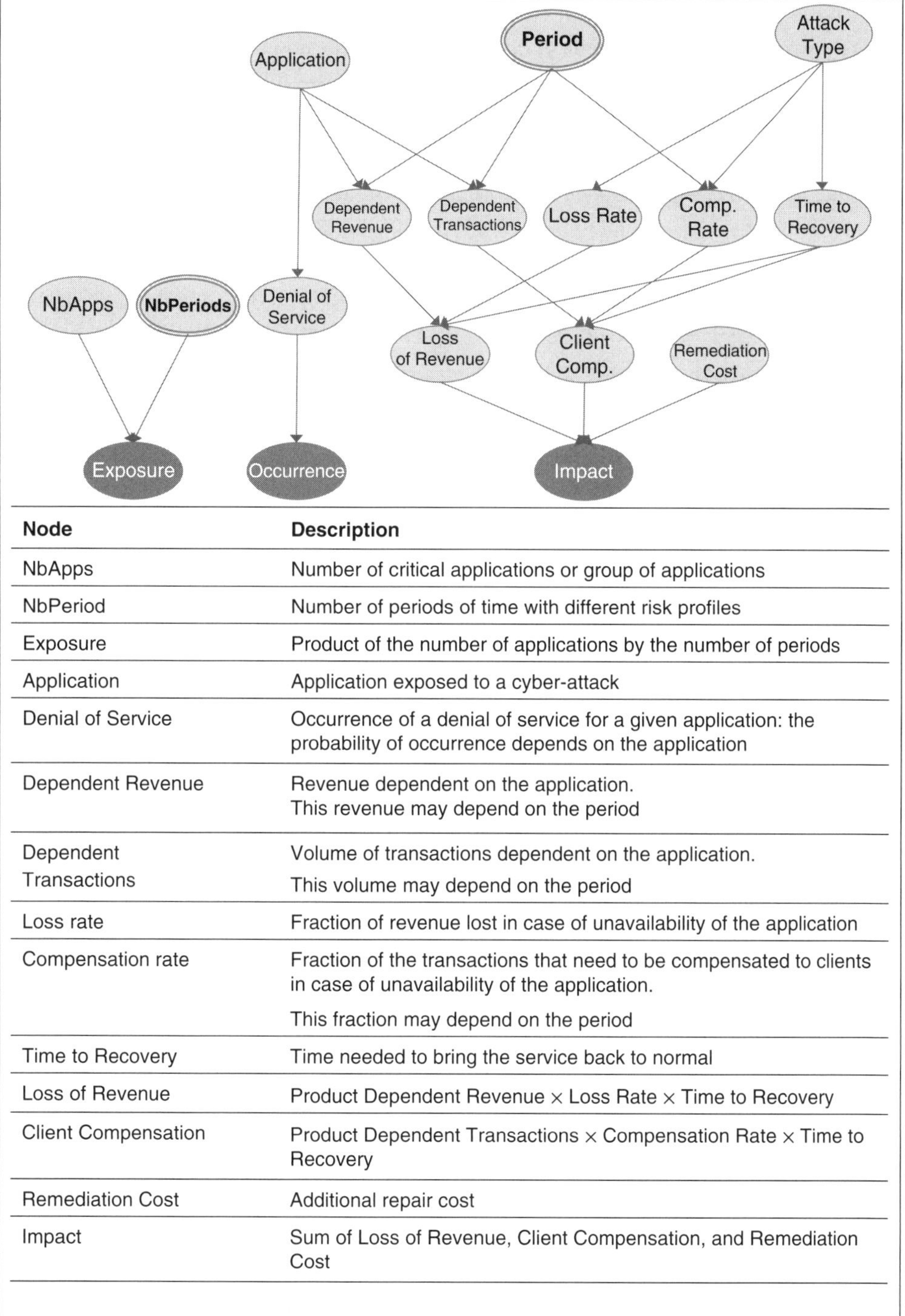

Node	Description
NbApps	Number of critical applications or group of applications
NbPeriod	Number of periods of time with different risk profiles
Exposure	Product of the number of applications by the number of periods
Application	Application exposed to a cyber-attack
Denial of Service	Occurrence of a denial of service for a given application: the probability of occurrence depends on the application
Dependent Revenue	Revenue dependent on the application. This revenue may depend on the period
Dependent Transactions	Volume of transactions dependent on the application. This volume may depend on the period
Loss rate	Fraction of revenue lost in case of unavailability of the application
Compensation rate	Fraction of the transactions that need to be compensated to clients in case of unavailability of the application. This fraction may depend on the period
Time to Recovery	Time needed to bring the service back to normal
Loss of Revenue	Product Dependent Revenue × Loss Rate × Time to Recovery
Client Compensation	Product Dependent Transactions × Compensation Rate × Time to Recovery
Remediation Cost	Additional repair cost
Impact	Sum of Loss of Revenue, Client Compensation, and Remediation Cost

FIGURE 19.4 Multiperiod XOI Model for a Cyber Attack Scenario

The answers to the above questions are:

- Yes, we can reuse XOI models designed for other applications, and
- No, we cannot interpret the projection of operational risk under stress as a percentile of the distribution of future losses.

Let's start with the second point. By nature, stress-test scenarios are neither forecasts nor expectations of what might happen in the future. Stress-testing scenarios are only reasonable but purely hypothetical assumptions to test the company's resilience.

These assumptions are not assigned any probabilities and therefore cannot be part of the sampling process we have described for assessment of the operational risk capital charge. The firm has to estimate the potential futures losses in the hypothetical context described by the stress test scenario.

Instead of a percentile calculation, the mathematical problem of operational risk stress-testing could be formulated as follow: *Estimate the conditional expectation of the distribution of the future operational risk losses over a time horizon given a set of assumptions.* The stressed operational risk capital is rather as the mathematical expectation of the stressed operational risk distribution.

Based on this formulation, the most appropriate usage of XOI models may depend on the stress-test assumptions. First, it is not easy to translate the assumptions of regulatory stress tests, which are mostly economic, into actionable assumptions for operational risk models. Indeed, operational risks are generally considered to be idiosyncratic or loosely coupled with economic drivers (see for instance Losses Projection in Part III.) As a result, the company may have to define its own set of contextual factors, more closely related to its operational risk profile. In fact, the company has no choice but to design, for different levels of stress, a set of assumptions specific to operational risks and consistent with its business profile.

Two types of assumptions can be made by the firm which will result in different ways of using XOI models.

The first approach is to select a subset of scenarios for each stress level. The company will select from the portfolio of risks it has already identified and modeled those that could reasonably occur for the level of stress considered. Each stress level would be assigned a set of operational risks, and the higher the stress level, the more severe the risks chosen should be.

This approach means that even if you have identified 50 material risks in your firm, you consider that a handful of them will occur. For example, a firm may specify a stress test as the occurrence of three major events as described in Table 19.1.

This approach is probably the easiest one to implement, but also the most arbitrary. The firm can legitimately consider that, among all the material risks it has identified, there is no logic in explicitly choosing which ones will occur.

TABLE 19.1 Selection of Plausible Scenarios

A major cyber attack on the payment-settlement system will occur.
The firm will be fined for a breach of antitrust regulation.
Investors will sue the firm for having misrepresented the financial health of a large company.

The second approach is to stress some factors that drive the entire portfolio of risks.

In this approach, the firm will define a set of specific operational risk factors, such as the regulatory environment, the level of cyberthreat, the level of natural disasters, and so on, and then describe for each stress level the set of assumptions relating to these factors.

We will now explain how the selection method (the first one) and the portfolio method (the second one) can be implemented with XOI models.

First of all, it should be remembered that, regardless of the method chosen to describe stress tests, the problem is to estimate a mathematical expectation. The good news is that mathematical expectations, unlike percentiles, can be added. This means that the conditional expectation of a set of risks is equal to the sum of the conditional expectations of the individual risks.

Since no complex aggregation is needed, the implementation of the methods can be described at the level of one single XOI model.

19.2.2.1 The "Portfolio" Method Assuming that a set of XOI models has been designed for each major risk, the following steps will be performed.

Frist, the firm must define a set of *stress factors*. A stress factor is a factor that determines the firm's operational risk profile. Each factor should cover an aspect of the firm's operational risk environment: cyber threat, regulation, climate, geopolitics, economy, market, controls, supply chain, IT infrastructure, and so on,

The choice of the best level of granularity is at the firm's initiative. However, we recommend starting with a small set (5 to 10 factors) and refining the list if the factors do not seem focused enough when trying to associate them with the XOI model drivers.

Second, the drivers used in the XOI models must be examined to link them to the stress factors they are influenced by. This matching ensures that the firm is able to propagate the stress-test assumptions to the model drivers. Some of the drivers may be either independent or loosely dependent on any of the stress factors. The matching would result in a table similar to Table 19.2.

Third, the stress-test assumptions will be defined as a set of consistent what-if assumptions on the stress factors. These assumptions could be represented by qualitative stress factor

TABLE 19.2 Mapping Stress Factors to Scenarios Drivers

XOI Model	Driver	Stress Factor
Rogue trading	Time to detection	Controls
Rogue trading	Concealed position	Controls
Rogue trading	Daily volatility	Markets
...	...	...
Employee class action	Class action	Economy, regulatory
Employee class action	Average settlement	Regulatory
...	...	...
Trading Algo Runaway	Error	IT, controls
...	...	...

assessments in the same spirit as the geo-strategic scenarios defined by the NIC in Part III[13], for example: "The regulator scrutiny is increased", "The level of cyber threat is moderate", and "The markets are highly volatile".

But based on the mapping matrix established previously, these assumptions should be translated into more quantitative assumptions about the factors influenced by stress factors. In practice, this ultimately means changing the distribution of the XOI model drivers. For example, if the stress assumption on the Market stress factor is "Markets are very volatile", since this factor influences the stock market volatility factor used by the Rogue Trading XOI model, an assumption should be proposed on this factor to reflect instability. If the default assumption for the stock market volatility factor is 1.5%, it could, for instance, be increased to 2.5% (see Figure 19.5).

It should be remembered that the assumptions of stress testing are not intended to provide expectations or forecasts of what the future state of the world will be like. As a result, SMEs have some flexibility to define sensible assumptions to describe what could be a more adverse environment for the firm.

Defining the stress factors and their different configurations is a high-level task that requires a 360-degree perspective and must therefore involve the company's senior management.

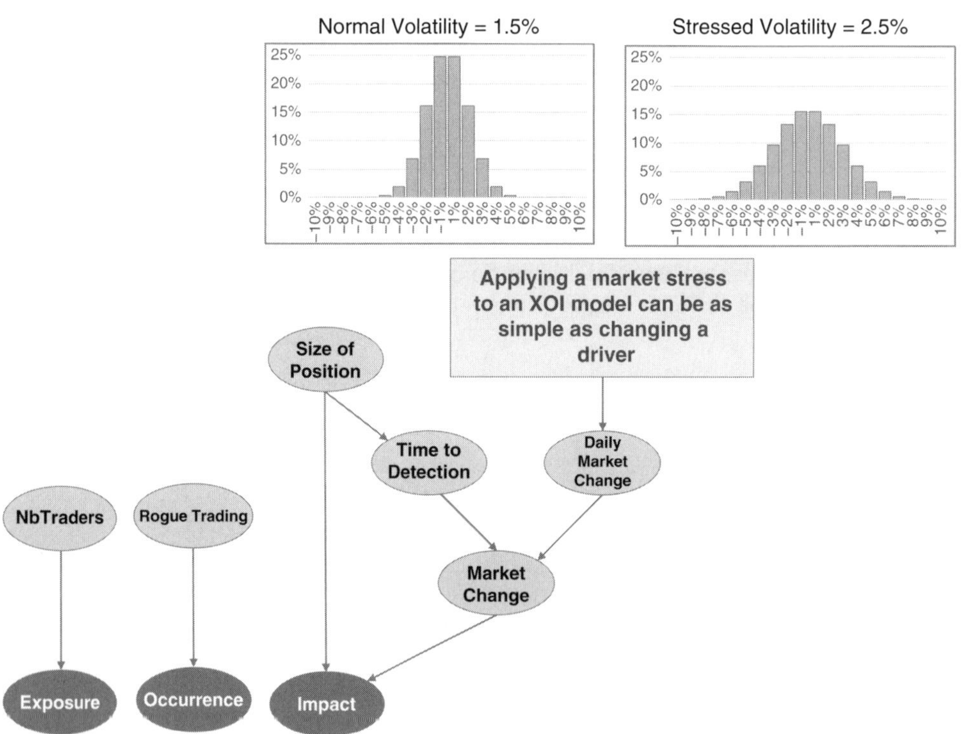

FIGURE 19.5 Applying a macroeconomic scenario to an XOI model

[13]See the "Scenario Analysis" chapter in Part III.

The translation of stress factor assumptions into hypothetical quantifications for drivers should be done by those involved in the design and quantification of XOI models to ensure consistency of quantifications. These quantifications should be plausible (for instance. a 10% daily stock market volatility would be outside the range of reasonable values) and consistent with each other.

Fourth, once the stressed version of the XOI drivers have been defined, each XOI model has to be sampled in the same way as it was to estimate the operational risk capital. The result of this process is a set of samples, one for each XOI model, that reflect the set of stress-test assumptions.

Fifth and final step, the mathematical expectations are calculated for each sample[14] and summed to obtain a figure that represents the stressed capital. Each set of stressed assumptions gives a different value for the stressed capital.

19.2.2.2 The Selection Method In the basic and simplest version, it is assumed that a subset of scenarios will effectively occur. For either of the selected scenarios, provided that a XOI model has been designed, the stress assumption is that the scenario occurs on any of its exposed units[15]. From the XOI model's perspective, this is simply equivalent to setting the occurrence variable to "true" and recalculating the distribution of the impact with Bayesian inference.

The stressed loss is the mathematical expectation of the conditional impact. It can be denoted by $E(Impact|Occurrence = True)$, where $E()$ denotes the mathematical expectation function.

It is not necessary to sample the XOI model as for the capital calculation problem. Only Bayesian inference is executed on the restricted Occurrence Impact model (see Figure 19.6).

An enhanced version of the selection method could rely on assumptions on a set of stress factors as presented in the "portfolio" method, but could also be more specific about the conditions of occurrence. For instance, in the case of a cyber attack scenario, one can also assume that the event will occur in volatile market conditions (stress factor assumption). This will be represented in the scenarios by setting to "High" the assumptions on the volume of transactions and on the compensation rate (see Figure 19.7).

It is also possible to consider that a scenario will occur several times on different exposed units. In that case, the same XOI model should be used several times with a different set of assumptions. For example, if the firm wants to express that a stress scenario on a cyber attack scenario would involve two attacks over the same period, the same XOI model should be used twice, with appropriate assumptions about the distribution of the model drivers, and the two resulting expected losses should be added.

For a given set of stress-test assumptions, the mathematical expectations of the impact distribution for each XOI model have to be summed to obtain the stressed capital.

[14]To calculate the expected loss of a XOI model, it is not necessary to sample the XOI model through Monte-Carlo simulation.The expected loss can be calculated directly through Bayesian inference.

[15]We will see later in this chapter that we can also specify that a selected exposed unit is hit by the event or that several selected exposed units are hit.

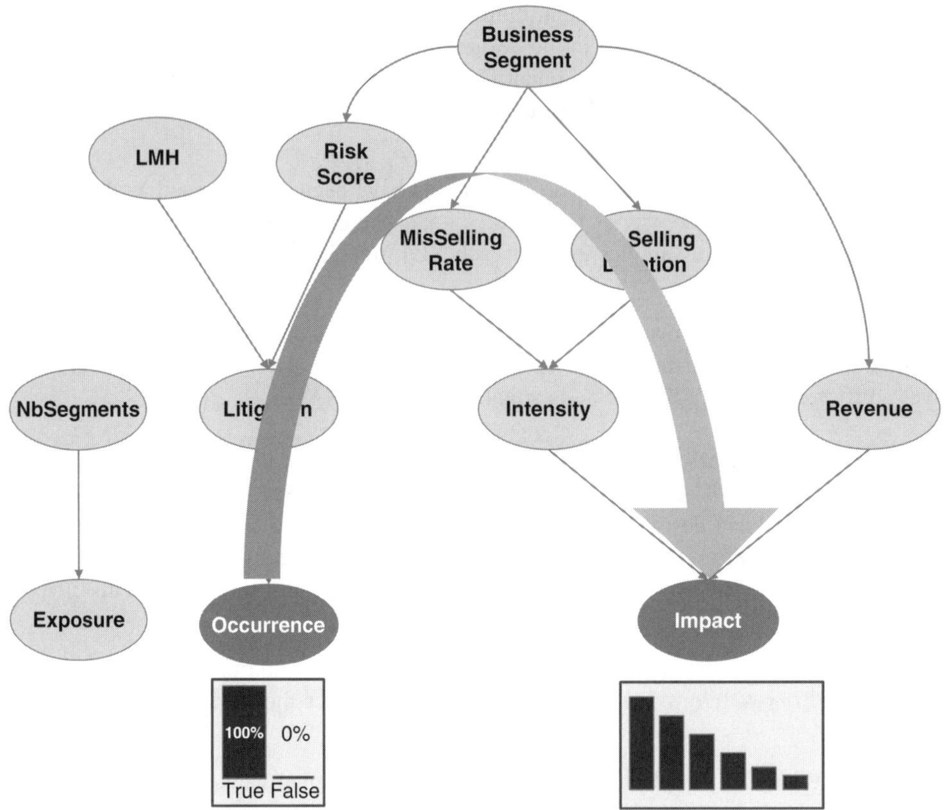

FIGURE 19.6 Selection Method for Stress Testing
Conditional distribution of impact, given the event has occurred.

19.3 RISK MANAGEMENT

XOI models decompose risks into three dimensions: Exposure, Occurrence, and Impact.

Controls, or more generally mitigation actions can have an effect on each of these dimensions:

1. Reducing the exposure to a scenario is "risk avoidance", at least partial.
2. Reducing the probability of occurrence of a scenario is "risk prevention"
3. Reducing the potential impact of a scenario is "risk protection"

In this chapter, we explain:

- How to identify controls from XOI models
- How to represent controls in XOI models

Furthermore, we will discuss why the representation of controls as barriers – as is done in industry – is not fully applicable for operational risk scenarios.

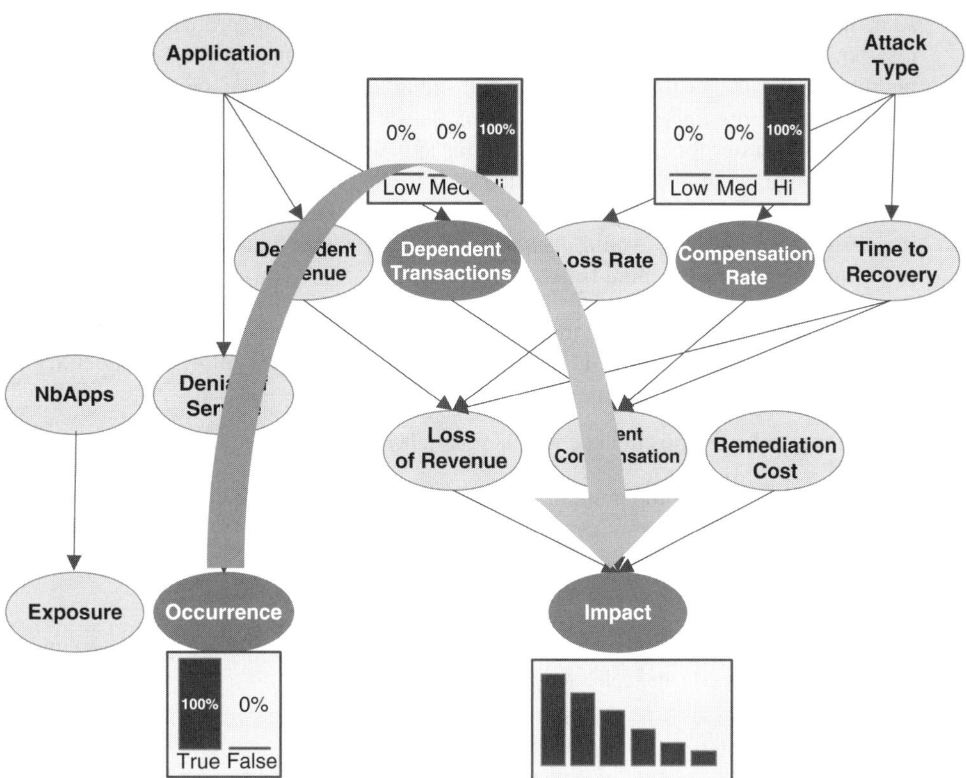

FIGURE 19.7 Enhanced Selection Method for Stress Testing
Conditional distribution of impact, given the event has occurred **and** the market is volatile.

19.3.1 Identifying Controls from XOI Models

The simple fact of analyzing a scenario in these three dimensions gives some directions for identifying controls:

1. *Can we reduce the exposure to this scenario?* This is often done at the cost of reduced business, and although generally not desirable, it can be considered. For instance, reducing the number of traders will certainly have an impact on the exposure to Rogue Trading, but it also has direct consequences on the trading revenue. On the other hand, trying to reduce the number of people having access to large volumes of customer data could reveal situations where the access rights granted to some people are not necessary for their job, and can be revoked with no or little impact on business.
2. *Can we reduce the probability of occurrence of this scenario?* Of course, this is usually the most desired type of control, as reducing the exposure has often a business cost, and reducing the impact implies that the event occurred anyway, which is always perceived as a failure. Not surprisingly, being able to identify controls that can reduce the probability of occurrence is as difficult as assessing the probability of rare events itself. It can be considered only in the situation where the probability of occurrence can be made dependent on

some feature of the exposed object. For instance, considering the probability of a natural disaster, it is dependent on the location of the building. Moving some of the most exposed buildings to a safer location is an action that should directly reduce the probability.

3. *Can we reduce the impact of this scenario?* This can be related to resilience analysis. It is generally easier for experts to consider the situations where the scenario has occurred and to imagine actions that could reduce its impact. For instance, considering a major card compromise, being able to identify the point of compromise early enough through improved expert systems would allow to stop all the cards that have been used at this point, and reduce the potential fraud.

Of course, this analysis is made even more powerful when the scenario dimensions have been made dependent on drivers. The same reasoning will apply to drivers, allowing to identifying more targeted and better-defined controls.

For instance, several scenarios include a “reaction delay” to the occurrence of the scenario:

- Time needed to identify the point of compromise in a major credit card compromise
- Time needed to switch to another supplier
- Time needed to detect a fictitious trading position
- Time needed to recover from an application disruption, and so on

Analysing how to reduce this reaction time is certainly a concrete discussion that can be undertaken with business experts and reflected in the scenario.

19.3.2 Representing Controls in XOI Model

An XOI model is a decomposition of the loss generation mechanism into exposure, occurrence, and impact, and the drivers that influence them.

This is a level of decomposition beyond the usual Frequency and Severity assessment, but this is not detailed enough to be able to represent barriers in scenarios, unless in specific cases.

The representation of controls in XOI models can therefore take the forms presented in Table 19.3.

19.3.3 Comparison with Risk Models Used in Industrial Safety

19.3.3.1 The Bow-Tie Model The representations used in industrial safety or dependability theory are very present in the way people think about representations of controls.

One of the popular representations in industrial safety is the so-called “bow tie” model (Figure 19.8).

According to this model:

- The “hazard” is the activity which bears risk by nature, such as “working with explosive materials”. In the banking industry, hazards are the activities that are risky by nature, such as “working with traders”, “acquiring merchants”, “selling products to clients”, and so on.
- The “causes”, also called threats, are the events which, alone or in combination, could lead to the transformation of the hazard into an event. For instance, this could be “loss of operator attention”, and so on.
- The “consequences” are, simply, what could happen after the event occurred.

TABLE 19.3 Representation of Controls in XOI Models

Type of Representation	Example
Representation of a control as a barrier	For some type of errors, there might exist a four-eye control above a given amount. In that case, the control can be directly represented as a node in the XOI model ("barrier").
Representation of the dependency of the occurrence to some category of the exposed object, and representation of the controls through the allocation of objects in categories	The probability of a natural disaster on a building is dependent on the location. A change in the repartition of buildings to increase their proportion in safer zones is a representation of the control. The probability of a card data compromise within a merchant can be considered as dependent of the merchant's PCI DSS[16] status. Increasing the proportion of PCI DSS compliant merchants through incentives is a control that can be represented in the model.
Representation of the controls in a node that can be subject to revision if the quality of controls is not maintained.	The fact that a firm has obtained from the regulator that a Consent order is lifted, is the acknowledged materialization of improved controls, and can be represented in the distribution of potential fines intensity. This representation is an incentive to maintain the quality of the controls. A similar reasoning could apply to the success of simulation exercises. If a rogue trading is simulated; than the time to detection of the position during the simulation can be used to assess the driver value. But it is recommended to keep a node to represent that this performance is guaranteed only if periodic simulations are performed.
What-if analysis	This representation is similar to the one above, but instead of being kept in the actual model, the representation of control alternatives is represented in a separate "what-if" analysis model.
Representation of all controls implicitly in the quantification of the XOI model drivers	The probability of occurrence of a wire transfer error is what it is because of all the controls in place: simply using the observed probability of error is a simple representation of controls, but is not visible.
Use of industry assessments	A trader going rogue is a very rare event and it is very difficult to assess the efficiency of controls on this event. Therefore, it is recommended to use the industry level assessment.

[16]Payment Card Industry Data Security Standard.

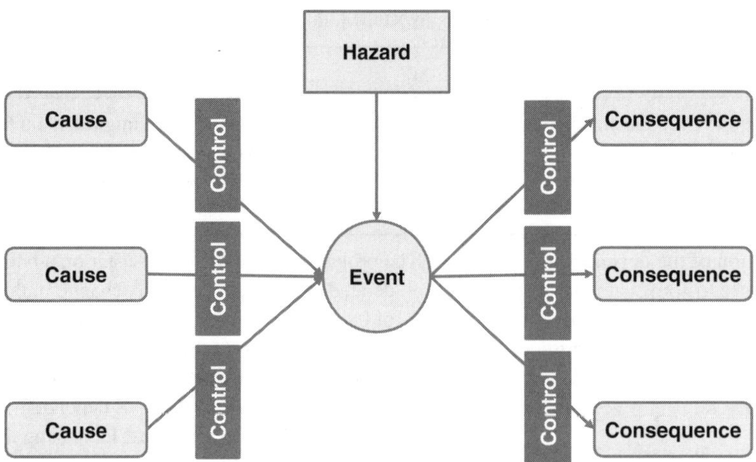

FIGURE 19.8 Representation of Controls in a Bow Tie Model

In this representation, *controls are viewed as barriers*. Controls stop potential causes to manifest, thus reducing their possible contribution to the occurrence of the event, or limit the consequences of the event. Therefore, control failures or inadequacies can be seen as the real causes of the events.

For this reason, it is natural to represent controls in the bow-tie graph.

19.3.3.2 The XOI Model The XOI model allows exactly the same type of representation, and even more powerful ones.

In the XOI model represented in Figure 19.9:

- The hazard is the exposure (remember: "working with traders", "acquiring merchants", "selling products to clients")
- The occurrence can be represented as a logical operation $AND(Cause, NOT(Control))$, which in that case would mean that the event would occur IF the Cause Occurred and the Control failed.

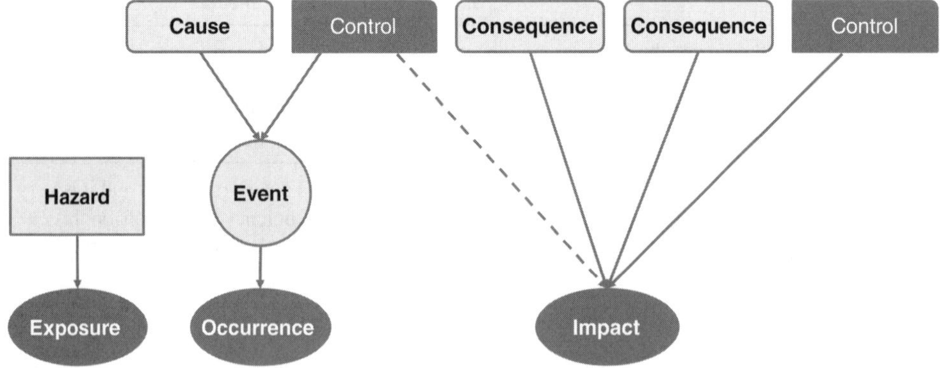

FIGURE 19.9 Mapping of a Bow-Tie Control Representation to an XOI Model

- The impact can be represented in various ways to account for controls, but it could be something like *IF*(*Control*, *MinorConsequence*, *MajorConsequence*), reading: if the control works, the consequences would be limited to minor impact, and could be major if the barrier fails.

The XOI model is potentially more powerful than the bow-tie representation because it allows to represent barriers having an effect on occurrence and on impact simultaneously.

19.3.3.3 Can We Represent Barriers in XOI Models? Having said that, why can't we represent controls this way in XOI models?

There are several reasons to this. In particular, there are no controls acting explicitly as barriers, in the sense that the simultaneous occurrence of the cause and the failure of the control will trigger the occurrence of the scenario.

Consider again the Rogue Trading scenario. The hazard is "Working with Traders", which exposes the firm to Rogue Trading. Some potential causes of a trader going rogue are:

- The trader wants to recover from past losses.
- The trader is in a difficult personal situation that he/she needs to solve.

We could very well write a Rogue Trading scenario this way, decomposing the occurrence into one of the two possibilities.

Then we could identify barriers for this:

1. Monitor traders' performance to identify those with recent bad results
2. Have periodic interviews with traders to detect their personal difficulties

The occurrence would therefore be represented as shown in Figure 19.10 above.

A Rogue Trading event occurs *if* one of the following two situations occur:

1. The trader has experienced high trading losses, is not identified by the performance monitoring program, and decides to go rogue
2. The trader faces a difficult personal situation, while his situation is not detected by periodic interviews, and decides to go rogue

In this situation, assessing the scenario would mean:

- Assess the probability that a trader experiences recurrent loss, and decides to recover from them by going rogue
- Assess the probability that a trader goes through a difficult personal situation (gambling debts, need to help a relative, etc.), and decides to go rogue to solve his/her problems

Then we would need to:

- Assess the probability that the monitoring of traders fails to identify a trader with significant losses
- Assess the probability that the periodic interviews fail to detect the difficulties

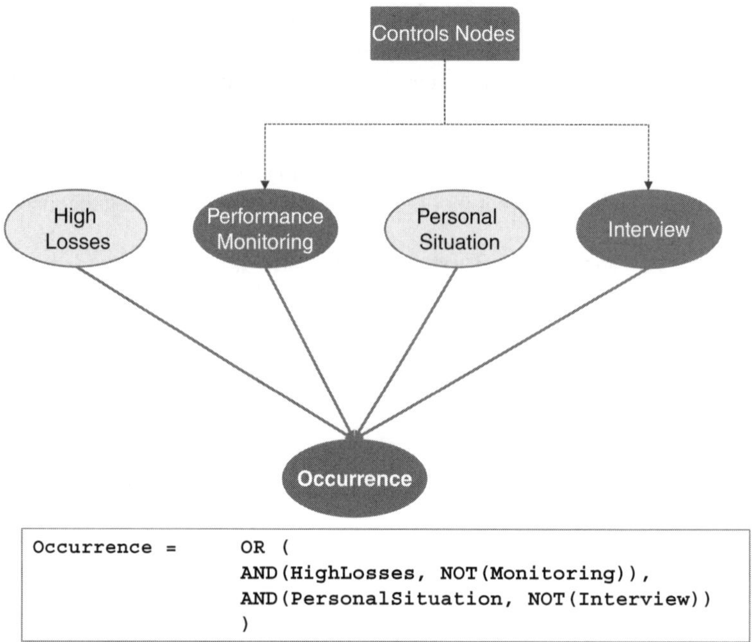

FIGURE 19.10 Representation of Barriers in an XOI Model

This works perfectly fine in theory. But of course, each XOI model would require a PhD thesis to assess these drivers. And of course, the list of causes is never guaranteed to be comprehensive.

19.3.4 Does One Model Fit All?

In this chapter, we have shown how XOI models can be applied to the major applications that are of interest in the operational risk field, whether regulatory or not. Actually, we have used the XOI models for other types of applications such as calibration of insurance program[17], splitting of a firmwide model between legal entities or business units through breakdown of the exposure. The range of applications that can rely on XOI models underlines the versatility of the XOI approach.

However, one question has not yet been clearly addressed: Does one single model fit all these applications? Can a model built for regulatory purpose also be used for risk management? We assumed the answer was "yes", but we need to come back to this question now.

The XOI approach aims at building scenario models with a structured approach, collecting all relevant knowledge related to the drivers of the risk. Which knowledge element to collect first depends on the application. In the case of regulatory capital assessment, an

[17]For a detailed description of insurance program modelling, see L. Condamin, J. P. Louisot, and P. Naïm (2006), *Risk Quantification: Management, Diagnosis and Hedging* (Hoboken, NJ: Wiley).

accurate understanding of the controls in place could be replaced by simple and conservative assumptions if the firm wishes to reduce the workload and cost of the project.

However, since a firm has to deal with multiple applications that require the use of risk scenarios over the course of a year, it is strongly recommended to use the same XOI models or at least share a common set of XOI models across all applications. It is recommended for consistency but also to optimize the overall cost of projects related to operational risk. In addition, it is likely that experts will eventually reject requests if they are approached several times on similar questions, but in different contexts.

Each new application should be seen as an opportunity to enrich the current version of the XOI model by raising new questions. Addressing the problem of regulatory capital would yield a first version of the XOI models. Examining the interdependences could allow to identify new drivers common to different XOI models. Thinking about the controls would improve the XOI model by adding new specific drivers. Working on stress tests allows you to investigate more extreme situations that might have been missed before.

This way, after one or more exercises, a robust library of XOI models would benefit from the contributions of all the applications and would, in return, give better results to each of them.

CHAPTER 20

A Step towards "Oprisk Metrics"

20.1 INTRODUCTION

In one of our projects, the firm Head of Operational Risk had a strong market risk culture. He hoped that one day he would be able to assess operational risks in the same way as market risks, by assessing risks on individual positions and then aggregating them.

We believe the exposure, occurrence, impact (XOI) models can be used to progress in this direction.

An XOI scenario is defined as a range of possible adverse events. As such, it differs from a usual scenario, as it is not viewed as a particular storyline.

For instance, a usual way of describing a cyber attack scenario would be:

> The trading application is down as the result of a powerful DDOS attack, and two days are necessary to go back to normal. During this period, most transactions fees have been lost, and some large institutional clients ask for compensation as some of their transactions could not go through.

The XOI version of this cyber attack scenario is different:

> One of the critical applications of the bank is down as the result of a DDOS attack, either powerful and limited in time, or weaker but lasting for several days. During the duration of the attack, part of the revenue dependent on the application is lost, and some clients need to be compensated.

One of the key differences here is that we consider all of the possible applications, that is, all of the possible "objects" or "units" exposed to the occurrence of the scenario.

This means that in order to build the scenario, we need to list all the exposed units for this scenario.

20.2 BUILDING EXPOSURE UNITS TABLES

Let us continue with the example of the cyber attack scenario.

In the version of the model detailed in this book, we considered five applications (see Chapter 16, "A Scenario in Cyber Risk"):

1. Cards
2. Transfers
3. Trading
4. Loans
5. Internet banking

The parameters needed to assess the scenario are:

- Probability of an attack for each application
- Time to recovery
- Dependent revenue for this application
- Loss of revenue rate
- Volume of transactions that depend on the application
- Transactions compensation rate

This means that the scenario would be entirely defined by building and maintaining the following Exposure Unit Table (Table 20.1).

A similar approach could be used for the mis-selling scenario (Table 20.2).

There are some scenarios for which the Exposure unit is too granular to be assessed individually. The Rogue Trading scenario falls in this category. For these scenarios, we prefer to use "groups" or "clusters" of exposed units rather than individual ones.

We propose an exposure table based on the type of derivative desk in Table 20.3.

TABLE 20.1 Exposure Units Table for Cyber Attack Scenario

Application \ Risk Driver	Probability of a Duration Attack	Probability of a Magnitude Attack	Time to Recovery from a Duration Attack	Time to Recovery from a Magnitude Attack	Dependent Revenue	Dependent Transactions	Loss Rate	Compensation Rate
Cards								
Transfer								
Trading								
Loans								
Internet Banking								

TABLE 20.2 Exposure Units Table for the Mis-Selling Scenario

Product \ Risk Driver	Product Revenue Range	Product Risk Score	Probability of a Litigation	Range of Mis-selling Rate	Range of Mis-selling Duration
Banking and Cards					
Home Financing					
Auto Financing					
Student Financing					
General Insurance					
Investment					
Life and Pensions					

TABLE 20.3 Exposure Units Table for the Rogue Trading Scenario

Traders \ Risk Driver	Number of Traders	Probability of Rogue Trading	Possible Size of Concealed Position	Time to Detection	Market Volatility
Equity Derivatives					
Bond Derivatives					
Commodities Derivatives					

Finally, there is a subset of scenarios for which the exposed objects are not "permanent" as applications, products, or trading desks, but "transient". These are all the scenarios for which the exposed object is of the nature of a transaction, as for instance a "fat finger" trading error scenario. For these scenarios also, we would rather use "groups" or "clusters" of exposed units rather than individual ones.

20.3 SOURCES FOR DRIVER QUANTIFICATION

We can now qualify the main source of the data to be assessed using some simple criteria:

- External
- Expert-based
- Business data
- Loss data

TABLE 20.4 Sources for Drivers Quantification

Risk Driver / Application	External Data				Business Data		Expert-Based Data	
	Probability of a Duration Attack	Probability of a Magnitude Attack	Time to Recovery from a Duration Attack	Time to Recovery from a Magnitude Attack	Dependent Revenue	Dependent Transactions	Loss Rate	Compensation Rate
Cards								
Transfer								
Trading								
Loans								
Internet Banking								

This would help in organising the data collection process. We need to keep in mind, however, that each piece of data has some dimension of expert-based assessment, as this is the nature of a forward-looking scenario.

Going back to the cyber attack scenario, Table 20.4 shows how we would characterize the fields of the Exposure Unit Tables.

The use of loss data appears generally marginal. This is normal as we are trying to assess major events for which very few occurrences have been observed.

However, loss events (not limited to the amount of the loss) are used in the early stages of the definition of the scenario to assess the loss generation mechanism. They are also used to help assessing the probability of a scenario.

20.4 CONCLUSION

The use of Exposure Units Tables is possible for all scenarios, provided we distinguish the scenarios for which the exposure units are individually named, from those for which only clusters of exposure units can be defined, as they are too many to be listed individually, or transient and cannot be used from one year to another.

The use of Exposure Tables has the following benefits:

- Clear definition of the exposed units
- Simple structure of data collection
- Possible industrialisation of business data collection
- Ease of communication and review
- Straightforward splitting of scenario for legal entities

Index